THE ART
OF
Rock

HERMAN'S HERMITS
SATURDAY, JUNE 12th 1:00 P. M.
AT THE **ACADEMY OF MUSIC**   3.50, 4.50, 5.50 (INC. TAX)
MAIL ORDERS ACCEPTED — ACADEMY OF MUSIC

THE DAVE CLARK 5
AT THE **ACADEMY OF MUSIC**   3.50, 4.50, 5.50 (INC. TAX)
FRIDAY, JUNE 18th 7:30 P. M.
MAIL ORDERS ACCEPTED — ACADEMY OF MUSIC

— FIRST AMERICAN CONCERT —
The Kinks & the Moody Blues
AT THE **ACADEMY OF MUSIC**   3.50, 4.50, 5.50 (INC. TAX)
SATURDAY, JUNE 19th 1:00 P. M.
MAIL ORDERS ACCEPTED — ACADEMY OF MUSIC

THE BEATLES
SUNDAY, AUG. 15th 8:00 P. M.
SHEA STADIUM
4.50, 5.10 5.65 (INC. TAX)   PLEASE ENCLOSE 25c FOR MAILING & HANDLING
BY MAIL ONLY!
SID BERNSTEIN ENTERPRISES, INC.
119 WEST 57th STREET
NEW YORK, N. Y. 10019

THE FIRST NEW YORK FOLK FESTIVAL
WITH 60 OF THE NATION'S TOP FOLK ARTISTS
— INCLUDING —
PHIL OCHS, CHUCK BERRY, JOHNNY CASH & BUFFY ST. MARIE
4 DAYS: JUNE 17th thru JUNE 20th
AT CARNEGIE HALL
ALL TICKETS AT CARNEGIE HALL BOX OFFICE
FOR FURTHER INFORMATION, PLEASE CALL: 679-8281

The apotheosis of the British Invasion. Poster for New York appearances, 1965. The Beatles drew 60,000 at Shea Stadium.

THE ART OF ROCK

Posters from Presley to Punk

PAUL D. GRUSHKIN

ARTWORKS PHOTOGRAPHED BY JON SIEVERT

ARTABRAS · A division of

ABBEVILLE PRESS · Publishers

New York · London · Paris

To

Bill Graham, Jane Eskilson, Tim Patterson,
and all the artists and collectors.

Jacket front artwork by Wes Wilson; posters on jacket back by Alton Kelley (*Dinosaurs*),
Art Chantry (*Tina Turner*), Rick Griffin (*Grateful Dead*), John Van Hamersveld (*Jimi Hendrix*),
David Singer (*Rolling Stones*), and Su. Suttle (*Talking Heads*); title-page hand lettering by David Singer.

Editor: Alan Axelrod
Designer: Philip Grushkin
Production Manager: Dana Cole

The Art of Rock was produced with the cooperation of the
Bay Area Music Archives, San Francisco.

Printed and bound in Hong Kong

Library of Congress Cataloging-in-Publication Data
Grushkin, Paul
  The art of rock.
  Includes index.
  1. Rock music—History and criticism—Pictorial
works. 2. Rock musicians—Portraits. I. Title.
ML3534.G78 1987   741.67'4'0904   87-11374
ISBN 0-89660-025-4

CONTENTS

PREFACE

A lot of time has gone by since the fall of 1965 when I began having posters made for the first musical events I produced at the Fillmore Auditorium in San Francisco. From day one, the posters have always had a very special meaning to me as they gradually evolved into a very exciting new art form. I still fully enjoy looking back over all of the posters through the years. I never, ever, tire of looking back at them; to me, they have always reflected personal, intimate expressions of lives spent in rock 'n' roll. For some of us, the memories are deep, and the emotions evoked are expressive of a very special time in history.

These posters are so much more than just historical documents or promotional tools for our business; they are *art*, as the music itself is art, and in many cases they are very fine, high art. These posters are no less significant in our modern culture than a timeless series of classic postage stamps; certainly they have come to command a similar passion and respect. I'm proud of having been involved with these posters, proud of the artists and printers who created them. Their work fully deserves the in-depth presentation this fine book provides.

It's my hope that everyone who explores this book will be struck by a similar awareness: that the field of rock poster art is a great deal more extensive—broader and richer—than most people expect. That so many unique, eye-opening pieces of poster art could be gathered together in one volume is a testament to the true passion felt by so many people—poster artists, printers, musicians, collectors, music industry professionals, and rock fans everywhere. Each of us will doubtless find his or her own special place in this book, a place that brings to life a particular memory of when the music first struck head-on, shaping our feelings and outlook about the world in which we've come to live.

Posters are pieces of rock music's expanding puzzle. They're a means by which we look forward to events with great anticipation; or, afterward, to hold on to our memories of the sights and sounds of the great nights, the wonderful bands that played, the camaraderie of all the people who were there. Posters are like the icing on the cake; on top of everything else you got that night, there's a beautiful poster to live with, to take home or to rediscover some-time later on. And posters tell such wonderful stories! Lenny Bruce *and* the Mothers of Invention. The Who *and* Woody Herman. The Grateful Dead *and* Miles Davis. Otis Redding *and* Country Joe & the Fish. These are among the reasons I never tire of looking at the posters. For me, they form a time machine, much like an old family photograph album; each poster creates instant recall of all the wondrous emotions I experienced at the events—the joy, the madness, and those magical results that created everlasting impressions for all of us.

Throughout the thirty years of rock 'n' roll, posters have reflected the state of the music at any given time. Fundamentally, rock music has a free-form character: for the members of the audience in their thinking and interpretation of what's unfolding, as well as for the musicians who create that energy onstage. So it is with the poster artists themselves, because they, too, delve into the new possibilities. I feel very *fortunate* to have been able to run an ongoing operation that enabled artists and printers to use their imagination and intuition to create lasting works of art.

The artistic integrity of all the people involved has always sustained my belief in having posters be a part of a musical event, even when they were no longer necessary as primary promotional vehicles to draw people to shows. Whether or not they were cost effective in the strictest business sense, posters had a place because they spread the word far beyond any one show. They were a part of the overall event, and they took the whole enterprise to another, higher level.

One of my basic theories in doing business always has been the desire to get to the point in your work where, if at all possible, *everybody* wins: the public wins, the musicians win, the producing organization wins, the business community wins, the poster artists and printers win, the people behind the refreshment counter win . . . and, if everybody wins, and there's a profit from all this work, you can *continue* doing business. Everybody wins, the music continues, and the posters keep on coming. Posters kept coming because we could afford to keep them happening and because we believed in them as part of our overall philosophy. Our idea was to do our work the best we could, with the most imagination, and always with an eye to giving people a little more than they might expect.

I've always felt that I'm a New Yorker who happened to find himself in San Francisco, in the right place, at the right time. I appreciate the good fortune, and I've tried to let things happen as they should, with my best efforts thrown in. The posters evolved in sync with the same growth I went through in my own business in the music world. People lived *with* the Fillmore years, the Avalon years, and a strong, creative lifestyle evolved, extending throughout the various art forms of those incredible years—the posters, the light shows, the clothing styles, and, of course, the poetry and music. People grew to love the posters because the art wasn't subjected to gross commercialization. The posters happened on their own, as they were meant to. They evolved from *nothing* into *something*. That's what really mattered—and that's what this book is all about. Enjoy!

Cheers,
Bill Graham

INTRODUCTION

A plague of crazed critics, curators, and graduate students will descend upon me if I declare that rock posters are great modern art. So what I'll tell you is that they inspire extraordinary love and passion and that, unlike most other modern artworks, they are truly popular: thousands of people all around the world now avidly collect them.

Many of the posters are exceptional graphic achievements, their printing having employed the highest skills, and the poster artists themselves having extended the limits of their medium. These artists and printers were innovators bent on bringing forth something manifestly new and exciting.

Rock posters have been around as long as rock music has— about thirty years. Not since Europe of the 1930s has poster art played so significant a role in promoting popular entertainment. Moreover, rock posters have become a leading popular art form that has been a major influence in such related graphic fields as advertising. Rock art is tied directly to the changing music of a thirty-year period; simply put, because there are rock concerts, there are inevitably rock posters. It is also true that rock music has reflected, even as it has helped to shape, its thirty-year span of American and international culture. And so the posters are a visual history not only of the music but also of a little bit of the world that produced the music.

Rock has many roots and branches, and what this book calls rock poster art also embraces other forms of popular music related to rock. Black music had an obvious and great effect, as did country. The posters help to tell how and why this is so. The book begins in the mid 1950s, when rock was very young and when for the most part black people were still setting the popular music trends followed by various white performers. By 1955, swing-jazz, jump bands, and early rhythm and blues had yielded to the likes of James Brown and, a little later, Elvis Presley. With the sixties came the Temptations and Aretha Franklin, then Bob Dylan, and the storming of America by "British Invasion" groups like the Beatles, the Rolling Stones, the Animals, Gerry and the Pacemakers, Herman's Hermits, and so on.

All the posters of rock's early period, 1955 to 1965, whether advertising white or black acts, were done in a "boxing style," with heavy emphasis on key words—usually names—done in woodblock. Plain pieces, these posters are nevertheless tremendously evocative. They have a luminous quality, a rich patina of age. They are not intentionally beautiful, but they capture rock's first, vanished era perfectly and bring back memories of music that was raw and authentic. Here, they say, is where it all began.

Next came the psychedelic era of the mid and late 1960s, extending into the very early 1970s. This was the Golden Age of the rock poster and one of the great flowerings of poster art generally. It came about as part of America's response to the British Invasion and began in San Francisco and Los Angeles, with such groups as the Charlatans, Country Joe and the Fish, the Byrds, the Doors, and the Grateful Dead. Then it came in a great rush from all other areas of the country. The new music led to a new school of rock poster art. Vivid and imaginative, it stands in dramatic contrast to the art of rock's earlier period. It was produced in great quantity and received with tremendous enthusiasm.

After the early 1970s, psychedelic music and art, associated with counterculture communities and hippie communes, began to yield to a mainstream increasingly dominated by music industry businessmen. By the mid 1970s, promoting rock was often a corporate rather than a communal endeavor, and mass-media appeals—newspaper and magazine ads—replaced much poster art. What posters there were displayed a professional maturity and often were effective translations of music into graphic terms. But, like the music itself, the rock poster, now more or less a corporate entity, had lost much of its appealing naiveté.

Beginning in the late 1970s and continuing in varying degrees into the present, a revolution has been under way, a move against the mainstream. Punks and new wavers became rock's cutting edge, and their aggressive sound has been accompanied by a return to street-scorching lamppost art. Unlike psychedelic art, punk and new wave posters aren't meant to promote inward exploration. Nor are they intended to be displayed in the bedroom or living room. They more closely resemble the early rhythm and blues bills and, like them, are meant to be seen outside, on the street. In some purely unconscious way, rock art has thus come full circle.

The thirty-year trail of rock art has opened up many a new door to people excited by modern graphics. For many collectors, rock posters bring back memories. The art helps them feel again what it was like to hear the music. Such collectors probably care more about the specific bands listed or where the shows took place than they do about the art as art. They like the feeling of history—*their own* history—that the rock poster reveals.

Many others collecting posters see their magic in the artwork. What is important to them is the design, the use of color and imagery, the technical sophistication of the printing process. More than the bands advertised, the artists who created the art are the heroes for these collectors.

In many respects, this book of posters is also the story of the collectors, the people who responded to the art by caring for it passionately. Why this is so has to do with the nature of rock art: it is there to elicit a response. It draws one in, just as the call-and-response mode of rock 'n' roll (originating in its black-music roots) pulls people out of their seats down to the front of the stage. If it's great rock music or if it's a great rock poster, it awakens emotion.

Rock 'n' roll has a powerful effect on peoples' lives, and how rock posters came to play their own role makes for deeply personal, often poignant stories. In every case, there was a *first time*, a moment in which something fresh and special was freely offered in the spirit of comradeship and generosity. Most rock poster fans turned on first to the San Francisco psychedelic works. These, after all, represented a whole new way of life for many American kids, a music and art unlike anything that had come before. Chris Coyle, today a band manager, recalls:

I got into it probably around March of 1966. I got into it because my father rented a boat in Sausalito, and we used to go there every Sunday and wander around. It was there my friends and I discovered rock posters—stuff far more compelling than even the dragstrip posters we'd earlier turned on to. There were posters for all these new groups and for all these new dance halls, like the Fillmore Auditorium and the Avalon Ballroom. And each time we'd go to Sausalito, I'd see another new one, and so I began to collect them. I made this huge collection even before the end of 1966. My bedroom was covered—every inch of white space was covered, the entire ceiling and all the walls. It was the greatest thing that had ever happened in my life. To be honest, I was an outcast in high school because I was so into posters. I was like

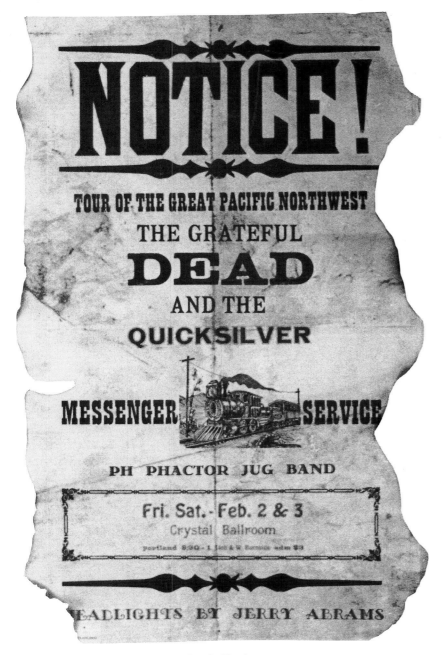

Grateful Dead: Tour of the Great Pacific Northwest
Rare blow-torched version, 1968. Artist: George Hunter

you hardly gave a thought to the value or even to the meaning of the posters. It was enough just to be obsessed with finding them and sticking them up where you lived. Posters were everywhere.

I remember in my early days going into the Psychedelic Shop on Haight Street, on Monday afternoons. It was part of a route I'd hit. I had a little Vespa scooter, and I'd run it up on the sidewalk and wait for the poster guy from the Fillmore or Avalon to walk in. He'd drop off a big stack on the counter, and I'd just grab like forty or fifty of them and split. I'd take them around to friends, or I might take some up to Ben Friedman and trade or sell a few to him, but basically the idea was to get them up on my wall as fast as I could.

Waiting for the poster man became the high point of the week for many early collectors. Harold Feiger, today a realtor, remembers Bill Graham's poster lady who served the East Bay and the University of California campus:

The lady would come each Friday afternoon, and the line of people waiting for her would be nearly down the block. I remember she told me why she wore gloves—she was handing out art so fast, the danger was getting paper cuts. Finally I got up enough nerve to ask whether I could help her give away the art. And then I became the poster man.

Some people even had an inside track, contacts who knew the artists or knew an employee at one of the print shops. Steve Brown, who helped run the Grateful Dead's record company and who is now a video producer, tells about his connection:

My ex-wife's father was an electrician, and one aspect of his job involved working with printing presses and print shops. So he was often called in by Levon Mosgofian at Tea Lautrec, or Double H Press out on Haight Street if there was a problem. My father-in-law knew I was into posters and if at all possible I wanted one of each. So if he was there as the posters were being printed, he'd always get me at least one—sometimes printer's proofs and test sheets, sometimes armloads of goodies.

After a time, Bill Graham and the Family Dog promoters no longer could afford to give away the large posters and instead sold them wholesale to stores, where the usual retail price, up through 1970 or so, was one dollar each. You could still get handbills—miniature versions of the posters—for free at the shows, but if you wanted the real thing, some searching was required. This was particularly true of those who arrived in San Francisco after the decline of the Haight community, beginning in 1968. Paul Getchell, a lawyer associated with a legal publisher, started collecting during those years:

The first stash of posters I ever came across was in Jack Carmel's art-frame store, out on Geary Boulevard, when I first came up to San Francisco in 1973 from college in Santa Barbara. One day, Jack had just gotten in a huge stack of Fillmore posters. It was the first time I'd ever seen such a big accumulation of them, and it gave me an idea these were something that could be collected. I

a rock 'n' roll fanatic when, unless you were into sports, were a jock, or member of the student council, you got your ass kicked. I felt like a renegade.

Poster collecting was something I did better than anyone. I was the king of my peer group—all the other people just then getting into rock. I was the king. I had every poster imaginable.

In the early days of the psychedelic scene, poster art was available even to the most casual rock fan. It was for sale in many stores, like the Print Mint, the Psychedelic Shop, or Ben Friedman's Postermat, all in San Francisco. It was also being given away by rock promoters like Bill Graham and by the Family Dog collective, both of whom even sent a poster man around to head shops, the Berkeley campus, and other likely places to distribute the posters. Graham's posters for his shows at the Fillmore Auditorium and the Family Dog's posters for their's at the Avalon Ballroom are especially prized today. Recognizing the artistic and historical value of the posters they were commissioning, both promoters began to

The original Ben Friedman Postermat, North Beach, San Francisco

bought four or five of them—three dollars apiece—mostly stuff that appealed to me graphically, or because I knew the bands.

The very first poster I picked out was Fillmore #259 (BG 259). I remember it vividly because it had the band Seatrain on it, and I was really amazed because there weren't many people who were into Seatrain at that time besides me. Now I was really curious about rock poster art, and I started looking around in earnest for a place where you could buy a whole lot of it.

Most in-the-know collectors of rock art would agree that the search inevitably ends at the historic establishment operated by seventy-five-year-old Ben Friedman, the wily proprietor of the Postermat. This is a legendary store—home of the last, nearly unlimited stash—now located on Columbus Avenue in San Francisco's North Beach, just down the street from where Ben opened his first shop in the mid fifties, on Grant Avenue.

Paul Getchell:

I saw this store, right on the corner. Ben had a huge wall of psychedelic posters—seemingly hundreds of Fillmores and Avalons on display—and he had a Rick Griffin "Aoxomoxoa" in the

window. That was the first time I ever saw that particular poster— surely one of the greatest, all-time classic pieces—and seeing it hung in such an available way in the man's store really did it for me. I was a client of Ben Friedman's for life.

Ben's own story of how he got into posters, if you ask him directly, is told over the course of several hours, since Ben is never in a great hurry. He was an egg man first, a major egg broker who worked independently and for large companies such as Nu-Laid.

The Grant Avenue store was sort of handed to me by accident. When I was an egg broker, I had time to mess around a little bit, and when a friend of mine, a bankruptcy goods buyer, said he'd found this great store in North Beach where nobody was paying the rent, I thought I'd invest. When we opened the store originally, it was mostly clothes and bankruptcy goods. All kinds of bargain stuff. This was at the end of the beatnik era, not quite the hippie time.

One thing led to another, and one day my partner and I bought a stock of records, like maybe 100,000 records that had gotten wet—the covers were sticking to the records. It was mostly show-tune material, and we sold them for thirty-nine cents. I put a tub of water out, along with some soap and towels, and I had all these fancy ladies from the night clubs coming in and washing records to take home.

I kind of liked having records in my store, and before long I was getting visits from people in the record business. First, they'd sell me promotional records to resell at one dollar. We were getting a good mixed crowd, and so I started buying the records, regular records from regular channels. The records themselves were a whole mixed bag, from that late 1950s early 1960s era. Some early rock, a whole lot of soul, then Chubby Checker's "Twist" came in, then surf music.

My partner was still selling clothes in his half of the store, but he didn't like the nighttime hours I was keeping. I told him, "Look, 90 percent of the business is coming in during the evening, especially for the records. If you don't like it, why don't you move out?" So, suddenly, there was this whole other half of the store empty. About that time, a guy from Portal Publications, a poster wholesaler, came along and said to me, "Listen, I can put posters on that wall over there—I can cover that wall, and you can make bins for the floor. You'll have a poster store—it'll go together with your records."

Well, I did what the guy told me to do. Suddenly, I was taking in much more than the two hundred dollars a month we were getting from the clothes—I was getting two hundred a week or in less than a week. And I didn't have to do hardly anything; Portal would give me new posters for my wall, and I kept restocking the floor bins.

Pretty early in 1966, just after things got started with the Family Dog and Bill Graham, Fillmore and Avalon posters were being dropped off in my store every week, for display, telling people what was coming up. It wasn't just my store, either—all the hip stores in North Beach got them. At first people just stole the posters out of my window, but later on they started asking me about them in a serious way. I put a whole bunch up on one of my walls fairly early on. I covered one stairwell in what must have been, I guess, the first forty Fillmore posters. Around that time, I made my first call to Bill Graham.

Bill said to me, when I phoned him, "Oh, I don't know. I don't want to bother with those posters—they're really for telephone poles, or I just give them away." I said to him, "Look, asshole (I'm not sure if I said exactly that), if you bring me fifty of each of the first forty posters, I'll give you a thousand dollars." Graham said, "Why? Why do you want to give me a thousand dollars?" I said, "Well, I figure I'm going to get two thousand—I'll sell them for one dollar apiece."

So, he brought down the two thousand posters personally and got his thousand dollars. He liked that. And then I started distributing them; I began to get them for forty cents apiece from Bill, and from Chet Helms over at the Family Dog.

I drove them all over the Bay Area—down to Menlo Park, over to Berkeley. People all over were calling for them. By late 1967 or so, it was really becoming a new business for me.

I made a whole wall of posters that responded to a "color organ" I got from some scientific supply house. The organ had different colored lights that lit in response to the store's stereo—high notes were red, low notes, blue, that sort of thing. When you played the Beatles, with their range of sound, the organ went crazy, and the wall of posters really popped. We also had a special room for black-light posters, which were very popular back then. People would come in stoned and look at those things for hours.

Despite the thousands of poster fanatics coming to the Postermat over some twenty years, Ben Friedman managed the impossible, to parcel out his stock so there'd always be rock posters left for him to sell. Nobody really knows if this was a conscious act on his part, whether he had a grand plan in mind, or if it was just *Ben*. The thing was, nobody could buy everything they wanted from him all at once, as Hewlett-Packard division manager Tim Patterson relates:

I'll always remember Ben trying to fill an order for you. You had just about all you could take of the evening's endless discussions, and it's time to move on, take care of business—time to come to terms about what you want and what he has on hand. It was always an adventure trying to get him to pull what you wanted out of those wooden drawers, late in the evening. And even while he's doing that, he's pulling out envelopes of letters from people in New York, England, Germany—letters requesting his assistance—and he says, "Oh, I've been trying to get to that order for weeks; just can't seem to get to the warehouse and get those things pulled." How many hundreds of time did I hear that? You wanted to reach around the counter and strangle him.

People on the trail of posters established contact with other collectors or searched for material from unlikely sources. Such encounters were often pivotal, chance meetings that helped expand everyone's horizons. Trades, barters, and major scores became the stuff of legend. Even if it's hard to get, it's out there;

Ben Friedman, 1984

Peace Rock I (original version)
Fillmore Auditorium, San Francisco, 1966

Peace Rock I (revised version)
Fillmore Auditorium, San Francisco, 1966

that's the poster hunter's maxim. You have to keep your eyes and ears open, and *work* at it.

Paul Getchell:

It seems like everything turns up eventually. On the average, you can figure there'll be two or three stashes of really great posters that'll turn up every year—and the thing that's really amazing to me is that even after all the years I've been into collecting, that rule of thumb has hardly changed—and I started doing this back in about 1973.

What's happened over the years is that you don't run into so many people with just a few things, but the big stashes keep coming out at about the same frequency. Of course, in order for any of this to happen, you have to dig a little harder than you once used to do, follow up contacts more carefully, make a point of really asking people who they were, or what they had, or what they'd seen.

Looking for posters, you can't consciously expect to find anything, but when you do, it blows your mind. You find them in these weird places, and you get the shakes. I remember the day over at the Marin Flea Market when I got a good part of my Fillmore collection, along with a whole lot of really rare miscellaneous stuff. This was a day I guess about seven years ago, the usual dull sort of day at the flea market. As I was wandering around, all of a sudden I looked down at one booth and saw piles and piles and piles of handbills. Most of them were pretty common, but they were there in bulk—hundreds and hundreds of certain numbers.

Finally, when I'm about halfway through the stash, I look up

and ask the guy, "Gee, by the way, do you have any posters?" He said, "Yeah, they're over here." And sure enough, there was a big portfolio about four inches thick with posters.

I started going through it, and it was mostly real oddball stuff, which I like. I got through about half the portfolio and picked out maybe five or six things, and the guy told me they were three to five dollars apiece, so I picked out maybe four or five more from the ones I first rejected. Then, I turn the page and what's staring me in the face but the Big Brother/Merry Pranksters poster from Sokol Hall—the Hells Angels party—which I'd never seen. I kept turning the pages and started hitting Fillmore posters I'd only dreamed about. They were all the early ones, and they were all there, every single one of them, all the ones I wanted. That's where I got most of my first #1 to #20 Fillmores—first printing "Batman," #2, #3, #4, all the way right up the line to about #25 or so. All in perfect mint condition.

I knew this was one batch where I got there first. By this time, you talk about shaking, I could barely stand up straight.

Probably thousands of people have been on the hunt for rock posters ever since San Francisco psychedelic art came to the forefront. But owing to the incredible profusion of the art, it seemed unlikely any one person could ever have been called King of the Collectors. Except maybe Randy Tuten.

Chris Coyle:

When I first met Randy, around 1969, he didn't have anything. He didn't have any posters at all, and I had like boxes and boxes, and I was even putting up posters at that time, for companies like

Soundproof, which commissioned Rick Griffin to do "Aoxomoxoa." But things sure changed in a hurry, once Randy got started.

As far as detective work went, Randy was probably the very best at uncovering things. He worked at it harder than anyone I know, and he built an unbelievable collection. I'll never forget his room when he lived in San Francisco—just stacks and stacks, everything different. He was the king at that point, and nobody ever had a collection as big as his.

Paul Getchell:

Walking into Randy's place was like walking into a museum. It seemed like he had everything in there. He had framed original art, printing plates; even just at first glance you could see he had rare, unbelievably beautiful pieces. Randy didn't have one of everything, he had more than one of everything. He had things you had never before seen in your life—things for which you could spend a lifetime visiting Ben Friedman's store and still never hope to attain. He had on one wall Griffin's original large-size "Hawaiian Aoxomoxoa," done for a show involving the Grateful Dead and It's a Beautiful Day. But the show was cancelled, and I'd heard most of the posters were destroyed by the printer. The poster just didn't exist, not in the real world. One of Randy's copies was casually tacked to the wall.

Tuten was himself a poster artist—he did a lot of work for Bill Graham, and for thé Family Dog when it was out at the Great Highway—and in one room he had his studio and drawing board, and in another room were his poster collections. There were posters on all the walls, and in this one room he had big piles in the middle of the floor; he had small tables with more poster piles, and it seemed all the piles were at least seven, eight inches thick.

Randy Tuten's studio, 1969

Not everyone who was into rock poster art lived in the Bay Area—although, talking to the top collectors, including Dennis King, Chris Coyle, Harold Feiger, Randy Tuten, Ray Andersen, Bill Schuessler, Eric King, Gilbert Levey, George Michalski, Stephen Braitman, Ron Schaeffer, Tim Patterson, Paul Getchell, Jacaeber Kastor, and others, it often seems like that. More recently, New Yorkers have been getting into the act, although they, too, had to come to San Francisco in order to find the best stashes. Tony Mongeluzzi, owner of Stargazers, a metaphysical head shop in Flushing, New York, is one outstanding example:

I'd have to say my interest in metaphysics got me into rock art in the first place. I thought all the better stuff had all sorts of underlying meanings.

I had a few Fillmore East posters. That pretty much got me into it. And then I learned there was a whole bunch more from the Fillmore West. My collecting wasn't too serious in the beginning. One here, one there. But it takes money to buy them, so instead of buying one here, one there, I would buy two here, two there. And I'd sell a few off, or trade, and I just built my collection that way.

I knew a fellow by the name of Muttzie who was really into collecting posters like I was, on the East Coast. Around 1978, I said to him, "You know, if we're really going to try and buy this stuff, why don't we go meet a few of the artists?" My thought was, they were the guys who drew it, they should have some of the old pieces. And so we flew out West and showed up on some peoples' doorsteps.

One of the first artists I met was David Singer. We hung out, stayed up a few days, and just bullshitted. He got to see that I was really all right, and I got to see he was really all right. We seemed to be into a lot of the same stuff—metaphysics—and our talks were about things deeper than just the collecting of the art. We rapped about where David got his images for the posters, their roots and sources, and got along great. From there, having made such good, meaningful contact, it was pretty natural I'd get to meet some of the other artists who were still around. David would call them up and say, "Hey, this guy's really all right. He's from New York, he's really into collecting," and so on. And it turned out I got along real good with the rest of the guys, too.

The price of rock art has appreciated considerably since the 1960s. Original art—drawings, paintings, artists' mechanicals (layouts from which posters are made)—now commands a hefty price, and quite a number of rare posters could cost a collector upward of five hundred dollars—even more, if the sale were taking place on the East Coast.

Chris Coyle:

Today, I'm mostly drawn to posters that are very eclectic, strange, and hard to get. But to be honest, if someone offered me the right amount of money, I'd probably sell all the posters I have. Even the original art pieces I collected. That was my investment; when I had a roll of money and I wanted to go out and buy something, I bought original art, just because I liked it. My favorite was the original for the Lenny Bruce Fillmore show—his last performance before he died—and the piece really had a life of its own. I mean, it was deep. And maybe that's one I do regret selling, that I wished I would have held on to. But I needed the money, and I sold it to Bill Graham. It hangs in his house, and I'm sure it gives him a really good feeling. It gave me a really good feeling.

Extremely rare black-and-white handbill: The Who; Poco Palladium, Hollywood, 1969. Artist: Rick Griffin

Tony Mongeluzzi:

The way I've been looking at it, there is a whole new art form here on this planet, which is rock 'n' roll art. Centuries ago, there were always people who took gambles with new artists, the new periods of art. Down the road, maybe fifty years after they made a purchase—maybe not even in their own lifetime, maybe not even in their children's lifetime—these became major pieces of art.

So when I got started—and also right now, too—I had the thought that this would be our shot at that kind of art. I thought it would come to have a history, that in time it would be worth a great deal from a purely financial standpoint—although first as a major artistic accomplishment. It was a good way for a guy like me, who didn't start out with much money, to buy things that would later turn out to be the Picassos of my era. Of course, who's to say? It's just my gut feeling.

Tim Patterson:

My wife Nancy and I were recently in New York, and we went to the Museum of Modern Art. The very top floor is dedicated to architecture, design, modern prints, and so on. They were exhibiting some wonderful things from their permanent collection— miniature models for skyscrapers, designer furniture, even a

hockey mask—and we turned one corner, and there on the wall was a Victor Moscoso rock poster, one of his Neon Rose numbers done for the Matrix. It was a great feeling to see it there—it was like the stuff had now taken its place, it belonged to the ages. You're in a world-famous museum, with a lot of important and stimulating objects everywhere in sight, and then you turn around and see something of yours. Amazing.

Fundamentally, however, rock art isn't "high art," isn't so exalted that it's out of the reach of even the novice collector, even a teenager in the 1980s just feeling his way into it. Yes, an entire Fillmore or Avalon set, bought intact with every rare numbered piece included, would set somebody back a good ten to fifteen thousand dollars. But you can still go to Ben Friedman's store and purchase most individual pieces for fifteen to fifty dollars. If you want to be a *collector*, and you want the rush that comes with turning up something wonderful and obscure and totally within your means, then patience and watchfulness are what's required.
Paul Getchell:

Persistence is the key. You have to be willing to put up with a fair amount. Basically, the thing is not to give up. I've had more than my share of missed appointments. I can remember driving sometimes hundreds of miles in a day, after getting off work early, trying to arrange my schedule so I could meet somebody's very weird schedule and then the person would not be there.

But I can't really blame people when the stash turns out to be much less than I'd wished for. That's part of the hunt.

So what is it about rock art that really grabs people by the gut? Is it the image? Is it the memory of a concert? Is it the identification with a social community, like the San Francisco Haight-Ashbury scene of the 1960s? Tim Patterson thinks it's a lot of things:

Number one, I think it's the people. There are a lot of fine people to meet in the rock art world—the artists, the collectors. It's just an adventure, really. It never comes to an end, and most of the time it's a real intellectual and artistic challenge.

It all flows together for me—the beauty of the pieces, the lettering, the bands that are being celebrated, the artists who are responsible for dreaming up the images, the times in which all this interaction was taking place. There's an honesty to it all. It's still important, even more important, somehow, the longer I live. It's come to mean something far beyond just the moment.

It's like knowing a secret that not everyone knows about, despite there having now been thousands of people who've been exposed to the art. All that matters to me is that the collection itself keeps growing and changing—the basic feelings that motivated me to start collecting haven't changed at all.

Paul Getchell:

There's still a whole lot out there to find. It's only if I keep searching for pieces I haven't seen—and they're mostly now in places far beyond California—I'm going to keep getting the thrills I first got when somebody would pull out a new Griffin poster, or something unbelievable by Mouse or Kelley or Moscoso. Sometimes I think it's just a matter of being another prisoner of rock 'n' roll—something Bruce Springsteen always says he is—but in my case, I guess it's just being another prisoner of rock 'n' roll art.

1

Roots: 1955–1965

I remember the first time I met the great bluesman, Howlin' Wolf, in 1966. He started talking about white blues singers, a new concept at the time. He liked Paul Butterfield, he said, also "that other boy—what's his name? Somewhere out in California, that 'Hound Dog' number." He was talking about Elvis Presley. But surely Elvis couldn't be considered strictly a *blues* singer, somebody pointed out. Maybe not, conceded Wolf in that great hoarse growl of his, but "he *started* from the blues. If he stopped, he stopped. It's nothing to laugh at. *He made his pull from the blues.*"

PETER GURALNICK
album liner notes (February 1985)
for Elvis Presley, *Reconsider Baby*
(RCA AFL1-5418)

Everything "makes its pull" from something. Rock 'n' roll made its pull from the blues and from other forms of black music and sometimes country music. The concert poster from rock's first golden era—the mid 1950s and early 1960s—made its pull from poster art advertising popular forms of entertainment from much of the preceding period. Rock has come to be known as a revolutionary musical art form that "set the world on fire." But the earliest concert posters that promoted rock were hardly revolutionary; they owe much to advertising art associated with carnivals, circuses, vaudeville, minstrel shows, Grand-Ole-Opry-style country music, and even big-band jazz.

Much of the poster art of the mid 1950s and early 1960s was developed in the print shops that had produced the earlier street advertisements. For printers accustomed to satisfying the needs of performers' managers, booking agents, and early show promoters during the twenties, thirties, and forties, developing for them standard window cards and telephone pole posters, it was an easy transition to the new promotions associated with rhythm and blues, early rock, and soul music.

These posters are highly valued for their scarcity and historical importance. However, while they are often eye-catching, they are not intentionally beautiful. Concert posters from the early days of rock and the glory days of rhythm and blues and soul were functional objects, colorful pieces of cardboard advertising that had a specific and unsophisticated function. For the very reason that the purpose of the posters was utilitarian rather than aesthetic, few survive today. But some *have* survived as living symbols of an earlier, more innocent era of rock 'n' roll. Such artifacts are often found in the collections of dedicated archivists, people like John Goddard, forty-year-old proprietor of Village Music, an overflowing floor-to-ceiling museum of American music history that masquerades as a record store in Mill Valley, California:

The first poster I ever brought home was from a show with James Brown, Hank Ballard, Ray Charles, and Jackie Wilson. It took place in 1959, my freshman year in high school. It was a poster I actually grabbed myself, off a telephone pole.

Poster art from the r & b period is some of my favorite stuff, but it's very, very hard to get, at least nowadays. I think I've pulled most of my posters down from telephone poles myself, although I've traded for some, too. The posters I've got hanging in my store are for shows I really like or groups I really like. The art's basically the same style on all of them—it's the billings that mean the most to me.

For some people, like John Goddard, the historic roll-call of names motivates their collecting. For others, it's the colors of the posters, or their overall feel. Clyde Woodward, a musician now living in Wylie, Texas, has vivid recollections of seeing posters in all the black neighborhoods he visited as a child, the same neighborhoods he cruised years later, looking for art to take home and share with his friends. The music these posters advertised was professional, but also very much of the grass roots. And while this music survived into the rock 'n' roll era of the 1960s, it predates white urban rock and figures as one of its primary rural sources:

I grew up in Nacogdoches, East Texas, part of what they call the Pine Belt, which stretches all the way to Georgia. I was hanging out in the black part of town from a real early age. My family's

maid and yard man—Zalma and Ludy Harris—especially meant a lot to me. My parents were always gone—they traveled—and I'd get dumped off at Zalma and Ludy's house for the weekend. It was there that I first saw the blues posters.

They were nailed up on telephone poles all over the neighborhood. They were printed in incredible colors: chartreuse, orange, pink. As a youngster, I was attracted to the colors. Later, when I got to know the music better, I would take the posters off the poles and drag them home.

I used to go to this place in Apple Springs, Texas, called the New Cinderella Club. Johnny Winter had a band there called "It and Them." This was in 1965. It was an all-black band; he was the only white guy. I used to go with my hometown bootlegger, a black man named Leroy Palmer. The New Cinderella, like a lot of clubs Leroy and I went to, was really rough. I'd generally stay right by the bandstand. Whenever there'd be a fight, the club management would always hustle me out the back; they'd get me and run me out the back door until the violence was over. I was going to see people like Z. Z. Hill in places where at first I didn't even understand why they were running me out the back—I mean, they were cutting and shooting in there. Hanging around people like Leroy warped me for life. It's the reason I'm not an insurance agent or something like that.

The clubs Woodward refers to were called "jukes," a term probably derived from *dzugu*, a Bambara word meaning "wicked," by way of the Gullah term *joog*, "disorderly." After the grind of a long work week, juke joints provided the setting for music, drinking, dancing, gambling, and love-making. Woodward continues:

Where I grew up, the Saturday night dance was known as a "bon temps." You can't get analytical about a bon temps. It's all real close to the surface: the food is killer, the dancing is killer, and the music just makes everybody sweat. Like, I still go to "zydeco" dances down in Houston. The people who go take them real seriously—and they're church-going Catholics. But man, when it gets time to "bon temps" on a Saturday night, they've got their half-gallon of Crown Royal, and they're dressed to the nines, and they don't make any bones about it.

I think even the term zydeco music has various connotations for people in Louisiana and East Texas. If you've seen many Clifton Chenier posters—and Clifton is the king of zydeco music—you'll notice zydeco is spelled many different ways, like it was community slang or something. You'll see it written zordeco, zydico, and maybe a few others, and of course that's because it's black Cajun French and a rude approximation of gonna-have-a-good-time-on-Saturday-night-dancing-to-some-hot-music-made-by-a-guy-playing-the-accordion.

Posters in East Texas and southern Louisiana were often real rough looking, crude in their style, like the zydeco and blues clubs themselves. Lots of times I'd see posters where the place and day of the gig were written in by hand at the top or bottom of the poster. The only actual printed part of the poster might be the musician's name in big letters, along with his photograph.

These posters were the only way gigs were advertised in places like Nacogdoches. The clubs couldn't or wouldn't get any newspaper advertising, and there were no radio stations around that catered to the black population. When Bobby Bland was coming

John Goddard's Village Music store, Mill Valley, California

to Nacogdoches, you certainly didn't read about it in the Daily Sentinel; you heard about it because you were driving past Connie's Cafe or Simon's Barbeque, and you saw the poster up on the wall or stapled to the telephone pole in front.

One time, I was at Simon's Barbeque, and some black guys came by and put up a poster on the telephone pole outside. This was in the mid 1960s. I was sitting inside eating greens, and right after the guys put up the poster and got in their car, some cops pulled up in back of them. They stopped the dudes' car right in the middle of the street—flashing lights, siren, everything. And the cops got out, tore down the poster, ripped it up into little pieces, threw the pieces in the street, got back into their police cruiser, and drove off. The poster obviously represented a lot more than just the Bobby Bland show.

That's the thing about blues music. It's an alternative, a different way, and to some parts of the community I guess it's still a threat. But to me, it's just the bon temps. Life's tough, but if you've got a scene going where there's a good little band playing, you can go dance, you can hustle a chick, a chick can hustle a guy, you can have a good time for one night, and that one night really carries you through the week. You see the poster all over town, and you

just know what's in store for you. The poster sets you up for what might happen.

The feeling of what-might-happen-on-Saturday-night is common not just in East Texas, but throughout the rural and settled Deep South and, of course, up North, too, in cities like Chicago and Detroit, where black music—and the black concert poster—flourished. During the 1940s the black population of the northern states increased dramatically. In 1940 there were 387,000 black people in Illinois; by 1950, there were 645,000. In Michigan the population increased from 208,000 to 442,000. Throughout the 1950s, the black migration continued, the new urbanites bringing into Chicago and Detroit the music of the rural South, music that would influence the sound of the city even as city life exercised an influence on it. Country-born singers of an urban blues, like Muddy Waters, played such clubs as Smitty's Corner, Thirty-fifth and Indiana Avenue, Chicago. Howlin' Wolf gigged at the Big Squeeze Club, on the city's South Side. And there were many more, all playing music hard driven by hard cities, but music nevertheless rooted in Mississippi mud, Georgia clay, and the Cajun woods of East Texas and Louisiana.

As they had in the South, posters went up all over Chicago, Detroit, and elsewhere in the urban North. They were often just as crudely and boldly composed as the posters Clyde Woodward grew up with, printed in the "boxing style," with heavy emphasis on names. Most failed to survive the glory years of the blues, the 1950s and 1960s, primarily because they were just plain outdoor advertising. Jim O'Neal, publisher and editor of Living Blues, a magazine out of Chicago, recalls how they were used:

Posters were the means of getting the word out in the black sections of Chicago. They were the main form—often the only form—of advertising for a lot of blues gigs. Unless it was a really big show, you wouldn't see any advertising in the newspapers, particularly in the 1960s. In the 1950s, you could find club ads in the Chicago Defender, *the black newspaper, but in later years it seems the clubs just didn't advertise that way. Radio was pretty hit or miss, too. They really just depended on the posters.*

The posters slowly changed with the times, not in their appearance so much as in the acts they promoted. Rhythm and blues and, later, soul became widespread throughout the 1950s and into the 1960s; new traveling acts were getting the boxing-style billing. As Arnold Shaw observes in *Honkers and Shouters*, the blues was "trouble music," and urban blues was the song of adjustment to the city, "but, r & b was good-time dance music. If the blues was rural song and urban blues city music, r & b was black ghetto music." It "brought vitality into pop music—such vitality that it overwhelmed a generation of teenagers, white as well as black, European as well as American."

The jukebox and the radio were important means of promoting rhythm and blues and soul. In some cases, people could rely on the disc jockeys to tell them about the important acts appearing in the clubs or tours coming into town. But for at least two decades posters were the most effective communication devices in the black community simply because no one could avoid seeing them. Thomas Eskilson, now president of the Dixie Dairy in Gary, Indiana, remembers his days as a route foreman, delivering milk in a predominantly black community during the late 1960s:

I was listening to WMPP, out of East Chicago Heights, Illinois, and they played all the r & b and soul. On radio, guys like "J. J." would promote a lot of shows, but I was made even more aware of the music by the posters in the streets. You just couldn't miss them. They were on every corner. So when you stopped at a stoplight, there was always one on the right. Every time. And every four ways you could look in an intersection, there'd be six or seven posters. A lot of times you'd see two or three from various shows—the new ones would be stapled right on top of the old.

What got me the most were the changes of color. The colors were incredible. And the names of the artists and the names of the clubs, those jumped out at you, too. Percy Sledge was real big in Gary, and I remember he used to play Joe Green's Club Woodlawn. That was a jumpin' spot, and also Barbara's Playhouse. Of course, the really big attraction in Gary was the Jackson Five. Down at the Dairy, people were always talking about the group— they were from Gary—but it was always in terms of "the little kid." How that "little kid could sing and dance." It was always "the little kid" to them. For a long time I didn't even know his first name: Michael. You know, if they really wanted to advertise Jackson Five shows in Gary, all they needed to say on the posters

was "the little kid." Everyone would have known what the poster was talking about.

A good blues, r & b, or soul poster actually says very little but speaks volumes. The few words leap out at you, the colors dazzle your eyes, as Clyde Woodward recalls:

The poster's got to catch your eye. That's the whole idea, that's the reason for the bright colors, the oranges, greens, yellows, pinks. I know it sounds strange, but it was the posters that really got me into the music. When I started listening to the music that the posters were talking about, it all just fit together. And then later, when I became a musician and started traveling, I saw posters in other towns. I was forever pulling posters off telephone poles. Every time I go into a new town, I go over to the black district and start looking for them. What gets me are the graphics—the look; that's what really slays me. I've got a friend with a poster stash as big as mine, Little Junior One-Hand, a Mexican guy who plays slide blues guitar. We cruise down to the black part of Houston a lot, and if we're driving around and see a big blurb of chartreuse or wild orange up on a pole, I just know we're going to look at it. Sometimes we have to wheel around the block, catch it a second time. We're just tuned into that sort of thing.

Next to the colors, what I love most are the names, the names of the artists, the names of the clubs. Z. Z. Hill. I mean, really, Z. Z. Hill? The first poster I ever saw for his show, his name, I swear, was half the poster. The letters were ten, twelve inches high, right across the middle. The name had so much authority.

The message has to jump out at you. A good example of that is the poster I've got of "Cookie and the Cupcakes." The poster explains the whole show to you in a matter of seconds, just lays it all out. It's got just enough pictures—one of Cookie, one of Shelton, one of their trio, one of their band—conveying what you're going to hear that night. And the type is real big, so the words that register are Cookie and Cupcakes. And if you look just a bit closer, the poster tells what some of their hits are, like "Matilda." And much of this is done—unconsciously, I'm sure— with a lot of humor.

Like, take that poster I've got for Guitar Slim. Look at that pose he's in: he's standing there with a big, wild grin on his face, he's holding his guitar, and he's bending over in this weird position. Something in all this has to make you grin yourself. If you already know something about Guitar Slim's music—that he's a real heavy guy, plays his guitar up real loud—the poster just reinforces that image. Seeing his name and that photo thrown together like that, you know it means fun. You know it means bon temps.

The hardest part about collecting black music posters is finding them, particularly those from the 1950s and early 1960s, which were rarely set aside as future museum pieces. Stimulated by the work of such people as Chris Strachwitz at Arhoolie Records, Les Blank at Flower Films, archivist Michael Ochs, writers Robert Palmer, Arnold Shaw, and Peter Guralnick, institutions like Nashville's Country Music Foundation and the University of Mississippi's Living Blues Center, and record companies like Rhino, Yazoo, and Rounder, interest in American traditional music has been revived, and much has been unearthed that might otherwise have been lost forever. Some musically oriented people have made a career of locating surviving bluesmen, discovering rare record masters, or simply documenting America's musical roots. Jim

O'Neal, of the magazine *Living Blues*, and his wife, Amy, are two such:

A lot of people view posters as transient objects, just advertising. But I guess there are always people, like Amy and me, who are archival by nature. The trick is to find people who felt that way at the time or who did some searching back before music history artifacts became collectible and expensive. In searching for people to trade with, we've dealt mostly with blues record collectors. From time to time we'll learn about someone like Jump Jackson, a booking agent here in Chicago, who had some posters left over from the 1950s. And some of the Chicago blues record companies, like Delmark, have posters on their walls.

Amy and I started our own collecting around 1969. The idea was we'd pick up things whenever we could, and a great many of our posters we got simply by driving around Chicago, on the South or West Side. You pull up to the curb, jump out real quick, and untie the poster or pull out the staples. I always felt a little funny about taking them, but I tried not to take anything until after the event. And when I'd travel down South—I grew up in Mobile— I'd take my staple remover along with me. That's how I got my big green "Howlin' Wolf" from the Harlem Dukes Social Club— our prize possession.

Sometimes the clubs would give me them directly; I didn't always have to steal them off the street. Musicians would give them to me, too, especially if I asked for them.

Amy and I like posters as documentation of events, because that's what our magazine, Living Blues, is heavily devoted to. But there are certain key acts we're always keeping our eye out for, particularly when trading. Posters for Howlin' Wolf and Sonny Boy Williamson are the most prized. B. B. King posters are much more common. Muddy Waters is somewhere in the middle.

The O'Neals have tried to track down the printers of the original posters, hoping there would be a stash left in a back room or a basement. For the most part, according to Amy O'Neal, no such luck:

The guy that printed most of the Chicago blues posters is in Earl Park, Indiana—the Tribune Press. It's about a hundred miles south of Gary. Jim and I trekked over there once; they had a whole bunch of wonderful cuts of dead blues singers. We also tried to make a deal with the guy to run us up some mock posters, using the cuts, but he wouldn't do that because he deemed it unprofitable and because we weren't the owners of the cuts. Well, who were the owners? The musicians, for the most part, were dead, and the promoters long gone. I suppose if we'd ordered a thousand copies of each poster, then they might have thought the job worthwhile. It was very frustrating.

The feeling among most printers has been that the old posters get in the way of current jobs. They are trashed. Sometimes a printer will dump tons at once, like the New Jersey company that had printed all of Harlem's Apollo Theatre work. Two or three decades of popular music history can thus vanish in an hour. This is not always the result of ignorance or callousness; often printers do appreciate the historical significance of their back stock, but they cannot locate an individual or repository to cart off what may well be a mountain of cardboard. Even the film negatives used to print offset posters are uneconomical for a printer to store. They don't take up a great deal of space, it is true, but their silver content represents a substantial investment that may be partially recovered by selling them to various firms that extract usable silver from old film. Zinc and magnesium cuts, the etched woodblock-mounted metal plates that are used to reproduce images in letterpress printing, are also valuable as scrap.

Despite all the reasons for discarding the poster heritage as dead stock, there is one press specializing in show posters that makes active use of its archival holdings and historic reputation, Hatch Show Print, of Nashville, Tennessee. The firm is currently reprinting many of its old posters, including material from the early days of rock 'n' roll, but its history dates from far before the era of Elvis Presley. The shop's first job was for the father of Harriet Beecher Stowe, Henry Ward Beecher, who was lecturing on the subject of freedom for black people. The lecture was given at the Grand Opera House—which later became the Grand Ole Opry. In the late nineteenth and early twentieth centuries, Hatch created posters for minstrel shows, carnivals, vaudeville—including black as well as black-face acts. Later, the company produced posters for big bands and, most important, for country music performers.

When master printer Will Hatch inherited the company from his father and uncle in the 1920s, the company began to produce some of its most elaborate work. Hatch Show Print's present-day general manager, Jim Sherraden, himself a skilled woodblock carver in the tradition of Will Hatch, explains:

A talented man like Will Hatch would be trusted to come up with a beautiful, artistic theme for a show promotion. And when Will Hatch was alive, carving woodblocks for these posters dominated his life. He never married, and the secretaries for the company at that time, who are of course very old people now, talk about how they'd always see him carving woodblocks in the back of the office after everyone else had gone home. And the way Will Hatch would do it was the way a real master would do it; he'd carve the image right on the block, without any intermediate tracing.

You actually can tell an early Hatch poster by the style of Will's art. But he also would have stock silhouettes of, say, black folk with one leg in the air, waving a baton. And he easily might transpose cuts from one poster to another, so not everything Hatch did each time out was totally "original." Also, show poster printers stole a lot from each other. We've seen posters printed in Texas that borrow our themes. And some performers liked all their printers to use certain thematic images to create an act's ongoing, personalized style. Printers always had to stay current, so their art and design actually might be based on something not of their own "original" creation. Will Hatch did have his own opinions as to how something ought to look, though. He and Col. Tom Parker, Elvis Presley's manager, would get into tremendous arguments over how an Elvis poster ought to look—how the design could best further Elvis's career.

As we will see, in the 1950s—by the time popular music posters were advertising rhythm and blues, soul, and early rock 'n' roll— various economic factors, together with changes in printing techniques, greatly affected poster design and production. Straightforward, simple, and unadorned "boxing-style" work supplanted the elaborate artistry of master printers like Will Hatch. Nevertheless, two characteristics of the Hatch-era printer survived into the 1950s and early 1960s: pride in craftsmanship and a kind of hardnosed, autocratic approach to the business of producing posters, typical of the period before the intricacies of psychedelic art demanded the services of an artist-designer in addition to a printer. Between the middle 1950s and roughly 1965, the printer was art director, artist, and production manager rolled into one. Charles F. Tilghman, Sr., the foremost black printer in California, handled much of the show poster work for the Pacific Coast states during more than thirty years. He recalls:

I tried to approach each job as something fresh. I used what I had—my borders, my colors, my types. I guess it'd be like a painter painting a picture. He's doing something new, but he's using some of the things from the past. You have to know what to display and what not to display. You have to feel something when you're designing a poster. That's the knack. Experience.

A poster should have the attraction, the date, and the place. Nothing really more than that. You should be able to read all the information from across the street, riding in a car going the other way. Good poster printing is just something that's born in a person, I guess. I don't know exactly how to explain it. To get a good printing job done right, you have to feel how it ought to look. And I printed posters for almost every name band you can think of— and our posters looked very good. You could see them a block away.

The 1950s–1960s were the days of letterpress printing, a process largely supplanted today by offset lithography. Offset is first and foremost a photographic process. Type is set, proofs (called "repro") are pulled, cut apart, and then arranged to create the poster; this layout is photographed, and the image is transferred to a cylindrical grained metal plate, which is specially treated so that water will adhere to the background areas but not to the image of the type. In the printing process the plate is wetted, and the ink adheres to the dry image-area only. In the printing press, the cylindrical plate revolves against a "blanket cylinder," which transfers— "offsets"—the image onto the posterboard.

In contrast to the essentially photographic offset method, letterpress printing is largely a mechanical operation. Type consists of raised metal or (as Tilghman used) wooden letters, and pictures are reproduced by means of mechanically and chemically etched metal "cuts" mounted on wooden blocks. Whereas the offset printer needs merely to cut out and paste down "repro" to create his layout, the letterpress worker has to assemble ("lock up") the type and cuts into a metal frame called a "chase." With all the type and cuts locked up, such a chase might weigh 150 pounds, and two strong men are required to carry it from the composing room to the press. Letterpress work takes about four times as long as offset. Tilghman had a man working six days a week printing letterpress posters, setting and printing four or five a day. Often handling a hundred poster jobs each month, many for promoter Charles Sullivan, the company would buy five to ten thousand pounds of board at a time. Charles F. Tilghman, Jr., describes the usual print run:

Two or three hundred posters was what we used to run for single attractions. A show in San Francisco, say, would use up that many posters. But maybe the promoter would be doing shows in Oakland also or down in San Jose, so the whole run ordered might be 5,000 or so. Generally, there'd be no top—or no bottom—to the poster. There was blank space left. What we'd do was "head them up," or imprint them before they left the shop. Sometimes, we'd send them out without any imprinting, so wher-

ever they went, the people would fill in the information themselves—handwrite it or even give it to a local printer.

At its best, the 1950s style was honest and straightforward, delivering its message with little if any embellishment. Jazz posters from the 1940s were often more consciously "arty" than early 1950s rock posters. Because 1940s era big band tours were often promoted by a single poster design, a good deal of time and money could be devoted to the poster, which was a collaboration between printer as well as artist. In contrast, the kind of posters Tilghman and others produced during the 1950s were generally created for individual shows. Time and production budgets were therefore limited, and promoters dealt directly with printers rather than with designers or artists. As Hatch's Jim Sherraden explains, other factors also contributed to the simplification of the early rock poster—the low cost of printing a photograph on the poster, which substituted for an artist's drawing; size limitations—space to put up posters in the streets was at a premium; and the disappearance of the master printer:

When you talk about a show poster of the 1950s, you have to understand the people making up the poster weren't Will Hatch— they were blue-collar workers, who slapped the poster together and went home to dinner. They knew an effective way of making the printed presentation, and that was that.

Lest economy and journeyman production result in dull posters, some printers of the period began to employ "split-fountain" and "day-glo" techniques to punch up their austere product. In split-fountain work, blocks are placed in the printing-press ink fountain, dividing it into segments. Two different-colored inks are used in the fountain, one in each segment. The process is explained by Dave Bowman, president of Campbell Printing, which now runs the Tilghman operation:

The way you place your blocks in the ink fountain gives you the two different colors in certain areas of the poster—you can highlight portions of the poster this way. As the inks merge, they actually create a sort of third color. As you run the press, the colors are moving; each poster that comes out represents just a moment of color merging within the run. No two posters are exactly alike. The longer the run, the more the colors blend. If you ran the press long enough, the poster would end up all one color.

Frank Cicero, of Baltimore's Globe Printing Company, explains how "day-glo" fluorescent inks, screen-printed in blocks of colors, were developed to great effect in his firm's work:

Globe introduced fluorescent ink into its posters about thirty years ago. That really gave our work a sort of rejuvenation. And to this day, many people know these posters as "day-glo." It's the kind of ink that does very well on an outdoor poster. You can see the colors a block or more away. Our panels of color really break down the poster's message for the reader. He doesn't even have to read the whole poster to get the gist of it, because each performer featured on the poster has his own panel, in a separate screen-printed color. You can get the message in an instant.

Tacoma, Washington, *News Tribune* ad (1 September 1957): Elvis Presley
Lincoln Bowl, Tacoma, 1957

Globe's supercharged colors came to be associated with black performers. Back in Nashville, Hatch Show Print was making a virtue of a more austere "American Gothic" style characterized by very thick or very narrow gothic typefaces often printed in reds or blues and always on white stock. This style became associated with much country music and early white rock 'n' roll, which, for a southern printer like Hatch, were intimately linked. General manager Jim Sherraden is currently researching his company's back stock:

I remember recently we came across a week somewhere in 1957 in which Hatch printed posters for country artist Eddie Arnold, the Silas Green Minstrels, and Elvis. It was right about then when a lot of changes took place that led directly to rock 'n' roll.

There are people all over America, many now in their early fifties, who date their lives from their first exposure to Elvis. Perhaps because the fame of Elvis, like that of the Beatles, burgeoned in such short a time, posters played a useful role as concert advertisements only very early in their careers. Beatles

concert posters and outdoor art promoting Elvis are very rare items today. Compared to the enormous concert success of these performers the number of posters associated with them is miniscule. What few exist have come into the hands of the very hardest-working collectors, whose efforts to amass memorabilia are legendary.

One of the most dedicated Elvis collectors is Judy Bickford of Napa, California. Judy and her husband Greg recently broke up their massive collection, but right up to the end they held onto a very special piece documenting Elvis's rise as only something from his earliest days could. It was printed for a 1955 country music event in Memphis, Tennessee. With barely his second or third single in circulation, Elvis is billed at the very bottom of the poster. He was just beginning to climb to the top. Judy Bickford remembers:

I first saw that poster in a box of items I got from one of the earliest hometown Elvis collectors. This gal lived in Memphis and went to all of Elvis's early shows. Well, a relative first put us in touch, and we began to correspond, and Greg and I visited her once when we came through Memphis on a vacation. After awhile, she would from time to time send me a box full of her old Elvis things. She wasn't well off, and her prices always were so low that I'd usually hold on to the entire lot and send payment for everything. What I didn't want myself, I'd trade to my other Elvis friends.

In one of the packages she sent was this simple, wonderful concert poster. I couldn't help but notice Elvis's name was at the very bottom. Now, you have to realize it wasn't very long before Elvis became ELVIS. Except at the very beginning of his career, he didn't take second billing to anyone.

The feeling I got displaying that poster in my house—it was one of the pieces Greg and I featured in our "Elvis room"—was the same I experienced hearing "Heartbreak Hotel" for the first time on the jukebox. I mean, when you grow up as I did, listening to "How Much Is That Doggie in the Window?" and "Red Sails in the Sunset" and then "Heartbreak Hotel" suddenly comes into your life, well, you're a changed person from then on.

The momentum Elvis gave to rock 'n' roll was accelerated by such visionary entrepreneurs as disc jockey Alan Freed and, later, Dick Clark. In 1951 Freed joined Cleveland radio station WJW and hosted the pioneering "Moondog Rock & Roll Party." As Michael Ochs notes in *The Rock Archives*, "Freed's playlist consisted primarily of rhythm and blues, but he chose to call it rock and roll to sidestep the stigma attached to black, or 'race' records." In March 1952, Freed staged the first large-scale rock show, "The Moondog Coronation Ball," at the Cleveland Arena. As Ochs reports, "When 25,000 fans showed up to claim 10,000 seats, the show was cancelled."

Freed moved to New York City radio station WINS in September 1954, and it was not long after that he began staging major all-star rhythm and blues *cum* rock 'n' roll events at the Brooklyn and Manhattan Paramount theaters. Freed relied less on concert posters than on theater marquees. As you walked past the ticket booth and headed for the auditorium doors, the entire outside lobby area blazed with oversize movie-style full-color posters—art more naturally associated with the theater than the street.

Freed's tours gave rise to rhythm and blues and rock 'n' roll "caravans" and "cavalcades" presented by promoters like Dick

Paramount Theatre, Brooklyn, ca. 1955

Clark and Murray the K. What few posters these tours generated were associated with the tour as a whole rather than with specific venues or events and, like Freed's, were used in or near the theaters. Motown Records' widely touring "Motortown Revue" of the early 1960s relied on similar promotional methods. Only when such a tour came to, say, New York's Apollo Theatre might a run of separate "street" posters be produced.

Much of the best 1950s art associated with the birth of rock 'n' roll was done for the movies of the period. Window cards, along with larger lobby cards were used by theaters across the country. The very titles of the movies—*Don't Knock the Rock*, *Rock Around the Clock*—incorporating hits by black acts like Little Anthony and the Imperials or white groups like Bill Haley and the Comets, inspired bold movie-poster art that lured teenagers by the thousands. But even as Elvis's own rock movies—the most successful of all—reached their peak, rock 'n' roll music was beginning its first decline. Out of this early 1960s slow-down came the great folk-rock poet Bob Dylan as well as the British Invasion and, paramountly, the overwhelming surge of Beatlemania.

Concert poster art served a workmanlike role in the lives of folk musicians. Folk music clubs like Folk City (New York), Club 47 (Cambridge), Ash Grove (Los Angeles), and Cabale Creamery and Jabberwock (Berkeley) issued handbills by the hundreds every week. But these are even plainer than the plainest of 1950s rock posters, and they are not collected much, except for billings that portend the rise of such giants as Dylan.

As with *Elvis* and *The Beatles*, the name *Dylan* often sufficed to sell tickets. Once his act became established, posters for Dylan concerts rarely appeared. There are some wonderful pieces that herald Dylan's first appearances in major cities. One great poster was created by folk musician Eric Von Schmidt for Dylan and co-performer Joan Baez. It was done *á la* Toulouse-Lautrec, strangely evocative of the time and place in which Dylan's impact was first felt. Another significant piece is the poster that announced Dylan's 1965 appearance at the Newport Folk Festival, where he stunned his large and faithful following by performing on electric instruments.

The cult that developed around the Beatles was of even greater consequence than what Dylan generated. The Dylan fan had nothing on the Beatlemaniac. A poster advertising any of the Fab Four's American concerts after their first State-side engagement in 1964 would have been superfluous. The pure emotion in the air, intensified by enormous press coverage, was enough to sell every ticket available. Musician Pat Jacobsen assembled a major collection of Beatles memorabilia as a San Francisco Bay Area teenager and remembers just how scarce concert posters were:

It seems to me the Beatles' promotion wing spent most of its money creating real-life drama to advertise concerts: just getting the Beatles out of their airplane, having them walk down the ramp in the middle of all that concrete, having them immediately mobbed.

I imagine that as a result of all this hysteria, anything you would put up on the Beatles, like an outdoor poster, would be instantly torn down. Anyway, everybody in America was promoting the living hell out of the Beatles, so they didn't need posters. You just didn't have to do any of the traditional things to promote them. You just said the word Beatles.

But there was one concert poster that had a great impact here in the States. It advertised the Beatles' "Command Performance," before the British royalty, at the London Palladium in 1963. It's a 1964 poster, printed in America.

Now why would a 1964 poster be printed in America featuring the Beatles at a British show in 1963? My understanding is that the poster was intended solely to promote the Beatles' American concerts in 1964, when they came over for the first time. It was a prepublicity stunt. It used the authority conveyed by "Command Performance" to get them attention in America.

The Command Performance poster, despite a wide early circulation, is a rare collectible piece today. Its original 1964 printing can fetch upwards of $250. But there is another Beatles poster that is *virtually* priceless today. It advertises the 1965 Shea Stadium concert. More widely known is the Beatles concert poster done by San Francisco psychedelic artist Wes Wilson for the Candlestick Park show in 1966—the concert that turned out to be their last fully public event.

Apart from a few unusual Beatles items, the bulk of the posters advertising "British Invasion" groups of the 1964–1966 period were simple letterpress jobs. These generally were multiple billings; the printer had a tough time fitting in all the information promoters felt necessary.

Charles F. Tilghman, Jr.:

I think promoters felt they couldn't draw enough people unless they included a great many acts, and so the posters got a lot busier. You had to run too much too small. You couldn't feature four bands equally and make a good poster.

I think the psychedelic poster, which came next, around 1966, was one way of making multiple attractions stand out. The style of art was bold enough to shock people into looking at the poster. Of course, the psychedelic poster was also a lot harder to read than the stuff we were doing at the Tilghman Press, but it started to appeal to a new kind of fan. You began to see psychedelic art in newspaper advertising, in magazines, and so forth. Psychedelic posters were a sign of new times, just as some of the earlier art had been in its day.

Elvis Presley

He will forever be known as the King of Rock 'n' Roll. But in February 1955, when the Faron Young poster was printed to advertise a local appearance at the Memphis Auditorium (1.1), Elvis was only just developing his wild rockabilly style. He was rightfully billed at the bottom. By October, he was on the brink of becoming a national sensation. Much of his success was due to the promotional savvy of his new manager, Col. Tom Parker, as well as the eagerness of RCA—which had bought his original Sun Records contract—to exploit a major discovery. In January 1956, RCA released "Heartbreak Hotel," which soared to the top position on *Billboard* charts. National television appearances followed, as did more hit singles, including "Hound Dog." Small wonder that Elvis's August 1956 appearance in Jacksonville, Florida, was heralded by a poster (1.2) altogether different in design and content from that of the year before.

From 1956 until his death in 1977, Elvis Presley was never less than a stupendous attraction. There was little need to depend on traditional street posters to sell out shows. The few surviving posters from Elvis's first years are particularly rare collectibles.

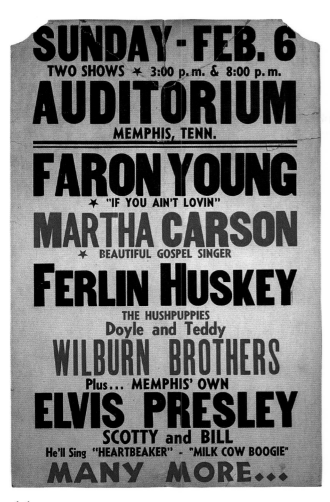

1.1

Faron Young; Elvis Presley
Memphis Auditorium, Memphis, 1955

1.2

Elvis Presley; Jordanaires. Florida Theater, Jacksonville, 1956
Artist: Hatch Show Print

Early Rock Movies

Early rock 'n' roll was given a tremendous boost by films featuring both white and black musical acts. MGM's *Blackboard Jungle* (March 1955), a serious social drama, featured Bill Haley and the Comets' "Rock Around the Clock," a song that lent its name to another film, released the next year. While the plot of the later opus was conventional enough, the rock 'n' roll soundtrack,

featuring Haley, the Platters, and controversial deejay Alan Freed, got the film banned in a number of cities—thereby assuring its popularity (1.4).

By 1956, Hollywood churned out rock 'n' roll films with regularity. But the standout was *Love Me Tender* (November 1956), starring Elvis Presley, who was fresh from national television

(continued on next page)

1.3

Lobby Card: *Don't Knock The Rock*—Bill Haley and the Comets
1956

1.4

Lobby Card: *Rock Around The Clock*—Bill Haley and the Comets
1956

1.5

Lobby Card: *Rock, Rock, Rock*—Frankie Lymon
1956

1.6

Lobby Card: *Let's Rock!*—Roy Hamilton
1958

1.7
Lobby Card: *Don't Knock The Rock*—Bill Haley and the Comets
1956

(continued from facing page) exposure. While critical response was favorable, audience reaction was overwhelming. A year later came *Jail House Rock* and *Loving You*, and in 1958, *King Creole*.

The lobby cards shown here are miniature versions of the much larger posters, usually vertical in format, with which theater managers decorated their lobbies. Despite the name, lobby cards were usually used outdoors, in showcase windows facing the street.

1.8
Lobby Card: *Shake, Rattle and Rock!*—Joe Turner
1956

1.9
Lobby Card: *Rock All Night*—The Platters
1957

"Cavalcades"

ALAN FREED

Disc jockey, promoter, music-industry pioneer, Alan Freed is often credited with giving rock 'n' roll its name. After a stint in Cleveland as deejay for WJW, Freed moved to New York's WINS in 1954. While *rock 'n' roll* had been used by blacks to describe boogie-woogie jazz—and as a euphemism for sex—Freed's WINS show, the *Rock & Roll Party*, was the first mass media use of the term.

In 1955, Freed began to produce regular stage shows, first at the

St. Nicholas Arena and then at the Brooklyn Paramount, always serving as emcee. The next year he started putting together touring "cavalcades." Ticket sales were generated mostly by decorating theater marquees with as many of the top names on the bill as possible, and by decorating the outer lobbies with gaudy posters similar in style to the art used to promote the rock films of the

(*continued on next page*)

1.10

Alan Freed Presents the Big Beat
Cincinnati Gardens, Cincinnati, 1958

1.11

Program: The Big Beat (inside)
1957

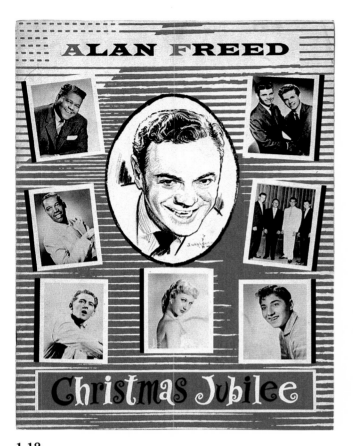

1.12
Program: Christmas Jubilee
1957

1.13
Program: Christmas Jubilee (inside)
1957

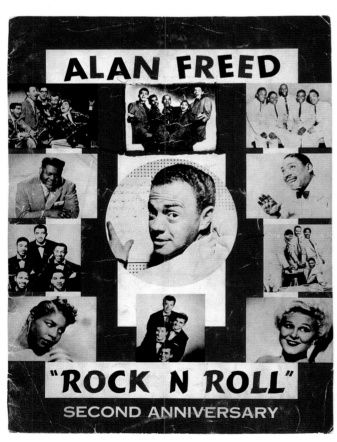

1.14
Program: Second Anniversary Show
1956

1.15
Program: Third Anniversary Show
1957

(*continued from facing page*) period. Few of the large lobby displays, and fewer still of any street posters that might have been printed for each stop on the tour, were preserved. Printed programs, sold at the shows, are the surviving artifacts.

OTHER TOURS

Independent companies like Super Attractions were among the earliest to produce tours of top rhythm and blues groups paired with white rock 'n' roll bands. Beginning very early in the 1950s and reaching maximum prominence between 1955 and 1960, these caravans criss-crossed the United States.

(continued on next page)

1.16

The 5 Royales; Tab Smith
ca. 1953
Artist: Globe Poster

1.17

The Biggest Show of Stars for '57
College of Puget Sound, Tacoma, Washington, 1957
Artist: Globe Poster

1.18

Winter Dance Party (Buddy Holly Final Tour)
Midwest, 1959

1.19

Jerry Lee Lewis; The Treniers
City Hall, Sheffield, England, 1956

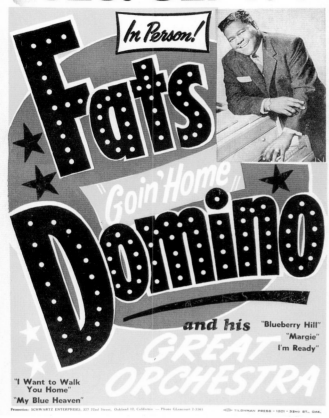

1.20

Fats Domino
Tri-City Center, Kennewick, Washington, 1964
Artist: Tilghman Press

1.21

The Biggest Show of Stars for 1957
Forum, Wichita, Kansas, 1957
Artist: Globe Poster

1.22

Program: The Biggest In Person Show of '56 (inside)
1956

(continued from facing page)

The poster from the 1957 Show of Stars (1.21), booked at the Wichita Forum, is one of the first tours to include the Crickets, the Lubbock, Texas, group fronted by Buddy Holly.

The Show of Stars continued into the mid 1960s. By 1964, posters and lobby displays revealed the first stirrings of the American response to the British Invasion(1.26).

1.23

The Biggest Show of Stars for 1961
Forum, Wichita, Kansas, 1961

1.24

The Biggest Show of Stars for 1962
Forum, Wichita, Kansas, 1962

1.25

The Biggest Show of Stars for 1963
Forum, Wichita, Kansas, 1963

1.26

Caravan of Record Stars for 1964
Forum, Wichita, Kansas, 1964

1.27
The Best Show in 1964
Ponce de Leon Ballpark, Atlanta, 1964

Black Music

Promoters like Alan Freed and touring cavalcades like the "Show of Stars" brought early rhythm and blues and pre-Soul-era bands to white audiences. Some black musicians even attracted a considerable white following as early as the mid 1950s—Chuck Berry and Fats Domino, for instance. Later on, many more whites were enjoying the music of Motown and Memphis Soul. But it was not until the late 1960s that whites en masse became aware of other black music styles, such as the urban blues. So that while black and white music were not wholly separated—even early on—there were distinct black and white tour circuits. "Blues masters," including Lowell Fulson (1.28), Joe Turner (1.30), T-Bone Walker (1.33), and Little Milton (1.31, 1.35), appeared frequently on the black tours. There are a number of acknowledged kings of the blues circuit: Clifton Chenier (1.34), master of the Cajun blues style; Big Joe Turner, celebrated as the greatest blues shouter of them all; Little Milton, who followed in Turner's footsteps; and T-Bone Walker, one of the most influential blues guitarists.

With very few exceptions, posters promoting appearances by black blues artists were designed in the print shop by foremen and pressmen. Up until the mid 1970s, these posters were produced primarily on letterpress, which gave them a distinctive look often termed "boxing style," as they resemble street posters advertising fights.

1.28

Lowell Fulson; Lloyd Glenn
Sunset Terrace Ballroom, Los Angeles, 1959

1.29

Buster Brown
Jack's Place, Fort Worth, Texas, 1955
Artist: Fred Marshall Press

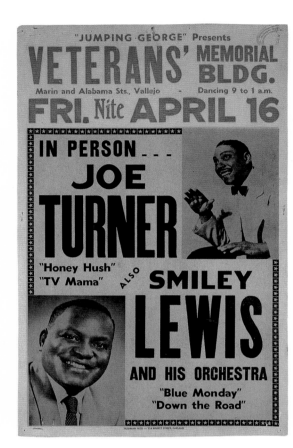

1.30

Joe Turner; Smiley Lewis
Veterans Memorial Building, Vallejo, California, 1965
Artist: Tilghman Press

1.31

Little Milton
G & M Pleasure Spot, La Marque, Texas, 1965
Artist: Fred Marshall Press

1.32

Big Jay McNeely
South Gate Arena, Los Angeles, 1952

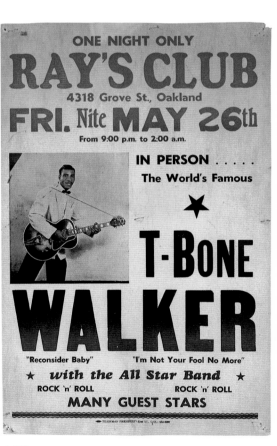

1.33

T-Bone Walker. Ray's Club, Oakland, California, 1967
Artist: Tilghman Press

1.34

Clifton Chenier. Paradise Auditorium, Mosswood,
Louisiana, 1966. Artist: Fred Marshall Press

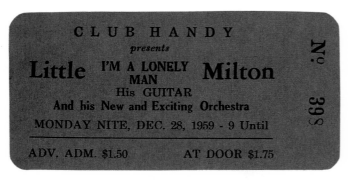

1.35

Ticket: Little Milton
Club Handy, Memphis, 1959

1.36

Advertising pass: Fats Domino
West Coast engagements, 1960

1.37

Ticket: Rufus Thomas
Club Handy, Memphis, 1964

1.38

Ticket: Ike and Tina Turner
Club Handy, Memphis, 1964

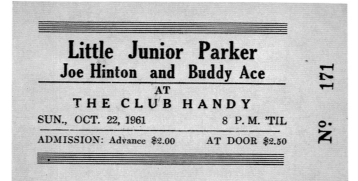

1.39

Ticket: Little Junior Parker;
Joe Hinton and Buddy Ace
Club Handy, Memphis, 1961

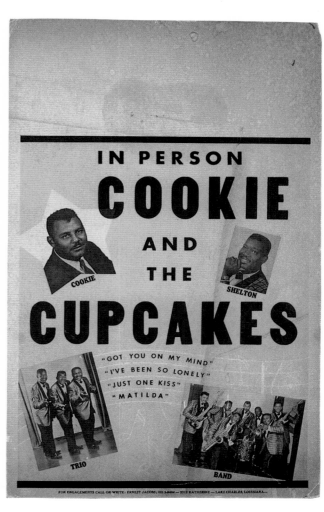

MEMPHIS AND NEW ORLEANS

The Club Handy was located in the Beale Street district of Memphis. B. B. King is among the artists who developed their technique and early repertoire at this and similar clubs.

Pianist Roy Byrd, dubbed "Professor Longhair," came to symbolize the uniquely soulful nature of the New Orleans black music style (1.40).

Throughout much of Louisiana and East Texas, Cookie and the Cupcakes are remembered with great fondness (1.41).

BOBBY BLAND

Bobby "Blue" Bland, while drawing on his Memphis and Houston roots, epitomizes the sophisticated modern blues-ballad singer.

(opposite top)
1.40
Willie T.; Professor Longhair
La Ray's, New Orleans, 1959

(opposite bottom)
1.41
Cookie and the Cupcakes
ca. 1960

1.42
Bobby Bland; Vi Campbell
Embassy Room, East Palo Alto, California, 1967
Artist: Tilghman Press

NEW-STYLE
BLACK POSTERS

Many veteran urban blues musicians enjoy current popularity among both black and white audiences. Only a change in poster style distinguishes their present-day activity from that of the past.

Until the early 1970s, posters promoting black-oriented entertainment were designed in a style that originated around the turn of the century, when minstrel show, vaudeville, and carnival posters were part of an ''American Gothic'' advertising tradition. But as silk-screen printing, particularly as developed by Globe Poster, Baltimore, has supplanted traditional letterpress, the posters have begun to take on a more modern appearance, with richer, more vivid ink coverage and greater freedom and flamboyance of design.

1.43
Z. Z. Hill. Beady's Club Fantasy,
Thibodaux, Louisiana, 1983
Artist: Globe Poster

1.44
Al Green. Longhorn Ballroom, Dallas, 1984
Artist: Globe Poster

1.45

Eddie Kendricks
J.R.'s Place, Mobile, Alabama, 1985
Artist: Globe Poster

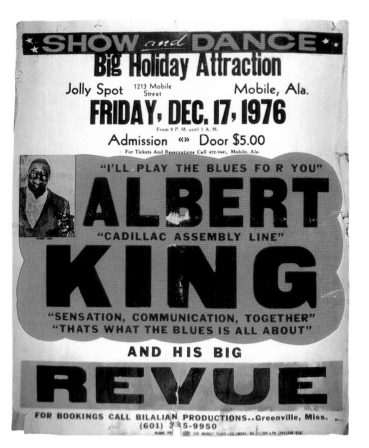

1.46

Albert King
Jolly Spot, Mobile, Alabama, 1976
Artist: Globe Poster

1.47

Joe Simon
Zodiac Club, Detroit, 1984
Artist: Globe Poster

1.48

Sam and Dave
Hide-A-Way Lounge, Nashville, 1980
Artist: Globe Poster

Few blues musicians have ever been accorded the widespread recognition that B. B. King enjoys. His success is the result of a life-long apprenticeship to his art, playing thousands of small clubs and dance halls beginning in the early 1950s. King's name has probably appeared on more posters than that of any other urban blues musician (1.49).

Like B. B. King, Chester Burnett—better known as "Howlin' Wolf"—grew up in the rural South and journeyed to Memphis, where he created a style all his own. Then, like King and many others, he went north to Chicago and there became a legend (1.50, 1.52).

While Wolf's career yielded many a classic blues, a contemporary, Muddy Waters, may have had more influence on rock. Waters's style was copied by such groups as the Paul Butterfield Blues Band, Led Zeppelin, the Rolling Stones, and the Yardbirds. He is also credited with helping Chuck Berry obtain his first major recording contract (1.52).

1.49

B. B. King
Pleasure Pier, Galveston, Texas, 1955
Artist: American Printing and Lithographic

1.50
Howlin' Wolf
Harlem Dukes Club, Mobile, Alabama, 1964
Artist: Globe Poster

1.51
Memphis Slim; Sonny Boy Williamson
Parkway Arena, Saginaw, Michigan, 1958

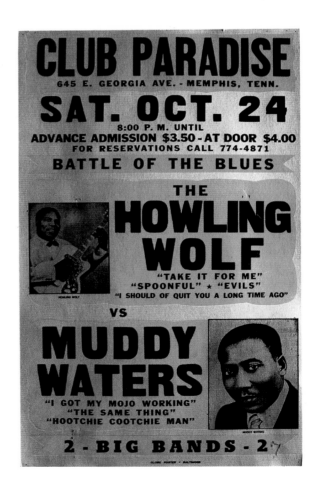

1.52
Howlin' Wolf; Muddy Waters
Club Paradise, Memphis, 1964
Artist: Globe Poster

Gospel has long been tied to rock 'n' roll. Professor Alex Bradford (1.55), pianist, organist, choir director, composer, influenced Ray Charles, Little Richard, and Sam Cooke.

Cooke is remembered as the greatest sex symbol in gospel history. He developed his first substantial following when he sang with the Soul Stirrers (1.55).

There were several versions of the Five Blind Boys (1.54), the most famous of which originated in Mississippi and featured leader Archie Brownlee, whose vocal strength was second only to Ira Tucker of the legendary Dixie Hummingbirds.

1.53

Big Gospel Train of 1964
Oakland Auditorium Arena, Oakland, 1964
Artist: Tilghman Press

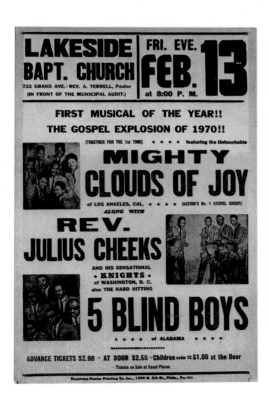

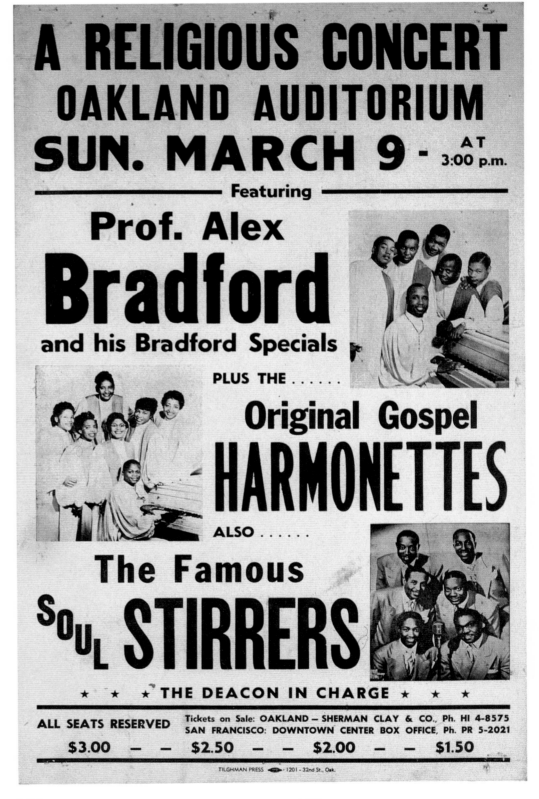

1.54 Mighty Clouds of Joy; Five Blind Boys
Lakeside Baptist Church, Shreveport,
Louisiana, 1970. Artist: Keystone Poster Printing

1.55 Professor Alex Bradford; Soul Stirrers
Oakland Auditorium, Oakland, 1958
Artist: Tilghman Press

JAMES BROWN

James Brown's influence is inestimable, since rock 'n' roll performers will probably never stop trying to be as wild as he.

Brown began with gospel, formed the Famous Flames in 1954, and rose to prominence in the early 1960s (1.56). He has had many chart-topping hits—"Papa's Got a Brand New Bag," "Say It Loud, I'm Black and I'm Proud," "Popcorn," "Hot Pants," "It's a Man's Man's Man's World"—and he has led some of the most exhilarating and well-drilled bands ever. But the legend comes down to the man himself, "Mr. Soul Brother Number One," nothing less than an electrifying performer, "so hot," according to one observer, "he literally sweats through his shoe soles."

1.56

James Brown; Sugar Pie DeSanto
Evergreen Ballroom, Olympia, Washington, 1961

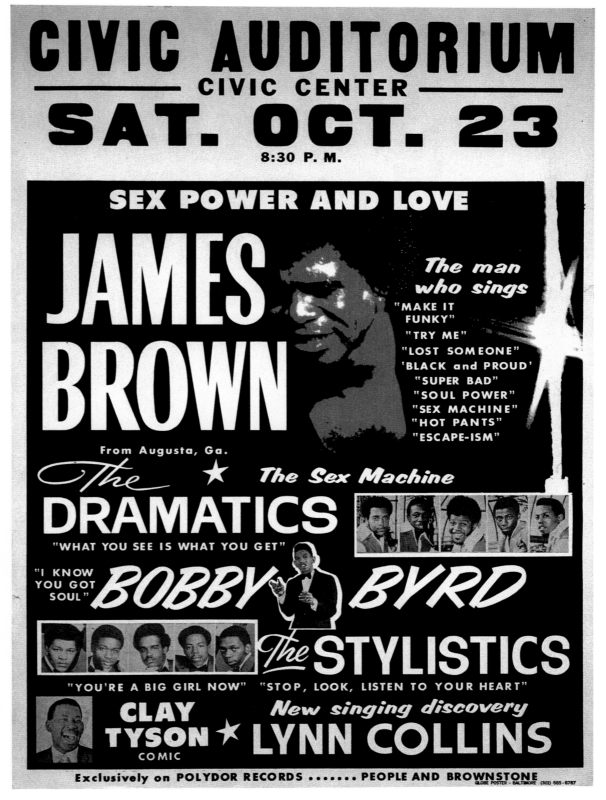

1.57

James Brown; The Dramatics
Civic Auditorium, San Francisco, 1971
Artist: Globe Poster

APOLLO THEATRE

The Apollo Theatre is synonymous with the greatest traditions of black music. Located in the heart of Harlem, the Apollo drew audiences who could make or break careers in the black entertainment world.

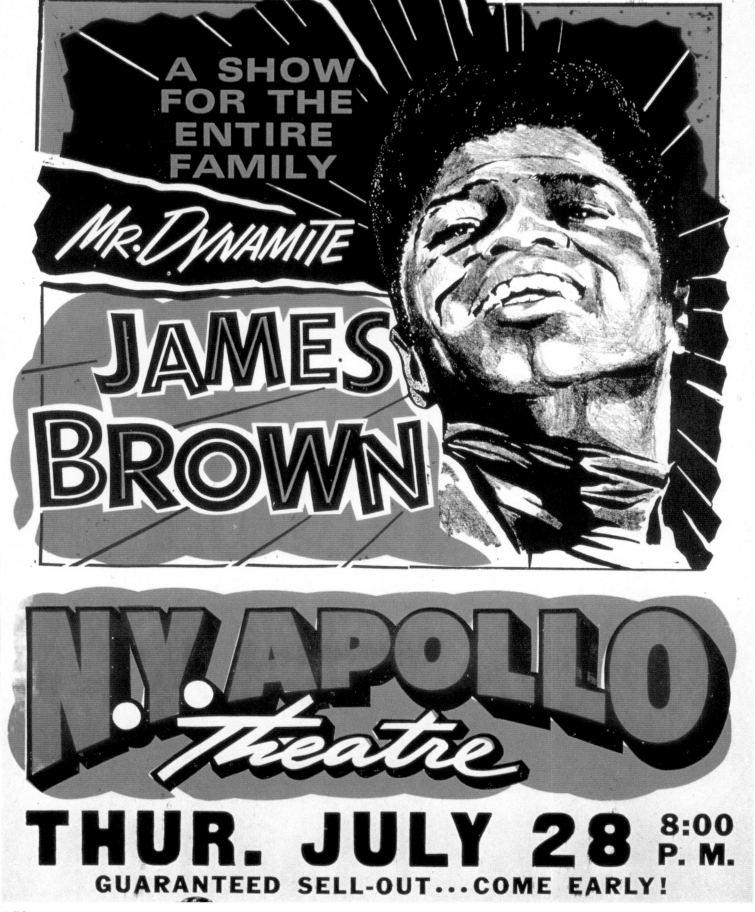

1.58

James Brown. Apollo Theatre, New York, 1966
Artist: Globe Poster

FILLMORE AUDITORIUM

The Fillmore Auditorium is as well known in rock 'n' roll as the Apollo is in black music. It is best remembered as the site of Bill Graham's first two years of dance concerts. But for many decades before Graham began his operation in 1966, it featured the best in black entertainment.

While Graham used psychedelic-style posters to advertise his shows, black shows at the Fillmore—even those that overlapped into the Graham years—were promoted by the traditional "boxing style" poster.

1.59
Temptations
Fillmore Auditorium,
San Francisco, 1966
Artist: Tilghman Press

Black dances at such venues as the Fillmore Auditorium and a host of night spots like Oakland's Continental Club were advertised with street posters like these, which were stapled to telephone poles throughout black neighborhoods. The posters shown here, heralding performances by Motown heavyweights like Marvin Gaye and the Four Tops, and Memphis soul great Otis Redding, were printed by the Tilghman Press, whose distinctive letterpress style, emphasizing crisp lettering and rich inks, established it as one of the most creative producers of posters.

1.60
Four Tops; Johnny Talbot
Fillmore Auditorium, San Francisco, 1966
Artist: Tilghman Press

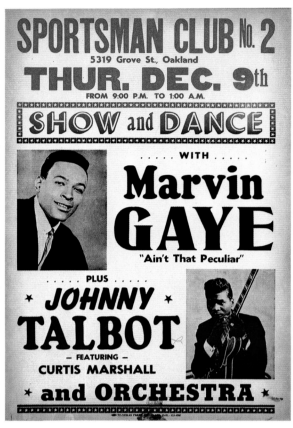

1.61
Marvin Gaye; Johnny Talbot
Sportsman Club No. 2, Oakland, California, 1965
Artist: Tilghman Press

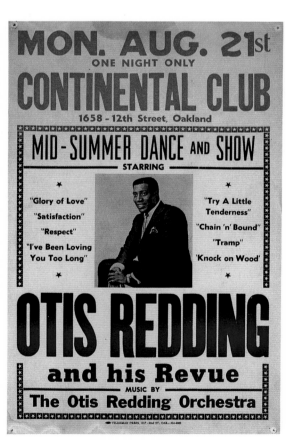

1.62
Otis Redding. Continental Club, Oakland,
California, 1967. Artist: Tilghman Press

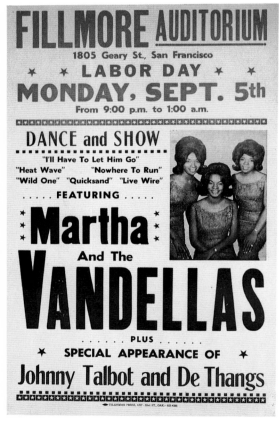

1.63
Martha and The Vandellas. Fillmore Auditorium,
San Francisco, 1966. Artist: Tilghman Press

1.64
Sam Cooke; Bobby Bland
Civic Auditorium, Richmond, California, 1964
Artist: Tilghman Press

1.65
Hank Ballard and the Midnighters
Kearney Bowl, Fresno, California, 1966
Artist: Tilghman Press

1.66
Jackie Wilson; The Upsetters
Evergreen Ballroom, Olympia, Washington, 1963
Artist: Tilghman Press

1.67
Mary Wells
Esther's Orbit Room, Oakland, California, 1965
Artist: Tilghman Press

1.68
Smokey Robinson and the Miracles
Continental Club, Oakland, California, 1966
Artist: Tilghman Press

1.69
Otis Redding
Fillmore Auditorium, San Francisco, 1966
Artist: Tilghman Press

CLASSICS AND TRENDS: MID 1960s

A number of artists from the 1950s continued to enjoy wide appeal as 1960s rock rose out of its early doldrums. These artists were joined by such up-and-coming Soul artists like Wilson Pickett (1.71) and groups like the Ike and Tina Turner Revue (1.72, 1.73), destined to play a greater role in the development of late-1960s rock.

1.70

Otis Redding; the Marvelettes
Civic Coliseum, Knoxville, Tennessee, 1966
Artist: Globe Poster

1.71

Wilson Pickett; Carla Thomas
Civic Coliseum, Knoxville, Tennessee, 1966

1.72

Ike and Tina Turner Revue
Oakland Auditorium, Oakland,
California; California Hall,
San Francisco, 1967
Artist: Colby Poster

1.73

Ike and Tina Turner Revue
Cocoanut Grove, Sacramento, California, 1962
Artist: Colby Poster

The Twist

The Twist was one of several music fads that livened up the dreary early 1960s. The best known of Twist artists was Chubby Checker (1.76), whose name is indeed synonymous with the dance.

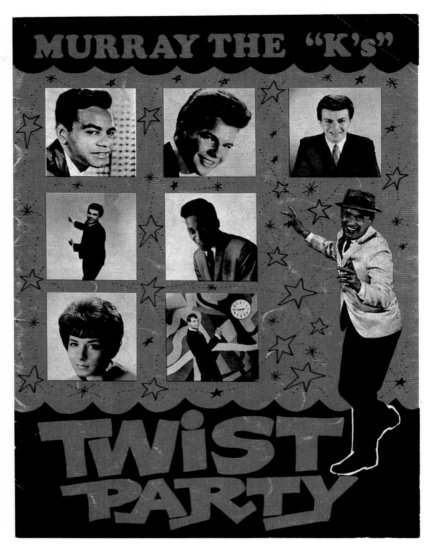

1.75
Program: "Murray The K's Twist Party"
1962

1.74
This Is It Cats!—Twist contest
Liberty Theater, Columbus, Georgia, 1962
Artist: Hatch Show Print

1.76
Lobby Card: *Don't Knock the Twist*—Chubby Checker
1962

Folk Music

Growing out of traditions established by people like Woody Guthrie and the Weavers in the 1940s and 1950s, folk music of the early 1960s was popularized by such musicians as Peter, Paul, and Mary, Joan Baez, Bob Dylan, and the Kingston Trio.

White folk music was also strengthened by the rediscovery of country artists like the Carter Family, and black country blues musicians like Lightning Hopkins (1.78), Mississippi John Hurt (1.85), Mance Lipscomb (1.80), Reverend Gary Davis (1.85), and Sonny Terry and Brownie McGhee (1.79). The folk community also embraced urban blues, made by the likes of Muddy Waters, Otis Spann (1.78), Howlin' Wolf, James Cotton, and Junior Wells.

The civil rights movement of the late 1950s and early 1960s gave birth to groups such as the Freedom Singers (1.77), who sang in conjunction with marches and sit-ins in the South and helped spread awareness of the black cause in northern communities.

Folk music, particularly of the "protest" variety, along with country blues and bluegrass, was featured at coffee houses and clubs in intellectual communities across the United States, including Gerde's Folk City in New York, The Club 47 in Cambridge, Massachusetts (1.81, 1.84), the Ash Grove in Los Angeles (1.77), and the Jabberwock (1.80) in Berkeley, California.

1.77

Freedom Singers; Alice Gunn
Ash Grove, Los Angeles, ca. 1962

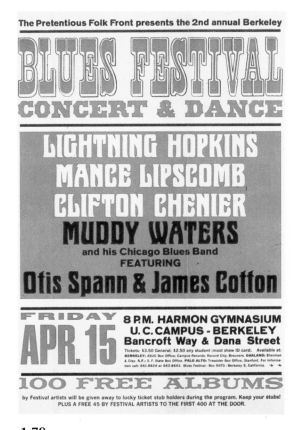

1.78
Second Berkeley Blues Festival
University of California, Berkeley, 1966

1.79
Sonny Terry and Brownie McGhee
Reed College, Portland, Oregon, 1961

1.80
Mance Lipscomb
Jabberwock, Berkeley, 1966

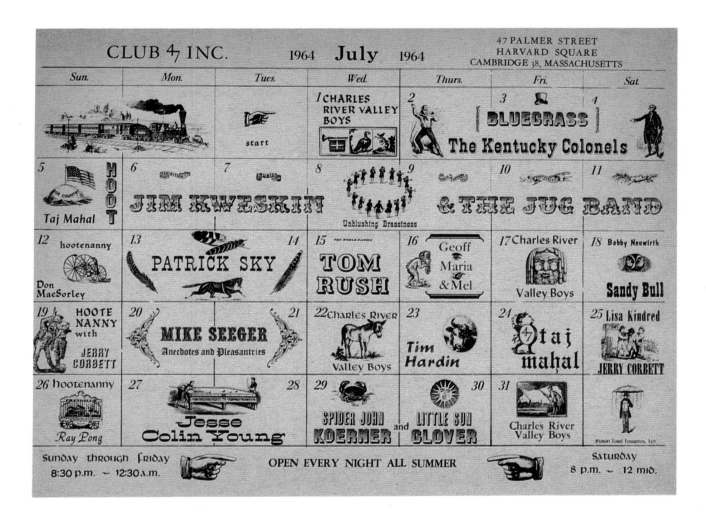

1.81
July Calendar
Club 47, Cambridge, Massachusetts, 1964
Artist: Byron Linardos

1.82

Willie Mae "Big Mama" Thornton
Masonic Temple / Savoy Club,
Richmond, California, 1966

1.83

Fifth Memphis Blues
Festival. Overton Park,
Memphis, 1970

1.84

July Calendar
Club 47, Cambridge, Massachusetts, 1965
Artist: Byron Linardos

1.85

Folk Blues and Gospel Concert
Hunter College, New York, 1964

1.86

Jimmy Reed
Masonic Hall, Richmond,
California, 1964
Artist: Tilghman Press

AMERICAN FOLK BLUES FESTIVAL

The American Folk Blues Festival was a highly successful tour produced for several years by the German concert promoters Lippmann and Rau, whose staff artist was Gunther Kieser, designer of some of the best-known European rock posters of the late 1960s and early 1970s.

1.87

American Folk Blues Festival '65
European tour, 1965
Artists: Michel, Gunther Kieser

BERKELEY FOLK FESTIVAL

Guitar teacher Barry Olivier is the founding father of the Berkeley Folk Festival. First presented at the University of California in 1958, it lasted ten years. The Festival featured prominent musicologists in addition to a who's who roster of folk musicians: names like Pete Seeger, Doc Watson, Joan Baez, Jean Ritchie, and Lightning Hopkins. By 1966, the Festival also showcased most of the early San Francisco psychedelic-era bands, which had their own roots in folk and blues music. These included the Jefferson Airplane (1.89), the Steve Miller Band, and Country Joe and the Fish.

1.88

Sixth Berkeley Folk Festival
University of California, Berkeley, 1963

1.89

Ninth Berkeley Folk Festival
University of California, Berkeley, 1966

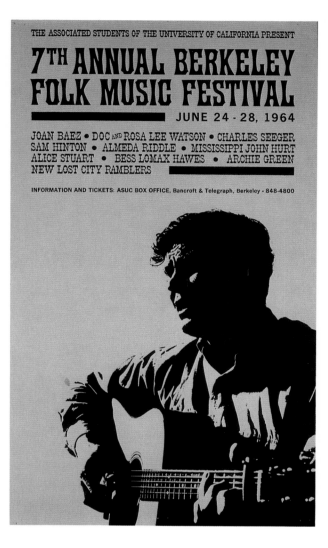

1.90

Seventh Berkeley Folk Festival
Greek Theater, Berkeley, 1964

1.91

First Berkeley Folk Festival
University of California, Berkeley, 1958

BLUEGRASS, FOLK, AND BLUES

Major country blues musicians like Lightnin' Hopkins (1.94) found a new home in the Bay Area, thanks in part to the activity of Arhoolie Records, founded by musicologist Chris Strachwitz.

While Bill Monroe (1.92) symbolized the bluegrass "establishment," there were by the mid 1960s, up-and-coming groups like the Kentucky Colonels (1.93), who invented new ways to approach acoustic country music. Led by Roland and Clarence White, the Colonels impressed a Bay Area banjo picker named Jerry Garcia, later lead guitarist for the Grateful Dead. Garcia helped book the Colonels into Palo Alto's Comedia Theater in 1964.

1.92

Bill Monroe
Napredak Hall, Santa Clara, California, 1963
Artist: Tilghman Press

1.93

Kentucky Colonels
Fugazi Hall, San Francisco; Comedia Theater,
Palo Alto, 1964

1.94

Folk Festival Fireside Concert
Greek Theater, Berkeley, 1965

1.95

Jimmy Reed; Reverend Gary Davis
Berkeley Community Theater, Berkeley, 1964

BAY AREA
FOLK

Many Bay Area rock musicians began their careers playing folk and blues in small clubs like the Offstage, in San Jose, the Tangent, in Palo Alto, and the Cabale and Jabberwock, in Berkeley. Some of these musicians gave guitar and banjo lessons. Featured instructors on the "Folio Broadsheet" for the Offstage (1.96) were Jerry Garcia, later of the Grateful Dead, and Paul Kantner and Jerry (Jorma) Kaukonen, later of the Jefferson Airplane.

1.96

September Broadsheet: Offstage Folk Music Theater. San Jose, 1964

FOLK FESTIVAL HEYDAY

The granddaddy of all the American folk music festivals is the Newport Folk Festival, first held in 1959 at the harbor-front Freebody Park in Newport, Rhode Island. The 1960 festival (1.98) included young Joan Baez, "commercial" folk groups like the Limeliters and the Tarriers, "traditional" artists like Robert Pete Williams, John Lee Hooker, and Mahalia Jackson, as well as the "parents" of the folk music movement—the Weavers, Oscar Brand, Theodore Bikel, and Pete Seeger.

After a two-year hiatus, the Festival returned in 1963 with Bob Dylan, who, two years later at Newport, broke with folk tradition by appearing with an *electric* band. While this scandalized traditionalists, it was a major step in the inevitable integration of folk and rock styles.

The Folk Festivals held at San Francisco State College (now University) were less ambitious, featuring far fewer nationally recognized names, but the annual event foreshadowed the rise of many San Francisco psychedelic rock groups.

The Second SFSC Festival (1.97), held in 1963, featured such performers as Jerry Garcia (later lead guitarist with the Grateful Dead), David Nelson (guitarist and leader of the New Riders of the Purple Sage), and Janis ("Janet") Joplin and Peter Albin (mainstays of Big Brother and the Holding Company).

An additional note of interest: the poster for the Fifth SFSC Folk Festival (1.99) was done by Michael Ferguson, charter member of the Charlatans, the rock group credited as the originator of the San Francisco psychedelic music community.

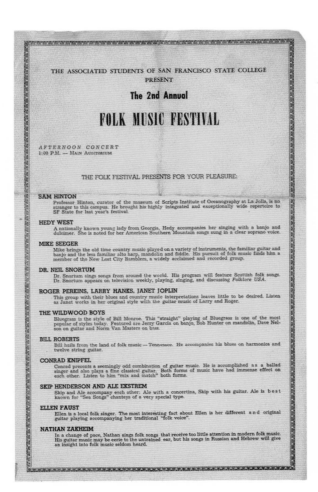

1.97

Second Annual Folk Music Festival (front). San Francisco State College, San Francisco, 1963

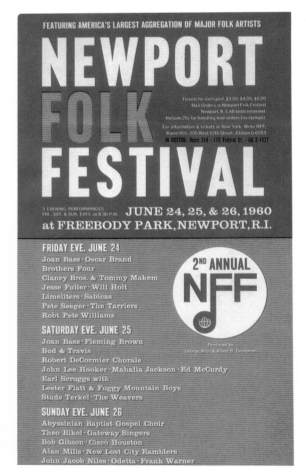

1.98

Second Newport Folk Festival Freebody Park, Newport, Rhode Island, 1960

1.99

Fifth Annual Folk Festival, San Francisco College, San Francisco, 1966
Artist: Michael Ferguson

JOAN BAEZ
AND BOB DYLAN

By 1965 Baez and Dylan were recognized as folk music's two brightest stars, so it was natural that they would team up, however briefly. As the two were about to embark on an East Coast tour, folk singer Eric Von Schmidt presented their managers with a concert poster he created in their honor (1.101). A homage to Toulouse-Lautrec, it *(continued on p. 60)*

1.100
Folklore Concert Series
multiple venues, Boston, 1963, 1964

1.101
East Coast Tour: Joan Baez and Bob Dylan. 1965
Artist: Eric Von Schmidt

(continued from p. 59)
has become one of the classic American posters. However, Dylan was not entirely pleased with it, and only a few were printed; fewer still actually carried a concert date and place.

Between 1960 and 1964, Baez and Dylan were featured attractions within a self-defined folk music scene. By 1965, the year of his electric stage appearance at Newport, Dylan had matured into his own singular stage presence. To some degree, this spelled the end of the traditional, close-knit folk community, whose music was now forced to contend with the huge commercial popularity of late-1960s rock.

1.102
Bob Dylan
Berkeley Community Theater, Berkeley, 1964

1.103
Bob Dylan
Wilson High School, Long Beach, California, ca. 1964

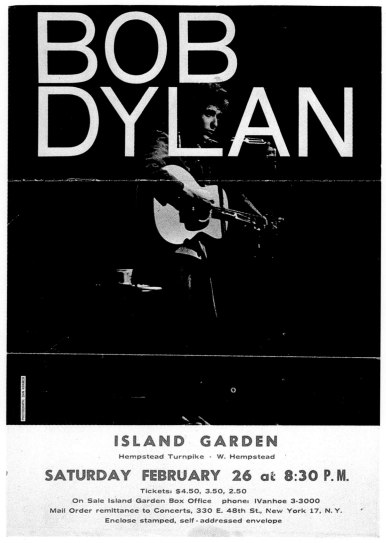

1.104
Bob Dylan. Island Garden, Long Island, New York, 1966
Photographer: Dan Kramer

British Invasion/American Response

The British Invasion of 1963–66 conquered the American popular music scene. Not since the mid 1950s, with Elvis Presley, Chuck Berry, and Buddy Holly, had rock made such an impact. By the early 1960s, American rock—despite fads like the Twist and regional trends like Southern California surf music—was in decline. The nation was ripe for invasion.

The Beatles' Royal Command Performance in November 1963 confirmed their status in England. Just before their first, 1964, visit to America, during which they appeared on the Ed Sullivan Show and played Carnegie Hall, the "Royal Command Performance" poster (1.111) was created. Printed in America and widely distributed, it became one of the earliest of Beatles icons. Between June and November 1964, the Beatles played over fifty cities on four continents, including twenty-six American concerts. The result of this touring, coupled with the release of chart-topping singles and albums along with their first movie success, Beatlemania achieved hysterical proportions. The 1965 tour was even more stupendous, an appearance at Shea Stadium in New York drawing 55,600.

Despite this success, the Beatles could not long sustain the physical, emotional, and creative strain of such tours. On August 29,

1966, San Francisco's Candlestick Park became the site of the last Beatles concert.

Probably the most sought-after American Beatles concert poster advertised the 1965 Shea Stadium appearance. While this was artistically very unimpressive, done in the ubiquitous "boxing style," the poster created for the 1966 San Francisco concert was a visual delight (1.115). Promoter Tom Donohue, who later founded the

(continued on page 64)

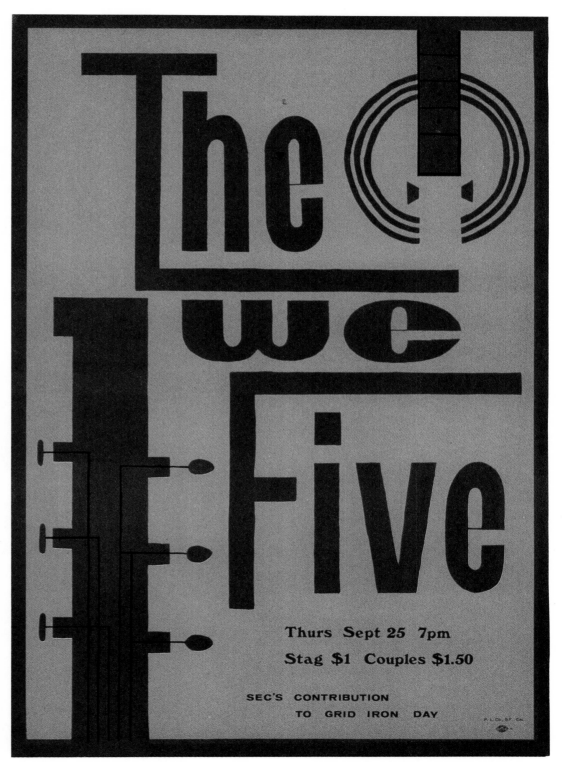

1.106

We Five
Gridiron Day, ca. 1965

1.105

Mitch Ryder and the Detroit Wheels
Civic Center, The Dalles, Washington, 1964
Artist: Tilghman Press

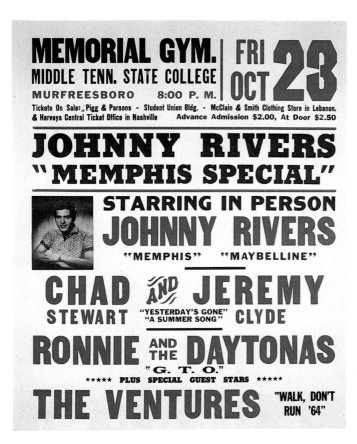

1.107

Johnny Rivers; Chad and Jeremy
Middle Tennessee State College, Murfreesboro, Tennessee, 1964
Artist: Hatch Show Print

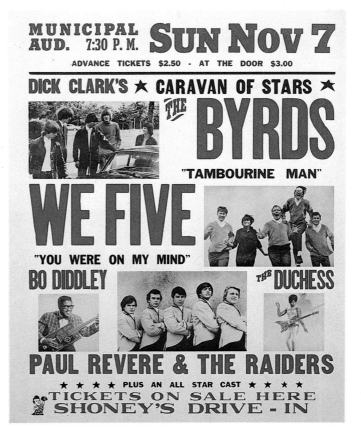

1.108

The Byrds; We Five
Municipal Auditorium, Nashville, 1965
Artist: Hatch Show Print

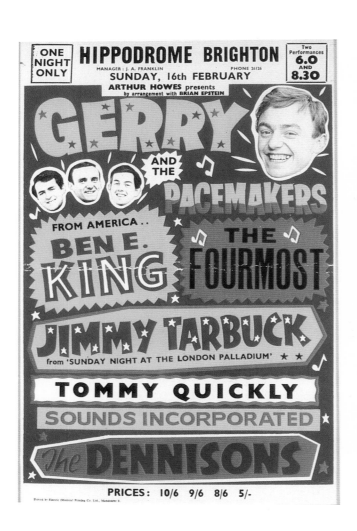

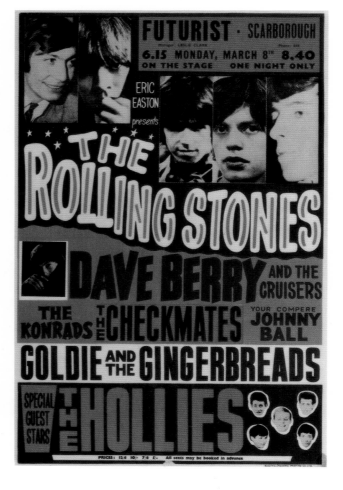

1.109 *(far left)*

Gerry and the Pacemakers; Ben E. King
Hippodrome, Brighton, England, 1964

1.110

Rolling Stones; Hollies
Futurist Hall, Scarborough, England, 1965

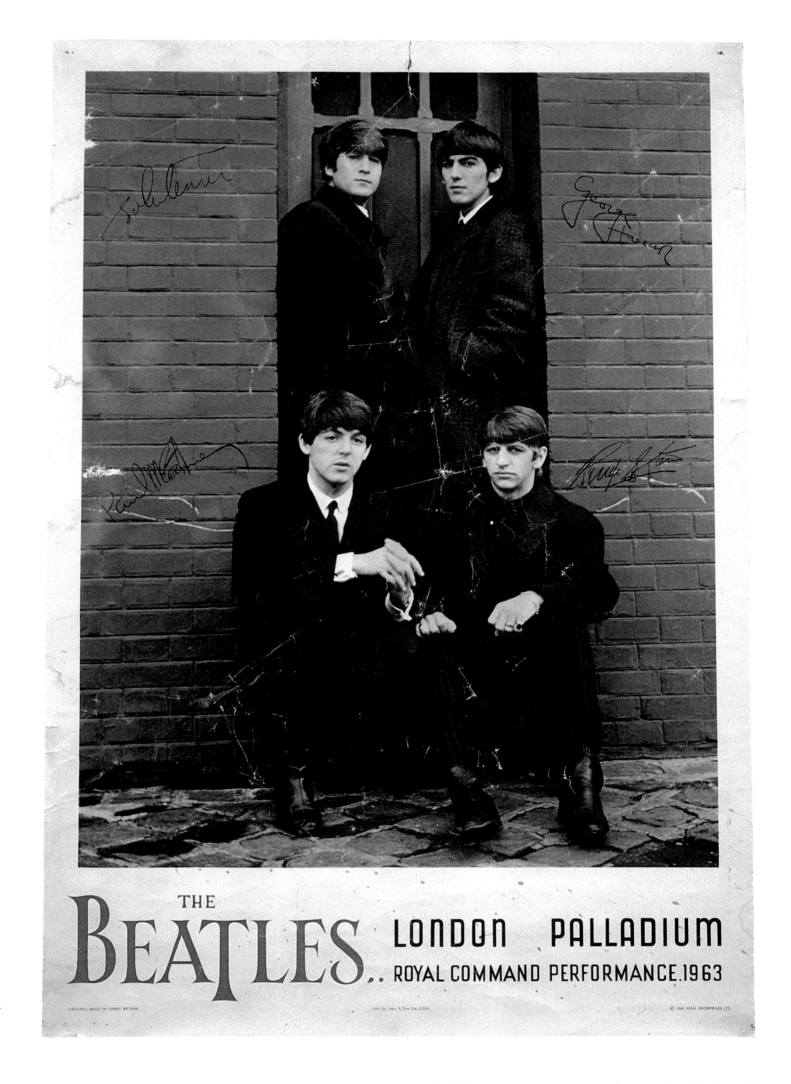

1.111

Command Performance—
The Beatles
Palladium, London, 1963

(continued from page 61)
pioneering San Francisco FM rock stations KMPX and KSAN, commissioned the poster from Wes Wilson, the man who did the first psychedelic posters for the Fillmore Auditorium and Avalon Ballroom, San Francisco.

Classic American rock from the 1950s influenced the Beatles' early work. To a much greater extent, American urban blues was the basis for the Rolling Stones' music. Where the Beatles were fresh, cheery, and melodically engaging, the Stones were hard edged. As the Beatles withdrew from the stage, and groups like the Rolling Stones and the Yardbirds developed in America an enduring respect for English-made rock, a second wave of groups, including the Who and Led Zeppelin, became mainstay attractions.

The American response to the British Invasion developed slowly. Groups like Paul Revere and the Raiders (1.108) and Jay and the Americans were on a par with English groups like the Dave Clark Five. but it took the rise of Bob Dylan and the emergence of such groups as the Byrds (1.108) along with solo standouts like Jimi Hendrix and the explosion of San Francisco-based groups to reinstate Americans as international contenders for rock's top honors.

1.112
Operation Big Beat #5
Tower Ballroom, New Brighton, England, 1962

1.113
A Night to Remember
Tower Ballroom, New Brighton, England, 1962

1.114
Another Beatles Christmas Show
Odeon Hammersmith, London, England, 1963

1.115
Final Concert Appearance: The Beatles
Candlestick Park, San Francisco, 1966
Artist: Wes Wilson

2

The Psychedelic Years in San Francisco: 1965–1971

The 1960s posters were where fine art and commercial art met. It was a great time—it meant breaking all the rules.

STANLEY MOUSE
to the San Francisco *Chronicle*
April 9, 1987

As the decade of the 1950s gave way to the 1960s, no sage foresaw the changes that were about to take place. The 1950s had seen some social rebellion, expressed popularly in such films as *Rebel Without a Cause* and even in early rock 'n' roll, but despite cold war, world unrest, and civil rights protests, America's mood was quiescent. It proved to be the lull before the storm.

As late as 1963, little new had erupted on the American rock 'n' roll front, and there were no new forms of concert poster art to suggest that a revolutionary era was in the making. But by the next year, quietly at first, clutches of radically minded young people had begun to establish themselves on the West Coast. During that same year, excitement over developments in British rock— especially the Beatles—was growing. Musically, the United States was about to be invaded by the British. That onslaught would in turn unleash American musical forces just as powerful.

What came to pass was heralded by a gradual, almost volition-less migration of hip young Americans to the beckoning haven of San Francisco. This gathering began to stoke up the sputtering fires of American rock 'n' roll. Part of this revitalization was the development of an entirely new genre of art: the psychedelic rock poster.

Among the first to make the trek to San Francisco just as the beatnik era began to give way to the hippie years was Michael Ferguson, piano player for the Charlatans, the city's pioneering bohemian rock band. With George Hunter, the Charlatan's stylish leader, he drew the very first concert poster in the new mode. Historian Walter Medeiros interviewed Ferguson shortly before the musician died in 1975:

Growing up in San Diego, very early on I was "the artist," or at least people thought I was during junior high and high school. I was always on the poster committee or making up signs for people running for class president and such. And, like so many people my age in the mid 1950s, I was drawing cars.

Later, curiosity brought me to San Francisco. I followed my on-and-off-girlfriend up there and moved into her house in Pacific Heights. Then one night someone took us for a ride up to North Beach, where the beatniks hung out. And looking at all the weird little shops and coffeehouses, and watching all the bohemian people trotting around, I saw for the first time in my life a scene I'd only known from reading Life and Time. It was a major turning point for me. I remember thinking: This is it!

So I grew a beard and bought a Navy workshirt and sweater and one pair of jeans and began hanging out in North Beach, just living on the street, really. I never totally appreciated the philosophy of the beats' scene—everyone being down all the time—but I made an effort to carry a sketchbook with me and record some of what I saw. San Francisco was so different from San Diego! Its history, its old buildings, its different neighborhoods. I got sucked into the past, and because of that I began collecting old stuff, castaway objects I'd see on the street, bringing them home to play with.

I was starting to meet all kinds of crazy people, going to weird parties and scenes that were all new to me. I made up my mind I was going to go along with whatever came along. At that time I was mostly watching—not playing piano like I'd done in a jazz combo in San Diego. Sometimes, though, just for kicks, I'd play a cheap little bamboo flute I got at Cost Plus, standing on the sidewalk in front of Enrico's, just to piss off the tourists.

In due course, I took my first trip down to Mexico. One of those classic On The Road journeys in an old panel truck, which we eventually abandoned. When I got back, I started working in a clothing store, and one day I was hanging around down at Aquatic Park, near Fisherman's Wharf. It was there I met a couple of young ladies looking for somebody to share the rent in a big house up on the hill. I got in their car to go check it out, and one of the girls lit up a joint and passed it back to me. I'd never turned on before, but I didn't want to appear a dummy. These girls turned out to be some of the earliest big "dealers," and within a day not only did I become a "head," I became a dealer as well. It was one of those instantaneous experiences San Francisco is so famous for.

So the three girls and I rented this house. And, in the course of dealing lids over a period of four years living in that house, I think I met all the very first "hip" people of the new scene. Bob Dylan, Allen Ginsberg, Tom Donohue. Artists, musicians. Everyone came to us to score. But at that point, 1963 or so, it was still kind of a secret society. Walking the streets, you couldn't immediately tell the people who were turning on.

This new scene was in a formative period. The musicians were still into folk, but you also could sense things were just on the verge of changing all around. And it was about this time I began to create my own style of "funk" art, which I call "assemblages." I've since learned there were a bunch of San Francisco artists doing art constructions—assemblages—in the 1950s, but I was mostly unaware of any art but my own. A few of the girls—who were into art—and I would walk the streets, very stoned, and collect huge amounts of things. Broken dolls. Pieces of machinery. And I used this stuff in making assemblages. Some of the pieces you could actually operate. You'd turn a dial, and a flag would pop up. One of my best pieces had a transistor radio built into it, and one day while we were listening to this assemblage, the announcement came over that Kennedy had been shot in Dallas.

Our house was in a classic San Francisco location, on Twentieth Street, just off Noe. A dead-end block, which meant the neighborhood was very quiet. The house was set back, and there were

Beatnik-era espresso bar menu, ca. 1959
Artist: Jerry Paulsen

THE WORD IS "ARTIST"..."NOT" BEATNIK"...

Self-portrait of Rick Griffin with eye patch, *Surfer* 5, no. 3 (July 1964).
Cartoon response to a reader's letter.

big trees all around. It had a view of the entire downtown and East Bay, and there was a glassed-in studio at one end overlooking everything.

At some point late in 1962, Chloe, one of my housemates, and I decided to open up a shop down on Divisadero Street. Chloe suggested the name, from Steppenwolf, by Hermann Hesse. We called it the Magic Theater for Madmen Only. I kind of treated the shop as one big assemblage, but it was more than a gallery, because you could buy things there. We lasted about two years, until sometime in 1964. The Beatles were the happening thing, and people were starting to grow their hair long and form garage-type rock bands.

Luria Castell, in the 1960s a student activist who had been to Cuba several times and who was shortly to become part of the first Family Dog collective, remembers the Magic Theater:

My introduction to a "high" psychedelic scene was through meeting the new hip people who'd begun to hang out together. These were people like Michael Ferguson, George Hunter, and Alton Kelley. Even back then it was a romantic, velvety, lacey, jeweled, pretty trip, and I related to these first experiences very happily. To me, the first truly "psychedelic" shop was the Magic Theater, which operated long before the Haight started going through changes. I remember the sign above the door that Ferguson made up and all the magic boxes and collages they had

inside. It was like the first really drug-oriented art scene I'd ever discovered.

Ferguson and his friends were not the only ones responding to a new and growing pulse. San Francisco's KYA radio station broadened its format with hearty doses of the emerging British rock along with classic r & b. In 1963 KYA's top disc jockeys Tom Donohue and Bobby Mitchell formed a partnership that led to their producing a sold-out show at the 18,000-seat Cow Palace; it headlined the Beach Boys, list-topping Motown acts, and classic fifties rockers. The show's success led Donohue and Mitchell to form Autumn Records, which recorded the Beau Brummels, San Francisco's first major post-1950s band. Donohue also briefly ran a rock club known as Mothers, where the featured attraction during one eye-opening week in 1965 was the Lovin' Spoonful, America's answer to Britain's Gerry and the Pacemakers. Even more importantly, that year San Francisco first heard the Rolling Stones, who really opened people's *ears*. This was May 14, 1965, and the city was about to find a new pet—a psychedelic canine known as the Family Dog.

It started with a very mod, stylish, American Edwardian named George Hunter, whom Luria Castell met in 1965, when she was a student at San Francisco State:

George Hunter was the first person I ever saw who I'd think of as a "hippie." But he was different from a beatnik, you know? He

Rolling Stones; McCoys
Memorial Auditorium, Sacramento, California, 1966

wasn't scruffy; he wasn't walking around with his head down. He had a concept about him, a certain style. His whole environment was a trip—everything about him was a trip. He was the first person like that who bowled me over.

Michael Ferguson:

George was the first hippie I ever saw in San Francisco. George was the one who turned everyone on out at State, and he turned on the Haight.

I remember he was the first person I saw wearing Beatle boots and Beatle suits. And when you walked into his pad, that too was a trip. I'd hung out in artists' pads before, but George's . . . he had gaslights in his house, and he was into a Victorian trip in a big way, totally. And I think he designed the band, Charlatans, to sound like and look like the things going around in his head. Part of our difficulty in sustaining the band was that George couldn't quite communicate the total vision to the rest of us.

While at San Francisco State, Hunter became involved with sophisticated audio electronics and produced a number of free-form "happenings." Then, meeting musicians Mike Wilhelm, Richard Olsen, and, later, Dan Hicks and Michael Ferguson, Hunter emerged as the leader of a folk-rock novelty band. According to Gene Sculatti and Davin Seay's *San Francisco Nights*, the Charlatans "sprung fullblown from Hunter and Ferguson's abiding love of the city's gas-lit past." "You'd go into these little thrift shops," Hunter recalled for Sculatti and Seay, "and find all kinds of things from the turn of the century: ladies' silver handbags, sequined dresses, frock coats, waistcoats, shirts without collars, collar buttons, cufflinks, straw boaters." So costumed, the Charlatans created something that Hunter calls "1920s country-folk music with something done to it."

In late spring 1965, Chandler Laughlin, bartender at the Red Dog Saloon in Virginia City, Nevada, began to look for a band that would fit into the Wild West dance hall that he and Mark Unobsky envisioned for the old Comstock House Unobsky had bought. Except for the fact that the group was just learning how to play musical instruments, the Charlatans were ideal. In June the band traveled to Virginia City and auditioned—on acid—to the great amusement of those gathered. The summer-long engagement that followed has become celebrated as the birth of America's psychedelic era.

Luria Castell:

How can I even describe what was taking place? When I visited the Red Dog for the first time, Carmella, who used to live with Boz Scaggs, was standing there in a velvet dress with tons of beads. And the Charlatans were playing on the bandstand. It was like taking a trip right back into the 1890s. But it wasn't the 1890s. It was now. It was this brand new, old-timey sense of being conscious of fine things well done and reliving a period when fine things were made good. There was just an aesthetic that I immediately recognized as an artistic expression of "highness."

As the Charlatans were beginning their engagement, the Red Dog was being reconstructed from the inside out. Many friends of the band came up to help. Among them was artist, helicopter mechanic, and former motorcycle racer Alton Kelley and the other people who became the original Family Dog collective. Kelley recalls:

Charlatans; Electric Chamber Orkustra
Sokol Hall, San Francisco, 1966. Artist: Alton Kelley

Oh, I was there, all right. I helped rebuild the place. We were all up there for the purpose of painting signs and helping decorate the joint in real funky Wild West style. It was a dynamite scene. There were people with long hair, wearing cowboy suits, packing guns. The Charlatans sounded real good, and the townspeople were getting off on the scene. People were taking acid all the time. Really getting looped. Bill Ham was there with his light-show boxes.

Michael Ferguson:

We got a little more cowboyish up there because we came across clothes that were a little more Western and less Victorian. But we still weren't cowboys—more gambler types or mining-camp Westerners.

Some of the pictures that were used on our posters during the following year were taken at the Red Dog, at the Gold Leaf Bar. It was all so authentic! Even down to the collars we wore. I had a few that were almost three inches high, which would literally cut your throat when you turned your head. And we'd be up on the bandstand, all stiff and very proper, sweating because it was real hot, and the audience would be having a real freak-out of a time.

It's true we actually auditioned on acid. What a rubbery experi-

ence! We were so nervous, and our songs really weren't together, and we had no idea how we were sounding. But as things progressed up at the Red Dog, we very seldom played on acid. We were always stoned, but from smoking grass. A few times we experimented and played on DMT, an intense but short-lived psychedelic you smoke.

People would come up to Virginia City to party. The Red Dog got to be a real popular place that summer, and the scene lasted until the early fall, when the weather began to turn and the townspeople began to get tired of it all. What I remember most about the Red Dog was all the guns. That's the only thing we spent our money on—bullets. One of my favorite things was going down to the dump and spending about an hour setting up cans and bottles then finding an old chair, sitting down, and plunking away. It was a real loose Western scene.

The Charlatans' Red Dog engagement occasioned the first rock poster of the psychedelic era. It was dubbed "The Seed" in *Art Eureka*, an early poster book, and the name has stuck.

In the catalog for the poster show he produced in 1976 at San Francisco's Museum of Modern Art, Walter Medeiros wrote: "The Seed is unique for being completely hand-drawn, in a densely-patterned format, and was much different from rock posters that existed then. Yet it is reminiscent of nineteenth-century carnival, medicine show, and music hall posters, in that it boldly heralds a spectacular event that shouldn't be missed. It has a 'funky' character about it, and 'funkiness' was one of the most prominent

Cartoon portrait of the Jook Savages, *Surfer* 8, no. 3 (July 1967)
Artist: Rick Griffin

characteristics of hippie sensibility. And the poster carries off this feeling because of the lightness and capriciousness which permeates the whole work."

George Hunter came up with the poster's distinctive logo incorporating the band's name, but it was piano player Michael Ferguson who drew the caricatures and decorations that create the old-timey feel. Ferguson recalls:

George had ideas about the lettering, and he also provided the slogan, "The Amazing Charlatans." He was very much into advertising and promotion, you know. But I had an inkling in my own mind of what it ought to look like as a complete piece. And I wanted to do it sort of Victorianish, with little oval frames around the caricatures. Like all rock posters, it was done at a late hour, in a big rush to get it finished. Actually, there are two versions, because our opening was delayed. The first printing was done in blue, which just didn't make it at all. It's much better in black, which was the final version. George did some of the crosshatching on the final piece, but all the little details, like the iron cross, the crescent moon, and the swastika, are mine. Looking at it from a distance of some years, I think that if there could have been more time taken with it, it could have been really a terrific poster. But it was the first.

As fall approached, there were stirrings of interest about putting on Red Dog-like happenings in San Francisco, stirrings that emanated partly from some people living cooperatively in a house at 2111 Pine Street, across town from the Haight. Those people became the Family Dog, which came to include people united by a common interest in ecology, politics, early protests against the Vietnam War, drugs, and—finally—music. In 1964, Alton Kelley left Connecticut and a job as a motorcycle mechanic to live in San Francisco. He became an early inmate of the Dog House, as Luria Castell recalls:

Back then, Kelley was into doing collages. The whole wall of his bedroom was covered with framed collages. And I remember Ellen Harmon used to lie on the bed, which was covered with an American flag, and read Marvel comics. Kelley also did things with day-glo paints. He would cover the little Victorian inset places in the house, all the nooks and things, and paint them day-glo, with giant lightning bolts and stuff. It was early psychedelic, you could say.

When the Family Dog decided to put on rock dances, Kelley was a natural to design the promotional posters.
Alton Kelley:

We named the first dance "A Tribute to Dr. Strange." I don't know why exactly—other than it was a groovy idea. Maybe because Ellen was so into Marvel comics at the time. It might have been because we were inspired by the names of the bands—the Jefferson Airplane, the Great Society, and all that. It was sort of a hip gimmick, and it worked out very nice.

We printed up a couple hundred handbills for the first dance, just as we did for the next two dances. I remember finishing the art right on top of the counter down at the printer, Joe Buchwald's Rapid Repro Shop. There also were a few special silk-screen posters done, not many at all, which would go up at places like the Committee Theater. We were running a pretty loose operation, including selling tickets on the street. We didn't have any idea *how many people would come to the dance or even if it would be popular. And so it was really amazing to me—amazing to all of us—that all these people showed. It was such a shock to see all these freaks; they must have come out of the woodwork.*

Luria Castell:

Kelley drew the first three handbills, and I think a lady named Amy did the first two silk-screen posters. Marty Balin, who founded the Airplane, might have had a hand in doing one of them, but that's only what people tell me. The second one was all in green, with sparkly letters, which was neat.

So then we did a second dance, which featured the Lovin' Spoonful, a band I'd first met down in Los Angeles. We borrowed some more money to do it. And then we did a third dance, with Frank Zappa and Mothers of Invention. But this one was kind of heavy—people started to fight, and Zappa was weird.

That third dance was not the same happy scene as when we'd gone into it. We still hadn't made any money, and nobody wanted to borrow more. Basically, people didn't want to do it any more. I moved out and went over to Hemlock Street, where Richie and Sue Olsen lived. Not too long after that, I put on another dance, with the help of Danny Rifkin and Rock Scully, who later helped manage the Grateful Dead. We did it with the Charlatans, at California Hall, and George Hunter keeps taking credit for it, although he only played a part. Ferguson and Hunter did the poster. I believe this dance was the one that finally made money—$1,500. So I decided to put on one more at the same place, also with the Charlatans, except what I didn't realize was that it was also the night of one of the acid tests, which cut into the attendance.

It was after this final concert, the fifth produced under the name Family Dog, that I decided to split the scene. I was going to leave for Nevada, to live in a cave with a guy I'd just met, but instead I went to Mexico.

With Luria's exit, the focus shifted to lanky ex-Texan Chet Helms. Helms managed Big Brother and the Holding Company. With partner John Carpenter, Helms staged shows featuring Big Brother at Berkeley's Open Theater. He wanted to try his chops on something more public and arranged with Castell to book Big Brother at a Family Dog dance in California Hall. But when Castell left, the date fell through, and Helms had to look for an alternative. He went to Carpenter's friend Bill Graham, who offered the Fillmore on alternate weekends. "Graham asked us what name we would use," Helms recalls in Sculatti and Seay's *San Francisco Nights*, "and we kind of looked at each other and said, 'Family Dog, I guess.' "

Helms and Carpenter approached Bill Graham because he had been producing successful dance benefits for the San Francisco Mime Troupe. He served as the Troupe's business manager and factotum after having left a lucrative management position with the Allis-Chalmers Manufacturing Company late in 1964. The next two years saw Mime Troupe shows and, in 1966, the epoch-making Trips Festival. Although naturalist Stewart Brand and Ken Kesey's Merry Pranksters, along with various leading musicians, actually conceptualized this three-day event—which firmly established psychedelia in San Francisco—it was Graham who capitalized on its possibilities. He went into business for himself. The weekend following the Trips Festival, he produced his first show, the poster for which makes prominent mention of the festival's

Alton Kelley, San Francisco, 1967

"sights and sounds," which people could experience once again at the Fillmore. Two weeks later, Helms and company produced their own first dance, and for the next two-and-a-half months, Graham and the Family Dog shared the Fillmore.

They also shared the same poster artist. Wes Wilson, who had attended San Francisco State and dabbled in philosophy, was working at Contact Printing, a small San Francisco press that had handled jobs for the Mime Troupe. Before doing the first Graham and Family Dog posters, Wilson had executed Helms's handbills for his Open Theater shows, as well as the handbill and program for the Trips Festival. Except for Graham's very first poster (done by Peter Bailey, another artist associated with the Mime Troupe) and perhaps one or two others, Wilson handled all of Graham's work through early May 1967. He also did eleven of the first twelve Family Dog pieces, printing the first four posters at Contact Printing. Wilson developed two styles during this early period, as collector Jeff Berger notes:

It's so interesting to look at the Wes Wilson Family Dogs and the Wes Wilson Bill Grahams. The same week he would crank out a super folksy type "conceptual" Dog, he'd put out a Graham with really interesting letters, but none of the theme.

The *theme* initially would come from Chet Helms, who often outlined culturally relevant images to be incorporated into the artwork. Wilson explained, in an interview with Walter Medeiros, how he and Helms worked together:

Chet did serve as a kind of art director at first. I wasn't that experienced in doing what I was doing, and so it would help that Chet would think up themes. For example, he'd find a picture, say, of Bernard McFadden, an early health and exercise guy. The picture was of McFadden showing people how to "exercise laugh"—you know, exercise by learning how to laugh. He actually told you how to laugh, by breathing properly, and so on. We got two different posters out of that, one of which we called the Laugh Cure.

Chet had some really far out ideas; he was quite a tripster with a very active imagination. And he'd come to me saying, "Wes, here's the name of the dance, and this is the theme. Let's do it like this."

Some of the thematically strong early Family Dog posters became known by such titles as "Euphoria," "Hupmobile 8," or "The Quick and the Dead." Later on, as the posters became more popular and were made available for retail sale, the Family Dog staff assigned code names, much like Helms's early titles, to all the posters in the series. The margins of some Family Dog posters also contain cryptic messages. Most famous of all is the one on FD 5: "May the Baby Jesus shut your mouth and open your mind." Helms claimed to have found it on a bathroom wall. The phrase was also keyed to the Family Dog's logo, which Wilson designed using as the central image a photo of an Indian fur trader, smoking a long-stemmed pipe that the artist modified to look like a joint:

I designed the logo on a little piece of paper, and I said, "Well, Chet, how about this?" And he went, "Wow! That's great. Looks sort of like a deputy sheriff's badge." It was a funky design, and it's hard to read that background lettering on the shield, which says "the," which some people don't realize. But the guy in the middle is outrageous, just right for the part. It was somebody Chet found in the American Heritage Book of Indians.

Not until late in 1966 did both the Family Dog and Bill Graham realize they were producing *works of art.* Initially, the posters were thought of as groovy and effective promotions. Dozens were placed in store windows or even stapled to lampposts.
Chet Helms:

The modern poster originated in belle epoque France. Contemporary accounts describe how avid collectors unceremoniously stripped opera and café posters from walls, even before the glue could dry. I believe we experienced a parallel evolution some eighty years later in San Francisco. It was very disconcerting to poster a whole street and then walk back a few minutes later and discover that 90 percent had been removed. But I soon learned that a stolen poster carried home and pasted on the refrigerator reached the audience I wanted.

My grandfather was a fundamentalist minister who started grass roots churches all over Texas. I learned the promotional techniques of evangelism from him. My uncles were printers of biblical tracts and advertisements in poster and handbill form for local businesses. Summers spent with my uncles as a printer's devil taught me to love printing, publishing, and graphics. My brothers

and I formed a bill-posting and canvassing service that served my uncles' clients. A large part of Family Dog's success was due to our bill posting and canvassing. My brother John Helms organized and supervised this critical function, becoming an ambassador-at-large for Family Dog. As he was always on the street he became an important conduit for feedback from the community. I sometimes took turns at postering to get this feedback directly.

Posters and handbills are a particularly democratic form of advertising and social expression. Posted in public places, they are available to virtually everyone at little or no cost. The parallels between the belle epoque poster and the psychedelic poster are obvious, but the 1960s posters also were rooted in the American free speech tradition of political and social phamphleteering. The central issue of the 1960s was civil liberty and personal freedom. The posters were vehicles for both, incorporating new graphic techniques and juxtaposing colors that traditionally were never printed side by side. The pioneering work of humanistic psychologists exploring psychological and physiological perception was appropriated and applied directly to the poster. Maslow and Perls taught us about gestalt and the principles of figure-ground reversal. Suggesting line or form by printing two opposite colors side by side was borrowed from the Impressionists and the more methodical color studies of Josef Albers. Figure-ground reversal lent itself to double entendre. The eye is not equipped to perceive red and blue simultaneously, so vibrant red-green, red-blue combinations served to simulate the shimmering world of the psychedelic experience. The values of this emerging culture were conveyed through verbal and visual double entendre, sexual innuendo, drug innuendo, and sometimes by merely placing two images near each other on the page and allowing the viewer to draw his own conclusions. In this way the unspoken was spoken, forbidden topics were discussed, suppressed feelings held in common were acknowledged.

Having grown up in the Eisenhower years, the era of the gray flannel suit, we had a great thirst for color and reclaimed it as a mode of expression. The joyless head-long rat race to the top was supplanted by the joyful, sensuous curves and gyrations of the dance, expanding in all directions.

Poster collector Jeff Berger was a high school student in the mid 1960s and remembers the excitement of acquiring each new poster as it came out:

Every day, the moment school ended, we'd head up to Telegraph Avenue, and then a whole ritual would begin. We would go into the stores that had posters in their window and ask the proprietor if we could sign the back with, say, "save for Jeff Berger." If they had the handbills on the counter, we'd grab a handful. But you've got to realize how intense this was. The crowd that was into this collecting scene would catapult out from school, go screaming up the avenue in order to be the first to sign the backs. And then, after we'd gone up and down the street, being real comradely about it, maybe finding the poster man and getting some, the daring guys who had to have them would sneak into the stores and pull them off the windows. And go tearing off again down the block.

The excitement on the streets was matched by the excitement inside the artists' studios. Wes Wilson had the most difficult role of anyone, since he had little to base his art on, save a growing intuition of what the music called for:

When I was a kid, or when I was back in high school, I thought dancing was stupid and dumb. Just didn't make any sense. But then the Trips Festival came along, and that turned into a major experience for me. There was music, there was drama, there were costumed people, there was Ken Kesey and the Pranksters, light shows, weird sound equipment. It was like this big "happening" for me, and I'd never experienced that kind of enthusiasm at a dance. It was just magic.

When I started doing posters, especially the posters in color, which followed the initial black and white "Tribal Stomp," I think I selected my colors from my visual experiences with LSD, along with what I'd learned as a printer. I was really trying to create exciting images, but when I first started out they really didn't flower as much as they did by the end of the year, in 1966. By then, I was able to do things that I thought were getting far out, and if I'd continued doing posters for a full year after that, I think they would have been really great.

Posters to me represented real departure points. I like the idea of filling up space, and I like to do my work freehand—no ruler and stuff. Just make it fit naturally. If I needed to make a letter a little wider, well, I would. So, early on, I was already headed in a certain direction, and when I found this catalog for the November 1965 Jugendstil and Expressionism exhibit at the University of California, which included Viennese Secessionist lettering, I was able to adapt it and use it on almost all my posters from that point on. It was the easiest type of lettering imaginable. You just draw the outlines and put in these little intrusions to make each space become a letter. Playing with foreground and background helped me work out patterns and shapes.

I'd sort of project myself into whatever I was doing. If I was in a good mood, I could do great things. And if I felt lousy, well, I'd still have to get it done by Friday or whenever the deadline was. All that pressure would get to me sometimes, I'd always do something that would just kind of "come out." From the point of view of psychology, I imagine the posters were like some kind of imprint, like a section of my mind at that time. And some of them were pretty weird, pretty strange.

A lot of my early posters for the Fillmore involve great masses of lettering, because lettering was really fascinating to me, especially using letters as "negative spaces," the way some woodblocks are done. But I always liked to draw women, loved to do nudes, and my work took me in that direction as well. What I'd sometimes do was to get my wife to pose for me, and then I'd disguise her,

Bill Graham in his Fillmore Auditorium office, 1966

just use the drawing as a form to put the poster together. My favorite, if I had to pick one, is "The Sound." The woman figure is reaching and twisting, one foot behind the other. She's spinning within the sound of the music.

It was like I was experiencing for the first time how you draw out of your head. I didn't have a studio, really, just a drawing board set up on a card table. And I generally finished each piece just before I had to have it in to the printer.

It was very hard to keep up the pace and deal with Bill Graham week after week, because back then he was a very volatile kind of personality. I mean, you can't imagine the dramatics— screaming and shouting—someone like Bill went through in order to get his way: "Too far out," he'd say. "The Jefferson Airplane is only this wide. The Grateful Dead is only this wide. Who cares about this lady in the drawing? They want to see the bands. You should have made the names much bigger." But I began to realize what he wanted actually wasn't so important, because I could see that people really were observing the posters, taking them home and really enjoying them. So, I would disguise the lettering in whatever way I felt necessary.

Bill Graham:

Wes was the first artist I dealt with on a regular basis. But with Wes, as with all the artists who worked with me, the difficulty was in making him understand—and I'm sorry it was that way—that you can't have total artistic freedom to do these posters. Because the basic point of the poster is to transmit information, to communicate information about concerts. But I understood their desire, in this wonderful, childish, scheming way, to bury all the pertinent information underneath all the oozes and ebbs and flows and liquidy movement on the poster. And so I would always say to Wes, and to everyone who came after, "Don't get me to the point where you're going to have total freedom, and then there'll be an asterisk somewhere pointing to the bottom of the poster, where there'll be an explanation of who's actually playing." However far out the artists wanted to go, they somehow had to get across that on those dates something was happening someplace. I would say to Wes, "Just watch people standing there, trying to read your poster!" Their bodies actually would be trying to follow the curvature of the words, the lettering.

Wes Wilson:

I finally quit doing posters when Bill and I couldn't agree on the money trip. I finally felt strong enough to tell him either to come forth with more money or find another artist. I realized that in a couple more months, I wouldn't have the option of that ultimatum. In the first year, I don't think Bill could have easily replaced me, but when we got to 1967, there were a lot more people around that could do what I was doing. In 1966 I could get my way, more or less, and do posters the way I thought they ought to be done. When I left, I could see a dozen people who were very capable of doing fine posters, and in styles very different from my own.

Unable to cut a continuing satisfactory deal with Bill Graham, Wilson executed his last poster for the promoter in May 1967. Leaving the Fillmore fold, Wilson found beyond San Francisco no ready market for his skills, even though the commercial art world recognized his pioneering role in poster design. After a time, he

Berkeley Barb ad (14 April 1967): Country Joe and the Fish
Artist: Tom Weller

began experimenting with enameled glass and various forms of fine art. Somewhat later, he moved his family to a farm in Missouri's Ozarks, where he still lives.

Wilson was succeeded by Bonnie MacLean, Graham's wife and Fillmore staff member. Apart from her weekly Fillmore chalkboard renderings of current and forthcoming attractions, MacLean had no experience as a poster artist. But she readily adapted to her new role and quickly built upon what formal art training she had before meeting Bill Graham, who tells the story:

Before we did the Fillmore, I hired Bonnie as a secretary when I worked for Allis-Chalmers. After an interview, I didn't want to hire her, but the agency called me back and said, "Mr. Graham, this woman is really miffed. She thought she'd had a good interview with you." So then I asked myself, "Why didn't I hire her?" And it flashed on me that the thing that had set me off was—I hated the color of her coat! She'd worn this awful turquoise coat! But I did interview her again, and she became my secretary. Sometime after that we began dating, back in 1963.

I can honestly say that if there was one person without whom the Fillmore wouldn't have happened, it was Bonnie. I don't mean just because of her artwork; she was such an integral part of the whole thing we went through—the difficulties with downtown, getting the permits, setting up the place right, making sure everything ran smoothly week to week. Bonnie was another critical eye for me. She was critical, and she was creative.

Bonnie always did the chalk art for the billboards at the Fillmore. One billboard featured the acts for the current show, the other promoted our show for the following week. Her chalk pieces were posters in themselves, conveying messages as the posters did— subtle, decorative, and amusing. The blackboards gave me the idea she could do posters for the Fillmore, and when Wes left, Bonnie took over. They say her style is derivative of Wes, but I think she evolved a style of her own very quickly. She was never anybody but her own person, with her own creative expression, and she was the person who kept the posters coming. And she did what she did for the right reasons. She and I both know we could have done a lot more to commercialize the poster art, even back in the beginning, but she wanted to remain within the confines of the scene developing all around us—she wanted to be true to that scene.

As Bonnie MacLean followed Wes Wilson at the Fillmore, one Stanley Miller, formerly of Detroit and better known as Stanley Mouse or simply ''Mouse,'' succeeded Wilson at Family Dog. Wilson had executed eleven of the first twelve Family Dog posters, Victor Moscoso did the twelfth, and Mouse began with FD 13, for a Captain Beefheart appearance at the Avalon in mid June 1966. He was responsible—alone or in collaboration with associate Alton Kelley—for twenty-six of the next thirty-six Family Dog posters during a nine-month period that firmly established the ''pyschedelic'' style as an expression of the times.

Mouse! Monster Club identification card. Detroit, ca. 1960
Artist: Stanley Mouse

Mouse was already highly regarded as an artist on the hot rod show circuit, before settling in San Francisco during the Haight-Ashbury heyday. His weapon of choice was the airbrush, with which he produced hot-rod-era cartoons that brought him early grassroots fame. The techniques he evolved on the road served him well when he turned his hand to rock posters. The artist explains:

Between age eighteen and twenty-five—1958–65—I went all over the country, airbrushing hot rod designs on t-shirts. That was on the weekends; I was also going part-time to the Art School of the Society of Arts and Crafts, in Detroit. My dad often went on the road with me, kind of managing the business, and my mom handled the mail-order end of things. When I was just getting started, I worked a lot of drag racing meets, setting up my easel around the stands or near the refreshment booths. But I got much better results at hot rod shows held indoors. What I liked most was working with the energy of the people who stood around my booth. They were sort of my art directors. They'd tell me what they wanted, but even more than that I could sense their involvement on a subliminal level. It was almost telepathy. I could tell, with my back turned, which of my pieces they were getting off on the most. I've never forgotten that feeling.

Grade school and high school were a nightmare for me. By the tenth grade, I just gave up and got kicked out. When I couldn't find anything else worthwhile to do—because nothing else turned me on—I went down to the art school. I found something in art school. I discovered there was meaning in what I could do. After a year there, I went back to high school, one of the better ones this time, and graduated as the school cartoonist. This was in 1959. I tried to go to college, like everybody else was doing, but it just wasn't for me. I was having better results airbrushing shirts on the hot rod circuit. What's more, even by 1963, I'd established my own corporation, Mouse Studios. We were not only handling t-shirts, we had a line of posters and decals. At the height of this period, Monogram Models used some of my most popular work for their model car kits.

I first came to California in 1964. I settled for awhile in Berkeley, where I lived in a little windmill on Telegraph Avenue, near the Oakland border. I sat inside the windmill and painted t-shirts, and I made my first trips over to San Francisco, where I met the first Family Dog people on Pine Street. I remember meeting Kelley. It was an empty room, empty except for a big pile of trash in one

Wes Wilson, San Francisco, 1966

Bonnie MacLean in front of her Fillmore chalkboard, 1967

corner. Kelley was sitting on top of the trash, talking a mile a minute. Talking, talking, talking. He was sitting up there like the King of Funk.

Although I was deep into the hot rod scene, I didn't know much about the California surfing community. I recall going down to a fair in Orange County, south of Los Angeles, to airbrush shirts like I always did. A little kid came up to my booth and said, "Hey, do me a Murph the Surf." And I said, "What's Murph the Surf?" The kid and about five of his buddies roared with laughter. I'd no idea Murph the Surf was one of surfing's most recognizable cartoon figures, or that it was a design of Rick Griffin's, who later came up to San Francisco and became one of the top poster artists.

I left California in 1965 because I got drafted, and I had to go back to Detroit, where I figured out an escape. In very early 1966, I made plans to return to California. I went to a drive-away place, which set me up with—of all things—a hearse. I said, "Perfect!" I threw all my stuff in, slapped a "Make Love, Not War" sticker on the back window, and drove across country with my girlfriend Suzi and a dog named Cigar.

I pulled into San Francisco, ending up right in front of Long-shoremen's Hall, the first night of the Trips Festival!

Once I got settled in a place up on Seventeenth Street, I ran into Kelley again, probably over at the Dog House. Kelley said to me, "Stanley, can you believe it? There are 5,000 crazy people here in San Francisco just like us!" And it was true, things were happening everywhere.

When I'd first come out, two years earlier, there was not much of a new art scene happening. I remember Michael Ferguson's "Magic Theater" store, and I think people were mostly into making funk art, assembling weird things together. But I didn't see any posters. But in 1966, it was much, much different. Posters for the early rock concerts were just beginning to appear, and there was an early feeling of excitement. Of course, up to the point where Chet Helms started producing the Family Dog dances, first at the Fillmore and then over at the Avalon, the posters had been done basically by Kelley and Hunter and Ferguson. The Charlatans were the big thing. And then Wes Wilson came in and did that Family Dog crest, working with Chet. I could see there was something for me to do in all this.

I came in around June and did a Captain Beefheart piece, my first. Then Kelley and I started working together. We did that great "Zig Zag Man" one, which I was terribly afraid would get us

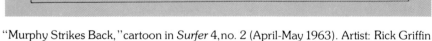
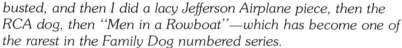

"Murphy Strikes Back," cartoon in *Surfer* 4, no. 2 (April-May 1963). Artist: Rick Griffin

busted, and then I did a lacy Jefferson Airplane piece, then the RCA dog, then "Men in a Rowboat"—which has become one of the rarest in the Family Dog numbered series.

A few others led us up to the Grateful Dead "Skull & Roses," which still gives me a lot of satisfaction, and then the Jim Kweskin "Girl with Green Hair," for which I borrowed the central image from a turn-of-the-century French poster artist, Alphonse Mucha.

In the early days, Kelley and I did a lot of collaborating, and what came out of that work was really good. Our poster art was more or less a conglomeration of everything we had learned—or had seen—up to then. Kelley had a good layout sense, and he found some fantastic images that we played with, but I handled most of the drawing. A lot of people say Kelley was the "idea man," and that I was the "executor," and I guess I'd have to say that rap is false in a lot of ways, and it's also true in a lot of ways. Kelley was just all the time finding neat things, and I'd get off on them. But, looking back, I feel a lot of pieces were mainly my work, and most of the posters carried the name "Mouse Studios," which was of course my trip from many years before.

According to rock-poster historian Walter Medeiros, while Mouse did the lettering and graphics, and Alton Kelley provided the photos and collages, "virtually all the posters signed 'Mouse Studios' were the combined work of both artists." Medeiros points out that, in the early work, because "Kelley was not yet a skilled draftsman, it is Mouse's hand that is most apparent." While

Kelley's specialty was the collage, this technique was used very little in Kelley-Mouse rock posters. What most characterized their work, Medeiros suggests, is "a healthy sense of irreverence toward narrow proprietary values." They freely appropriated classic trademark images, as in "Zig Zag Man," which exploited the Zig Zag cigarette paper logo. For them, such commercial pop "images . . . existed out in the world . . . like words in a dictionary." Dominy Hamilton, in Mouse and Kelley's 1976 retrospective art book, reported that the artists drew on what they called the "image bank," the "graphic flea market." "Reproductions of old masters, movie stills, and comic books were all considered potential visual material. Mouse and Kelley applied the same criteria to the finely wrought artifacts of ancient civilizations as to the homely or poignant truths revealed by the camera." In an interview with Blair Jackson, editor and publisher of *The Golden Road*, a Grateful Dead fanzine, Kelley elaborated:

We had no real direction [in our early work]. It was wild and wide open, and anything went. We just wanted them to be real visual and real noticeable. There really hadn't been any posters since World War II—those were the last real visual posters that anyone had put out, and they were all war propaganda—so there were no rules. We went to libraries looking for everything. And there was so much wonderful stuff! So we just started doing it on our own, trying to make [each poster] different.

There were just a few of us doing it—me and Stanley. Wes

Wilson. Victor Moscoso. Rick Griffin. We all knew each other, and we'd always watch for the other guy's poster to come out. It was always like, "Let's see what Victor has done!" Victor was fantastic; all that stuff he did for the Matrix; they were just killer. Everyone had his own style. Victor was heavy on the color. Wes had that zig-zaggy weird lettering. Rick had the weird imagery, and Stanley and I had these bold images. There were all these distinct styles that were all connected in a way.

It was Mouse and Kelley's Family Dog posters that apparently triggered Rick Griffin's interest in rock art and induced him in 1966 to move to San Francisco from Los Angeles. His art was influenced by the culture of the American West; as Walter Medeiros reports, Griffin's father was an amateur archaeologist who collected artifacts from Indian sites and ghost towns. Another key influence was surfing. Born near Palos Verdes, on the Southern California coast, Griffin came to love the sport at a very early age. He was also a grade-school cartoonist, and by the end of high school, in the late 1950s, had developed his own surfer cartoon figure called "Murphy." After graduation, Griffin joined the staff of filmmaker John Severson's *Surfer Magazine* and briefly attended art school. There he met a group of traveling artist-musicians called

Alton Kelley and Stanley Mouse, San Francisco, 1967

Stanley Mouse, San Francisco, 1967

the Jook Savages, an early hipster tribe that influenced some of his later thinking. Meanwhile, the Murphy character appeared in *Surfer*—and before long was to become the best-known cartoon figure in the surfing movement, reaching all corners of the globe via decals and t-shirts.

While still in Los Angeles in early 1966, Griffin and the Jook Savages took part in one of Ken Kesey's experimental gatherings, the Watts Acid Test, which featured the newly emergent Grateful Dead. Griffin describes the Acid test as "Really crazy. *Totally crazed.*" Combined with his exposure to Mouse and Kelley's work, it whetted his appetite for the new San Francisco scene, and he headed up the Coast. In 1965 he had seen the Charlatans at the Red Dog Saloon and was therefore acquainted with some of the leading members of San Francisco hip society, but what was happening now, in the fall of 1966, really turned his head around. Griffin tells the story in an interview with British historian John Platt published in *Zig Zag Magazine*:

The Jook Savages finally made the trip up the coast together. And all of us arriving from Los Angeles was something of an event.

We just fell right in. Our band played at a few small concerts, and then we were invited to put on an art exhibition at the Psychedelic Shop, in Haight-Ashbury. I did the poster, which was my first, and while I was taking it down to the printer, I met the organizers of the Human Be-In. And they asked me to do a poster for this real special event which took place in January 1967, and that was the second piece I did in San Francisco.

When Chet Helms, who was running the Avalon for the Family Dog, saw my Jook Savages poster and my Human Be-In poster, he said to me, "Hey man, you've got to do posters for the Family Dog, too. We really want you to do our posters." And that's how I got started doing regular dance posters.

The art school I'd attended down in Los Angeles didn't give me much encouragement to do the pen and ink drawing I really like. So in San Francisco, doing posters on a regular basis was like going to my own art school. It was like having some kind of incredible lithography class, with all the equipment there for my use. And I gained a tremendous education as a result, and looking back, I can see my early ones were really experimental, and how later on I began realizing all the possibilities that were available. . . . My first pieces were in black and white, but pretty soon I started experimenting with color. I was figuring out the process as I went along, first in two colors, then in three, then in four. I was educating myself about the basic principles involved in printing color, how to mix colors, how to gear the overlays, how to work up tones, and ultimately how to predict what the final version would look like.

Pacific Ocean Trading Company: promotional artwork
San Francisco, 1967. Artist: Stanley Mouse

Walter Medeiros sees affinities between Griffin's art and that of the Charlatans' George Hunter and Michael Ferguson as well as Mouse and Kelley. All explored the revival of nineteenth-century graphics and American advertising motifs:

Griffin especially enjoyed take-offs, or puns, on advertisements and commonplace labels, and his humorous approach, while similar to that of Mouse and Kelley, brings to his posters a particular spirit of adventure. . . . One of Griffin's classic pieces, done for the Denver Family Dog, actually incorporates mushrooms, peyote buttons, seven major 'characters' from other rock posters (five of which are Mouse's), the Zig-Zag Man, Elsie (the Borden cow), the Quaker Oats man, the Sunmaid Raisin girl, the Cream of Wheat man, Mr. Peanut, the sailor on Players cigarette packs, the Lipton Tea man, the girl carrying biscuits from the Clabber Girl Baking Powder label, the Royal Baking Powder can label, corn, wheat, pumpkins, a camel, the sword in the anvil, the pearl in the oyster, the artist's pen breaking through an egg, hearts, and radiant suns.

Bill Graham compares Griffin to Mouse:

You can't say one artist is better than the other. But what you

Alton Kelley, San Francisco, 1967

can say is that each of them had particular strengths. When I think of Stanley Mouse, for instance, I think of his open-eyed fascination with the world around him, and if I were to pick a half dozen of the definitive 1960s people, Stanley would be one of them. If the earth were parting in front of Stanley, he'd probably say, "Heeeey, look at that!" I think of Stanley as a smiling blotter, picking up everything.

Rick Griffin was also lighthearted, but along with that he took a very serious approach to his art. What Rick had were those searing color combinations. I look at his "Eyeball," or his "Heart and Torch," and I see beautiful, beautiful color, even over and above the beauty of his drawings. He was so skilled with the pen, but what I think made his posters so wonderful was his exuberant use of color. So rich. So warm. Rick had a very delicate strength, and his posters have a special, distinctive look.

One other San Francisco poster artist achieved renown for his use of striking, shimmering bright color. This was Victor Moscoso, a transplanted New Yorker who was one of the few psychedelic artists with extended and substantial formal art training. Like Griffin, Moscoso produced posters that have an instantly apparent "feel" all their own. He arrived in San Francisco in October of 1959, having graduated from Cooper Union, in New York, afterward completing a master's degree program at Yale. In San Fran-

Murphy cartoon character on a *Surfer* cover, 1962
Artist: Rick Griffin

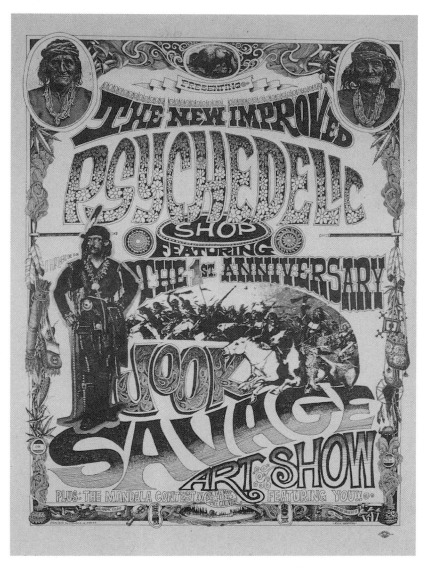

The New Improved Psychedelic Shop and Jook Savage Art Show
San Francisco, 1966. Artist: Rick Griffin

cisco, he continued studies at the Art Institute and became an instructor there. He was painting primarily, but saw the beginning of the Family Dog scene and watched what Bill Graham was doing at the Fillmore. Moscoso went to his first dance at the Avalon, and decided to "make some money doing posters for these guys." He considered Wes Wilson's first posters rather crude, and thought he could do better—especially after all the schooling he'd had.

But the artist soon discovered that training was not enough, that the new art form required a certain reliance on instinct, a willingness to let go. In his subsequent work for the Family Dog, Moscoso set about violating many hard-learned formal rules in an effort to overcome self-conscious inhibition. He used clashing, vibrating colors and deliberately illegible psychedelic lettering to hold—to demand—attention, so that a viewer would "have to spend at least three minutes figuring the thing out." Moscoso played with the viewer's faculties of perception—faculties often heightened or at least altered by drugs.

One of Moscoso's greatest poster-making accomplishments was the series he designed for the small but key Matrix, a San Francisco night spot founded in fall 1965 by Marty Balin, who organized the Jefferson Airplane and debuted the band there. Sometime in late 1966 or early 1967, Moscoso visited the Matrix and offered to design a poster series for upcoming events, which he would publish and distribute under his own imprint, Neon Rose. These posters are characterized by vibrating edges and borders and by bright, intense colors inspired in part by Moscoso's study with Josef Albers at Yale.

Back at the Family Dog during this time, Chet Helms was taking a less active role in art directing poster output; that responsibility was turned over first to Phil Hammond and then to Jack Jackson and Mac McGrew. Jack Jackson, better known as Jaxon, was not only the Family Dog art director during many of its most successful months, but helped develop the distribution system that gave San Francisco poster art national and international exposure:

Like Chet, I came from Texas. Long before I made a place for myself out in San Francisco, I'd been involved in the first psyche-delic happenings in Texas, which had a great effect on me. After I finished college in south Texas, I came to Austin in 1962, because I'd heard there was the beginning of a new scene there. I had a degree in accounting, which later served me well handling the poster distribution business at the Family Dog. During the day I led a very straight life, while at night I was hanging out with the tail end of the beatnik crowd. That was when I met poster and

"Renaissance or Die." Oracle Productions, San Francisco, 1966
Artist: Rick Griffin

comic book artist Gilbert Shelton and went to all the folk music things, including those that involved Janis Joplin. It was in Austin that I first met Chet, a few years before the first big migration to the West Coast began.

Chet was one of the brave souls who went out first, to check out the poetry scene, which he was interested in, and he sent back favorable reports. I came out in the spring of 1966, liked what I saw, went back to Texas, and returned sometime in July. There was a large Texas contingent in San Francisco, just as there was one from Detroit. There were at least three to four hundred people I had first met in Texas—a tribe—and our tribe became part of the San Francisco scene.

I got me a straight accounting job down on Montgomery Street and worked there for six months. Surprisingly, I wasn't really aware of the ballroom scene. That is, until the day Chet called me up and asked if I wanted to go to work for him setting up a poster distribution system. They were printing up several thousand posters, along with handbills, every week. Large quantities were left over and, with all the new interest in the posters, the thought was to make them work in a larger, more creative way than just to promote the current event.

So, sometime early in 1967, around the time FD 40 was coming out, I quit the straight life and joined Family Dog. I forget exactly how many posters they had as surplus, but what I saw were big piles, stack after stack, in an adjoining office. Family Dog hadn't realized any commercial good out of them, apart from their adver-tising value. Now they began to see potential.

But nobody at the Dog really had any business experience, so this is where my accounting background came in handy. I set up an office next to Chet's and began thinking up ways to market the posters. I started making contacts with established distributors, like the Berkeley Bonaparte over in the East Bay, and shops like the Print Mint and Ben Friedman's Postermat, in North Beach. I also set up a mailing list of people interested in getting posters on a regular basis. Initially, we had quite a few posters left over from the original printings, and I don't think we actually reprinted anything until some of the bigger deals were struck with music companies, which picked out some of our strongest, most repre-sentative items.

Rick Griffin, San Francisco, 1967

The Family Dog had two business accounts then: the ballroom account and the poster account. As I began accumulating quite a bit of money in my poster account, frequently the Family Dog would need money to settle with the bands that were booked. Our poster operation played a big role in keeping the Avalon Ballroom concert operation afloat.

The poster distribution grew enormously in a very short time. I felt there was really something very significant happening when our first little office ran out of room to exhibit what we had. All the walls were covered, and we were starting to go after the ceiling. We began to compile lists of our best-moving posters—the top twenty, you might say—and we gave them special code names on the order form. For many months in 1967, there was tremendous excitement marketing our posters, and we were constantly getting enthusiastic reports from our distributors and retailers. But the poster operation got out of hand, and then there was a glut on the market. All sorts of entrepreneurs were coming out with "love" posters and every kind of derivative, exploitative thing. By early 1968, even the Haight-Ashbury shops were heavy into promoting their own poster series. So we became just one of many.

I quit managing the poster operation after about a year and a half, and turned the management over to an old friend, McGrew. But when he got going, there just wasn't the money to do full-color posters on a regular basis, and there was kind of a disappointing end to things. The final posters in the series were black and white.

But while our scene was running well, there was a great flow of talent involved in the Family Dog posters. I think we commissioned every one, making the order with a particular artist. The commissioning process caused a few problems: regular artists—our reliable, always available artists—resented new, unknown artists coming in and getting assignments. But I felt it was a good thing to keep the medium expanding and to try out new people, who might do new, inventive things with their assignment.

The Family Dog's first two posters, I believe, were printed at Contact Printing. But then Chet went to Double-H, a little shop up on Haight Street. Then Family Dog did a whole slew of things with Bindweed Press, a few more at Double-H, and then we turned the work over to Cal Litho, which did the great majority of the Family Dog posters. Cal Litho was responsible for a great many technical breakthroughs that affected the quality of our posters. They treated each job as a labor of love.

While Family Dog ended its numbered series of posters late in 1968, Bill Graham carried his production into the summer of 1971. As was the case with Family Dog and Cal Litho, Graham developed a strong personal relationship with his printer, Levon Mosgofian, owner of Tea Lautrec Litho. Moreover, Mosgofian developed close working relationships with the artists Graham commissioned. Whereas the printer was virtually autonomous in the prepsychedelic days of the rock poster—before 1965 taking on the roles of art director, artist, and printer—the complexities of psychedelic art called for sensitive collaboration among promoter, artist, and printer. Bill Graham explains:

Levon Mosgofian is a direct extension of the creative process I became so involved with when I started issuing posters on a regular basis. Levon is himself an artist. He has compassion for the poster artists, and has a tremendous passion for the art of printing itself. I never expected anything but the best from the man,

Rick Griffin, San Francisco, 1967

and he always surprised me by doing the work even better than what I imagined could be done. He had great respect for all the artists he worked with. He respected what they were attempting to attain, to accomplish. If the artist's intention was to combine this lettering with those colors, or this collage with that design, you could rely on Levon to come up with solutions that worked.

Levon Mosgofian, now in his late seventies, is clearly proud of the key role he played in bringing so many of the best San Francisco rock posters to life:

My work as a printer goes way back, starting in 1925. I did some of my early work on stone, just as Toulouse-Lautrec had done back before the turn of the century. And the adaptation of his name, calling my own print shop Tea Lautrec, is sort of done in homage. My earliest years were spent in Los Angeles, but when times got tough following the stock market crash in 1929 and

Jaxon (Jack Jackson), San Francisco, 1967

through the Depression, I made my way up to San Francisco, which was a big printing town. I had to wrestle with the union to get work, but I was able to because I was a skilled pressman as well as a mechanic. Then the war came. After it, I went back into printing, into offset lithography. Eventually I settled into a shop called Neal, Stratford and Kerr, where I worked for some twenty years. They had a fine reputation as letterpress printers, but no reputation for lithography—which provided me with great opportunity. I handled some of their toughest jobs, and advised in buying their large offset machines. Our offset reputation grew rapidly, to the point where we became known as one of the best shops in the city.

I got to Bill Graham through my friend Joe Buchwald, a printer who is Marty Balin's father. Marty, of course, founded the Jefferson Airplane. Graham and I struck up a very good acquaintance. We always busted our butts working for Bill, and we were never—and I mean never—late with an order. All the artists Bill gave his poster jobs to came to appreciate all the care we took to get things right.

We worked with almost every significant artist of the period. In the beginning it was Wes Wilson, Rick Griffin, Stanley Mouse,

Alton Kelley, and Victor Moscoso. Then there was Bob Fried, Lee Conklin, and finally David Singer. They were all individuals. Rick Griffin was a good man to work with—very conscientious. Fried was tougher, because he'd never quite complete his art; I got the sense he'd rather we did it. And Kelley and Mouse were like that, too, in the beginning. Singer used to drive us crazy, trying to get exactly the colors he had in mind.

Starting with Bill Graham poster #66, the printer's credit appears as Neal, Stratford and Kerr. But Mr. Stratford, one of the nicest people in the printing industry I ever worked for, was beginning to get concerned about some of the social aspects connected with the poster work. I think he was embarrassed by the barefoot hippies coming into the shop, sitting on the floor, and so on. I said to him, "Why don't we set up a division within the company? We could call it 'Toulouse Lautrec Posters, a Division of Neal, Stratford and Kerr.' That way, it would seem to your other clients that the rock poster work was being handled separately."

But I knew the name I'd chosen was just too long, and maybe some descendant of Lautrec himself might object. So then it was "T. Lautrec," and not long after a young friend of mine said, "Hey, Levon, why don't you spell it out? Have it read 'Tea Lautrec.'" Of course, "tea" was another word for pot, going back to the jazz days.

Even while we were still officially Neal, Stratford and Kerr, some of our posters began to carry the Tea Lautrec credit. Later that year, management decided to liquidate the company, and they approved my taking the Tea Lautrec name for my own business.

Our shop did a lot of innovative things for Bill Graham. For example, for a long while he was using rather plainly printed admission tickets, which could be forged easily. People were starting to rip him off. So I came up with an idea that Bill liked very much. I said to him, "Give me posters for two shows at one time. I'll print them two-up on one sheet, which will save you money. And we'll have another sheet on which we'll print eight postcards of each poster, and where the ninth postcard would go, we'll print different-colored tickets for each night." The idea saved money, time, and put an end to counterfeiting—except for one absolutely classic incident, which Bill and I love to tell about. One day Bill calls me up. He says, "Jesus Christ, Levon, look at this. It's counterfeiting!" I went up to his office. "Bill, show me these counterfeit tickets." He gave me one. That's all there was. Some guy had stayed up all night long, coloring a ticket from a freehand drawing. But he made a mistake and put it on thin paper, which he had to glue onto card stock. It started to peel, and that alerted the guard at the door. When I saw this, I laughed and laughed, and said, "Bill, go find that guy and tell him he's welcome anytime. Come on in, fella, you've earned it!"

Of course, Levon Mosgofian saw poster work as a fine business opportunity. But, like many others who were becoming associated with the San Francisco psychedelic scene—printers, promoters, store owners, as well as artists—he also saw himself as a part of something important, a new look for a good new culture. Bob Fried's experience is typical of the period. Trained as a commercial artist, he came to San Francisco from New York to study at the Art Institute and to work as a free-lance designer. But this was 1966, and his conventional art training had been supplemented by friendship with the likes of "beat" poet Allen Ginsberg and LSD advocate Dr. Timothy Leary. He began to look at the rock posters that were starting to appear throughout the Bay Area. Encouraged by Victor Moscoso, whom he met at the Art Institute, Fried began to create his own posters:

By early 1967 the ballroom scene was exploding, and posters were coming from every direction. There was somebody out there always ready to commission you to do a work. I saw it as a throwback to Lautrec's time, what with the artists and printers working together, the people in the audience and the bands up on stage serving as weekly inspiration, the costumed people in the street, and colors, colors, colors, everywhere.

The posters were just a part of a much larger cultural event, but as it was happening it was hard to put it all in perspective. When something so significant comes up that fast and hits you so squarely on, you have no conception of whether it's a passing thing or will go on forever. It just seemed an alternate way of thinking. And for my part, as an artist, I was using a printing press to communicate my ideas, instead of painting.

I don't think I was any different from other artists in wanting to

put out my own ideas, establish a firm, direction, and style of my own. I wanted to create new posters. I wanted to keep them simple, and I wanted them to have entrances and passages. I wanted my posters to convey feelings of dimensional space, like what you feel when you trip on acid. Passing from one reality into another. I wanted to express a kind of space network, rushing, floating, going through time. I wanted people to feel in my posters the sense of discovery I myself was experiencing.

The cultural status of the work of Fried and other poster artists was further enhanced by a distribution operation known as the Berkeley Bonaparte. Its cofounder, Cummings Walker, today a commercial art director, tells the story of the enterprise:

I went to the University of California at Berkeley, hitchhiked around Europe for a year and a half, and then joined the Peace Corps, where I met Louis Rappaport. Louis moved to Berkeley, where I was living when the Haight scene was just getting started, and we

"The Printer": portrait of Levon Mosgofian. San Francisco, 1982. Artist: John D. Moran

began hanging out together once again. We'd always talked about doing something, a bookstore, a coffee house, the traditional sort of avant-garde trip. Louis called me one day, toward the end of 1966, and said, "Cummings, you know what? It's going to be posters. That's where it is." And so the trip started.

At first, our poster distribution activity was a mail-order operation. Louis advertised photo posters, the first being either Lenin or Trotsky, and when the first orders came in, we ran down to the printer and had a quantity made up. And we came up with a name for our business, Berkeley Bonaparte, because the post office insisted that the company have a name.

Then we started looking at the dance poster artists, because we were thinking of serving as their distributor. The first non-political poster we offered was Rick Griffin's "In God We Trust." We met Rick through the man who ran Double H Press, on Haight Street. He said, "You're doing posters? Then you've got to meet this guy!"

We started going through Rick's sketchbook, and I was absolutely blown away. I think it was Louis who found out Rick and his wife Ida were living out of their van and didn't have hardly any money. So we immediately got Rick into doing posters for Berkeley Bonaparte. We were into sharing money ourselves, and everybody got paid at least something, I don't know, fifty bucks a week, and all the dope you could smoke. Something crazy like that, right in tune with the time.

When we took time to think coherently about what our operation could do as a business, it was to present an opportunity for artists like Rick to create art in their own style that could be marketed apart from the normal concert posters. We were reacting against what establishment there was—Bill Graham, the Family Dog—and trying to take care of the artists on another level. And while things went well for us, we distributed some of Victor Moscoso's things, we produced a whole lot of Bob Fried's pieces, and Mouse and Kelley did a few things as well, like their Sierra Club poster.

Right along with the artists themselves, we were learning about the nature of printing, what could be done with predictable success and what was out of bounds. We had to discover how posters

Bob Fried, San Francisco, 1967

The Berkeley Bonaparte, 1967

were actually produced. And if you look at some of our earliest pieces, you'd see what rank amateurs we really were. Take Rick's first piece, "In God We Trust." The printer said to me, "You're going to have to cut overlays for that." And I looked at him and said, "What do you mean by overlays?" And it so happened that that day I was stoned out of my mind, and now I had to cut overlays, so that the poster could be printed in color. It wasn't a very professional job. I still cringe to this day. But then Moscoso and Fried came along and began to get a sense of all the technical particulars that make an imaginative rock poster possible from the standpoint of printing.

Around the time Louis and I came to a parting of the ways, in 1968, I decided I wanted to do a poster book that would reflect all the poster accomplishments up to that point. The book came out late in 1968. I think Art Eureka ended up selling some twenty to twenty-five thousand copies and was the first reference and pictorial work of its kind. It became a treasured classic in its day and turned a lot of people on to what was available at the time.

I asked Rick Griffin to do the book's cover, a take-off on a Disney-type character, and I loved it immediately. It was understood that Rick owned the original art for the cover, and in due course I went up to his house to return the piece after the book

had been printed. As I gave it back to him I said, "Boy, Rick, you know, someday when I'm flush with cash, I'd really like to buy that back from you." And we shared a couple of beers, talked for awhile, and I got in my car to leave. Then Rick says, "Wait a second, Cummings. Hang on." And he hands me a paper bag and walks away, back to the house. I thought maybe he'd made me a sandwich or something, because I think I'd said that I was hungry. When I got to my first stoplight, I opened up the bag, and there's the art! And Griffin had signed the piece, "To Snick from Rick," because that was my nickname. That's the kind of person Rick Griffin is.

The end of 1968 saw not only the liquidation of Berkeley Bonaparte, but the ouster of the Family Dog from its Avalon Ballroom venue when city officials withdrew its hall permit. Ben Friedman, owner of San Francisco's Postermat store, gathered in much of the fallout, amassing stocks of Berkeley Bonaparte and Family Dog posters. Earlier, Friedman had acquired Bill Graham's first excess poster stock, left over after Graham moved from the original Fillmore to the Carousel Ballroom, rechristened the Fillmore West.

Before these major poster stocks changed hands, many Bay

Fans at the Fillmore, San Francisco, ca. 1967

Area record stores, head shops, and related businesses were distributing posters. One of them, the Print Mint—with stores in Berkeley and San Francisco—achieved worldwide recognition when it was featured in a September 1967 *Life* magazine cover story on the poster explosion. Print Mint co-owner Alice Schenker remembers:

In the beginning it was a very naive, open-eyed venture, or should I say adventure, because I basically just started looking for interesting graphics to sell. I was buying stuff from state agricultural departments, weird things from all over, and then one day I spotted an ad in the Village Voice *that offered large photo posters of people like Marlon Brando. This was the beginning of the famous "Personality Poster" operation, and we were one of its very first clients. This was in late 1965.*

Early the next year, I began to see the first Avalon and Fillmore posters tacked to telephone poles and kiosks along Telegraph Avenue. I tried to run these dance posters down, but it was very difficult. No one knew what was going on. No one knew that this was art, not just promotional material. That was early in 1966; by the end of the year people in the Bay Area—people who were hip, people who were turning on—came for the dance posters. We were constantly being asked about them.

Then there was the Life *article, in 1967, which featured all the*

San Francisco rock poster artists. Our store was depicted, and people came to us in droves, people from all over the country. We made a ton of money, but it wasn't something we could have ever predicted. When the Haight-Ashbury scene was going good, we were just another one of the classic businesses that were gathering points, central locations in the midst of all the chaos. The whole San Francisco operation—employees giving away posters in the midst of selling them, cops busting crowds of people in front of our store, and all the wonderful art on our walls and ceilings—was a great, great thrill to be part of, and when the Haight began to deteriorate as a community, we were sad to close up shop and consolidate in Berkeley. Then, as with many of the original poster artists working for the Avalon and Fillmore, we began to make our way into underground comix.

There was an innocent spirit to all the good, wonderful things that emerged as art in San Francisco during the psychedelic sixties. That a store like the Print Mint could do fantastically well with Fillmore and Avalon posters was in some ways incidental and a lucky accident. Not everyone involved was as fortunate financially, especially the artists. Take Wes Wilson:

I did dance posters pretty steadily into 1967, and it was early in the summer of 1967 when I stopped. I thought maybe I could make as much as $60,000, which was a great, great deal at that time. Of course, I was aware of Peter Max, maybe the one artist who actually did make it. But he was in New York, the central location for graphic art, the hub of publishing and all that. And it's in New York where there are people who would put a lot of money into new graphic art. So Peter Max got into doing posters that were in the psychedelic style, and the New Yorkers would print up 250,000 copies of each design. And all he was doing was putting designs together—basic images like Buddha, and rainbows—and ended up selling them all over the world and made tons of money.

Out here in San Francisco, even though we'd invented this new art, it was a much different situation. I learned people were not likely to invest a lot of money backing my particular art. My stuff was very personal, and it had a lot of meaning for awhile, but it wasn't the kind of art that could have meaning on such a broad scale as Peter Max's. What Max turned out was art on a very basic level, and it had a common appeal. I guess what I was doing was too specialized, and that's why I never made any real money. I

Next week's Posters are late because Poster Artist's wife is giving birth.

August 19th & 20th

Bill Graham presents

THE YOUNG RASCALS

(Good Lovin')

With the

QUICKSILVER MESSENGER SERVICE

FILLMORE AUDITORIUM, SAN FRANCISCO

Get your tickets at regular ticket outlets

Interim handbill: Young Rascals; Quicksilver Messenger Service
Fillmore Auditorium, San Francisco, 1966

Wes Wilson on the cover of *California Living*
(November 1966; Collection of Steven D. Lewis)

don't think I ever made more than $14,000 in a year, and that was in 1967, the height of the whole thing.

Bill Graham paid me on a poster by poster arrangement. Generally, I'd get about $100 apiece. We did work out a modest royalty arrangement, but it was never followed through on properly.

When I left Bill Graham, I found myself in a rather weird position. I really couldn't be a regular commercial artist because I just didn't have the portfolio of techniques you need for work like that. I did go to New York one time and talked to some reps. They told me if they ever had a need for something like what I did, they'd contact me, but they also said that in terms of the kind of art I was noted for, they could find in New York a hundred artists who could do it as well, or better. I knew that was probably true. What made things sad was that I could never really capitalize on all the success I was having out in San Francisco.

Corny as it may seem at this cultural remove, the posters were a labor of love. Most of the people associated with them failed, or refused, or were somehow reluctant to translate the posters into a salable commodity. No one can deny the business acumen of Bill Graham, but even he seems to have had trouble seeing his posters just as items for the marketplace:

I never set out to make my posters a successful business in themselves. When you succeed at something like our posters, people

Chalkboard art by Bonnie MacLean
Fillmore Auditorium, San Francisco, 1966

ized in the manner of other American icons. It is possible still to feel a special reverence for them, and even as the posters were being created, those involved in their creation as well as all those standing by felt a sense of kinship with the poster artists at work. David Getz, drummer for Big Brother and the Holding Company, himself a painter, saw firsthand that a movement was in the making:

Big Brother had a rehearsal place on Pine Street, in the same area as the original Family Dog house. But then we had to find something better, and we heard that Mouse had something, a great studio over on Henry Street. It was an old firehouse, and inside it looked like a big empty barn. There was a loft somebody had built into a bedroom, and we started rehearsing there, in Mouse's loft. Janis Joplin first rehearsed there with us.

This was all happening in late April, May, and June of 1966, at the time Chet Helms had gone from Wes Wilson doing the first Avalon posters to asking Mouse, and then Kelley and Mouse, to do posters for the Dog. We'd be rehearsing at Mouse's firehouse, and I'd always be watching Mouse and Kelley turning out those posters. I'd see them from inception to completion. I was fascinated by what they were doing. I'd graduated with honors from the San Francisco Art Institute—I first met Victor Moscoso at the Art Institute—I was a Fulbright Scholar, and I'd taught painting. But I knew right away the art Mouse and Kelley were doing wasn't art that I could do. There was something they were seeing, something in their approach that I didn't understand and that really fascinated me. It was all intuitive. They laughed their way through the whole thing.

Alton Kelley:

The posters were real things in a real time, a really far-out time. The posters were for dances, and the dances were special. It was like Toulouse-Lautrec doing posters for the Moulin Rouge—each of his things was for a dance that really turned him on. And because I was doing posters, I got to go to all the gigs, got in for nothing, met all these far-out musicians and all these far-out people, and got involved in a totally new art scene. I feel real lucky having gotten into it. And I'm glad people like the posters, because I still like them. I can look back at the very first ones and remember how it all got started, and what it felt like. Looking at posters is like tripping out on time.

say, "Well, that man is a sharp entrepreneur." But I was never just that. I never went into the music business, much less the poster business, just to expand and exploit. All it is—you have eyes, you have ears, and you follow your nose.

I remember how many times printing companies and stationery companies would offer me a fortune for the Fillmore posters. There were Japanese import/export houses that offered to buy all my leftover Fillmore tickets. But I never went into anything like that because I never wanted to bastardize what meaning the posters have for me.

If I were strictly a businessman, pure and simple, a guy who's in the business because of supply and demand, I'm sure I would have gone the Peter Max route. You would have seen Fillmore posters used as book covers. I took a much more low-key approach. I worked it out so stores could have them for sales, and we sold some at our own rock shop at Winterland, so people could take something home after a concert. Later we opened up a real rock 'n' roll store of our own.

The rock posters of the psychedelic years were not commercial-

Business card: Bill Graham, ca. 1966

The Red Dog Saloon

CHARLATANS

The explosion of new rock music in San Francisco was the first significant American response to the British Invasion of the mid 1960s. First came the Charlatans, led by George Hunter, who, with his band, affected an Edwardian persona that foreshadowed the San Francisco hippie scene.

In June 1965, the Charlatans were hired to take their embryonic folk-rock music—more accurately, their own version of 1920s country honky tonk—to the Red Dog Saloon in Virginia City, Nevada. Tales of their antics in a modern-day Wild West filtered back to San Francisco, where the first Charlatans poster circulated hand to *(continued on page 90)*

2.1

"The Seed"
(traditional version)
Red Dog Saloon, Virginia
City, Nevada, 1965
Artists: George Hunter,
Michael Ferguson

(continued from page 89)
hand. It became known as "The Seed" and seemed to germinate into a new music and life-style as well as a funky new graphic tradition. Hunter created the distinctive Charlatans logo; Michael Ferguson, the group's pianist, drew the body of the piece.

Because the group's opening at the Red Dog was announced and subsequently delayed, two versions of the first poster were produced (2.1, 2.2). Despite their relative antiquity, the first- and second-version original art and second-version original plate survive.

BIG BROTHER

Big Brother originated in late 1965 jam sessions held at 1090 Page Street, San Francisco, an apartment building managed by the brothers Albin. Peter Albin and Detroit émigré James Gurley founded the band, soon adding Sam Andrew and David Getz. In June 1966 Janis Joplin joined.

2.2

"The Seed" (original version)
Red Dog Saloon, Virginia City, Nevada, 1965
Artists: George Hunter, Michael Ferguson

2.3

Big Brother and the Holding Company
Red Dog Saloon, Virginia City, Nevada, 1965. Artist: Dennis Nolan

Joplin, a Texan who had visited the Bay Area in 1963, returned home after a brief stint as a folk and blues singer. Fellow Texan Chet Helms, Big Brother's first manager, urged her to come out to California a second time. A portrait of Helms, drawn by Dennis Nolan, is seen in the middle of Big Brother's early "generic" handbill (2.3) used to promote appearances like that at the Red Dog.

The Acid Tests

Acid Tests were free-form events, principally the work of novelist Ken Kesey and a group of provocateurs known as the Merry Pranksters. The first official Acid Test poster appeared in December 1965. According to music archivist Glenn Howard, Kesey maintains that only the orange version of the Acid Test poster circulated at the beginning. Howard's own copy (2.5) was lifted off the wall of the Big Beat Club, an obscure Palo Alto venue where the fourth Acid Test was held on December 18. Many years later, Howard obtained the signatures of some of the Test participants (2.6).

The original Acid Test poster is also shown here in a rare handbill version (2.4) hand colored years later by one of Kesey's children.

2.4

Can You Pass The Acid Test?
Muir Beach, California, 1965
Artist: Norman Hartweg (hand coloring: Sunshine Kesey)

The Merry Pranksters And Their Psychedelic Symphony, Neal Cassady Vs. Ann Murphy Vaudeville, The Grateful Dead Rock'n'Roll, Roy's Audioptics, Movies, Ron Boise And His Electric Thunder Sculpture, The Bus, Ecstatic Dress, Many Noted Outlaws, And The Unexpectable.

(far left)
2.5
Can You Pass The Acid Test?
(Big Beat Club), Palo Alto, California,
1965. Artist: Norman Hartweg

(above)
2.6
Signatures (detail of plate 2.5)
(Big Beat Club), Palo Alto, California,
1965. Artist: Norman Hartweg

(left)
2.7
Can You Pass The Acid Test?
San Francisco, ca. 1966
Artist: Wes Wilson

Family Dog

THE EARLIEST CONCERTS

The original four-person Family Dog collective produced three dances held late in 1965 at Longshoremen's Hall, San Francisco. One partner, Ellen Harmon, a devoted reader of Marvel comics, helped dedicate the first dance to "Dr. Strange, Master of the Mystic Arts" (2.8. The second and third dances were dedicated to "Sparkle Plenty" (2.11, 2.12) and "Ming the Merciless" (2.9, 2.10), 1940s comic book characters. The Family Dog's Alton Kelley executed the first three handbills and helped with the posters.

The fourth and fifth Family Dog dances, held early the next year, were mainly the work of partner Luria Castell and her friends the Charlatans, two of whom, George Hunter and Michael Ferguson, did the poster art.

2.8
Handbill: A Tribute to Dr. Strange
Longshoremen's Hall, San Francisco, 1965
Artist: Alton Kelley

2.9
Handbill: A Tribute to Ming the Merciless
Longshoremen's Hall, San Francisco, 1965
Artist: Alton Kelley

2.10
A Tribute to Ming the Merciless
Longshoremen's Hall, San Francisco, 1965
Artist: Alton Kelley

2.11
Handbill: A Tribute to Sparkle Plenty
Longshoremen's Hall, San Francisco, 1965
Artist: Alton Kelley

2.12
Foil poster: A Tribute to Sparkle Plenty
Longshoremen's Hall, San Francisco, 1965
Artist: Alton Kelley

THE NUMBERED SERIES

This landmark series (February 1966–November 1968) included the work by San Francisco's best-known artists, among them Rick Griffin, Stanley Mouse, Victor Moscoso, Wes Wilson, and Alton Kelley. By the end of 1967, other artists, including Bob Fried, Bob Schnepf, Dennis Nolan, Jack Hatfield, and "San Andreas Fault" were contributing work.

Most poster experts agree there are at least 147 pieces in the series proper, with an additional thirteen separately considered as "Denver Family Dog" pieces. (Of 147 San Francisco posters, five are also associated with Denver events.)

Perhaps five to ten additional pieces might be considered adjuncts to the traditional set. These include limited-edition printings, a few rejected designs that somehow circulated, and possibly some graphics recycled for more than one show.

Seventy of the best are presented here. See the Appendix at the back of the book for captions.

FD 1

FD 2

FD 3

FD 4

FD 5

FD 6

FD 7

FD 8

FD 9

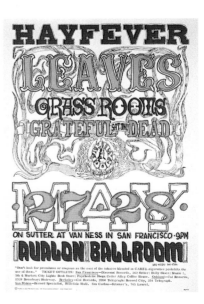

FD 10

FD 12

FD 13

FD 14

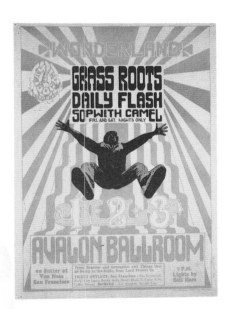

FD 15

FD 16

FD 17

FD 17A

FD 18

FD 19

FD 20

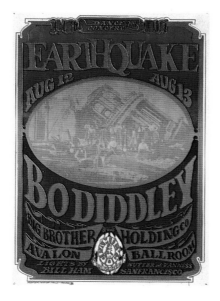

FD 21

FD 22

FD 23

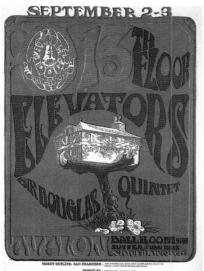

FD 24

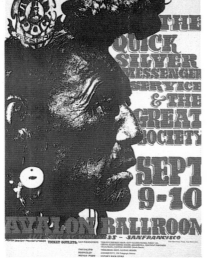

FD 25

FD 26

FD 27

FD 28

FD 29

FD 30

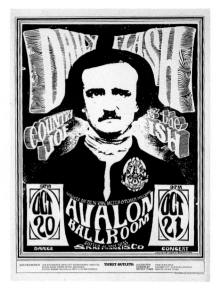

FD 31

FD 33

FD 35

FD 39

FD 41

FD 43

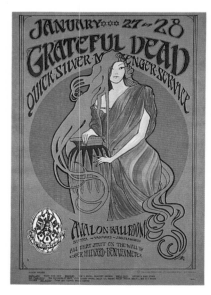

FD 45

FD 52

FD 54

FD 56

FD 58

FD 60

FD 62

FD 65

FD 69

FD 78

FD 79 (D – 1)

FD 85

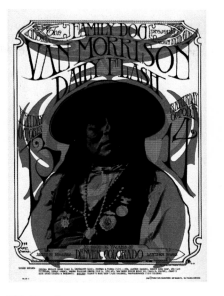

FD D-6

FD 88

FD D-7

FD 89

FD D-8

FD D-9

FD D-11

FD 96

FD D 15

FD D 18

FD 101

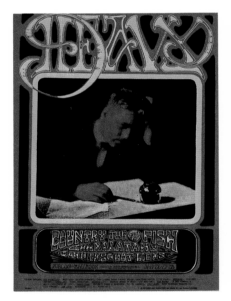

FD 103

FD 109

FD 110

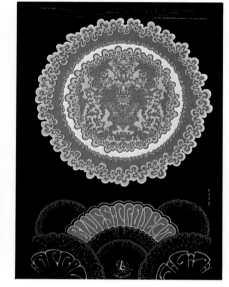

FD 113

FD 116

FD 139

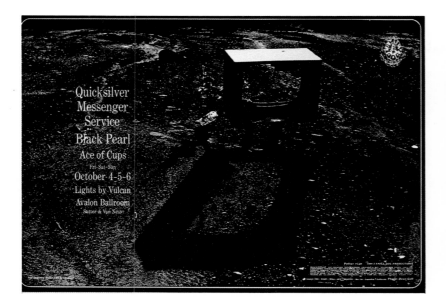

FD 140

FD 142

FD 143

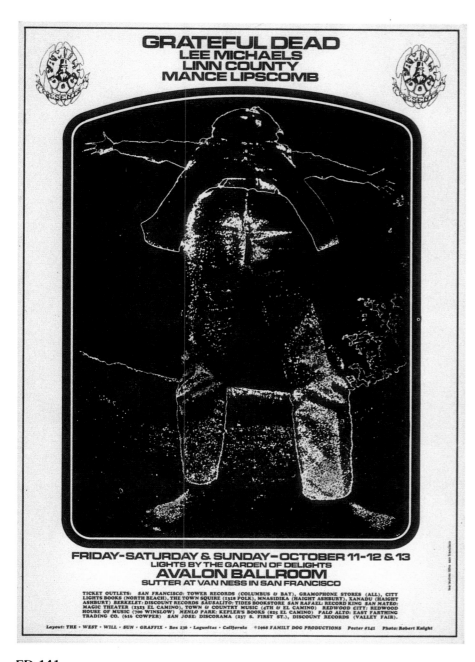

FD 141

FD 144

UNUSUAL EPHEMERA

Much artwork was incidental to the Family Dog numbered series. This included limited-edition silk-screen posters (2.13), color-variant handbills progressive proofs of posters, and uncut poster, handbill, and ticket proofs.

The first several Family Dog posters were printed in black and white, but the Family Dog staff often colored portions of these batches by hand. At this time, Wes Wilson, who created many of the earliest Family Dog pieces, was himself doodling on a copy of his black-and-white FD 1. The hand-colored piece that resulted was an inspiration for the subsequent printing of full-color posters (2.13).

2.13
Hand-colored FD 1
Fillmore Auditorium, San Francisco, 1966
Artist: Wes Wilson

2.14
Silk-screen poster: FD 27
Avalon Ballroom, San Francisco, 1966
Artists: Stanley Mouse, Alton Kelley

UNUSUAL AVALON SHOWS

Community-oriented, the Avalon Ballroom was often the site of obscure local concerts and benefits. One of the wildest was the reading and dance benefit for the Straight Theater, *(continued on next page)*

2.15
Handbill: Straight Theater Reading and Dance Concert. Avalon Ballroom, San Francisco, 1966. Artist: Linda Nimmer

2.16
Straight Theater Reading and Dance Concert
Avalon Ballroom, San Francisco, 1966
Artist: Jacob

2.17
Quicksilver Messenger Service: Big Brother and the Holding Company
Avalon Ballroom, San Francisco, 1967
Artist: P. Kibhall

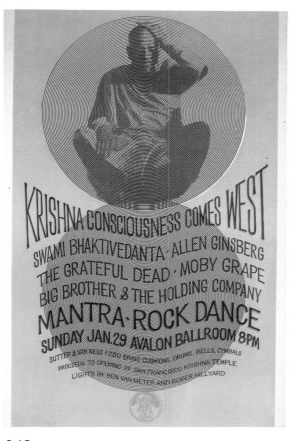

2.18

Krishna Consciousness Comes West
Avalon Ballroom, San Francisco, 1967

2.19

Turkey Trot
Avalon Ballroom, San Francisco, 1967
Artist: Rick Griffin

2.20

Kaleidoscope; Magic Sam
Avalon Ballroom, San Francisco, 1968
Artist: San Andreas Fault

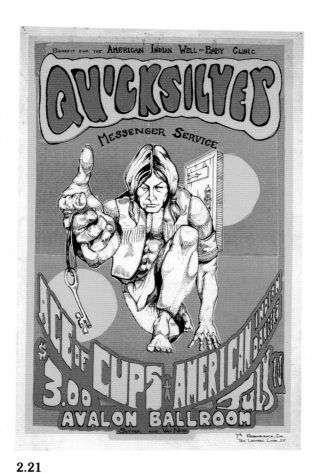

2.21

Benefit for American Indian Well-Baby Clinic
Avalon Ballroom, San Francisco, ca. 1967
Artist: 7th Resemblance, Inc.

(continued from facing page)
which featured among much else, provocative one-acts by radical black playwright Ed Bullins. Both a poster and handbill were created (2.15, 2.16).

Artist Rick Griffin did many of his finest pieces for Avalon Ballroom events, including the Thanksgiving Day "Turkey Trot" handbill for Family Dog (2.19). It is typical of his work from this period: intricate, humorous, intimate.

The presence of the widely recognized "Mr. Natural" character on plate 2.20 suggests that the handbill was the work of noted underground comic book artist R. Crumb. Actually, it was a homage to Crumb executed by an artist who signed his many pieces "S.A.F." or "San Andreas Fault."

SOUNDPROOF SHOWS AT THE AVALON

Soundproof Productions was the first company to produce rock shows at the Avalon after the Family Dog's departure. The first event, in January 1969, was a Grateful Dead dance accompanied by Rick Griffin's self-titled masterwork, "Aoxomoxoa" (2.24). Later that year, the Dead adopted Griffin's title and art for the cover of their third record album.

Even as Soundproof issued one of the greatest posters of all time, it also commissioned one of the grossest. Known as "Dead Chickens" (2.26), it is available in three equally unattractive color variations. A much finer poster (2.25) also heralded this particular Grateful Dead show, but is much more scarce than "Dead Chickens."

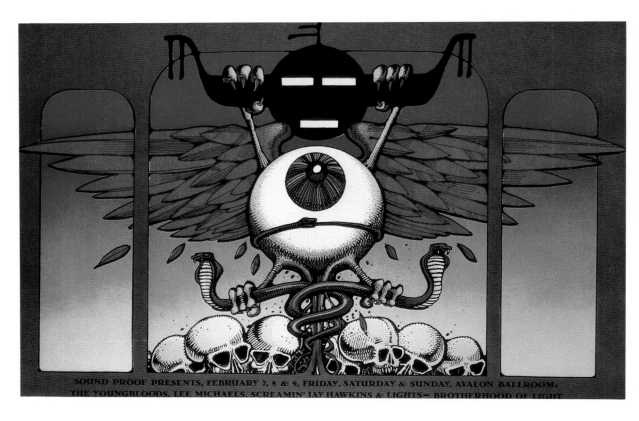

2.22 (left)
Youngbloods; Screamin'
Jay Hawkins
Avalon Ballroom,
San Francisco, 1969
Artist: Rick Griffin

2.23 (below)
Van Morrison; Black Pearl
Avalon Ballroom,
San Francisco, 1969
Artist: Rick Griffin

2.24 (opposite)
Grateful Dead;
Sons of Champlin
Avalon Ballroom,
San Francisco, 1969
Artist: Rick Griffin

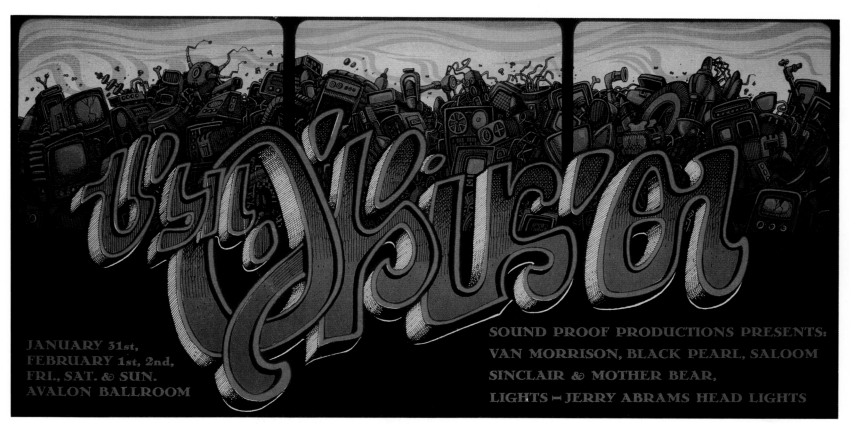

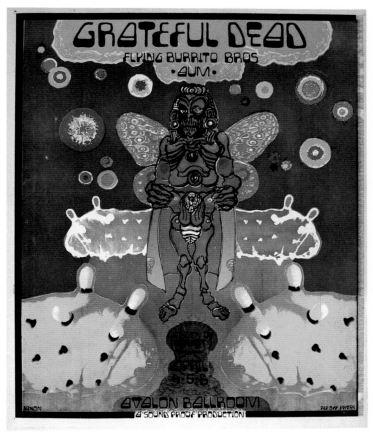

2.25
Grateful Dead; Flying Burrito Brothers
Avalon Ballroom, San Francisco, 1969
Artist: Jaxon

2.26
Grateful Dead; Flying Burrito Brothers
Avalon Ballroom, San Francisco, 1969

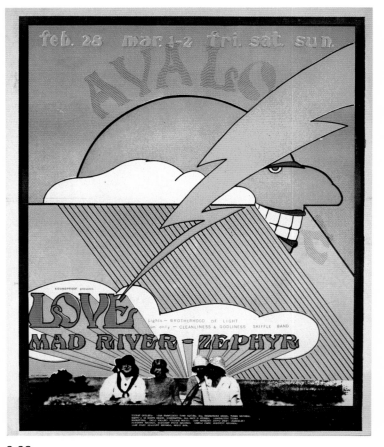

2.27
It's a Beautiful Day; Country Weather
Avalon Ballroom, San Francisco, 1969
Artists: R. Crumb, Gilbert Shelton

2.28
Love; Mad River
Avalon Ballroom, San Francisco, 1969
Artist: Bill Holloway

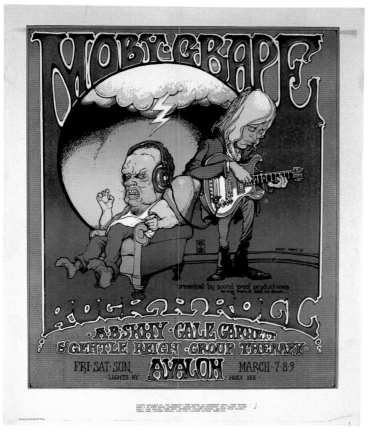

2.29

Moby Grape; A. B. Skhy
Avalon Ballroom, San Francisco, 1969
Artist: Greg Irons

2.30

Steve Miller; Allmen Joy
Avalon Ballroom, San Francisco, 1969
Artists: Alton Kelley, Stanley Mouse

2.31

Santana; Sons of Champlin
Avalon Ballroom, San Francisco, 1969
Artist: Bob Fried

Bill Graham Presents

MIME TROUPE SHOWS AND BENEFITS

Bill Graham left the Allis-Chalmers Manufacturing Company to join this San Francisco theatrical group's management. Late in 1965, Troupe founder R. G. "Ronnie" Davis was indicted for performing in public parks without a permit. In response, Graham mounted the first Mime Troupe fund-raising benefit (2.35). Its success prompted two more, in December 1965 (2.36, 2.37) and in January 1966 (2.38, 2.39). For the third benefit, Graham invited a new band, which he knew as the Warlocks. He didn't like it when the band told him they'd just changed their name, and he commissioned a poster that gave greater play to the group's old name (2.39). As far as can be determined, it is the only poster that billed the Grateful Dead by their prior appellation.

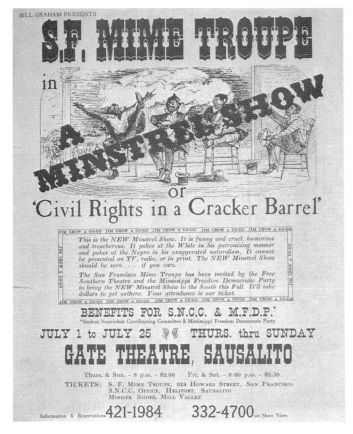

2.33
"Civil Rights In a Cracker Barrel"
Gate Theater, Sausalito, 1965

2.32
"Civil Rights In a Cracker Barrel"
Little Theater, Berkeley, 1965
Artist: Erik Weber

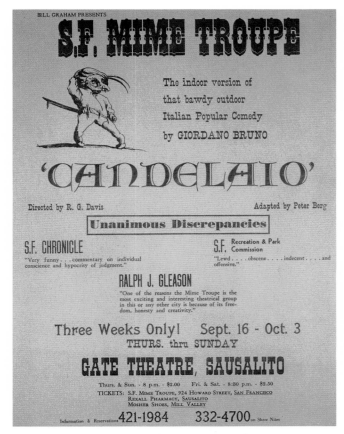

2.34
"Candelaio"
Gate Theater, Sausalito, 1965

S.F. MIME TROUPE
WILL HOLD AN
'APPEAL' PARTY
924 HOWARD STREET (BETWEEN 5ᵗʰ & 6ᵗʰ STS.)
SAT. NIGHT – NOVEMBER 6
FROM 8 P.M. TILL DAWN

Entertainment, Music, Refreshments!

DONATION: AT LEAST $1⁰⁰

Engagement, Commitment & Fresh Air!

R. G. Davis, director of the San Francisco Mime Troupe, was found guilty on November 1 of performing in the public parks without a permit. The four-day trial was pointless because the court did not allow the only relevant issue, freedom of speech and assembly, to be considered.

The trial settled nothing. The Mime Troupe is determined to fight until the parks are returned to their only "owners," the people of San Francisco.

For this is what it is all about: Who owns the parks? Chairman Walter Haas and his fellow members of the Recreation and Parks Commission? They apparently think so, for they revoked the troupe's permit on the grounds the Mime Troupe's commedia dell'arte production of "Il Candelaio" was not in "good taste" or "suitable" for "their" parks. The troupe defied the ban to test a constitutional issue: the commission's power to interfere with free expression. Then Municipal Judge FitzGerald Ames ruled that the commission's revocation power was "a matter of law" and not for the jury to decide. Thus the commission's powers were not allowed to be contested, and Davis was found guilty.

The only legitimate purpose for issuing permits is to schedule events properly – preventing time or place conflicts. The contents of performances is not a matter for the commissioners to judge. And Walter A. Haas's idea of good taste is NOT a "matter of law"!

There are adequate laws to handle any crime committed in the parks. Was the Mime Troupe accused of being disorderly? No. Of creating a public nuisance? No. Of obscenity? No. It was banned because it did not conform to the commissioners' standard of "good taste" (whatever that may be). If the commissioners believe the troupe violated any law, then let them charge the troupe with a violation of that law.

WHO OWNS THE PARKS? The people of San Francisco. The parks are very large and there is room for us all -- room for any expression of any idea. Freedom of speech and freedom of assembly do not stop where Mr. Haas's good taste begins.

What is the effect of the commission's action and the court's failure to confront the issue? Our freedoms are lessened, for when one means of expression is cut off, who knows what will be next? The 20,000 persons who enjoyed the troupe's free park performances in the past four years will no longer have that opportunity, thanks to the "good taste" of six commissioners.

THE CREATIVE LIFE OF SAN FRANCISCO IS NOW DIMINISHED AND THE PARKS ARE CONSIDERABLY LESS JOYFUL.

The following artists will appear at the APPEAL PARTY on behalf of the San Francisco Mime Troupe:

JEANNE BRECHAN	THE FAMILY DOG	JOHN HANDY QUINTET	JIM SMITH
SANDY BULL	LAWRENCE FERLINGHETTI	JEFFERSON AIRPLANE	ULLETT & HENDRA
THE COMMITTEE	THE FUGS	SAM HANKS	& OTHERS WHO CARE

FOR FURTHER INFORMATION, CALL GA. 1-1984

2.35

Handbill: San Francisco Mime Troupe Appeal I
924 Howard Street, San Francisco, 1965

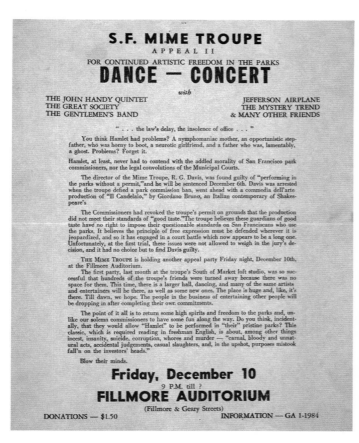

2.36

Handbill: San Francisco Mime Troupe Appeal II
Fillmore Auditorium, San Francisco, 1965

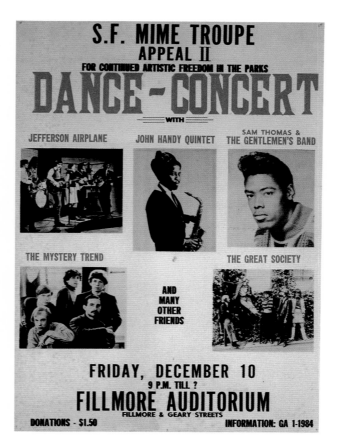

2.37

San Francisco Mime Troupe Appeal II
Fillmore Auditorium, San Francisco, 1965

2.38

Handbill: San Francisco Mime Troupe Appeal III
Fillmore Auditorium, San Francisco, 1966

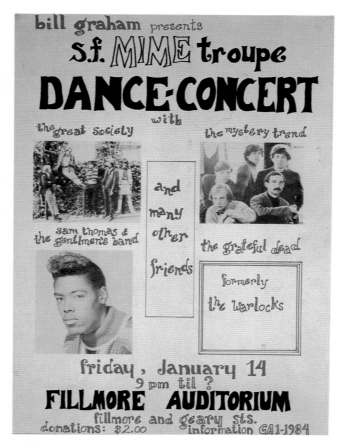

2.39

San Francisco Mime Troupe Appeal III
Fillmore Auditorium, San Francisco, 1966

TRIPS FESTIVAL

The three-day Trips Festival, held late in January 1966, was
first imagined by Stewart Brand, photographer, naturalist,
(continued on page 116)

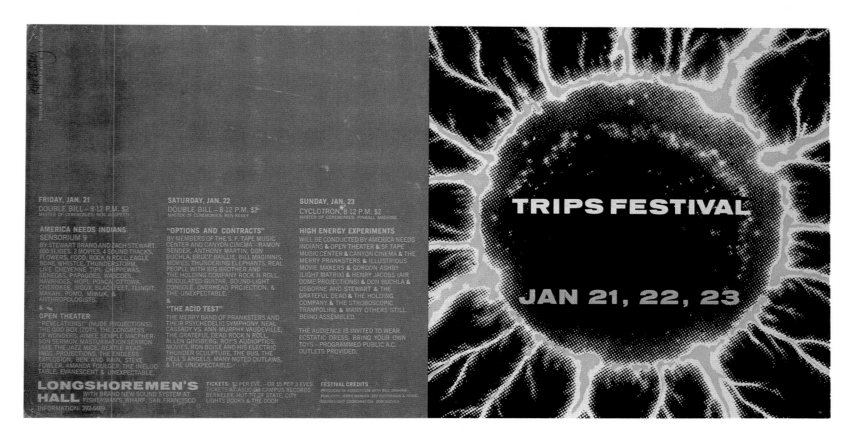

2.40
Trips Festival
Longshoremen's Hall, San Francisco, 1966
Artist: Peter Bailey

2.41
Program: Trips Festival (inside)
Longshoremen's Hall, San Francisco, 1966

2.42

Flier: Trips Festival (front)
Longshoremen's Hall, San Francisco, 1966
Artist: Wes Wilson

(continued from page 115)
and Merry Prankster, who later founded the *Whole Earth Catalog*. Ken Kesey and the Pranksters joined Brand in the initial plans, as did members of Big Brother and the Holding Company and the Grateful Dead, poet Allen Ginsberg, and others. Bill Graham was brought on as coordinating producer. This event inspired him to begin his own rock bookings at the Fillmore.

this is the FIRST gathering of its kind anywhere. the TRIP -- or electronic performance--is a new medium of communication & entertainment.

FRIDAY, JANUARY 21
america needs indians, sensorium 9 - slides, movies, sound tracks, flowers, food, rock'n'roll, eagle lone whistle, indians (senecas, chippewas, hopi, sioux, blackfeet, etc.) & anthropologists. open theatre - "revelations" - nudeprojections. "the god box" by ben jacopetti. the endless explosion, the congress of wonders, liquid projections, the jazz mice, the loading zone rock'n'roll, steve fowler, amanda foulger, rain jacopetti, & the unexpectable.

SATURDAY, JANUARY 22
ken kesey, members of the s.f. tape music center, big brother & the holding company rock'n'roll, the don buchla sound-light console, overhead projection, anthony martin, ramon sender, bill maginnis, bruce baillie. "the acid test", the merry pranksters & their psychedelic symphony, neal cassady vs. ann murphy vaudeville, the grateful dead rock'n'roll, allen ginsberg, roy's audioptics, movies, ron boise & his electric thunder sculpture, the bus, hell's angels, many noted outlaws, & the unexpectable.

SUNDAY, JANUARY 23
high energy experiments conducted in the cyclotron of dome-shaped longshoreman's hall by america needs indians, open theatre, s.f. tape music center, the merry pranksters, gordon ashby (light matrix), henry jacobs (air dome projections), kqed, don buchla, the grateful dead, the loading zone, big brother & the holding company, & many others still being assembled. since the common element of all shows is ELECTRICITY, this evening will be programmed live from stimuli provided by a PINBALL MACHINE. a nickel in the slot starts the evening.

the general tone of things has moved on from the self-conscious happening to a more JUBILANT occasion where the audience PARTICIPATES because it's more fun to do so than not. maybe this is the ROCK REVOLUTION. audience dancing is an assumed part of all the shows, & the audience is invited to wear ECSTATIC DRESS & bring their own GADGETS (a.c. outlets will be provided).

design:
Wes Wilson

printing:
Contact Printing Co.

TICKETS - $2 PER EVENING
$5 FOR SERIES
AT CITY LIGHTS, S.F., ASUC
AND CAMPUS RECORDS,
BERKELEY; HUT-T-I, S.F.
STATE- INFO: 392-5489

THE NUMBERED SERIES

Because Graham's first period of work lasted several years longer than that of the Family Dog, his world-renowned poster series (1966–71) includes many more pieces, represents a much wider range of musical attractions, and involves many more poster artists, including—among the best—Wes Wilson, Rick Griffin, Stanley Mouse, Alton Kelley, Bonnie MacLean, Lee Conklin, Greg Irons, Randy Tuten, and David Singer.

Most poster experts agree the traditional Graham numbered series concludes with BG 287. Based on a reexamination of posters graphically or thematically related to the numbered set, eight to twelve additional works might be included.

All of the numbered series are presented here. See the Appendix at the back of the book for captions.

BG 1

BG 2

BG 3

BG 0

BG 4

BG 5

BG 6

BG 7

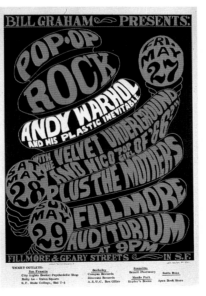

BG 8

BG 9

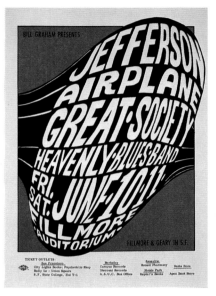

BG 10

BG 11

BG 12

BG 13

BG 14

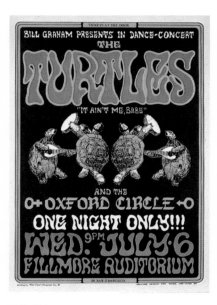

BG 15

BG 16

BG 17

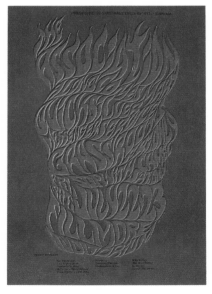

BG 18

BG 19

BG 20

BG 21

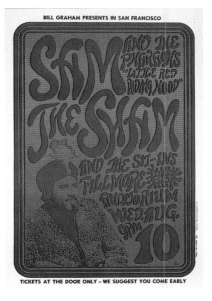

BG 22

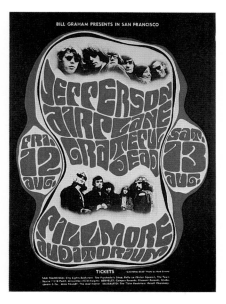

BG 23

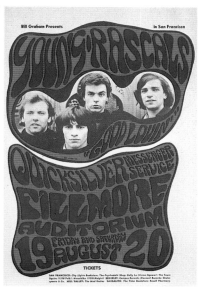

BG 24

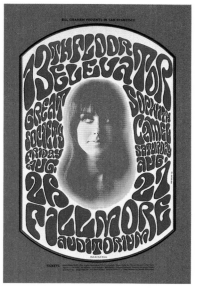

BG 25

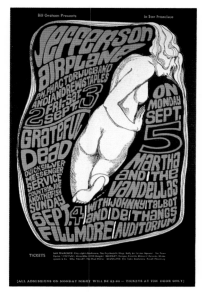

BG 26

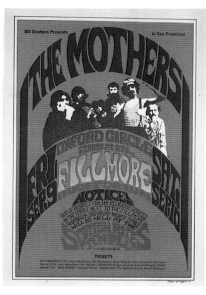

BG 27

BG 28

BG 29

BG 30

BG 31

BG 32

BG 33

BG 34

BG 35

BG 36

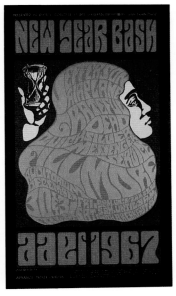

BG 37

BG 38

BG 39

BG 40

BG 41

BG 42

BG 43

BG 44

BG 45

BG 46

BG 47

BG 48

BG 49

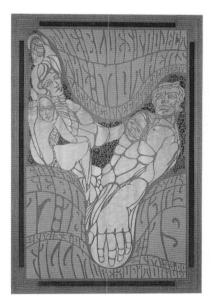

BG 50

BG 51

BG 52

BG 53

BG 54

BG 55

BG 56

BG 57

BG 58

BG 59

BG 60

BG 61

BG 62

BG 63

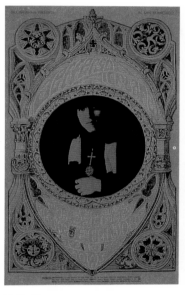

BG 64

BG 65

BG 66

BG 67

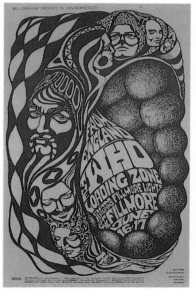

BG 68

BG 69

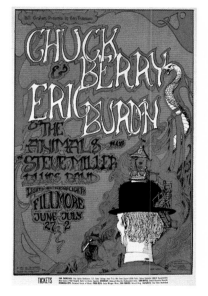

BG 70

BG 71

BG 72

BG 73

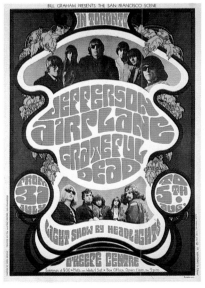

BG 74

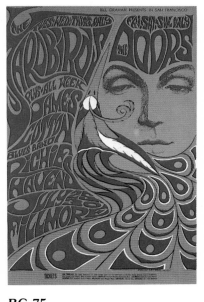

BG 75

BG 76

BG 77

BG 78

BG 79

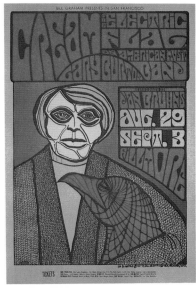

BG 80

BG 81

BG 82

BG 83

BG 84

BG 85

BG 86

BG 87

BG 88

BG 89

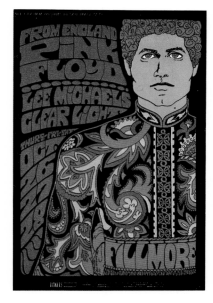

BG 90

BG 91

BG 92

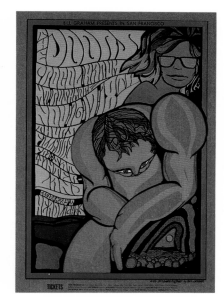

BG 93

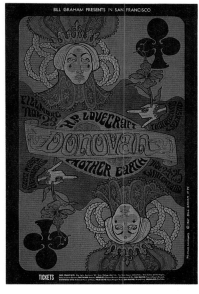

BG 94

BG 95

BG 96

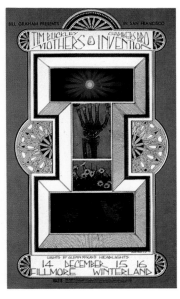

BG 97

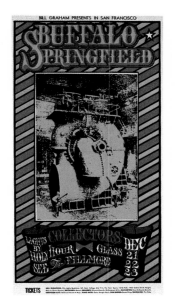

BG 98

BG 99

BG 100

BG 101

BG 102

BG 103

BG 104

BG 105

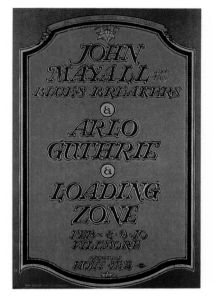

BG 106

BG 107

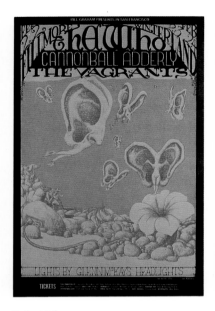

BG 108

BG 109

BG 110

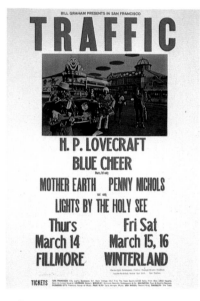

BG 111

BG 112

BG 113

BG 114

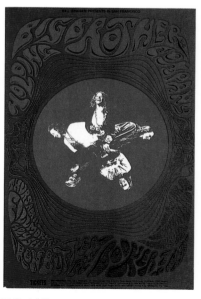

BG 115

BG 116

BG 117

BG 118

BG 119

BG 120

BG 121

BG 122

BG 123

BG 124

BG 125

BG 126

BG 127

BG 128

BG 129

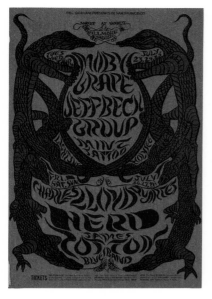

BG 130

BG 131

BG 132

BG 133

BG 134

BG 135

BG 136

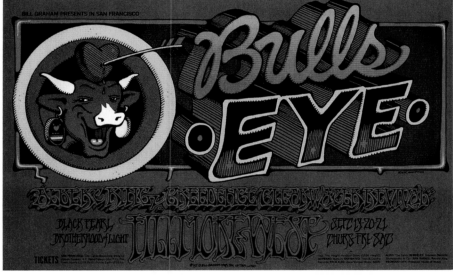

BG 137

BG 138

BG 139

BG 140

BG 140A

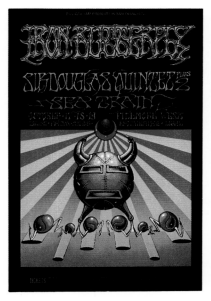

BG 141

BG 142

BG 143

BG 144

BG 145

BG 146

BG 147

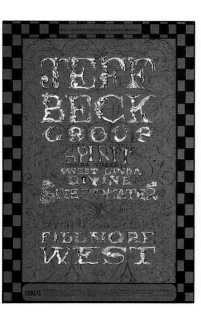

BG 148

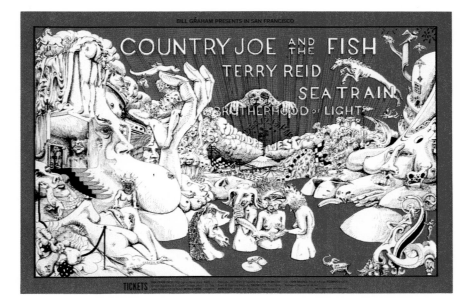

BG 149

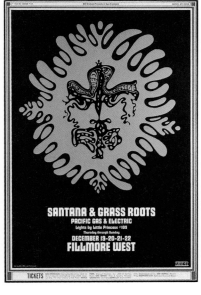

BG 150

BG 151

BG 152

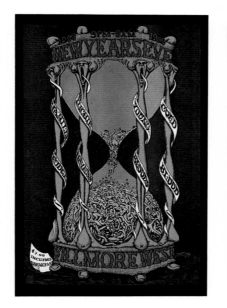

BG 153

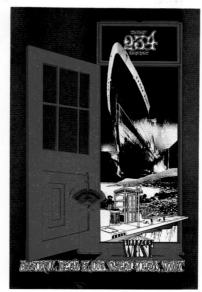

BG 154

BG 155

BG 156

BG 157

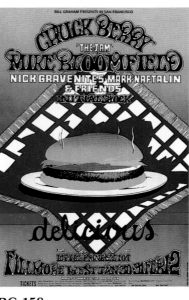

BG 158

BG 159

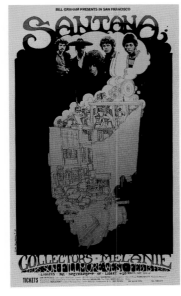

BG 160

BG 161

BG 162

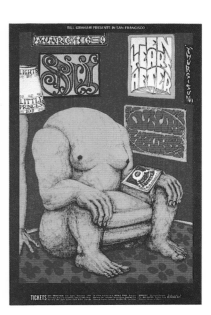

BG 163

BG 164

BG 165

BG 166

BG 167

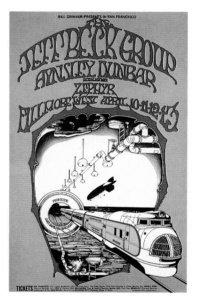

BG 168

BG 169

BG 170

BG 171

BG 172

BG 173

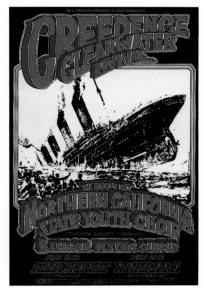

BG 174

BG 175

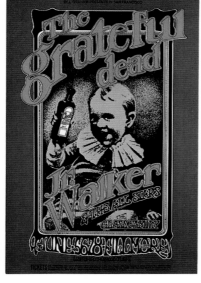

BG 176

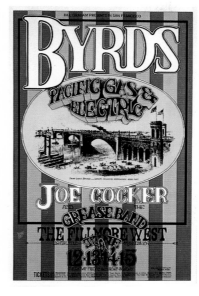

BG 177

BG 178

BG 179

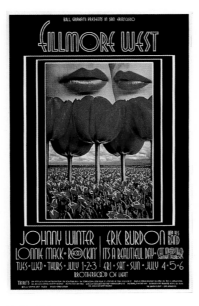

BG 180

BG 181

BG 182

BG 183

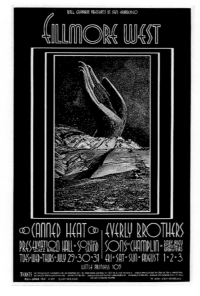

BG 184

BG 185

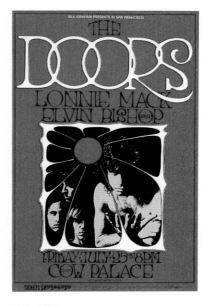

BG 186

BG 187

BG 188

BG 189

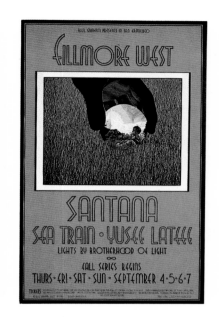

BG 190

BG 191

BG 192

BG 193

BG 194

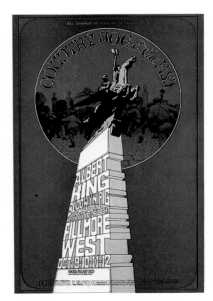

BG 195

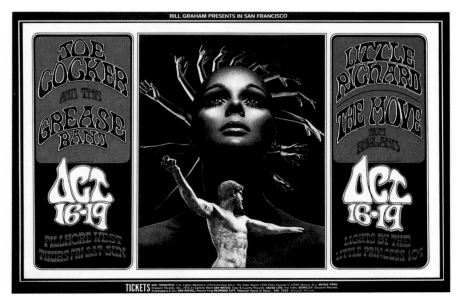

BG 196

BG 197

BG 198

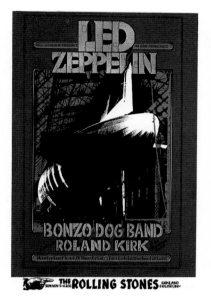

BG 199

BG 200

BG 201

BG 202

BG 203

BG 204

BG 205

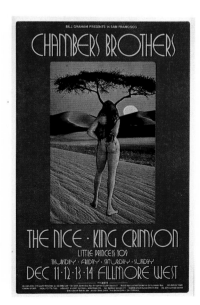

BG 206

BG 207

BG 208

BG 209

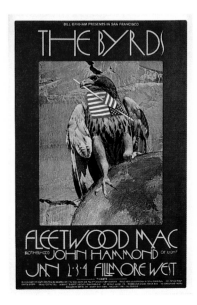

BG 210

BG 211

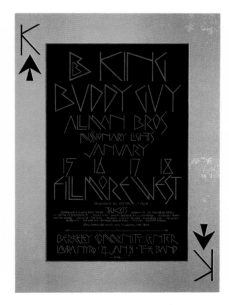

BG 212

BG 213

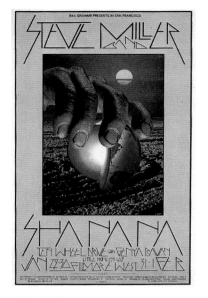

BG 214

BG 215

BG 215A

BG 216

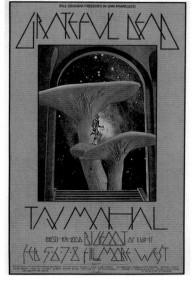

BG 217

BG 218

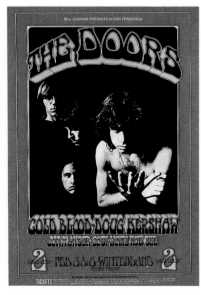

BG 219

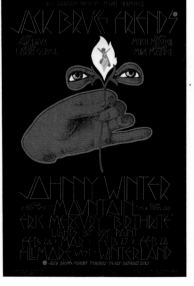

BG 220

BG 221

BG 222

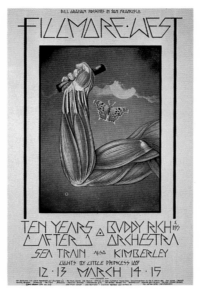

BG 223

BG 224

BG 225

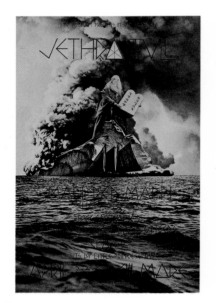

BG 226

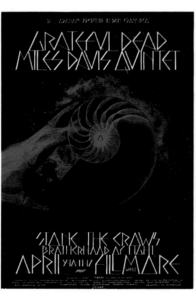

BG 227

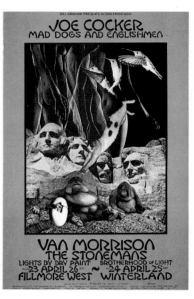

BG 228

BG 229

BG 230

BG 231

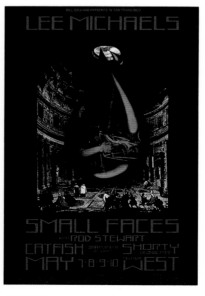

BG 232

BG 232A

BG 233

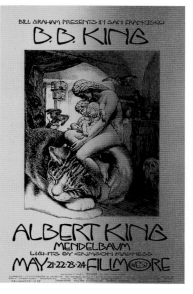

BG 235

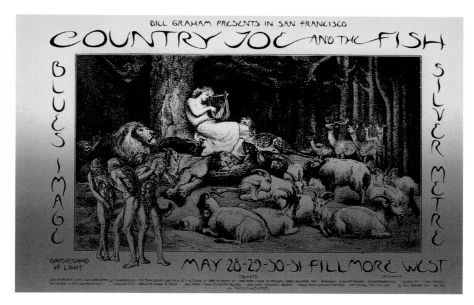

BG 236

BG 237

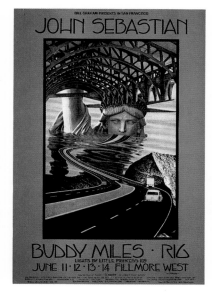

BG 238

BG 239

BG 240

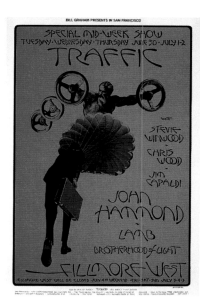

BG 241

BG 242

BG 243

BG 244

BG 245

BG 246

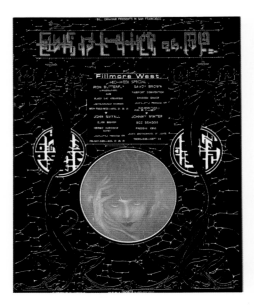

BG 247

BG 247A

BG 248

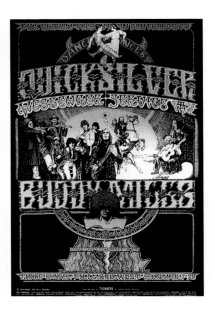

BG 249

BG 250

BG 251

BG 252

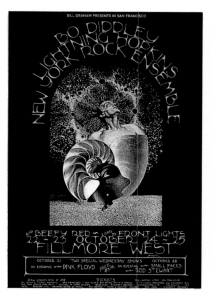

BG 253

BG 254

BG 255

BG 256

BG 257/8

BG 259

BG 260

BG 261

BG 262

BG 263

BG 264

BG 265

BG 266/7

BG 268

BG 269

BG 270

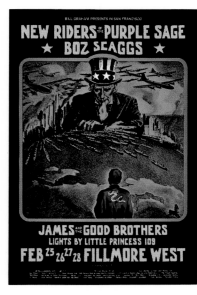

BG 271

BG 272

BG 273/4

BG 275

BG 276A

BG 277

BG 278

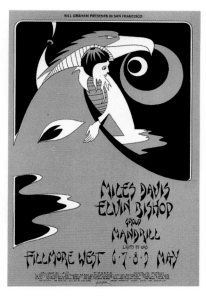

BG 279

BG 280

BG 281

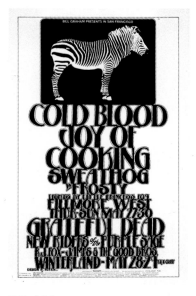

BG 282

BG 283

BG 284

BG 285

BG 286

BG 287

UNUSUAL EPHEMERA

Almost all Bill Graham posters were accompanied by handbills, most of which were very similar—if not identical—to the posters. There are, however, color, design, or printing variants, desirable because of scarcity.

Building a complete set of handbills is a great collecting challenge. An ephemeral commodity, this art has sometimes survived in far fewer numbers than posters. Up through BG 24, the handbills were produced as monotone prints on very light twenty-pound stock similar to typing paper. Beginning with BG 25, handbills were printed in full color like the posters, but still on light paper. By BG 53, handbills appeared on stiffer stock, produced in a format termed the oversize—or "continental"—postcard, with mailing information on the back. The previous handbills were then reprinted in the new format.

Some of the more unusual artifacts from the Fillmore poster days include uncut printers proofs (2.48–51), limited edition commemorative pins (2.52–54), early bumperstickers (2.55, 2.56), and the original art from which posters were made (2.58–61). Original art, which includes pencil sketches, pen-and-ink drawings, and pasted-up mechanicals, reveals detail sometimes lost in printing. This is particularly true of Lee Conklin's intricate work (2.61).

Like all concert promoters, Bill Graham was faced with the problem of identifying the proper night's ticket at the door, as well as recognizing counterfeit tickets. Levon Mosgofian, owner of Tea Lautrec Lithography, developed a solution. Since

(continued on p. 146)

2.44

Handbill: Otis Redding; Grateful Dead
Fillmore Auditorium, San Francisco, 1966
Artist: Bonnie MacLean

2.45

Band-generated poster: Quicksilver Messenger
Service. Fillmore Auditorium, San Francisco, 1966

2.46

Silk-screen poster: Quicksilver Messenger Service
Fillmore Auditorium, San Francisco, 1966
Artist: Bob Collins

2.47

"Phoenix Dance" Benefit
Fillmore Auditorium, San Francisco, 1967

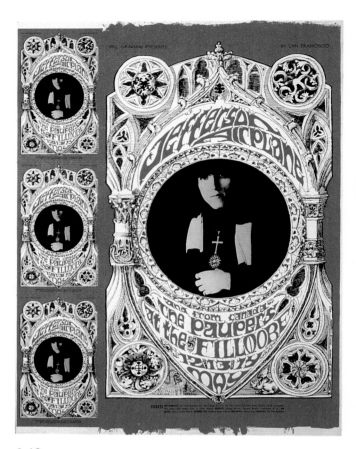

(continued from p. 145) color printing is a three-color (plus black) process —the colors adding up to create a full-color image —it is an easy matter to reproduce only one color at a time instead of combining them. Thus one piece of poster art can yield three different-colored tickets, solving identification problems at the front door, particularly when the same band appears on successive nights.

2.48

Uncut progressive proof: BG 63
Fillmore Auditorium, San Francisco, 1967
Artist: Bonnie MacLean

2.49

Uncut progressive proof: BG 48
Fillmore Auditorium, San Francisco, 1966
Artist: Wes Wilson

2.50

Uncut progressive proof: BG 57
Fillmore Auditorium, San Francisco, 1967
Artist: Wes Wilson

2.51

Uncut proof of second printing: BG 105
Fillmore Auditorium, Winterland, San Francisco, 1968
Artist: Rick Griffin

2.52

Button: Jefferson Airplane; Grateful Dead
O'Keefe Centre, Toronto, Canada, 1967
Artist: James H. Gardner

2.53

Button: Blues/Rock Bash II
Fillmore/Winterland, San Francisco, 1966
Artist: John H. Myers

2.54

Button: Rock/Blues Bash
University of California, Berkeley, 1966

2.55

Bumper sticker: Blues/Rock Bash II
Winterland/Fillmore, San Francisco,
1966. Artist: John H. Myers

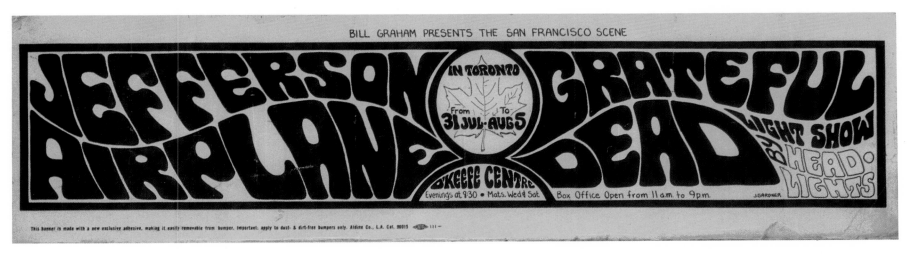

2.56

Bumper sticker: Jefferson Airplane;
Grateful Dead. O'Keefe Centre, Toronto,
Canada, 1967. Artist: James H. Gardner

2.57

Bumper sticker: Fillmore West
San Francisco, ca. 1970

2.58
Original art:
BG 136
Fillmore West,
San Francisco,
1969.
Artist:
Rick Griffin

2.59
Original art: BG 226
Fillmore West, San Francisco, 1970
Artist: David Singer

2.60
Original art: BG 80
Fillmore West, San Francisco, 1967
Artist: Jim Blashfield

2.61
Original art: BG 152
Winterland, San Francisco, 1968
Artist: Lee Conklin

2.62

Tickets: BG 136
Fillmore West, San Francisco, 1968
Artist: Rick Griffin

2.63

Tickets: BG 141. Fillmore West, San Francisco, 1968
Artists: Rick Griffin and Victor Moscoso

2.64

Tickets: BG 170. Fillmore West/Winterland, San Francisco, 1969
Artist: Randy Tuten

2.65

Tickets: BG 280. Fillmore West, San Francisco, 1971
Artist: David Singer

2.66

Tickets: BG 216. Fillmore West, San Francisco, 1970
Artist: David Singer

2.67

Tickets: BG 220. Fillmore West/Winterland, San Francisco, 1970
Artist: David Singer

FILLMORE AUDITORIUM BENEFITS

Dozens of benefit events, for a wide variety of causes, took place at the Fillmore. Graham is given credit for sponsoring many of them, even when his name does not appear on the actual posters. Among serious collectors, the benefit concert posters are referred to as "non-numbered pieces" in the Graham series.

2.69
Delano Strike Benefit
Fillmore Auditorium, San Francisco, 1966
Artist: Wes Wilson

2.68
Third Annual Children's Adventure Day Camp Benefit
Fillmore Auditorium, San Francisco, 1966
Artist: Mary Kay Brown

2.70
SNCC Benefit
Fillmore Auditorium, San Francisco, 1966

2.71
"Busted"—San Francisco Mime Troupe Benefit
Fillmore Auditorium, San Francisco, 1967
Artist: Stanley Mouse

2.72
Stop-the-Draft-Week Defense Fund Benefit
Fillmore Auditorium, San Francisco, 1968

2.73
Benefit for the Council for Civic Unity
Fillmore Auditorium, San Francisco, 1967
Artist: Hank Lelo

2.74
Benefit for the BOTH/AND Club
Fillmore Auditorium, San Francisco, 1966

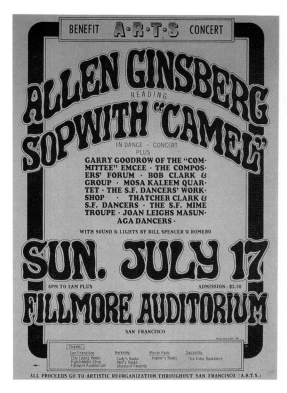

2.75
A.R.T.S. Benefit
Fillmore Auditorium, San Francisco, 1966
Artist: Wes Wilson

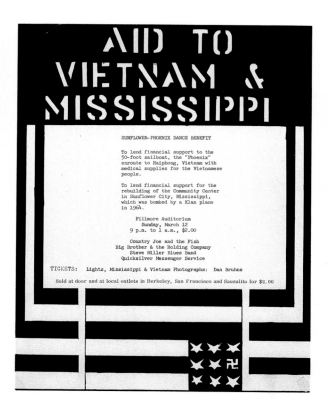

2.76
Sunflower-Phoenix Dance Benefit
Fillmore Auditorium, San Francisco, 1967

2.77
Andrei Voznesensky; Jefferson Airplane
Fillmore Auditorium, San Francisco, 1966
Artist: Bonnie MacLean

2.78
Grape Workers Strike Benefit
Fillmore West, San Francisco, 1969
Artist: Lee Conklin

2.79
KPFA Benefit
Fillmore Auditorium,
San Francisco, 1967
Artist: Devore

Bill Graham maintained a tight hold on Fillmore Auditorium, but it was possible for independent producers to claim the hall on odd dates. The Associated Students of San Francisco State College was able to produce its homecoming "Edwardian Ball" at the Fillmore (2.81). Graham himself produced Fillmore shows apart from those represented by his numbered poster series. An example is the "Magic Sam Memorial Concert" (2.86). He also produced occasional private party events for his staff and friends, such as the memorable 1969 Thanksgiving Eve celebration at the Fillmore West (2.88).

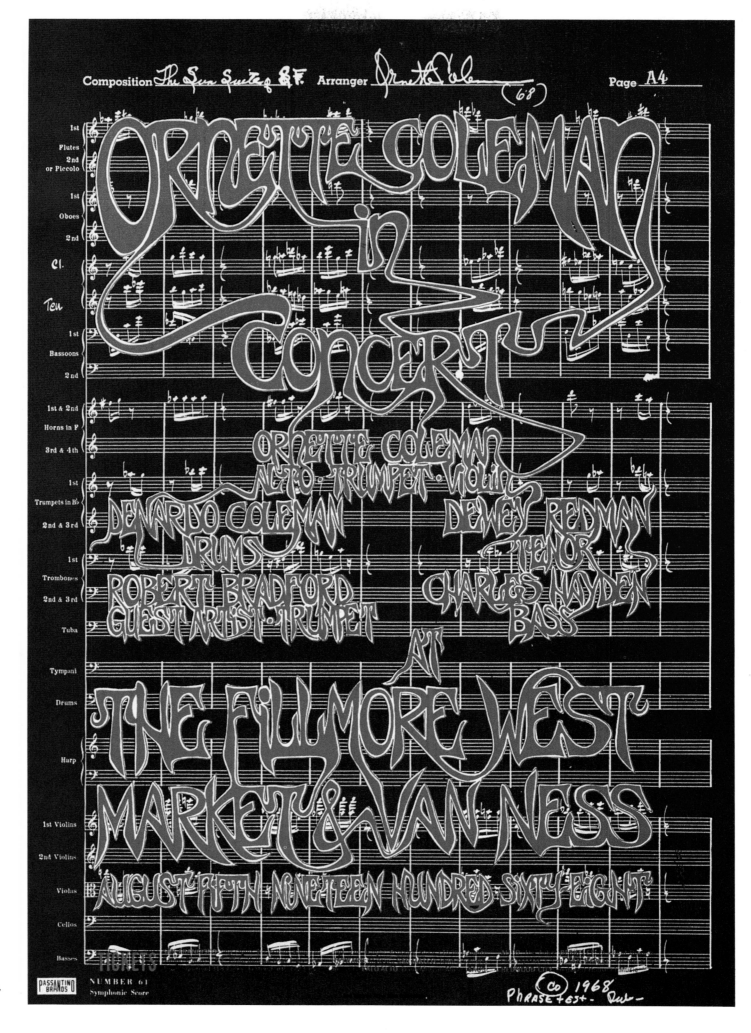

2.80

Ornette Coleman
Fillmore West, San Francisco,
1968. Artist: Doré

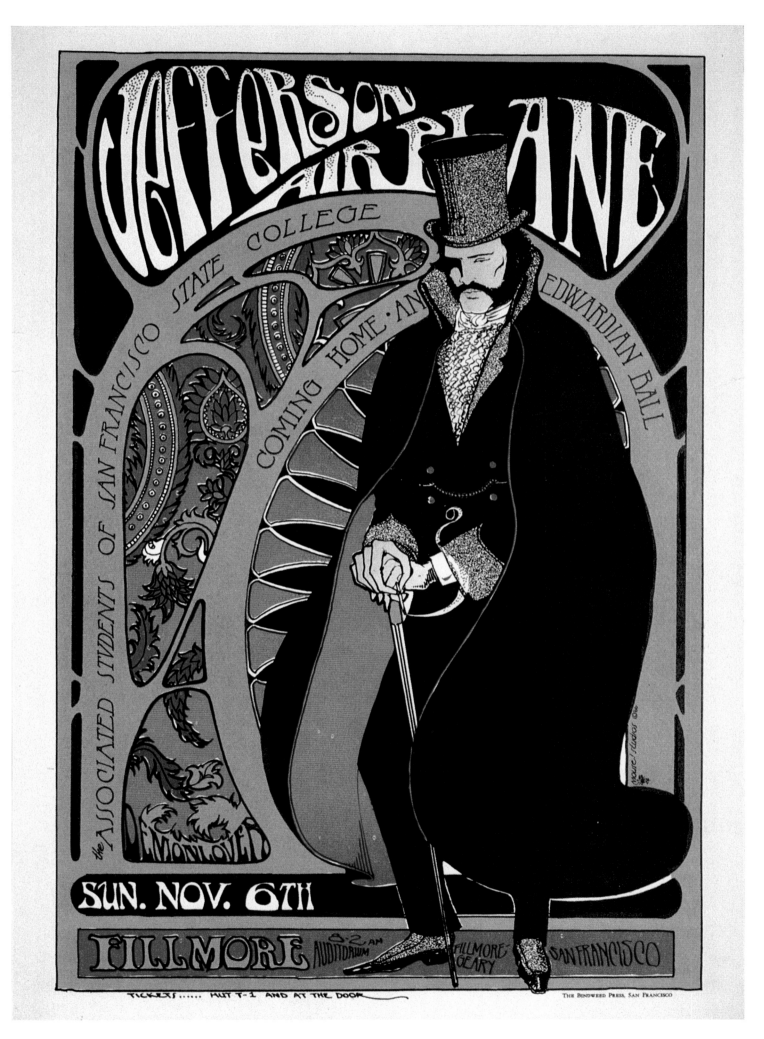

2.81

Edwardian Ball
Fillmore Auditorium,
San Francisco, 1966
Artists: Stanley Mouse,
Alton Kelley

2.82
Light-Sound-Dimension Easter Voyage
Fillmore Auditorium, San Francisco, 1967

2.83
Vanguard Records Party Invitation for Country Joe
Fillmore Auditorium, San Francisco, 1967
Artist: Tom Weller

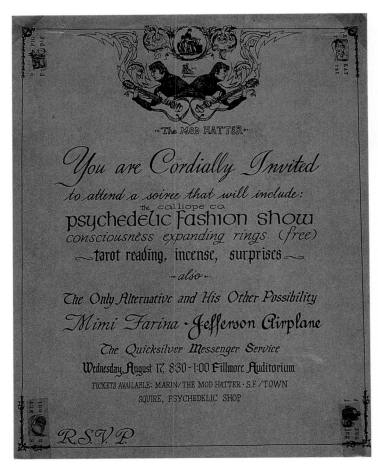

2.84
Psychedelic Fashion Show
Fillmore Auditorium, San Francisco, 1966

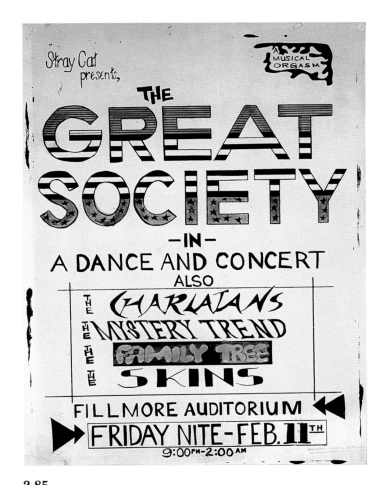

2.85
The Great Society; Charlatans
Fillmore Auditorium, San Francisco, 1966

2.86
Magic Sam Memorial Concert
Fillmore West, San Francisco, 1970
Artist: John Van Hamersveld

2.87
Jefferson Airplane; Quicksilver Messenger Service
Fillmore Auditorium, San Francisco, 1966
Artist: Gut

2.89
Proposition "P" Benefit
Fillmore Auditorium, San Francisco, 1967
Artist: Jim Blashfield

> With This Ticket Consider
> Joining Us As Our Guest   Admit One
>
> At the Fillmore
> on
> **THANKSGIVING EVE**
> WEDNESDAY, NOVEMBER 26, 1969 — 9 P.M. - 2 A.M.
>
> *For the Basics of Life—*
> *Food, Drink, Music and the Pleasure of Companionship.*
> —*Bill Graham and the Fillmore People*
>
> FILLMORE WEST • Market and Van Ness • San Francisco

2.88
Guest ticket: Thanksgiving Eve Party
Fillmore West, San Francisco, 1969

FILLMORE EAST
AND ELSEWHERE

The posters for the New York shows never evolved into an extensive series comparable to the San Francisco numbered series.

Graham staged most of his productions in San Francisco initially, then in New York as well, but one fondly remembered presentation was the Grateful Dead and Jefferson Airplane in Toronto. The Canadian poster, BG 74, is the scarcest of all Graham's numbered pieces. The Toronto show produced an equally rare handbill, a concert program (2.100), a commemorative pin (2.52), and a bumpersticker (2.56).

Graham did not regularly produce shows in Los Angeles, but one event held there was advertised by a take-off on an earlier Fillmore poster in the numbered series. This piece refers to Graham by his real name, Wolfgang Grajonca (2.101).

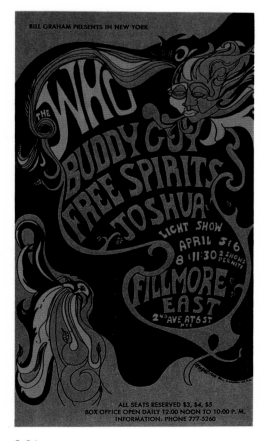

2.90

Jimi Hendrix Experience
Fillmore East, New York, 1968
Artist: Fantasy Unlimited

2.91

The Who; Buddy Guy
Fillmore East, New York, 1968

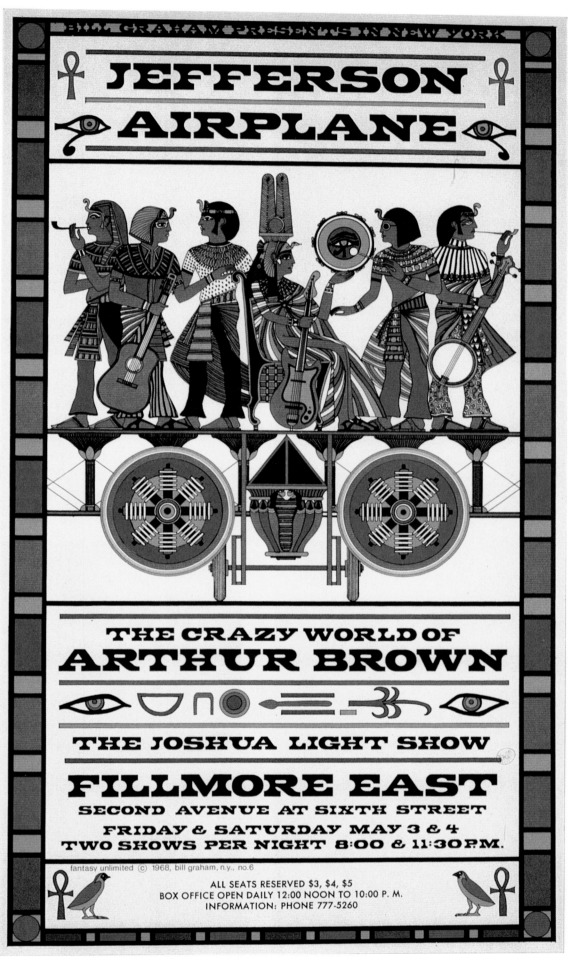

2.92

Jefferson Airplane; Crazy World of Arthur Brown
Fillmore East, New York, 1968
Artist: Fantasy Unlimited

2.93

Final Concerts
Fillmore East, New York, 1971
Artist: David Byrd

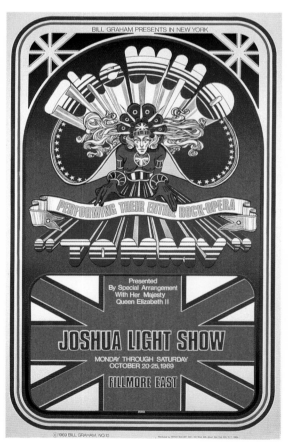

2.94

The Who Perform *Tommy*
Fillmore East, New York, 1969
Artist: David Byrd

2.95

Jefferson Airplane; The Who
Tanglewood, Lenox, Massachusetts, 1969

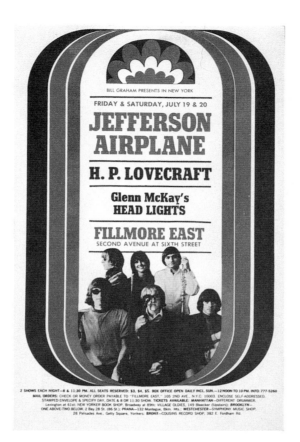

2.96

Handbill: Jefferson Airplane; H. P. Lovecraft
Fillmore East, New York, 1968

2.97

Handbill: Big Brother and the Holding Company;
Staple Singers. Fillmore East, New York, 1968

2.99

Big Brother and the Holding Company; Tim Buckley
Fillmore East, New York, 1968
Artist: Charles Brandwynn/Photographer: Linda Eastman

2.98

Butterfield Blues Band; Charles Lloyd
Fillmore East, New York, 1968
Artist: Jon Stahl

2.100
Program: BG 74
O'Keefe Centre, Toronto, Canada, 1967
Artist: James H. Gardner

2.101
Wolfgang Grajonca Presents
Olympic Auditorium, Los Angeles, 1969
Artist: Bonnie MacLean

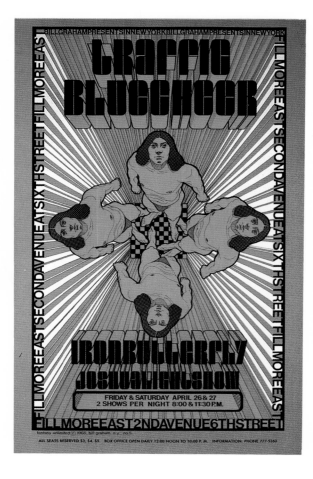

2.102
Traffic; Blue Cheer
Fillmore East, New York, 1968
Artist: Fantasy Unlimited

The Matrix

The Matrix bridged folk-rock and the swiftly developing psychedelic rock of 1965–66. The club was the creation of Marty Balin, one of the Jefferson Airplane's founders. He managed the Matrix briefly, but soon devoted his energies exclusively to the Airplane.

Despite a limited budget, the Matrix flourished for six years under a succession of managers. Shows were promoted by weekly handbills, a body of art exceeded in volume only by the poster production of the Fillmore and Avalon.

In 1966, the Matrix served as a proving ground for bands like Big Brother and the Holding Company and Quicksilver Messenger Service. Later on, Boz Scaggs appeared, following his leaving the Steve Miller Band. Grateful Dead band members appeared under a variety of guises, including the New Riders of the Purple Sage. Bruce Springsteen made his 1970 San Francisco debut there as a member of Steel Mill, a short-lived New Jersey band.

2.103
Opening
The Matrix, San Francisco, 1965

2.104
Lightning Hopkins; Jefferson Airplane
The Matrix, San Francisco, 1965

2.105

New Riders of the Purple Sage
The Matrix, San Francisco, 1970
Artist: Mark T. Behrens

2.106

February Calendar
The Matrix, San Francisco, 1971
Artist: Mark T. Behrens

2.107

Moby Grape
The Matrix, San Francisco, 1966
Artist: Heinrich Kley (drawings)

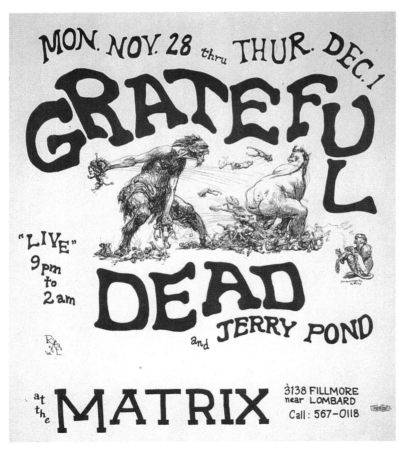

2.108

Grateful Dead; Jerry Pond
The Matrix, San Francisco, 1966
Artist: Heinrich Kley (drawings)

2.109

Big Brother and the Holding Company
The Matrix, San Francisco, 1966
Artist: Heinrich Kley (drawings)

2.110

Big Brother and the
Holding Company
The Matrix,
San Francisco, 1967
Artist: Leidenthal

2.111

Big Brother and the Holding Company
The Matrix, San Francisco, 1966
Artist: Stanley Mouse

2.112

Jefferson Airplane
The Matrix, San Francisco, ca. 1966
Artist: Tom Weller

2.113

The Great Society; Dan Hicks or Don Garrett
The Matrix, San Francisco, 1966
Artist: William Reid

2.114

The Yellow Brick Road
The Matrix, San Francisco, 1967
Artist: Leidenthal

2.115

Flamin' Groovies
The Matrix, San Francisco, 1967
Artist: Leidenthal

2.116

Howlin' Wolf
The Matrix, San Francisco, 1967
Artist: Leidenthal

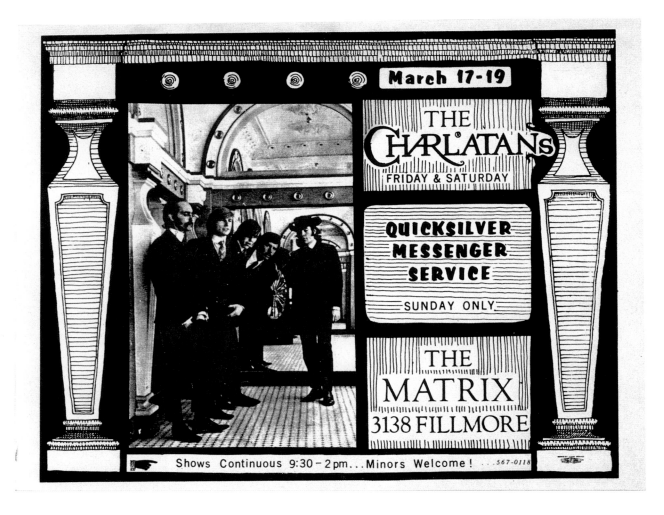

2.117

Charlatans; Quicksilver Messenger Service
The Matrix, San Francisco, 1967
Photographer: Herb Greene

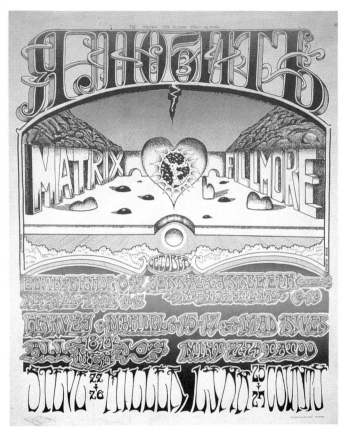

2.118

October Calendar
The Matrix, San Francisco, 1969
Artists: George Chacona, Marty Rice

2.119

Seatrain; Spooky Tooth
The Matrix, San Francisco, 1968
Artists: George Chacona, Marty Rice

2.120

Sandy Bull
The Matrix, San Francisco, 1967
Artist: Timothy

2.121

Andrew Staples
The Matrix, San Francisco, 1966
Artist: John H. Myers

2.122
Blues Project
The Matrix, San Francisco, 1966
Artist: Jon Adams

2.123
Little Walter; Quicksilver Messenger Service
The Matrix, San Francisco, ca. 1966
Artist: Ray Andersen

2.124
The Great Society
The Matrix, San Francisco, 1966
Artist: Ray Andersen

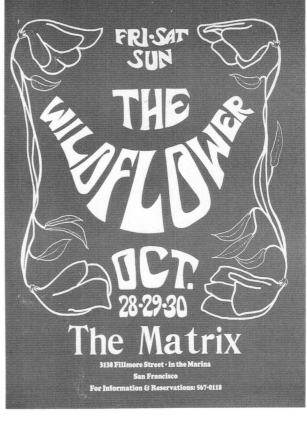

2.125
The Wildflower
The Matrix, San Francisco, 1966
Artist: Tom Weller

THE NEON ROSE SERIES

Victor Moscoso, along with Wes Wilson, Alton Kelley, Stanley Mouse, and Rick Griffin, pioneered and defined the San Francisco psychedelic poster style. One of his most significant achievements is a series of posters for the Matrix, one of the first departures from the usual practice of working only on assignment from Bill Graham or the Family Dog. Moscoso recognized that the Graham and Family Dog series were destined to become sought-after classics—from which, however, the poster artists would receive little financial reward beyond the original commission fee. Moscoso decided to create and distribute his own series, which would promote shows and also serve afterward to commemorate events held at Matrix. The artist called his independent company Neon Rose. Moscoso's Neon Rose concert posters stand as some of the boldest and most stylistically developed art in rock's thirty-year history and have held up particularly well in the years since their creation.

2.126

Big Brother and the Holding Company. The Matrix, San Francisco, 1967
Artist: Victor Moscoso; Photographer: Lisa Bachelis

2.127
The Doors
1967
The Matrix, San Francisco,
Artist: Victor Moscoso

2.128
Chambers Brothers
The Matrix, San Francisco,
1967.
Artist: Victor Moscoso

Charlatans

The Charlatans inaugurated the San Francisco psychedelic rock era. In 1965, at the Red Dog Saloon in Virginia City, Nevada, they began a summer-long run that would focus attention on a new period of music-making and social development.

While the Charlatans were soon eclipsed by the bands that followed them, many posters promoting their first two years are early gems. The best-remembered is the triptych commissioned by the Family Dog, based on photographs by Herb Greene and designed by Rick Griffin, aided on the third poster by Bob Fried.

Pianist Michael Ferguson, one of the Charlatans' leaders, developed a particularly whimsical style (2.131). Some of the band's later pieces were done by Terré, a street-wise Haight-Ashbury artist who served as the Charlatans' manager in their waning days (2.129).

2.130
Grope for Peace
The Ark, Sausalito, 1966
Artist: Stanley Mouse

2.129
Uncut sheet: Charlatans
Marigold Ballroom, Fresno, California, 1968
Artist: Terré

2.131
Charlatans; Mystery Trend
California Hall, San Francisco, 1966
Artist: Michael Ferguson

Jefferson Airplane and the Great Society

The Jefferson Airplane first symbolized hippie culture for much of the nation. Even with their strong original lineup, it is often said that the band achieved maturity only after the Great Society's Grace Slick joined.

2.132
Ninth Berkeley Folk Festival
Greek Theater, Berkeley, 1966
Artist: Barry Olivier

2.133
Jefferson Airplane; Patty Phillips
St. Mary's College, Moraga, California, 1966
Photographer: Barry Olivier

2.134
Jefferson Airplane; William Penn and His Pals
Civic Auditorium, San Francisco, 1966

2.135
Larry Hankin; Jefferson Airplane
University of California, Berkeley, 1966
Photographers: Edmund Shea, Jim Smirich

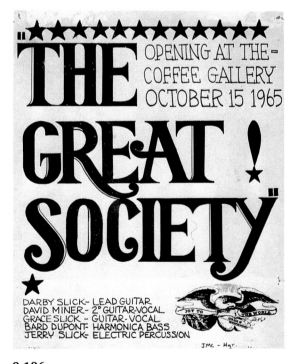

2.136
Great Society
Coffee Gallery, San Francisco, 1965

California Hall

California Hall was one of several smaller San Francisco concert venues that competed with Bill Graham at the Fillmore and the Family Dog at the Avalon.

Big Brother and the Holding Company virtually made the Hall its home, but many lesser-known Bay Area bands, like the Baytovens, the Hedds, and Friendly Stranger performed there frequently during 1965–67.

2.138

Steve Miller; Sunshine Company
California Hall, San Francisco, 1967
Artist: Greg Irons

2.137

Port Chicago Vigil Benefit   California Hall, San Francisco, 1967 Artist: Stanley Mouse

2.139

Big Brother and the Holding Company; Charlatans
California Hall, San Francisco, 1967
Artist: Greg Irons

2.140

Strange Happenings
California Hall, San Francisco, 1967
Artist: Greg Irons

2.141

The Hedds; The Friendly Stranger
California Hall, San Francisco, 1966

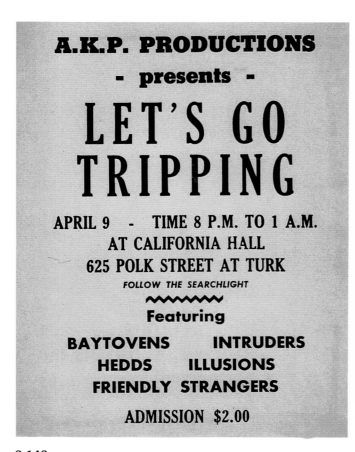

2.142

Let's Go Tripping
California Hall, San Francisco, 1966

2.143

Dance of Death Costume Ball
California Hall, San Francisco, 1966

2.144

Jefferson Airplane; Quicksilver Messenger
Service. California Hall, San Francisco, 1966
Artist: Bob Collins

2.145

The Hedds; The Styx
California Hall, San Francisco, 1966

2.146

Benefit for Legalization of Marijuana (LEMAR)
California Hall, San Francisco, 1966
Artist: Tom Weller

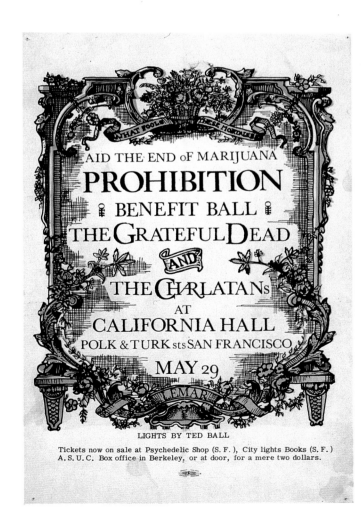

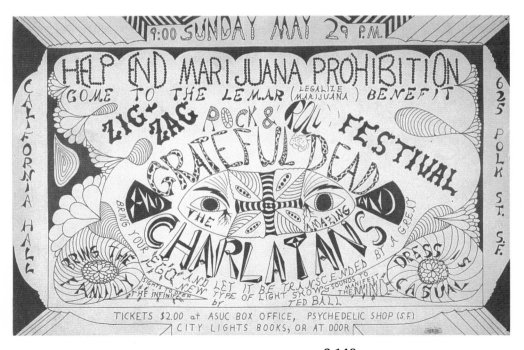

2.148

LEMAR Prohibition Ball Benefit
California Hall, San Francisco, 1966

2.147

Handbill: LEMAR Prohibition Ball Benefit
California Hall, San Francisco, 1966

2.149

Spirt of '67
California Hall, San Francisco, 1967
Artist: Michael Wood/Pyxis Studios

2.150

A Tribute to J. Edgar Hoover
California Hall, San Francisco, 1967
Artist: Soot Productions

2.151

Charles Lloyd; Big Brother and the Holding Company
California Hall, San Francisco, 1967
Artist: Michael Wood/Pyxis Studios

2.152

Big Brother and the Holding Company;
Big Mama Thornton
California Hall, San Francisco, 1967
Artist: Michael Wood/Pyxis Studios

2.153

Handbill: Bedrock One
California Hall, San Francisco, 1967
Artist: R. Crumb

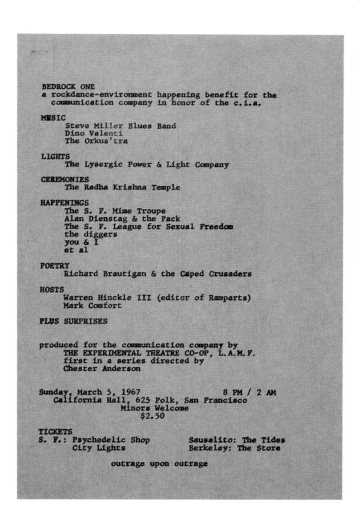

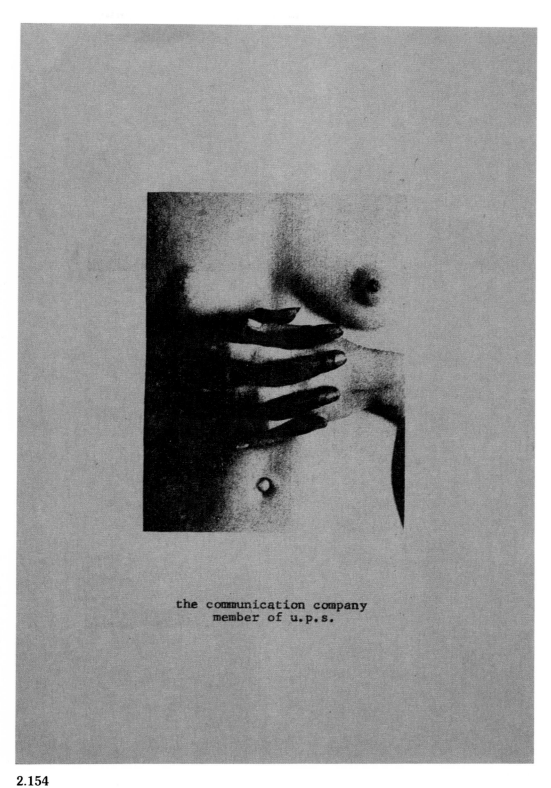

the communication company
member of u.p.s.

2.154

Flier (front): Bedrock One
California Hall, San Francisco, 1967

2.155

Flier (back): Bedrock One
California Hall, San Francisco, 1967

2.156
Bilbo's Birthday
California Hall, San Francisco, 1966
Artist: Passalaqua

2.157
Steve Miller; The Sparrow
California Hall, San Francisco, 1967
Artist: Michael Wood/Pyxis Studios

2.158
Big Brother and the Holding Company; Quicksilver
Messenger Service. California Hall, San Francisco, 1967
Artist: Michael Wood/Pyxis Studios

2.159
Charlatans; Mystery Trend
California Hall, San Francisco,
1967. Artist: Jack De Govia

Carousel Ballroom

As the El Patio Ballroom, the Carousel had been a major swing-band venue. In 1967 several San Francisco bands—among them the Grateful Dead and the Jefferson Airplane—joined together to produce dances independently of Bill Graham and the Family Dog. Inexperience led to poor management, and in 1968 Bill Graham took over the hall, abandoning the original Fillmore Auditorium, and renaming the Carousel the Fillmore West.

During the Carousel's independent period many fine posters were commissioned, including important works by Alton Kelley and Stanley Mouse, along with creations by such "unknowns" as Steve Catron, Rick Shubb, and the Crazy Arab, the latter actually world renowned for his racing-car pinstriping.

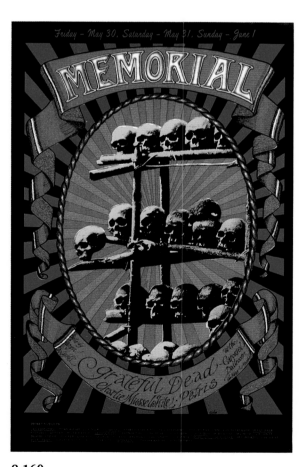

2.160
Memorial: Grateful Dead
Carousel Ballroom, San Francisco, 1969
Artist: Alton Kelley

2.161
Moby Grape; It's a Beautiful Day
Carousel Ballroom, San Francisco, 1968

2.162

Santana Blues Band; Frumious Bandersnatch
Carousel Ballroom, San Francisco, 1968
Artist: Steven Catron

2.163

Grateful Dead; Chuck Berry
Carousel Ballroom, San Francisco, 1968
Artist: Steven Catron

2.164

Big Brother and the Holding Company; Clara Ward
Singers. Carousel Ballroom, San Francisco, 1968
Artist: Crazy Arab

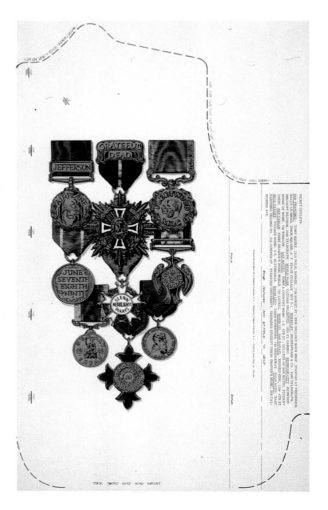

2.165

Grateful Dead; Jefferson Airplane
Carousel Ballroom, San Francisco, 1968
Artist: Patrick Lofthouse

2.166

Electric Flag
Carousel Ballroom, San Francisco, 1968
Artist: Rick Shubb

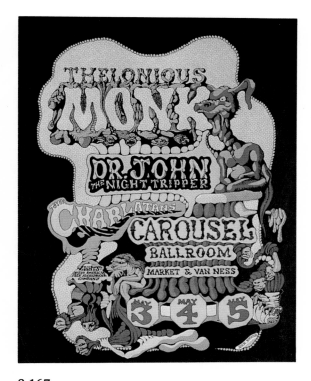

2.167

Thelonious Monk; Dr. John
Carousel Ballroom, San Francisco, 1968
Artist: Rick Shubb

2.168

Steve Miller; Sons of Champlin
Carousel Ballroom, San Francisco, 1968
Artist: Rick Shubb

2.170

Tuesday Night Jam
Carousel Ballroom,
San Francisco, 1968
Artist: Stanley Mouse

2.169

Grateful Dead; Quicksilver Messenger Service
Carousel Ballroom, San Francisco, 1968
Artist: Gut

2.171
People's Radio Benefit
Carousel Ballroom, San Francisco, 1970
Artist: Miranda Bergman

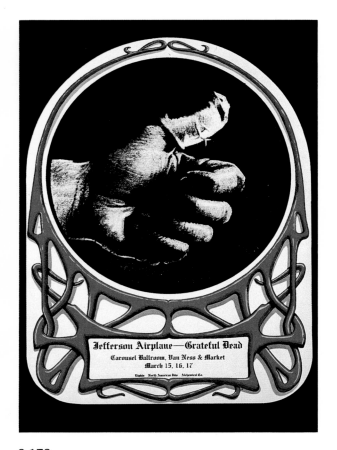

2.172
"Sore Thumb"
Carousel Ballroom, San Francisco, 1968
Artist: Alton Kelley

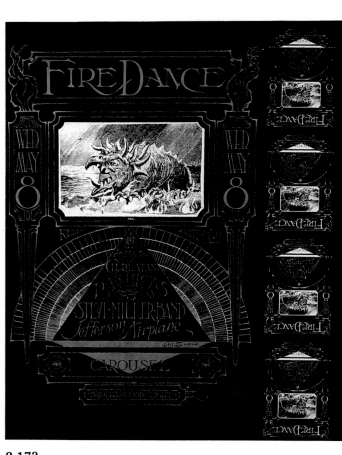

2.173
Uncut sheet: Fire Dance (Alton Kelley Benefit)
Carousel Ballroom, San Francisco, 1968
Artist: Stanley Mouse

2.174
Be Mine: Valentine's Day Dance
Carousel Ballroom, San Francisco, 1968
Artist: Stanley Mouse

2.175

Ticket: Friday night
Carousel Ballroom, San Francisco, 1968
Artist: Crazy Arab

2.176

Ticket: Saturday night
Carousel Ballroom, San Francisco, 1968
Artist: Crazy Arab

2.177

Ticket: Sunday night
Carousel Ballroom, San Francisco, 1968
Artist: Crazy Arab

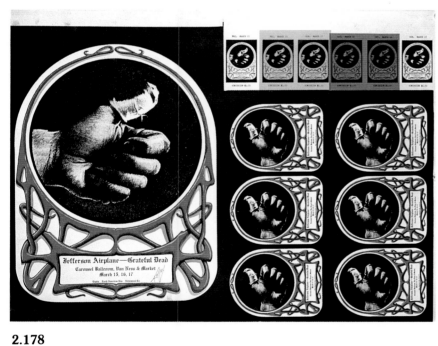

2.178

Uncut proof: "Sore Thumb"
Carousel Ballroom, San Francisco, 1968
Artist: Alton Kelley

2.179

Uncut proof: Memorial
Carousel Ballroom, San Francisco, 1969
Artist: Alton Kelley

2.180

Ticket: Blackman's Free Store Benefit Dance
Carousel Ballroom, San Francisco, 1968
Artist: Ovid P. Adams

Grateful Dead

More San Francisco poster art is devoted to the Grateful Dead than to any other band, and that art has evolved into a special field of collecting. One particularly sought-after piece is the 1967 Halloween poster known as "Trip or Freak" (2.183). Many of the other pieces included in this section are equally scarce. Only a string of providential circumstances could have turned up a poster as obscure as the one heralding the three-day 1966 San Francisco State Acid Test (2.188). Other cherished items include Bob Fried's "see-thru" translucent poster (2.190). It was issued in limited quantity because of a technical problem—difficulty producing posters without cracking them. Printed in even fewer numbers was the poster promoting the release of the Grateful Dead's first single, on the defunct Scorpio label. Only one oversize handbill is known to have survived the twenty-plus years since the record's release (2.191).

2.181

Zenefit—Zen Mountain Center Benefit
Avalon Ballroom, San Francisco, 1966
Photographer: Robert Bono

2.182

Hindustani Jazz Sextet; Grateful Dead
Fillmore Auditorium, San Francisco, 1966

2.183

Trip or Freak
Winterland, San Francisco, 1967
Artists: Stanley Mouse, Alton Kelley, Rick Griffin

2.184

Grateful Dead
Pioneer Ballroom, Suisun City, 1966

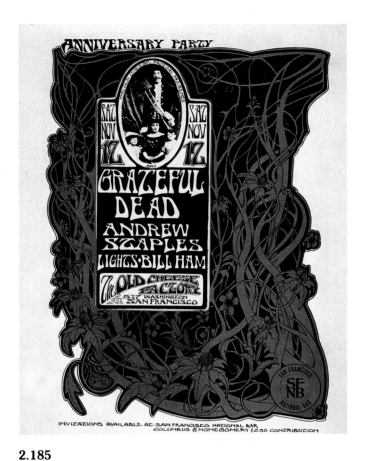

2.185

Anniversary Party: Grateful Dead
The Old Cheese Factory, San Francisco, 1966
Artists: Stanley Mouse, Alton Kelley

2.186

Bicycle Race and Folk-Rock Festival
IDES Hall, Pescadero, California, 1966

2.187

Trips Festival 196?
Longshoremen's Hall, San Francisco,
1966

2.188
Three-day Acid Test
San Francisco State College, San Francisco, 1966

2.189
Promotional packet: First Grateful Dead Album
San Francisco, 1967
Artist: Rick Griffin; photographer: Gene Anthony

2.190
Translucent poster: Grateful Dead. 1967
Artist: Bob Fried

2.191
Promotion: First Grateful
Dead Single
San Francisco, 1965

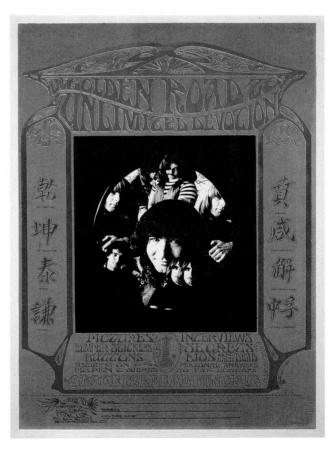

2.192
Grateful Dead Fan Club. San Francisco, 1967
Artists: Alton Kelley, Stanley Mouse

Miscellaneous San Francisco Events and Venues

Between 1965 and 1968, during the ferment of Haight-Ashbury, many unusual events were staged in a variety of halls, some of which were large and well established, such as Winterland, regularly used by promoters like Bill Graham, and others now only obscure footnotes to musical history, like the Whisky A-Go-Go, short-lived counterpart to the more famous Whisky in Los Angeles (2.195).

2.193

Week of the Angry Arts—Vietnam Mobilization
Longshoremen's Hall, San Francisco, 1966

2.194

The First Annual Love Circus
Winterland, San Francisco, 1967
Artist: Herrick

2.195

Doors; Peanut Butter
Conspiracy
Whisky A-Go-Go,
San Francisco, 1967

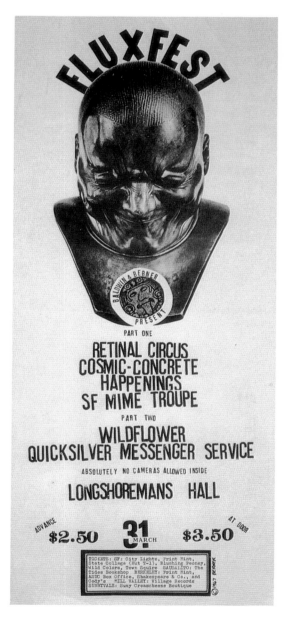

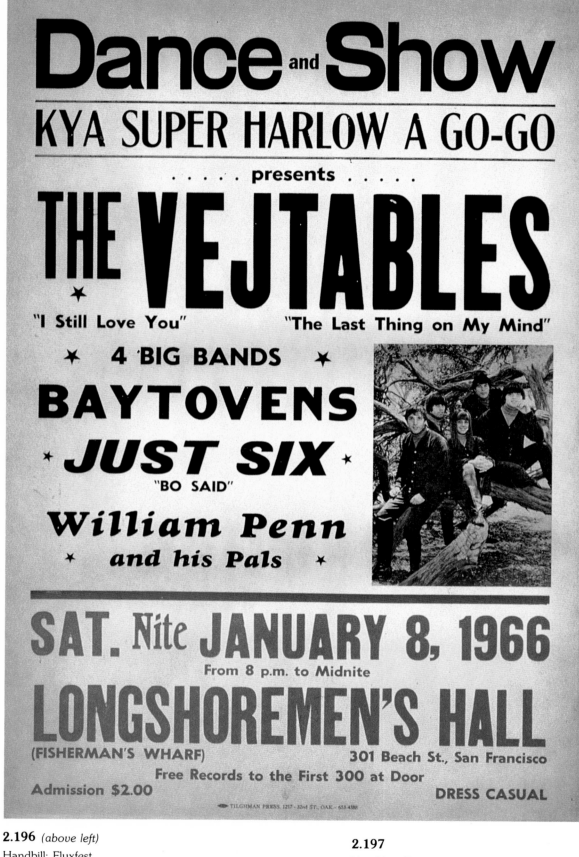

2.196 *(above left)*
Handbill: Fluxfest
Longshoremen's Hall, San Francisco, 1967

2.197
Vejtables; Baytovens
Longshoremen's Hall, San Francisco, 1966
Artist: Tilghman Press

2.198
Fluxfest
Longshoremen's Hall, San Francisco, 1967
Artist: Berner

Western Front

Western Front was a short-lived club located in San Francisco's outer Tenderloin district. It is chiefly remembered for a number of excellent posters produced by Stanley Mouse and Greg Irons (who subsequently gained renown for his spectacular tattooing).

2.199
Morning Glory; Indian Head Band
Western Front, San Francisco, 1967
Artist: John Thompson

2.200
Charlatans; Frumious Bandersnatch
Western Front, San Francisco, 1966
Artist: Stanley Mouse

2.201

Lobby poster
Western Front, San Francisco, 1967
Artist: Stanley Mouse

Promotion
Western Front, San Francisco, ca. 1967
Artist: Greg Irons

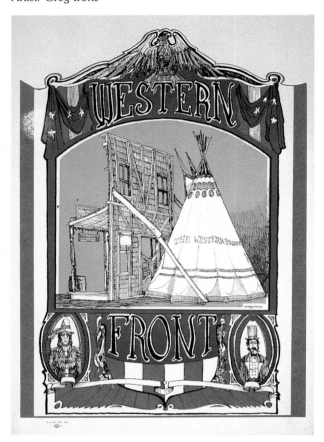

2.203

Grand Opening
Western Front, San Francisco, 1967
Artist: Greg Irons

Winterland

Winterland Arena stood as a San Francisco landmark for several decades, a place where rock concerts alternated with boxing matches and ice-skating revues.

Bruce Springsteen, the Rolling Stones, Sex Pistols, Who, and countless others have appeared at Winterland, but perhaps the Grateful Dead is most closely associated with the venue. During the mid and late 1970s it served as their home base; they presided over closing night itself, New Year's Eve, 1978.

Winterland was also the site of pivotal benefits, notably that held in 1969 following the Berkeley People's Park demonstrations (2.204). Ken Kesey's abortive "Acid Test Graduation" was an early—1966—Winterland event (2.209).

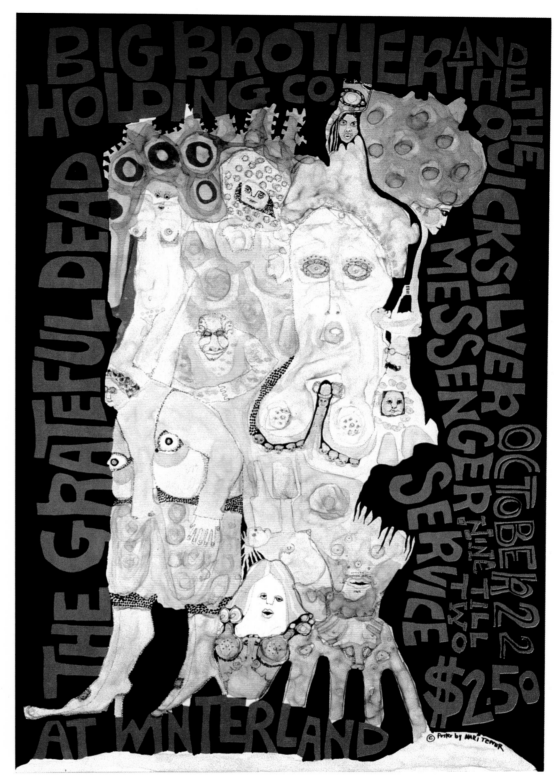

2.204 *(upper left)*
People's Park Bail Ball
Winterland, San Francisco, 1969

2.205
Big Brother and the Holding Company; Grateful Dead
Winterland, San Francisco, 1966
Artist: Mari Tepper

2.206
Benefit for the Haight-Ashbury Legal Organization
Winterland, San Francisco, 1966
Artists: Rick Griffin, Alton Kelley, Stanley Mouse

2.207

Quicksilver Messenger Service
Winterland, San Francisco, 1967
Artist: Gut

2.208

Mojo Men; Vejtables
Winterland, San Francisco, 1966
Artist: Mari Tepper

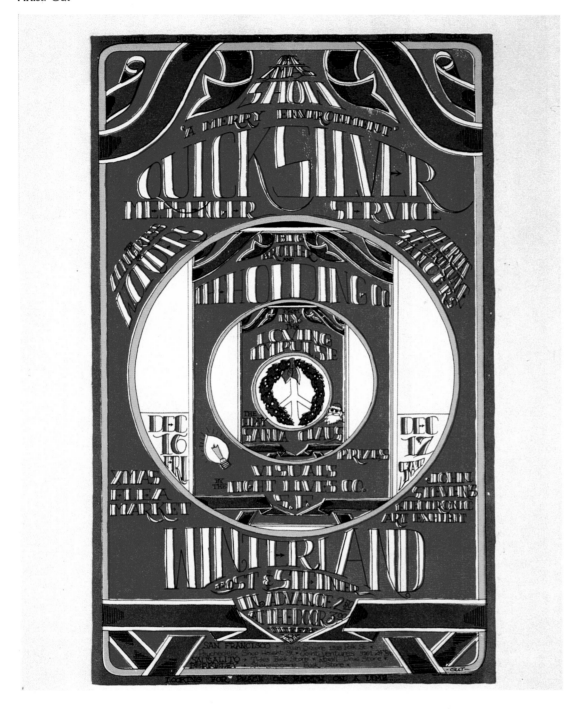

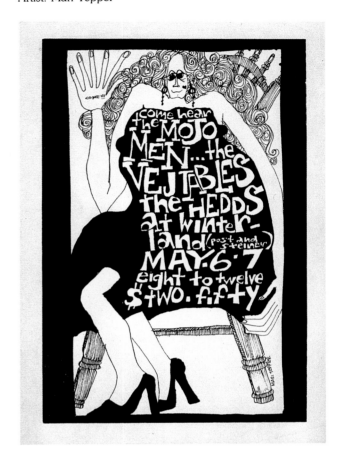

2.209

Acid Test Graduation
Winterland, San Francisco, 1966
Artist: Gut

Firehouse

The Firehouse operated only a short time, but was especially notable for the light shows staged there by Elias Romero and Ray Andersen. Andersen, who managed the Matrix in 1966, founded the Holy See Light Show, one of several mainstays at the Fillmore Auditorium and Avalon Ballroom.

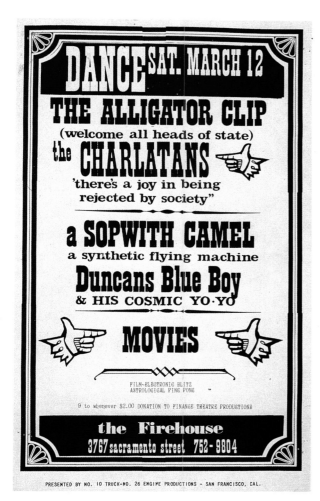

2.210
Charlatans; Sopwith Camel
The Firehouse, San Francisco, 1966

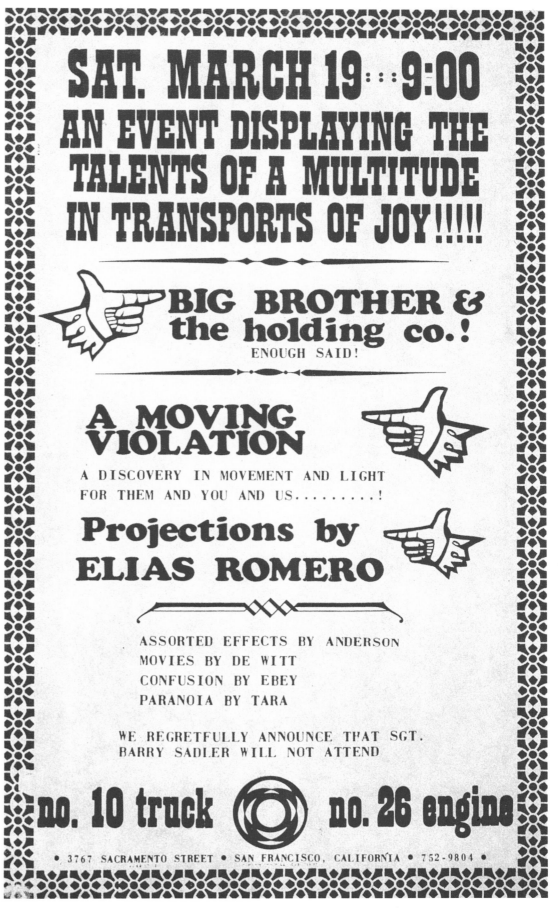

2.211
Big Brother and the Holding Company
The Firehouse, San Francisco, 1966

Rock Garden

Like the Firehouse, the Rock Garden is but a footnote in San Francisco rock history. The few posters and handbills done for shows there were designed in an unusual diamond configuration, apparently the only diamond-shaped series produced by any club or production company in San Francisco or elsewhere.

2.212
Grateful Dead; Charles Lloyd
Rock Garden, San Francisco, ca. 1967
Artist: Michael Wood/Pyxis Studios

2.213
Buffalo Springfield; Electric Chamber Orkustra
Rock Garden, San Francisco, 1967
Artist: Michael Wood/Pyxis Studios

2.214
Big Brother and the Holding Company; Love
Rock Garden, San Francisco, 1966
Artist: Michael Wood/Pyxis Studios

Human Be-In

The Human Be-In took place on a sunlit January day in 1967 at Golden Gate Park. A pivotal event in the history of hippie culture, it ushered in the 1967 "Summer of Love," when thousands of young people from all parts of the United States converged upon San Francisco to create a life-style that would transform social values across the entire country.

Two artists, partners Stanley Mouse and Alton Kelley, by this time well established locally, were among those who created posters and handbills for the event. But they were disappointed with the resulting work, partly because the central "guru" image was foisted on them by others and also because the color of the most widely circulated version of the piece was an ineffective blue green. The color variant reproduced here is unusual (2.217), a collector's prize.

In contrast, Rick Griffin's poster gained him recognition as a new artist to be reckoned with on the scene (2.215). His Human Be-In poster, printed both in black and brown inks and on variously colored papers, was his second major piece, after a black-and-white poster made for Haight-Ashbury's Psychedelic Shop. On the strength of the Be-In poster, Chet Helms invited Griffin to contribute to the Avalon Ballroom series, and he then rapidly rose to prominence.

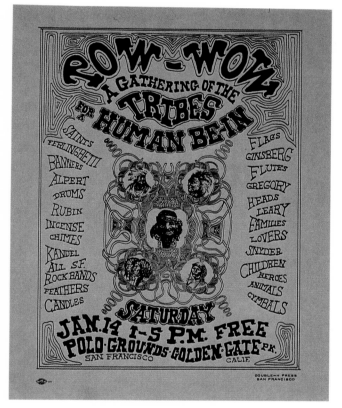

2.216

Handbill: Human Be-In
Golden Gate Park, San Francisco, 1967
Artist: Michael Bowen

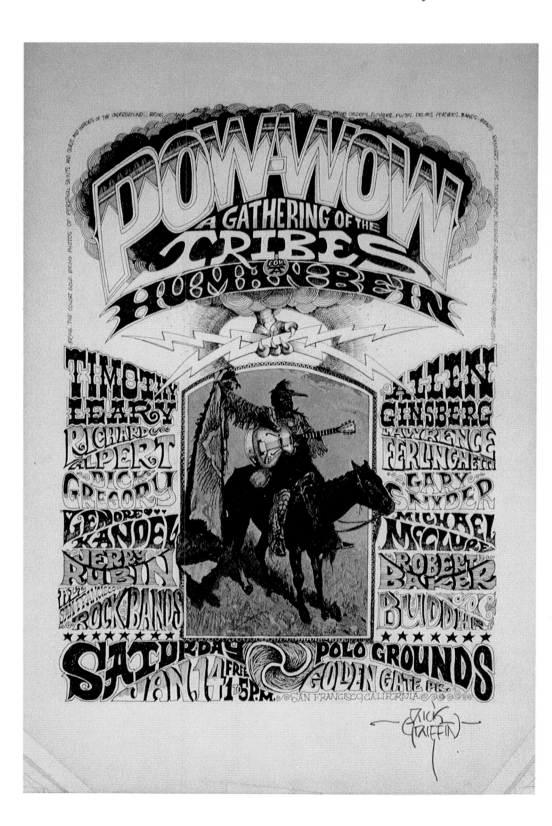

2.215

Human Be-In
Golden Gate Park, San Francisco, 1967
Artist: Rick Griffin

2.217

Color-variant handbill: Human Be-In. Golden Gate Park, San Francisco, 1967
Artists: Stanley Mouse, Alton Kelley, Michael Bowen
Photographer: Casey Sonnabend

Straight Theater

The Straight Theater (formerly the Haight Theater) was a hippie-run alternative to the commercially operated Fillmore Auditorium and Avalon Ballroom. Several hundred landmark rock shows (many featuring the newly formed Santana Blues Band), film screenings, poetry events, and the like were held at the Straight. But the operation was shaky from the start. When the city government withheld the essential dance permit, the Straight promoted a number of rock shows as "dance classes," with the Grateful Dead as the first instructors (2.224, 2.225).

Detroit artist Gary Grimshaw lived in San Francisco for a time, having gone "underground" following an arrest in Michigan for alleged marijuana possession. Grimshaw's one San Francisco concert poster, headlining a 1969 appearance by his hometown rock band, the MC 5, was done for the Straight Theater (2.227).

2.218

Mad River; Santana Blues Band
Straight Theater, San Francisco, 1967
Artist: C. Braga

2.219

The End of the War
Straight Theater, San Francisco, ca. 1967

2.220
Grand Opening
Straight Theater, San Francisco, 1967
Artist: Frank Melton

2.221
Steve Miller; Little Richard
Straight Theater, San Francisco, 1967
Artist: Randy Salas

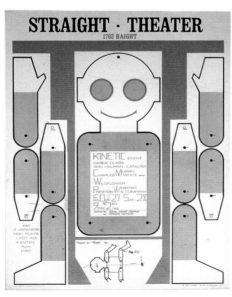

2.222
Kinetic Event
Straight Theater, San Francisco, 1967
Artist: Terré

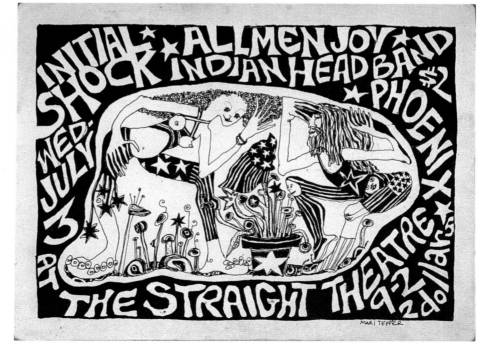

2.223
Allmen Joy; Initial Shock
Straight Theater, San Francisco,
1968
Artist: Mari Tepper

2.224

Grateful Dead; Sons of Champlin
Straight Theater, San Francisco, 1967
Artist: C. Braga

2.225

Handbill: Grateful Dead; Sons of Champlin
Straight Theater, San Francisco, 1967

2.226

Equinox of the Gods
Straight Theater, San Francisco, 1967
Artist: Randy Salas

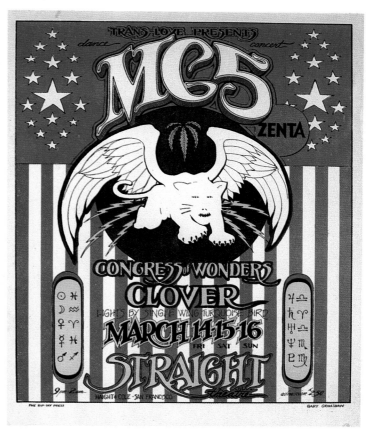

2.227

MC5; Clover
Straight Theater, San Francisco, 1969
Artist: Gary Grimshaw

2.228

Big Brother and the Holding Company;
Freedom Highway. Straight Theater, San Francisco, 1967
Artist: Randy Salas

2.229

Charlatans; Cleveland Wrecking Company
Straight Theater, San Francisco, 1968
Artist: Terré

2.230

Second Annual Grope for Peace
Straight Theater, San Francisco, 1967
Artist: Rick Griffin

2.231

Charlie Musselwhite; Dan Hicks
Straight Theater, San Francisco, 1968
Artist: San Andreas Fault

The Wild West and Other San Francisco Events

The Wild West was planned in 1969 as a West Coast sequel to Woodstock. Disputes among the organizers led to its cancellation at the planned-for Kezar Stadium site; it was held later at the Fillmore West and the Great Highway (2.233). A festival held the previous year at the Palace of Fine Arts in San Francisco was a greater artistic triumph (2.237–39).

One of the rarest festival posters was done for the 1966 Artists Liberation Front Free Fair, at which the Grateful Dead made a memorable appearance (2.244).

The appearance by the Jefferson Airplane and Buffalo Springfield at the University of San Francisco gym in 1967—sponsored by the students of St. Ignatius High School—was not a festival, but it did generate more separate art than many of the festival events.

2.232
Steve Miller; Jesse Fuller. North Face Ski Shop, San Francisco, 1967. Artist: Weyman Lew

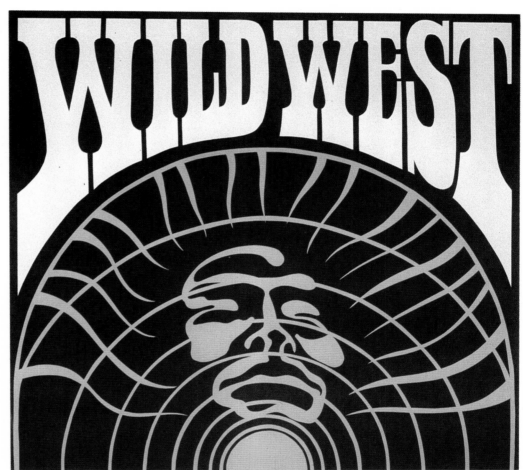

2.233
Wild West Festival
Kezar Stadium, San Francisco, 1969
Event canceled

2.234

Righteous Brothers; Nino Tempo and April Stevens
University of San Francisco, San Francisco, 1966
Artist: Wes Wilson

2.235

Eric Burdon and the Animals
Civic Auditorium, San Francisco, 1967
Artist: Sparta Graphics

2.236

Benefit for the Fellowship Church
Unitarian Center, San Francisco, 1969
Artist: Don Black

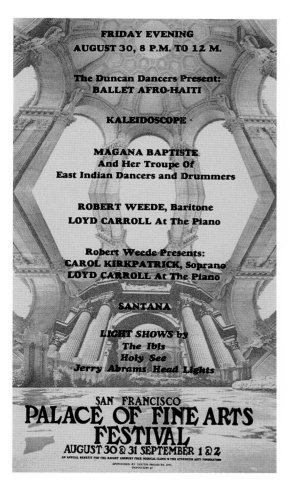

2.237

Palace of Fine Arts Festival (Friday)
Palace of Fine Arts, San Francisco, 1968

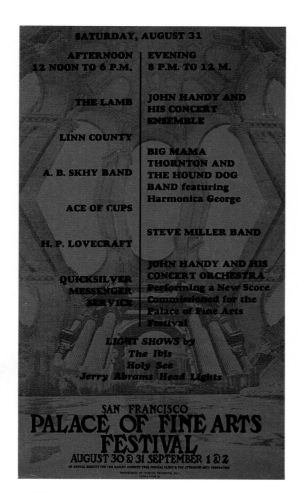

2.238

Palace of Fine Arts Festival (Saturday)
Palace of Fine Arts, San Francisco, 1968

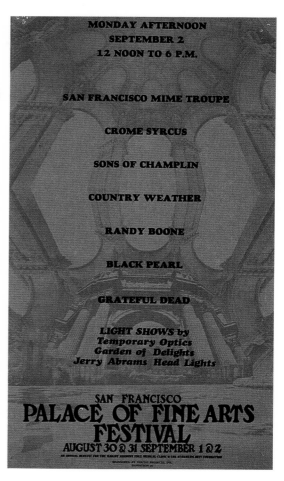

2.239

Palace of Fine Arts Festival (Monday)
Palace of Fine Arts, San Francisco, 1968

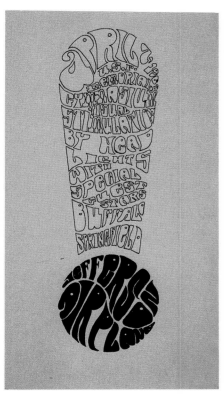

2.240

Handbill: Jefferson Airplane;
Buffalo Springfield. University of San Francisco,
San Francisco, 1967

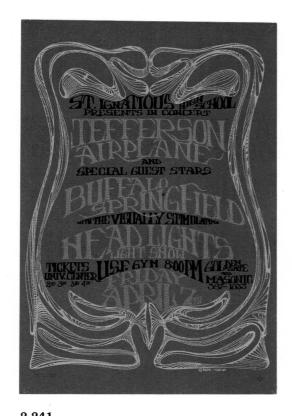

2.241

Jefferson Airplane; Buffalo Springfield
University of San Francisco, San Francisco, 1967
Artist: Gut

2.242

Handbill: Jefferson Airplane; Buffalo Springfield
University of San Francisco, San Francisco, 1967

2.243

Haight-Ashbury Festival
Golden Gate Park Panhandle, San Francisco, 1969
Artist: Wes Wilson

2.244

Artists' Liberation Front Free Fair
Golden Gate Park Panhandle, San Francisco, 1966

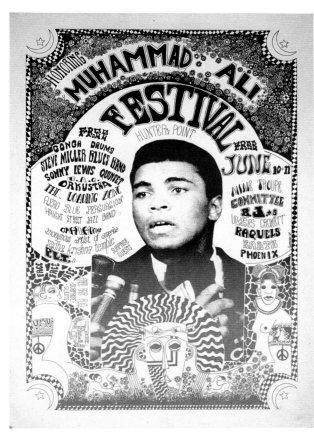

2.245

Muhammad Ali Festival
Hunter's Point, San Francisco, 1967
Artist: Gomez

2.246

P.H. Phactor Jug Band
Cedar Alley, San Francisco, 1966
Artist: Paul Basset

Hells Angels Events

The Hells Angels motorcycle club, among the most maligned of all California institutions, was befriended by Ken Kesey and the Merry Pranksters during the first Acid Tests (1964–65). Subsequently, an uneasy alliance was struck up between the bikers and hippies in Haight-Ashbury. Each year, the San Francisco and Oakland Hells Angels chapters held parties featuring— by 1966—prominent San Francisco rock bands, particularly Big Brother and the Holding Company.

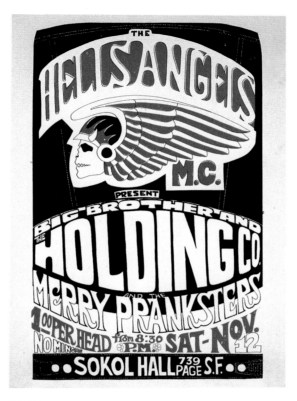

2.247

Hells Angels Dance
Sokol Hall, San Francisco, 1966

2.248

Hells Angels Dance
California Hall, San Francisco, 1967
Artist: Gut

2.249

Hells Angels Dance
Carousel Ballroom, San Francisco, 1968

2.250

Ticket: Hells Angels Dance
Sokol Hall, San Francisco, 1966

2.251

Wake for Chocolate George
Golden Gate Park, San Francisco, 1967

2.252

Ticket: Hells Angels Dance
California Hall, San Francisco, 1967

KMPX/KSAN

In March 1967, Tom Donohue—disc jockey, promoter, nightclub owner, record company manager—believed there was an adult audience ready for a new kind of radio, and at KMPX he put together the first hippie station. KMPX was unique for playing album cuts without regard to length—an entirely new concept at the time—along with unissued tapes and test pressings often provided by the bands themselves. The station featured music ignored or rejected by the traditional Top 40 AM circuit. In a short time, KMPX established "underground" FM rock radio, and had national impact.

At first, the staff worked mostly for the love of it, accepting meager wages. But then, despite the station's success, no salary increases were forthcoming, prompting a walkout in 1968. Many

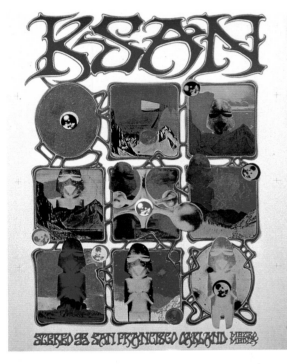

2.253

Proof: KSAN Radio Promotion
San Francisco, 1969
Artists: Rick Griffin, Alton Kelley

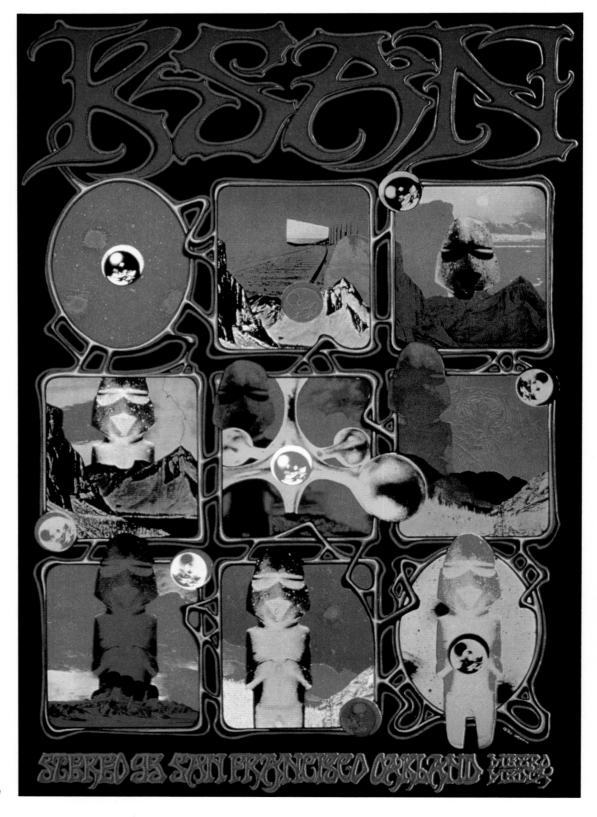

2.254

KSAN Radio Promotion
San Francisco, 1969
Artists: Rick Griffin, Alton Kelley

of the strikers lived on the street while picketing the station. The strike ended when Donohue, with the entire staff, left KMPX for the larger KSAN, owned by Metromedia.

KSAN bridged late-1960s hippie idealism and 1970s mainstream commercial programming. Ultimately, Metromedia ended a decade of experiment by abruptly changing KSAN's format to country music.

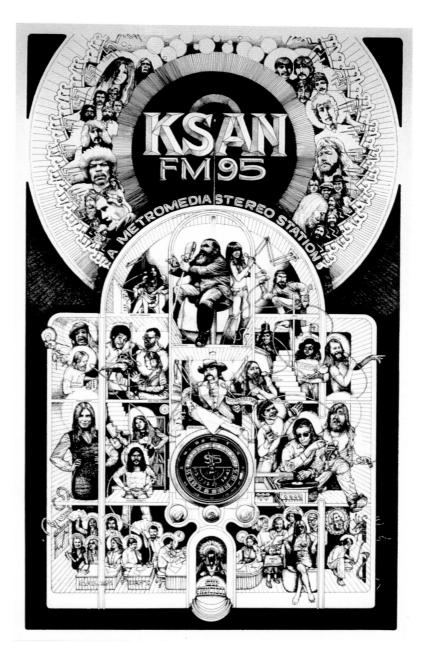

2.256
KSAN Radio Promotion
San Francisco, ca. 1969
Artist: Norman Orr

2.255
Handbill: KMPX Radio Promotion. San Francisco, ca. 1967
Artist: Bob McClay; Photographer: Baron Wolman

2.257

Invitation: KSAN Radio Family Freakout (front)
Avalon Ballroom, San Francisco, 1968
Artist: Michael Ferguson

KSAN, *the home of* FREE FORM FAMILY
RADIO, *invites you to a* FREE FORM
FAMILY FREAKOUT.

WHERE: Avalon Ballroom, Sutter and Van Ness
WHEN: Monday, July 1, 1968 — 6:00 - 8:30 P.M.
WHO: *Music by* "Creedence Clearwater Revival"
and "West"

LIGHT SHOW — FOOD — DRINKS — FUN
Reply to KSAN, Stereo Radio 95 — 986-2825
This Invitation Will Admit Two

2.258

Invitation: KSAN Radio Family Freakout (back)
Avalon Ballroom, San Francisco, 1968
Artist: Michael Ferguson

2.259

KMPX Radio Promotion
San Francisco, 1967
Artists: Stanley Mouse, Alton Kelley

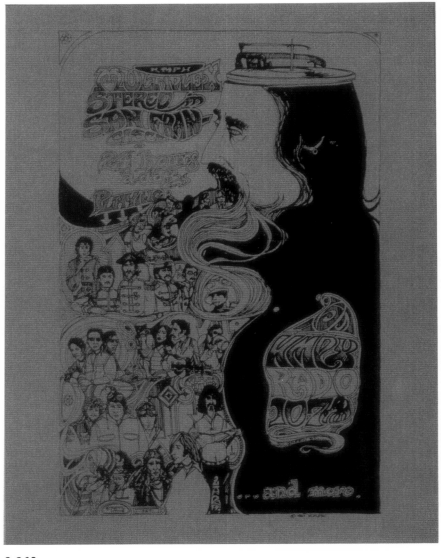

2.260

Handbill: KMPX Radio Promotion
San Francisco, 1967
Artist: Greg Irons

East Bay

Northern California rock developed not only in San Francisco proper, but also across the Bay, an area known as the East Bay, which includes Berkeley, Oakland, and Hayward, as well as rapidly developing suburban Contra Costa County.

Probably the best-known East Bay bands were Creedence Clearwater Revival, whose hometown was El Cerrito, just to the north of Berkeley, and Country Joe and the Fish, associated with Berkeley itself. Like Cambridge, Massachusetts, Berkeley boasted many influential folk music clubs and coffee houses, among them the Jabberwock, remembered as the first home of promising young 1970s bands like the Joy of Cooking.

The University of California at Berkeley also hosted concerts, most notably at the open-air Greek Theater. Other significant sites were the large high school auditorium, the Berkeley Community Theater, and the Oakland Auditorium, both used by Bill Graham extensively after the close of Fillmore West.

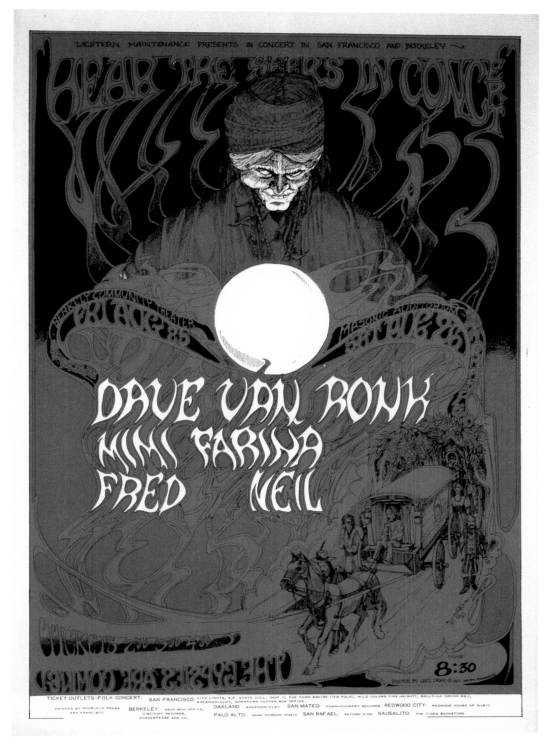

2.262

Dave Van Ronk; Fred Neil
Berkeley Community Theater, Berkeley, 1967
Artist: Greg Irons

2.261

The New World Hits Oakland
Leamington Hotel, Oakland, 1967
Artists: Stanley Mouse, Alton Kelley

2.263

Purple Earthquake; The 5th Dimension
Maple Hall, San Pablo, 1966
Artist: Henry Beer

2.264

Purple Earthquake; Zephyr
Berkeley High School, Berkeley, ca. 1966

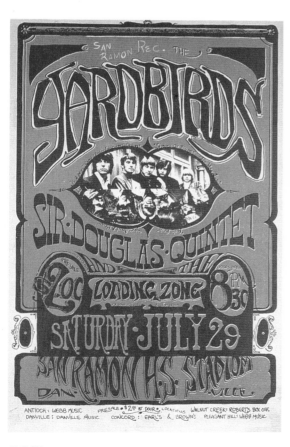

2.265

Yardbirds; Sir Douglas Quintet
San Ramon High School, Danville, 1967
Artists: J. N. Bower, R. Van Krugel/Haffbad

2.266

Potpourri
Greek Theater, Berkeley, 1967

2.267
Byrds; Stone Poneys
Berkelely Community Theater, Berkeley, ca. 1967

2.268
Peace Feast. Ligure Hall, Oakland, 1967
Artist: Drexhage

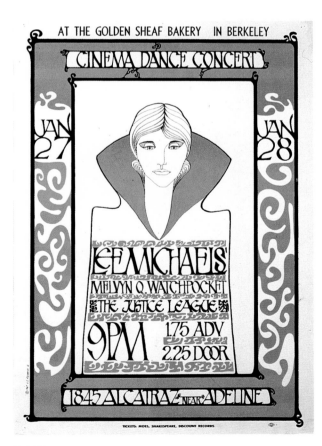

2.269
Lee Michaels; M. Q. Watchpocket
Golden Sheaf Bakery, Berkeley, 1967
Artist: Loren Rehbock

2.270
Country Joe and the Fish; The Wildflower
Finnish Brotherhood Hall, Berkeley, 1967
Artist: Loren Rehbock

2.271

Festival of Peace and Love
Live Oak Park, Berkeley, 1968
Artist: John Thompson

2.272

Youngbloods
New Orleans House, Berkeley, 1967
Artist: B. Linsky

2.273

Mystery Trend
Peter Voulkos Studio, Berkeley, 1965

2.274

Teen Drop-In Center Benefit
Acalanes High School, Lafayette, 1968

2.275

Vietnam Day Committee Peace Trip
University of California, Berkeley, 1966

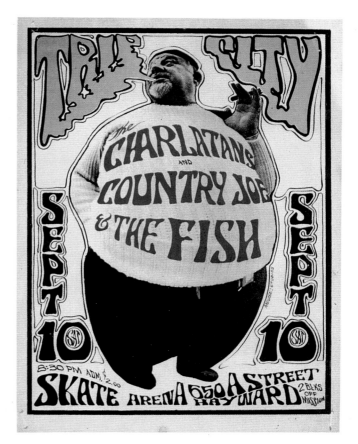

2.276

Trip City
Skate Arena, Hayward, 1966
Artist: Stanley Mouse

2.277

Them; Association
Oakland Auditorium, Oakland, 1966
Artist: Tilghman Press

2.278

First Annual Hippie Fair and Bazaar
University of California, Berkeley, 1967

COUNTRY JOE AND THE FISH

This group's music was more provocative than most, partly because of Country Joe McDonald's background in folk and protest music. The band began and developed in Berkeley clubs like the Jabberwock.

Tom Weller produced a graphically linked series of posters and handbills that were an important part of the band's program to create a self-image. Weller recalls how he and Wes Wilson visited a German Expressionist art exhibition at the University of California in 1966 and were impressed by a particular lettering style they encountered there. This experience led them, separately, to develop the "psychedelic" lettering characteristic of so much late-1960s graphics.

Country Joe and the Fish took an active role in marketing their records, and a significant portion of Tom Weller's art for the band was connected to these releases (2.287–90). An unusual Weller effort was the creation of oversize calendars intended as homespun promotions (2.280).

2.279

Country Joe and the Fish
Moe's Books, Berkeley, 1966
Artist: Tom Weller

2.280

February Calendar: Country Joe and the Fish
Berkeley, 1967
Artist: Tom Weller; Photographer: Michael Wiese

2.281
Country Joe and the Fish
Jabberwock, Berkeley, ca. 1967
Artist: Jon Adams

2.282
Country Joe and the Fish
Jabberwock, Berkeley, 1966
Artist: Beck

2.283
Country Joe and the Fish; Blues Project
Tilden Park, Berkeley, 1966
Artist: Tom Weller

2.284
Country Joe and the Fish
Jabberwock, Berkeley, 1966
Artist: Tom Weller

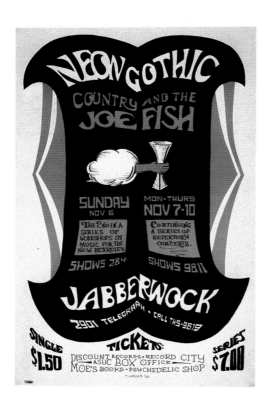

2.285
Country Joe and the Fish
Jabberwock, Berkeley, 1966
Artist: Tom Weller

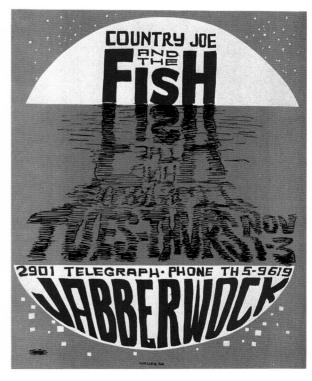

2.286
Country Joe and the Fish
Jabberwock, Berkeley, 1966
Artist: Tom Weller

2.287
Rag Baby EP—Third Pressing
Berkeley, 1966
Artist: Tom Weller

2.288
Rag Baby LP—Fourth Pressing
Berkeley, 1967
Artist: Tom Weller

2.289
Vanguard Album Promotion
Berkeley, 1967
Artist: Tom Weller

2.290
Vanguard Album Promotion
Berkeley, 1967
Artist: Tom Weller

BILL QUARRY

Bill Quarry worked mostly out of East Bay venues like the Rollarena, in San Leandro. His efforts were quickly eclipsed by Bill Graham and the Family Dog, but Quarry, who got his start promoting rock dances at his high school in the late 1950s, deserves much credit for booking bands from outside of the Bay Area, like Buffalo Springfield, the Young Rascals, the Byrds, and the 13th Floor Elevator, as well as English groups like Eric Burdon and the Animals, and the Yardbirds.

Quarry worked closely with Don Ryder, who had little experience as a graphic artist, but nevertheless over a two-year period drew several hundred posters and handbills for Quarry's Teens 'n' Twenties rock dances.

(above left)
2.291
Beau Brummels; Tame Greens
Rollarena, San Leandro; Carousel, San Francisco, 1966
Artist: Don Ryder

(below left)
2.292
Buffalo Springfield; Peter Wheat and the Breadmen
Longshoremen's Hall, San Francisco, 1967
Artist: Don Ryder

2.293
Yardbirds; Harbinger Complex
Rollarena, San Leandro; Carousel,
San Francisco, ca. 1966
Artist: Don Ryder

2.294

Eric Burdon and the Animals; Association
Oakland Coliseum, Oakland, 1967
Artist: Don Ryder

2.295

13th Floor Elevator
Rollarena, San Leandro, 1967
Artist: Don Ryder

2.296

Young Rascals; Country Joe and the Fish
Oakland Auditorium, Oakland, 1967
Artist: Don Ryder

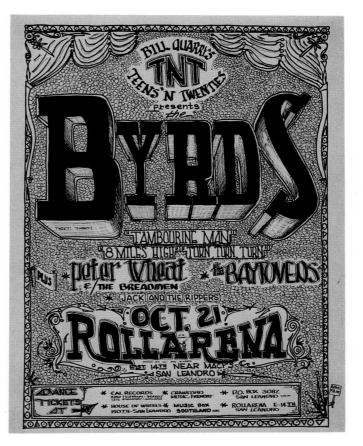

2.297

The Byrds; Peter Wheat and the Breadmen
Rollarena, San Leandro, 1966
Artist: Don Ryder

Marin County

Marin County hosted fewer rock dances than the other areas surrounding San Francisco Bay, but among its more notable venues were Fairfax Park, Muir Beach (where a legendary Acid Test took place), the Ark, and the Mt. Tamalpais outdoor amphitheater. One of the most memorable events was the Cosmic Car Show, held at Muir Beach. Stanley Mouse, who drew both the silk-screened poster (2.298) and the entry-kit handbill (2.302), was one of the show's judges, along with his partner Alton Kelley. Both artists had long associations with hot-rodding and related t-shirt art.

2.299

Grand Opening—The Mod Hatter
Mill Valley, 1966
Artist: Cervenak

2.298

Cosmic Car Show
Muir Beach, Marin County, 1967
Artist: Stanley Mouse

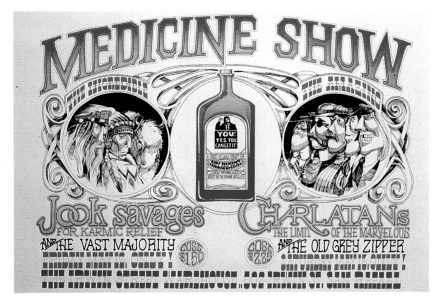

2.300

Medicine Show
Irwin Street Warehouse, San Rafael, 1967
Artist: Rick Griffin

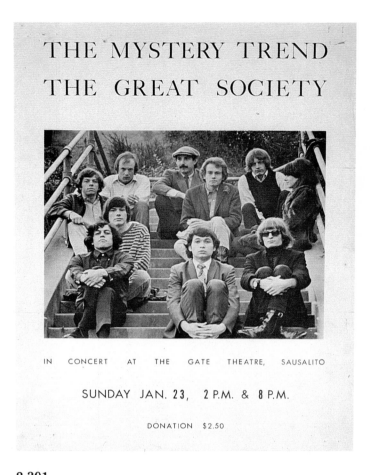

2.301

Mystery Trend; Great Society
Gate Theater, Sausalito, 1966

2.302

Entry kit: Cosmic Car Show
Muir Beach, Marin County, 1966
Artist: Stanley Mouse

2.303

Country Joe and the Fish; Baltimore Steam Packet
Fairfax Park, Fairfax, 1967
Artists: J. N. Bower, R. Van Krugel/Haffbad

2.304

Country Joe and the Fish; Baltimore Steam Packet
Fairfax Park, Fairfax, 1967
Artists: J. N. Bower, R. Van Krugel/Haffbad

2.305

Charlatans; Universal Joint
Fairfax Park, Fairfax, 1967
Artists: J. N. Bower, R. Van Krugel/Haffbad

THE ARK

The Ark, located in the bay-front town of Sausalito, was distinguished during the early psychedelic period as an after-hours hangout for bands, which would sometimes play a regular gig at a club or ballroom and then come over for an early-morning set. Big Brother and the Holding Company made many such appearances. Another significant feature of The Ark's operation was its large run of miserably designed and executed posters, detested by most collectors. The least objectionable pieces are the silk-screened posters for obscure groups like the Jungle Peach Blues Band.

2.306

Womb; Santana Blues Band
The Ark, Sausalito, ca. 1967

2.307

Steve Miller; Curly Cooke's Hurdy Gurdy Band
The Ark, Sausalito, 1966
Artist: Dave Brown

2.308
Big Brother and the Holding Company;
Human Beings. The Ark, Sausalito, 1967
Artist: Brighton Goodfellow

2.309
Big Brother and the Holding Company; Jack the Ripper
The Ark, Sausalito, 1967

2.310
Big Brother and the Holding Company;
Moby Grape. The Ark, Sausalito, 1967

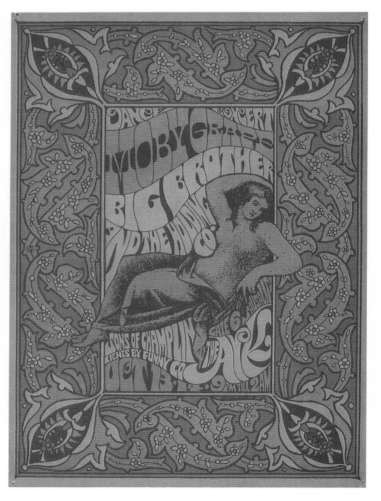

2.311
Moby Grape; Big Brother and
the Holding Company
The Ark, Sausalito, 1967

SANTA VENETIA ARMORY

Santa Venetia is a Marin County district close to San Rafael, the city where the Grateful Dead now make their home. In 1966, the Santa Venetia Armory featured a series of rock dances note-worthy for the two types of poster art they generated. One set of posters was produced by the Tilghman Press in the old letterpress style, the other in a loose, hippie, psychedelic style. The letterpress editions are today some of the rarest Bay Area rock posters, since, by this time, few such jobs were being handled by the older printing shops.

2.312
Big Brother and the Holding Company; Moby Grape
Santa Venetia Armory, San Rafael, 1966
Artist: Cervenak

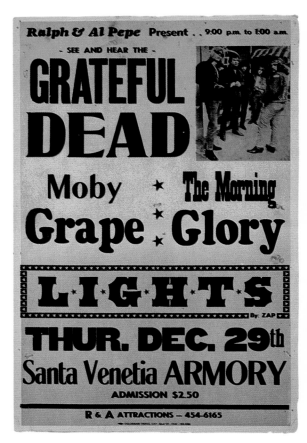

2.313

Grateful Dead; Moby Grape
Santa Venetia Armory, San Rafael, 1966
Artist: Tilghman Press

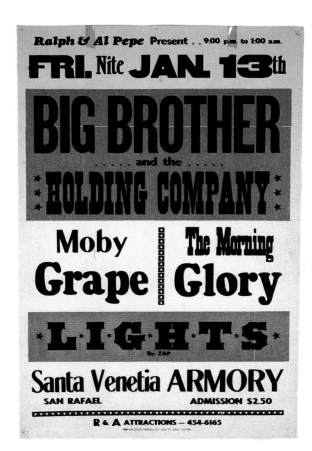

2.314

Big Brother and the Holding Company;
Moby Grape. Santa Venetia Armory, San Rafael,
1967. Artist: Tilghman Press

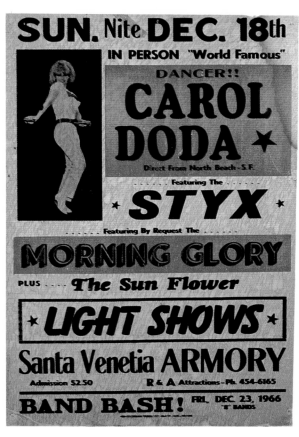

2.315

Carol Doda; The Styx
Santa Venetia Armory, San Rafael, 1966
Artist: Tilghman Press

2.316

Quicksilver Messenger Service;
Freedom Highway
Santa Venetia Armory,
San Rafael, 1967
Artist: Tilghman Press

MAGIC MOUNTAIN
FESTIVAL

The Magic Mountain Festival, promoted by AM radio station KFRC, was one of the most highly publicized events of its kind in 1967. It took place during the middle of the "Summer of Love," when thousands of young people flocked to San Francisco to take part in the hippie experience. Despite the profusion of art created for Magic Mountain—two posters, a handbill, a program, and other material—the event was not a total success.

Not all the groups announced—Wilson Pickett, for instance—actually played Magic Mountain, but the crafts fair did go on (among the booths was one manned by poster artists Kelley and Mouse), and attendees did ride "Trans-Love Buslines" to the mountain amphitheater.

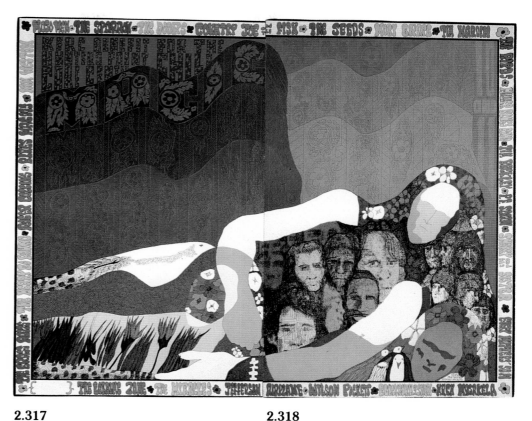

2.317
Magic Mountain (left half)
Mt. Tamalpais, Marin County, 1967
Artist: Jack Hatfield

2.318
Magic Mountain (right half)
Mt. Tamalpais, Marin County, 1967
Artist: Jack Hatfield

2.319
Magic Mountain Festival
Mt. Tamalpais, Marin County, 1967
Artist: Stanley Mouse

2.320
Handbill: Magic Mountain Festival
Mt. Tamalpais, Marin County, 1967

2.321
KFRC radio promotion: Magic Mountain Festival. Mt. Tamalpais, Marin County, 1967

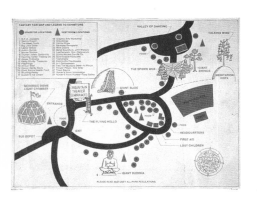

2.322

Program: Magic Mountain Festival (front)
Mt. Tamalpais, Marin County, 1967

2.324

Program: Magic Mountain Festival (inside)
Mt. Tamalpais, Marin County, 1967

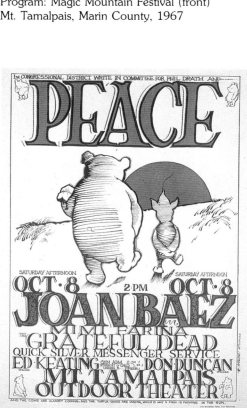

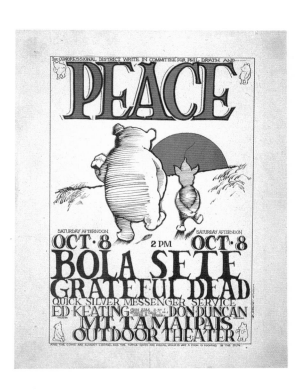

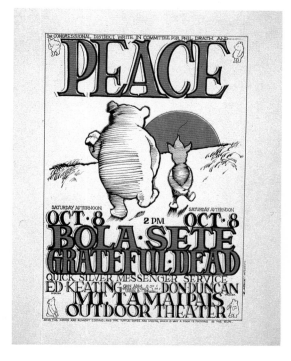

2.325

Peace (version 1)
Mt. Tamalpais Outdoor Theater, Marin County,
1966. Artists: Stanley Mouse, Alton Kelley

2.326

Handbill: Peace (version 2)
Mt. Tamalpais Outdoor Theater, Marin County,
1966. Artists: Stanley Mouse, Alton Kelley

2.327

Peace (version 3)
Mt. Tamalpais Outdoor Theater, Marin County,
1966. Artists: Stanley Mouse, Alton Kelley

Sonoma County

The Russian River resort area in Northern California's Sonoma County has long been a favorite of Bay Area residents. One fondly remembered site for rock dances was the Rio Nido Ballroom, but probably more events took place at the Fairgrounds outside of Santa Rosa, the largest city in that region.

2.329

Hot Tuna; Grateful Dead
The Barn, Rio Nido; Veterans Memorial Building,
Santa Rosa, 1969
Artist: Lee Conklin

2.328

Russian River Rock Festival
Rio Nido Ballroom, Rio Nido, 1967
Artist: Melinda Gebbie

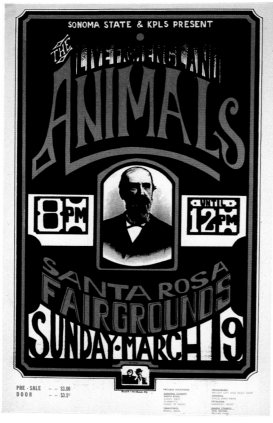

2.330

The Animals
Fairgrounds, Santa Rosa, 1967
Artists: J. N. Bower, R. Van Krugel/Haffbad

2.331

Quicksilver Messenger Service; H. P. Lovecraft
Fairgrounds, Santa Rosa, 1968

2.332

Canned Heat; Bronze Hog
Fairgrounds, Santa Rosa, 1968

2.333

It's a Beautiful Day; Cold Blood
Fairgrounds, Santa Rosa, 1969
Artist: Larry Noggle

The Peninsula and South Bay

Like Marin County, the areas south of San Francisco known as the Peninsula and South Bay, saw far fewer rock events than San Francisco or the East Bay—this despite the presence of Stanford University in Palo Alto, whose Frost Amphitheater occasionally featured groups like the Jefferson Airplane and Sly and the Family Stone. Palo Alto also had El Camino Park, a popular concert site for young bands, but little or no poster art was generated by gigs there.

Equally surprising is the paucity of art from San Jose and environs. While some memorable events were held at San Jose's Civic Auditorium, only the San Jose Human Be-In (inspired by the San Francisco event of that name) and shows at obscure clubs like Losers South occasioned significant posters. The piece Stanley Mouse and Alton Kelley created for the Jefferson Airplane's appearance at Losers South in 1966 is one of this team's rarest works (2.378).

2.334

Chocolate Watchband; Generations
National Guard Armory, San Bruno, 1966
Artist: C. Thayer

2.335

13th Floor Elevator; Inmates
National Guard Armory, San Bruno, 1966
Artist: C. Thayer

2.336

Jefferson Airplane; Big Brother and the Holding Company
Losers South, San Jose, 1966
Artists: Stanley Mouse, Alton Kelley

2.337

San Jose Human Be-In
10th and Alma Streets, San Jose, 1967
Artist: Dennis Nolan

2.338

Grateful Dead; Jaywalkers
Veteran's Hall, San Jose, 1966
Artist: Wes Wilson

2.339

Benefit—Haight-Ashbury Medical Clinic
Family Park, San Jose, 1967
Artist: Mari Tepper

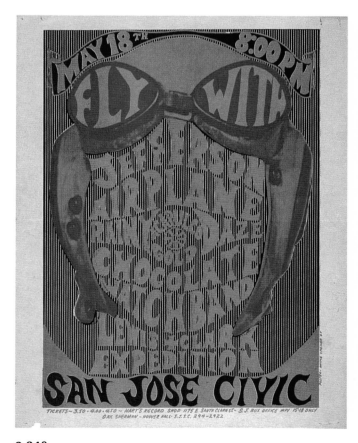

2.340

Jefferson Airplane; Chocolate Watchband
Civic Auditorium, San Jose, 1967
Artist: Mike Spenar

2.341

Northern California Folk-Rock Festival
Fairgrounds, Santa Clara, 1968
Artist: Carson-Morris Studios

CONTINENTAL BALLROOM

The Continental Ballroom was the South Bay's answer to San Francisco's Fillmore and Avalon. It featured all of the important San Francisco psychedelic-era bands, but also more obscure groups popular in the San Jose area, including the Count Five, Harpers Bizarre, and the Chocolate Watchband.

2.342

Big Brother and the Holding Company; Morning Glory
Continental Ballroom, Santa Clara, 1967

2.343

Grateful Dead; The Real Thing
Continental Ballroom, Santa Clara, 1967
Artist: Cannon

2.344

Big Brother and the Holding Company;
Mt. Rushmore. Continental Ballroom,
Santa Clara, 1967. Artist: Shem

2.345

Grand Opening
Continental Ballroom, Santa Clara, 1967
Artist: Grasshopper

2.346

Mojo Men; Harper's Bizarre
Continental Ballroom, Santa Clara, 1967

Joint Show

As the major San Francisco poster artists rose to prominence, they began to feel that their art deserved exhibition in a traditional gallery setting. The five most important artists at that time—Wes Wilson, Rick Griffin, Victor Moscoso, Stanley Mouse, and Alton Kelley—were approached by the Moore Gallery to organize a show, which opened on July 17, 1967. Everyone important on the scene made an appearance.

Each of the five artists celebrated at the Joint Show created a commemorative poster, but, except for Rick Griffin's piece, the efforts were not as enthusiastically received as might have been expected. Griffin's poster, however, has come to serve as a symbol for the era (2.347).

2.347
Joint Show
Moore Gallery, San Francisco,
1967. Artist: Rick Griffin

2.348
Joint Show
Moore Gallery, San Francisco, 1967
Artist: Stanley Mouse

2.349
Joint Show
Moore Gallery, San Francisco, 1967
Artist: Wes Wilson

2.350
Joint Show
Moore Gallery, San Francisco, 1967
Artist: Alton Kelley

2.351
Joint Show
Moore Gallery, San Francisco, 1967
Artist: Victor Moscoso

Rock-Related Posters

Rock poster artists did not limit themselves to producing art for concerts, and not all psychedelic graphic works were rock posters. Nevertheless, posters advertising special events, restaurants, head shops, and so on often resembled rock concert posters during the psychedelic period. Some of the artists who executed such pieces—for example, John Thompson (2.354)—later became major illustrators in the underground comix movement. But most of the pieces were anonymous.

Especially interesting is the poster for a theatrical group known as the Pitschel Players, which shows a sign painter covering over a Wes Wilson-like concert poster (2.352).

2.352
Pitschel Players Theatrical Satire
120 Julian Street, San Francisco, ca. 1967

2.353
Opening—San Francisco Store
Print Mint, San Francisco, 1966

2.354
Hire the Hip
Haight-Ashbury Job Co-Op, San Francisco, ca. 1967
Artist: John Thompson

2.355
Feel Free to Communicate!
The Hearth, San Francisco, ca. 1967
Artist: Jim Blashfield

2.356
Neiman-Marcus Poster Show. Exhibition Hall, Dallas, 1967
Artist: Victor Moscoso

PROMINENT ARTISTS

The "Big Five" San Francisco poster artists—Rick Griffin, Stanley Mouse, Wes Wilson, Victor Moscoso, and Alton Kelley—created many non-concert posters, including artistic spoofs (2.359), broadsides (2.362), promotional pieces (2.364), and advertisements for Haight-Ashbury stores. Bob Fried was another prominent rock poster artist who did non-concert work, such as his Family Dog billboard (2.367).

2.357
Man From Utopia Comic Book
ca. 1970
Artist: Rick Griffin

2.358
Hog Farm Celebration
Cinematique 16, Los Angeles, ca. 1969
Artist: Rick Griffin

2.359
Silk-screen poster: Mescalito
Berkeley, 1967
Artist: Rick Griffin

2.360
Canablis
Berkeley Bonaparte Poster, Berkeley, 1967
Artist: Rick Griffin

2.361
Light/Sound/Dimension
Museum of Art, San Francisco, 1966
Artists: Stanley Mouse, Alton Kelley

2.362

Allen Ginsberg Broadside
San Francisco, 1967
Artist: Wes Wilson

2.363

Are We Next?
Berkeley, ca. 1964
Artist: Wes Wilson

2.364

Opening
The Red Hat Restaurant, Palo Alto, 1966
Artist: Wes Wilson

2.366

California Shakespeare Festival
University of Santa Clara, Santa Clara, 1967
Artists: Robert Hollis, Stanley Mouse, Alton Kelley

2.365

Wilderness Conference
Hilton Hotel, San Francisco, 1967
Artists: Stanley Mouse, Alton Kelley

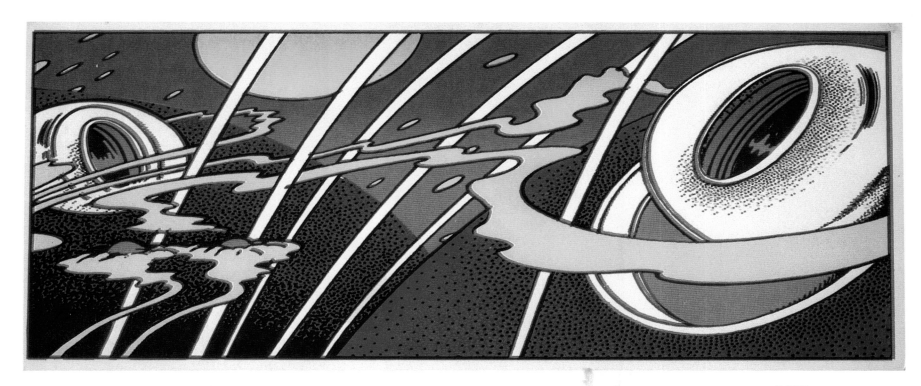

2.367
Billboard design
San Francisco, ca. 1967
Artist: Bob Fried

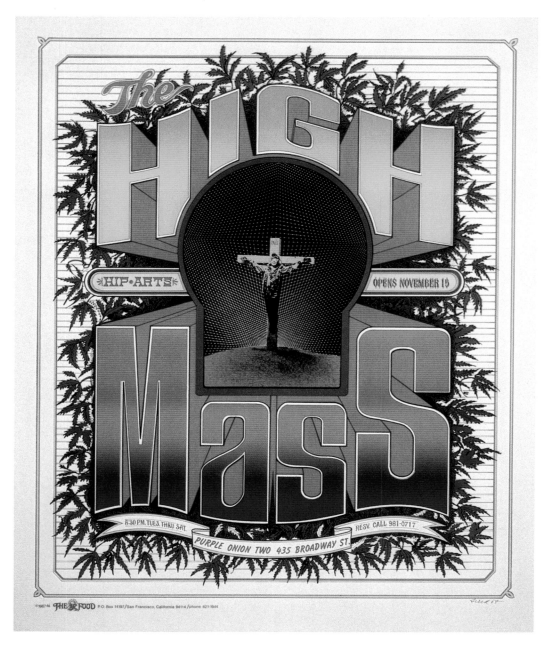

2.368
The High Mass
Purple Onion Two, San Francisco, 1967
Artist: Bob Fried

3

The Psychedelic Years in Southern California and the Rest of the World: 1965–1971

This time it was the native American bands which took us the one huge step closer to the future we had always been headed for. It was the Jefferson Airplane, the Grateful Dead, Big Brother and the Holding Company, Country Joe and the Fish, Quicksilver Messenger Service, the Great Society, the Fugs, the Mothers of Invention, Captain Beefheart and his Magic Band—all these great weirdo conglomerations of native-born maniacs who seemed to rise out of nowhere to sing the new truths which we had already begun to live.

JOHN SINCLAIR
Guitar Army

It was West Coast rock in 1965 that first posed a threat to the British Invasion. Then, over the next two years, American "psychedelic" rock swept across the country. Young people everywhere were caught up in a massive reorganization of values and life-styles, and the cultural influence of psychedelic rock would far surpass the impact of 1950s rock 'n' roll.

By mid 1965, Los Angeles had produced the Byrds, the first real challenge to the British, but, as we have seen, it was San Francisco that was the seedbed of national psychedelia. It wasn't very long before music-conscious cities like Detroit, Chicago, and Austin began to spawn their own rock cultures.

Detroit especially understood the possibilities of the new music. Indeed, it exported a host of key personages to San Francisco, including artist Stanley Mouse and guitarist James Gurley, soon to be a Big Brother and the Holding Company mainstay. As early as 1966, a Detroit subcommunity was emerging within the San Francisco hippie scene. However many Detroit natives made the journey west, an even greater number remained at home, becoming the nucleus of a vibrant American counterculture community with a social and artistic signature all its own.

The most prominent social activist in Detroit was John Sinclair, who became widely recognized in the late 1960s for his protests against police repression and unjust court rulings affecting him and the various counterculture communal groups he helped build. One of the first activists to see the late-1960s rock music as a new and highly powerful force for social change, Sinclair wrote *Guitar Army*, a personal manifesto and a call to action.

The public authorities pursued Sinclair with unusual zeal. Imprisoned for the first time early in 1966, he was released later that year into a world witnessing the emergence of a "hip self-determination movement . . . first expanding its scope to try and deal with needs of hordes of teenage hippies who were exploding onto the scene in great numbers every week. But even then, in late 1966, the Detroit hip community was still minuscule—the first year's dances at the Grande Ballroom . . . averaged maybe 300 people a night—but it was constantly growing as more young brothers and sisters dug how beautiful it was and started deserting the suburban wasteland they had been trapped in."

Detroit had played host to all the touring cavalcades of white rock 'n' roll and black rhythm-and-blues stars, and the city was next to earn a permanent niche in popular music history by serving as the birthplace of Motown soul. But in white youth circles, psychedelic rock was to provide the greater opportunity to break loose.

Most important to the fostering of psychedelic music in Detroit was the opening of the Grande Ballroom as a rock dance palace. The ballroom had been active since the 1920s, but it was often closed in the late 1950s and early 1960s. Then Russ Gibb found it, in the middle of 1966.

John Sinclair:

Russ had gone to San Francisco during the summer of 1966. He saw what Bill Graham was doing and what the Family Dog offered. He came back to Detroit and found the Grande available. Russ Gibb wasn't as hip as Bill Graham, but in Detroit, in those days, he was hipper than the average guy. He was like a nutty uncle.

The bulk of Detroit people who attended Grande events lived in two areas: the West Side, where the teenagers came from, and the Wayne State University area, the cultural locus for the hip and

the weird. These were the neighborhoods where you'd see psychedelic posters advertising the Grande shows.

I really think posters made the Grande. There just wasn't any other advertising medium that could be used effectively to reach the Grande audience. Russ Gibb realized their value. Certainly he'd have been wasting his money if he took out ads in the Detroit Free Press, the big newspaper, because he had to reach a whole different crowd.

When I came out of prison in August 1966, there was tremendous new activity on the hip front and a lot of focus on the opening of the Grande. It wasn't long before I met with the guys from the band MC 5 and with the people putting out The Fifth Estate, Detroit's radical underground paper. Through one of its writers, Frank Bach, I met artist Gary Grimshaw, which was the beginning of a friendship and a political and professional association that developed into our current partnership.

I remember seeing one of Grimshaw's first posters for the Grande—one of the first psychedelic posters I'd ever actually seen—and I was just wigged. It really was different, really a departure. It showed in his distinctive lettering, which flowed in some altogether new way, and in the combination of colors, which he came to work with more and more as his poster art developed.

"Guerrilla Lovefare." Grande Ballroom, Detroit, 1966
Artist: Gary Grimshaw

working in Detroit. He was fortunate enough to have come along at a pivotal point in rock history, he also took great pride in his personal history—in the graphic and design traditions of his Detroit-based family:

My grandfather was a stylist at General Motors, my uncle a printer, my aunt an illustrator. The tradition of graphic art in our family includes my father's work as a mechanical engineer. I was born in 1946, and like a lot of Detroit kids I grew up in the car-dominated 1950s. I doodled cars and trucks in school, and along with my friend Rob Tyner, who became the lead singer in the MC 5, I did some t-shirt art in high school, although nothing on the scale of Stanley Mouse, who also went to high school in the Detroit area and airbrushed hot rod t-shirts at custom car shows. Whereas Mouse worked mostly with an airbrush, I concentrated on line art. My work is done with Rapidograph pens—I'm really into fine lines and cross-hatching—and with graphic arts film.

I always thought I would be an artist, but I went through a lot of other experiences before getting into poster work. I went to college

"Third Eye"
Grande Ballroom, Detroit, 1967
Artist: Gary Grimshaw

Most of Grimshaw's psychedelic dance posters were done in two or three colors. And he did wonderful things with just those two or three colors. He made them seem like eight. His creative sense was especially important in those first years, because so many of the posters were produced out of penury. Gary had to work with basic, bare-bones resources: he knew he wasn't going to be able to go whole-hog with the printing. The saddest thing about Gary's Grande posters was how few were printed of any one design. A thousand copies would be about the limit: the usual was around five hundred.

Gary is a quiet, reserved person who has always been an active music connoisseur interested in hearing obscure, up-and-coming bands. He's always enjoyed the challenge that comes with new music of any period. The thing about Grimshaw is, he's always trying to articulate a new vision.

By late 1966, with the opening of the Grande, Gary Grimshaw became the most widely recognized psychedelic poster artist

Scott Richard Case; MC5. Grande Ballroom, Detroit, 1967
Artist: Gary Grimshaw; Photographer: Magdalene Sinclair

Yardbirds; Frost. Grande Ballroom, Detroit, 1968
Artist: Gary Grimshaw

Cream. Grande Ballroom, Detroit, 1968
Artist: Gary Grimshaw

for a year, but I just didn't like it. I enlisted in the Navy and served in 1965 and 1966 on an aircraft carrier off Vietnam. My last ship was stationed in San Francisco, in 1966. The day I got my first liberty after Vietnam was the day of a big peace march going from Berkeley into Oakland. I took a bus over to the East Bay and walked in the march. What an introduction to the new culture! But I'd been reading Jack Kerouac and Allen Ginsberg since I was twelve, so I guess I was intuitively prepared.

While I was in San Francisco, I started going to Avalon and Fillmore shows. I lived in a rooming house out near the Panhandle, off Golden Gate Park. It was a classic time, and I did some work for the great hippie paper, The Oracle (there's a bunch of my artwork in issues 7 and 8). I sold Oracles at night to support myself.

Late in the summer 1966 I returned home to Michigan, and my

first real job was doing dance posters for the Grande Ballroom. I returned at exactly the right time. I was staying at Rob Tyner's house when Russ Gibb, who started things going at the Grande, hired him for a gig. This was about a month before the Grande actually opened, and Gibb asked Rob if he knew any graphic artists. I happened to be sitting there at Rob's kitchen table, so I got the job.

Over the next eighteen months or so, my main work for the Grande was the posters, though I also put together the hall's first light show.

All of us had a great time working at the Grande and making it happen. It had a sort of Moorish look outside, with a lot of ornate plaster work. It was built as a ballroom in the 1920s, and it never had seats. It featured a suspended dance floor built over big coils that provided dancers with an added sense of movement.

I loved doing the Grande posters, because I learned so much over a short period. I'm not sure what I think of my first half-dozen posters; I didn't really know what I was doing technically. Every time I'd design something and bring it to the printer, he'd tell me, "Gary, you just can't do that." And I'd describe to him what I was trying to achieve, and he'd work with me, showing me how to create art by using all the basic processes. Within a year or so I finally got to the point where I could make my posters look the way I wanted them. I found it hardest to deal with multiple colors, and one of my key tasks was learning mechanical separations and how to obtain effects with the necessary film overlays.

The Grande posters were almost all done under an absurdly tight schedule. A lot of times, I'd get the final information about the concert the night before everything was due at the printer. And with all this rush effort I was never paid much more than $75 for any one.

I produced most of my Grande posters in 1967. The next year was different: a marijuana possession charge was leveled against me, which resulted in an arrest warrant. I was in no position to fight the charge at the time, so I left the state and went underground, first to Boston and then, early in 1969, back to California. Just before my difficulties came down, I had started alternating some of the graphic work for the Grande with another artist, Carl Lundgren. Carl really cared about the work. He wanted

Canned Heat. Grande Ballroom, Detroit, 1968
Artist: Carl Lundgren

"Eagle." The See, Detroit, 1967
Artist: Gary Grimshaw

to do a beautiful job, and he certainly did. When I left, it became a full-time gig for him, which lasted through the end of the Grande's classic period, until Russ Gibb decided he didn't want to continue spending money on posters.

Grimshaw drew most of his posters, while many of Lundgren's best efforts were collages. The contrasting techniques helped develop the Grande posters into perhaps the finest body of psychedelic concert art outside San Francisco.

Carl Lundgren:

I don't think I ever wanted to be an artist as a kid, but at some point I knew I had to do something with my life, and I just picked art. Maybe it was a mistake—I thought for a long time I made a

"The Spirit of Love." Grande Ballroom, Detroit, 1967
Artist: Carlin/Warlock Studios

wrong choice, a wrong decision—but I stuck with it. And then I began to enjoy my work as an artist.

I was born in 1947, and through most of high school I listened to folk music. I was really into the hootenanny scene, and I worked my ass off learning how to play the guitar. In my last years of high school, I played professionally in clubs, but I decided to become an artist when I was about seventeen, and I gave up thinking about music as a career. Around that time I helped make some underground films, but my real interest was in reading and collecting science fiction books, art books, and comics. I especially loved comic books—the DC comics and the old horror comics—and I became as big a fan of science fiction as I'd been of folk music. Science fiction has had a lot of influence on my work as an artist. Rock 'n' roll of the 1950s was never as important for me as folk music, but when the Beatles appeared, I started getting into rock.

When I graduated from high school, I was accepted by the University of Southern California. When the USC registrar asked me what I wanted to do, I said, "I want to be an illustrator!" He told me, "Carl, we don't teach that here," and referred me to the prestigious Art Center School, where I was turned down flat because my portfolio "was too cartoony." But I was accepted by the-not-so-prestigious Hollywood Art Center, where I studied for one semester until I ran out of money. I even enrolled in the Famous Artists Correspondence School, but I gave up after the eighth lesson. All this goes to show why I consider myself largely self-taught.

It was while I was living in California that I turned on to the rock scene, the hippie scene. So when I returned to Detroit in 1967, I knew all about the new art—I knew about Wes Wilson, I knew about the Avalon and the Fillmore, and I'd met the people hanging out in San Francisco. I loved the psychedelic art, and I collected as much of it as I could—hundreds of posters and handbills. That art told me I could do it myself, and when I got back to Detroit I got my chance.

I didn't know Gary Grimshaw before I left for California, but I'd heard about his work, and I knew he was a guy you had to talk to in Detroit about rock 'n' roll posters. When I started doing Grande posters in the fall of 1967, Gary was still active. There was a period of about nine months in which we alternated pretty regularly. But at the time I got involved, there were a lot of other guys doing poster art, too. One was named Carlin, who started Warlock Studios with Gary. And there was Don Forsythe, also known as Donny Dope: I got him in, sort of like Gary got me in. Sometimes there would be collaborations between me and Donny, or me, Donny, and Jerry Younkins. I was like the ringleader. I would get these guys into the business and help them out.

Gary got a lot more posters printed than I did, but that's because he got started earlier—back in 1966, when Russ Gibb was still new to the business. By the time I came abroad, the Grande hardly ever printed posters. I don't think there were more than six of mine ever printed as posters—all the rest were handbills.

I particularly liked doing collage work because I didn't feel entirely comfortable drawing. And I also knew people who could do collages, people I enjoyed collaborating with. I'd always be saying to my friend Jerry, "Hey, gimme a good collage." And then I'd spend hours coloring it, because I knew how to do that real well. I was especially good at making overlays, doing burns, and making creative use of color.

I did okay during the Grande period. I think I was paid about $95 for each of my posters—$80, $95, something like that—and at that time, you know, if I did a couple a month, I could get by. Practically make a living. It got me off to a good start as an artist, and I feel I was lucky in many respects. I fell into the hippie thing when it was popular. It'd be a drag if I were doing it now, because the opportunities just aren't there for a young man starting out. There was a counterculture to get involved with—not just a commercial scene.

Grimshaw, Lundgren, and their friends created a body of art that rivaled the best of San Francisco, whereas Denver, St. Louis, Baltimore, Washington, Pittsburgh, Philadelphia, New York, and Chicago produced no distinctive schools. In those cities, newspaper and radio ads largely supplanted poster production.

Chicago, nevertheless, did boast several excellent rock venues comparable to the Grande Ballroom, including the Aragon Ballroom and the Kinetic Playground (better known to Chicagoans as the Electric Theater). As in San Francisco, creating a weekly schedule of rock events in a dance hall during the psychedelic period brought together restless, talented young people hungry for new experiences. One such was Mark Behrens, who got his start as a poster artist working for the Kinetic Playground:

I was born in 1947, and grew up in the Midwest. I became involved with a couple of other artists, and we tried to start a lightshow, but we never could find backing. I was filled with a general sort of restlessness, and my dreams were larger than Minneapolis. After my twenty-first birthday, I left Minneapolis and moved to Chicago. No sooner had I arrived than, within days, President Johnson made his big announcement that he wouldn't run for another term. A few days later Martin Luther King, Jr., was assassinated, and all of Chicago just seemed to explode. I was virtually trapped inside my apartment for three days because I didn't know how to get anywhere without running into trouble. It was total pandemonium in the streets, and I was scared like I'd never been before in my life.

Shortly after I settled in, I started working on the lightshow at the Electric Theater, which later changed its name to the Kinetic Playground, but I always knew it as the Electric Theater. It was a ballroom meant for dancing and freaking. It was a major scene, a

February and March shows. Kinetic Playground (Electric Theater), Chicago, 1969
Artist: Mark Behrens

great place. All the big important bands came, the groups from San Francisco, from L.A., New York—and the English bands played, too. And the Theater had one advantage peculiar to being in Chicago: there were all the great Chicago blues bands and blues musicians, mostly from the South Side.

The Electric Theater was operated like the Fillmore and the Avalon back in San Francisco. We were booking shows five days a week. There was never a dead weekend. It contrasted somewhat with what was going on at the Aragon Ballroom, another one of Chicago's classic rock venues. There weren't regular shows at the Aragon, mostly spot gigs. They'd even alternate rock and soul shows, and altogether the Aragon seemed to draw an audience different from ours, sometimes even a violent "greaser" crowd.

The Theater always tried to book shows as far ahead as possible, up to six weeks in advance. If we had that much information locked up, socked away solid, a poster would be commissioned. That's why almost every Electric Theater poster was designed in a calendar format—to cover a month of shows.

The Theater did almost no advertising in the Chicago papers, due to the cost of display ads, and also because our audience wasn't their readers. In any case, the major Chicago papers waged a relentless war against rock and the hippies from the start. This was not San Francisco! You'd constantly be reading editorials in The Chicago Tribune decrying the evil of our scene and badgering the public authorities to shut us down.

Most of our concert art was a stream of handbills, although on occasion several thousand posters of a particular lineup might find their way onto the streets, into record stores, clothing boutiques, and head shops. Chicago's Old Town district was an area we often hit hard, since it was roughly equivalent in its day to San Francisco's Haight-Ashbury. But despite audiences, I don't think posters played nearly the same role in unifying or identifying a community as they had in San Francisco, Detroit, and Boston. In the year and a half I worked for the Electric Theater, roughly from March 1968 to August 1969, I don't remember more than twenty large posters distributed in any major way.

Right around Memorial Day 1969, I had a vacation coming, an actual paid vacation, which was rare for employees of an irregular operation like the Electric Theater. I went to San Francisco for two wonderful weeks. It measured up to everything I'd been hearing since 1966. For so long so many of us in the Midwest had heard the whisper and then the shout: San Francisco, San Francisco, San Francisco. And friends of mine would come back from there to Minneapolis or Chicago with a head full of tales and an armload of posters.

Actually seeing the San Francisco posters gave me the ambition to try something similar. By the time I visited the city, the Family Dog's Avalon operation had ceased, but Bill Graham was in full swing at the Fillmore West and Winterland. At least on his end there was still regular poster production, though the scene had changed somewhat since its heyday. Bands were still playing all over, all the time, and posters were still everywhere. Bizarre events were still taking place, and the streets themselves were theatrical.

My visit had a massive effect on what happened next. Within two days of my return to Chicago, I broke up with my girlfriend, packed my stuff, used my savings to buy a car, and made arrangements to relocate my life completely.

As notable Midwesterners migrated to the Coast, so did a number of Texans, among them Janis Joplin and Chet Helms, head of the Family Dog. There was a special connection between San Francisco and Austin, home of the University of Texas, whose students and former students became the state's first psychedelic adventurers early in the 1960s.

Austin proved as strong a base for rock as Detroit, and in San Francisco there were distinct communities of friends hailing from both cities. Poster art played a strong role in popularizing the new music in Austin. Don Hyde was cofounder of Texas's first psychedelic dance hall, the Vulcan Gas Company:

The Austin scene started with the folk movement, around 1960 or 1961. The first time I heard Janis Joplin was at the University of Texas at the student union in 1961, playing autoharp and singing "Railroad Bill"—two or three guys and she. They called them-selves the Waller Creek Boys. Janis sang in front.

The Waller Creek Boys had a little place, like an apartment house. There were a dozen or fifteen people who lived there, and everybody called it "The Ghetto." There were incredible parties there all the time. These were the first people—the first white people in our age group—who smoked marijuana in Texas. Then, around 1961, I heard that one of them had taken peyote. That started the psychedelic scene in Austin.

Austin actually preceded the West Coast and New York on the

Grateful Dead; Daily Flash. Eagles Auditorium, Seattle, 1967

Freddie King. Vulcan Gas Co. Austin, Texas, 1969

psychedelic scene. Texans were taking peyote and mescaline for five or six years before LSD came into general circulation. Austin had a head start over everybody, even though the dance hall scene didn't come about until 1966 or so.

It's hard to say exactly who started the dance hall movement or precisely when it started, but it grew out of the folk music trip, and out of something called the Electric Grandmother, a group headed by Gary Scanlon and Houston White. Houston and Gary had long hair back in 1963—I mean they had hair halfway down their backs—and that was outrageous. They'd walk down the street and traffic would stop. They were close friends with Janis Joplin and Chet Helms. By 1964 or early 1965, people from Austin were starting to make trips to San Francisco, bringing back rumors of a new thing beginning to happen.

I believe the Electric Grandmother did one show and then became the Vulcan Gas Company, which was Houston, Gary, and myself. I was the only one of the three who had any money— about $1,500, which seemed a fortune at the time—and I was able to secure a lease on a building and buy lumber to build the stage and paint the inside of the place.

Our very first show was filled to capacity, about 950. We opened in September or October of 1967, and I stuck with it through 1968. Then I turned it over to some other people, who ran it until maybe late 1969 or early 1970.

We never had to compete with the Armadillo—Austin's most famous dance hall, featuring rock and country rock. Eddie Wilson opened the Armadillo only after the Vulcan died. They found an old armory, which could hold 3,000. It was a lot more successful. The Vulcan could never even get a beer and wine license; we sold apple juice. All the money collected at the door went to the bands. We should have made money on the concessions, but we never could—we never could sell enough of anything to make money.

The only form of advertising we could obtain was getting posters made and putting them inside store windows up and down the main drag in front of the university. The Vulcan posters were really huge mothers—bigger than your average rock concert poster. I don't think we did more than a hundred, and quite a number of local artists did them for us, and so there wasn't much of a coherent style or form about them—not like the San Francisco thing. But the Vulcan posters did feature some of cartoonist Gilbert

Grateful Dead; Quicksilver Messenger Service. Eagles Auditorium, Seattle, 1968
Artist: John Moehring

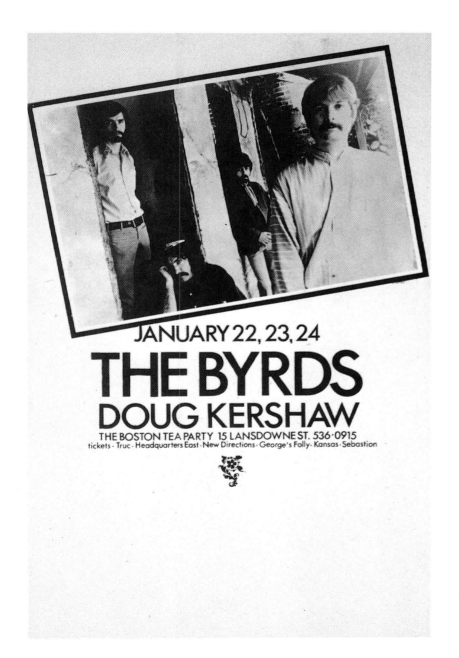

Byrds; Doug Kershaw
Boston Tea Party, Boston, 1969

Shelton's earliest public work. I had met Gilbert back in 1961 or 1962, during the folk music explosion. He, Jack Jackson (later known as Jaxon), and Tony Bell were editors of a Texas humor magazine called The Ranger. Gilbert had gone to school with them. By 1963 the magazine was publishing some great, really funny issues, but it wasn't until three or four years later, when the Vulcan posters began to happen, that Gilbert's work really went on full public display.

The scene around the Vulcan, in its heyday, was as casual as anything happening at the Avalon. We used to get kids coming in from Arkansas, Oklahoma, and New Mexico—hip kids, kids who had heard rumors, on the lookout—because we were the only thing like it within a thousand-mile radius. People stoned on acid and people smoking pot openly on the dance floor—there was nothing like that anywhere else in Texas. I imagine it must have been what Eagles Auditorium was to the people of Seattle—something completely different from anything that existed before in popular culture: the stoned versus the straight.

The Vulcan was like the Crystal Ballroom in Portland and the Denver Dog in Colorado—both operated by San Francisco's Family Dog—and like the Eagles Auditorium in Seattle or the Hippodrome—managed by Trans Love Airways Productions—in San Diego. All were venues that ushered in the psychedelic era in formerly straight communities.

Trips Festival. PNE Garden Auditorium
Vancouver, Canada, 1966

But places like the Hippodrome paled by comparison to Los Angeles's Kaleidoscope. It was the most amazing *building* of them all, the Fillmore and Avalon in San Francisco and the Electric Circus in New York notwithstanding. Located near Sunset and Vine in the heart of Los Angeles, it was built in the 1930s by showman Earl Carroll, who named it after himself. It featured an eighty-foot revolving stage with an additional six-foot outer ring that could revolve in the opposite direction. There was a "rainfall" curtain and jets that spat fire, along with an elevating orchestra pit. It had all been built to accommodate extravaganzas of naked women—especially the revolving stages. Local laws prohibited stripper-style entertainment, which, however, was narrowly defined as nude women in motion. In Carroll's theater, the women stood stock still; it was the stages that moved.

The Earl Carroll Theater next became the Moulin Rouge, then the stage set for the "Hullabaloo" live-music TV shows, then the Aquarius Theater, and, along the way, the site of many 1950s TV game shows, including "Queen for a Day." Happily, through all these metamorphoses, Carroll's array of stage equipment remained in place when the hippie production trio of John Hartmann (later manager of Crosby, Stills, and Nash), Skip Taylor, and Gary Essert took over.

John Hartmann:

We took out all the seats from the dance floor, put in some phenomenal lighting equipment, hung four giant Altec speakers from the ceiling, surrounded the dance floor with dozens of other speakers, and created the largest p.a. system ever in a nightclub. It was the best rock 'n' roll sound of all time. And we used the revolving stages to great effect. On one night that we featured the Jefferson Airplane, we had on the outer six-foot ring a live elephant—within three feet of the audience. And the time we produced a benefit for striking radio disc jockeys, we were able to put on fifteen acts in one evening, because we could set up three acts at once, shift the stage around, with only sixteen seconds between bands.

The only problem was capacity; we just never could make any money selling no more than a thousand tickets.

The Kaleidoscope posters and tickets were unique because they were all round. No other concert operation featured round *posters, but then no other psychedelic dance hall was a theater in the round. The posters spun off the whole theater concept.*

The Kaleidoscope and the Pinnacle concerts, whose home was the Shrine Auditorium, were the most noteworthy psychedelic concert operations in Los Angeles, easily rivaling what was going on in clubs like the Whisky and the Troubador. But while the shape of Kaleidoscope art was unique, its artistic content was often prosaic compared with the highly imaginative Pinnacle graphics by John Van Hamersveld:

I'm a Californian in nearly all respects. I've lived and worked here almost my entire life. I grew up in Palos Verdes, a suburb west of Los Angeles, out at the ocean's edge. The ocean always intrigued me.

My family background influenced my becoming a commercial artist. My grandfather, who'd been in California during the 1930s, was a famous industrial designer. He worked on the two-hundred-inch telescope up at Mount Palomar, and I remember him visiting us in the 1950s and taking us to see it. My father was a mechanical

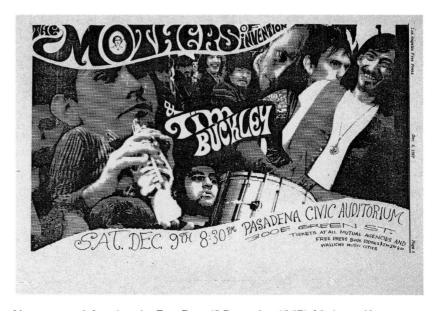

Newspaper ad, *Los Angeles Free Press* (8 December 1967): Mothers of Invention; Tim Buckley. Pasadena Civic Auditorium, 1967

Country Joe and the Fish. The Bank, Torrance, California, 1968

engineer who settled in California because he was involved in building the "Flying Wing" airplane for Northrop. He helped me become aware of the graphic arts; one of my childhood memories is watching him at work building forms. And then there is my mother, who painted watercolors, mostly landscapes. I picked up some basic techniques by watching her sketch seascapes.

High school provided basic art classes, but I wasn't doing what the other kids who had an interest in art were doing—sketching planes and hot rods, that sort of thing. I was more attracted to the ocean, and the sea began to merge with my new interest in black music and early white rock 'n' roll. Black music was like a secret message, one of the first musical experiences that contrasted with my basically bland home environment. There was one Long Beach station I got in real well on my little bedside radio—and it happened to feature black-styled bandleader Johnny Otis. Meanwhile, on TV, I saw Elvis for the first time. I even started going to R & B variety shows, the "Touring Cavalcades of Stars." And one of the biggest moments in my young life was watching them film the car crash scene from Rebel Without a Cause on the cliffs

at Rocky Point, in Palos Verdes. My hometown! And I loved teen movies.

In high school I was greatly affected by progressive folk music, groups like the Kingston Trio, Peter, Paul, and Mary. Folk music was an accessible poetic interpretation of the beatnik sensibility, and I was one of the L.A. kids watching that scene closely. It wasn't long before Joan Baez and Bob Dylan became important, and then I heard the Byrds. There was the beginning of a new American style, folk-rock, merging poetry and folk sensibility with progressively electrified sound. Immersed in folk, I was nevertheless aware that a lot of my friends were now listening to the British Invasion. It was impossible for an American teenager like me to ignore the Beatles, the Stones, the Kinks, and the Yardbirds, but, as someone from Los Angeles, I could see how the Byrds and then the Doors were emerging with a sound all their own. Even back in 1965 you could hear the first efforts of Stephen Stills, David Crosby, and Neil Young, all working the early L.A. club scene.

I really liked this L.A. music, a wholly new synthesis of jazzed-

"Earthquake Warning!"
University of California, Berkeley, 1965

few Acid Tests were held down our way—our first exposure to crazy people like Ken Kesey and his Merry Prankster friends and to way-out bands like the Grateful Dead. Then several Love-In events took place, and psychedelic rock really began to take hold.

I made my own entrance into the psychedelic world out of a characteristically Southern California surfing environment. Art school occupied only half my spare time; I was mostly fascinated by surfing. In fact, I consider myself first and foremost a surfer. It's a life-style I first got involved with back around age thirteen, and for the next twenty years or more, my graphic art bore some relationship to surfing. The sport also put me in touch with Rick Griffin. We began sharing our interest in art and began trading designs and ideas, most of which had to do with surfing.

Griffin, of course, went on to invent the Murph the Surf cartoon character, which began appearing in comic-strip form in John Severson's Surfer magazine in the fall of 1960. By August 1962, Murph made the cover of Surfer, and Griffin became a regular contributor to the magazine. I joined Surfer as art editor in February 1963. I handled ten issues and left for Bill Cleary's Surf Guide in July 1964. I look back at that period as a sort of graduate art school experience, because that was when I learned almost everything there is to know about commercial printing for magazines.

By early 1964, I was surfing and lunching with an agent friend of filmmaker Bruce Brown, known worldwide for his impressive surfing documentaries. Finally I met Bruce himself, started hanging around with him and talking about some of my own work. I told him about an idea I had, a graphic involving three surfers and their surfboards on a brilliant orange beach, silhouetted against a

John Van Hamersveld
staff photo in Surfer 4, no. 2 (April-May 1963)

up, laid-back blues coupled with electrified folk. I could hear in this music some very intelligent interpretations of classic American traditions, except that it had a new bite; my development as a graphic artist had a great deal to do with it. In art school I started to meet painters and visit art galleries. I became aware that there was a separate world of visual art, but that it also tied in very neatly with the new music scene. Girls near my age were beginning to date singer-songwriters. There were people on the fringes of my scene, like writer Eve Babitz, who were being photographed with art-world celebrities attached to the Pasadena Art Museum, people like Marcel Duchamp. There was the beginning of a groupie scene—art groupies. And groupie people like Eve would be both a part of the art scene and the music scene. She began going out with Stephen Stills, and while they were dating, she'd say to him, "hey, let's go to a gallery." So there was a merging of art and rock, and this merging affected what happened to me.

A few of the art schools and galleries held some of L.A.'s first psychedelic dances at Elks Hall, over by Otis Art School. One of the area's best-known bands, Love, got their start this way; they were a homegrown version of the Rolling Stones. Early in 1966, a

T-shirts commissioned by *Surfer*. Left: Murphy character by Rick Griffin; right: surfer Kemp Alberg in the "soul arch position" by John Van Hamersveld.

John Van Hamersveld during the Pinnacle years, Los Angeles, ca. 1968

yellow sun set off against a neon pink sky. We went and set up an actual shoot, and the photo had some real possibilities.

Around this time I was again going to art school at night. In one of my classes there was a lot of discussion about day-glo, and I brought it back with me to my drafting table. It became an essential element in what I was creating, an oversize, brilliantly produced, commercially appealing surfing poster. I particularly wanted the piece to read well—to slow people down, even to stun them. It would be perfect for the high school crowd. Then, around January 1965, my poster became the key graphic promoting Bruce Brown's surfing epic, The Endless Summer. The movie followed two young American surfers around the world to beaches in Senegal, South Africa, Australia, Tahiti, Hawaii, and California. The poster sold—boy did it sell—year after year, well into the late 1960s, in excess of several hundred thousand units.

I considered going back to art school, but then a teacher friend, Pat Blackwell, told me about an opening at Capitol Records. I brought The Endless Summer poster to the interview and the job was mine. In the course of my one year at Capitol, beginning late in 1965, I worked on the Beach Boys album, Wild Honey, the Beatles' Magical Mystery Tour, handled a great many other record packages, a considerable amount of work for the trade papers, and even a few visually hip billboards.

Without question, my work on Magical Mystery Tour was a personal achievement as well as a successful graphic accomplishment for the company. The artistic vision it produced opened my eyes. It was then, late 1966, that I began seeing some of the first psychedelic dance posters exported from San Francisco. I started to get wind of what was happening in Haight-Ashbury by reading Ramparts and listening to friends. I was about twenty-five when I

Magazine ad for *The Endless Summer* documentary film. From the poster by John Van Hamersveld.

finally decided to see these things for myself, and so I boarded my very first plane and flew off north to meet up with my old Surfer friend Rick Griffin, who by now had transplanted himself from L.A. to San Francisco.

That very first day, Rick brought me by Stanley Mouse's studio (a converted turn-of-the-century firehouse) and gave me some basic orientation. Then I went off by myself, eventually over to the Golden Gate Park panhandle, where, within minutes, I ran into an old skiing buddy of mine who happened that day to be filming Ken Kesey. And standing alongside Kesey was Country Joe McDonald, just hanging out. That first day in San Francisco I felt ushered into a whole new trip.

I considered moving to San Francisco, but I didn't want to give up my job at Capitol. What San Francisco did suggest to me were the possibilities of producing dance concerts in Los Angeles. Earlier I had shared a house with two friends of mine, students at the USC Business School, and the three of us were throwing parties constantly. We began to rent another place, an old restaurant, for some of the larger parties, and these went on and on, becoming little "happenings" in themselves. It was still early in the L.A. psychedelic era, the art scene was in full force, a few of the Love-Ins had just happened. Meanwhile, our parties started to get out of hand; they were getting too large and too crazy. It was logical to think in terms of producing actual "shows," dance events patterned after those at the Fillmore and Avalon. We just decided to take our parties to a higher level, a pinnacle: Pinnacle Productions.

We met with the manager of a band called Blue Cheer—a Hells Angel named Gut (also a poster artist, as it turned out)—and then the Grateful Dead, who said yes. That was the real coup. We approached Buffalo Springfield because they were the strongest regional band on their way up, not as established (or as costly) as the Byrds. Buffalo Springfield became our first headlining act, even though the Dead battled with us over their position on the bill.

Chambers Brothers; Velvet Underground. Shrine Auditorium, Los Angeles, 1968. Artist: John Van Hamersveld

My posters for Pinnacle's first two events, "Amazing Electric Wonders" and the Hendrix show, were not thematically related. But the next three posters, headlining Jefferson Airplane, Cream, and Traffic, were stylistically and graphically linked. A key element of one found its way into the next. The "Indian" (the graphic for the Airplane show) became part of the Cream poster; and the girl in the Cream poster became part of the Traffic poster. Later on, a few of the Pinnacle posters—the "Indian" and the Jimi Hendrix piece—were picked up by Personality Posters for national distribution. That's how kids from New Jersey learned about Pinnacle concerts at the Shrine.

It proved impossible to sustain Pinnacle as a successful financial operation. After awhile my partners even began to question the usefulness of posters—after first complaining about their "illegibility," like all good promoters. By the summer of 1968 I wasn't

Grateful Dead. Shrine Exposition Hall, Los Angeles, 1968
Artist: John Van Hamersveld

I did the poster for our first show, which took place in November 1967. I titled the piece "Amazing Electric Wonders," and I think six to eight hundred copies were printed. I used some of the techniques I'd first pulled together while doing Magical Mystery Tour. The fun was in stripping all the bits of film together, creating multiple images.

Pinnacle became the focus of an entirely new hip community in L.A.; it managed to embody both an art scene and a music scene. Filmmaker George Lucas at one point was on the lightshow crew, and there were people involved in our productions who later became well-known lawyers, designers, and even world-famous conceptual artists. People found their roots while working at Pinnacle. And everybody on the scene walked through my house where we worked and lived. I mean everybody, everybody who was hip. The Velvet Underground. Jimi Hendrix. Wavy Gravy of the Hog Farm, who introduced me to Gut, the past president of the San Bernardino Hells Angels. The Jefferson Airplane hung out with us a lot. I once asked Grace Slick if she wanted to go to the movies with me. Everything was so innocent back then.

After the Dead/Blue Cheer/Buffalo Springfield show, we booked Jimi Hendrix and sat up all night counting the cash from the door. Our earnings made possible a string of shows over the next several months; that's how we were able to introduce some of the best English acts, like Cream and Traffic. All of these shows were accompanied by poster art.

Pinnacle Concert Calendar. Los Angeles; 1968
Artist: John Van Hamersveld

Portion of John Van Hamersveld's mural for the 1984 Summer Olympics, Los Angeles

even doing all the poster work. We farmed out some fine things to people like Rick Griffin, Victor Moscoso, Bob Schnepf, and Neon Park.

Pinnacle went bankrupt. Sep Donahower reformed it under a new name, Pacific Presentations; then, during the 1970s, it became Avalon Attractions, which it remains today.

The first to go during the reorganization process was the light-show, and then the posters—or at least the highly imaginative, oversize ones. People who had hung around our house during the original days of Pinnacle became assistants in the new production company, and my girlfriend at the time, Honeya, started making the posters: rudimentary typographic efforts—lots of line shots and Letraset, usually just using promo stills of the bands provided by the record companies.

It was a far cry from a few years before, when the Pinnacle posters really were a new art form. Then it had been possible to create great sensations of depth, as if you could actually walk into the pieces. I thought that was particularly true of my Traffic poster. It was such a hallucination—so spatial, so unreadable. I think that had to do with my visual process. I'm a left-hander, and I have this right hemisphere thing going on, and I think the combination of the two gives me tremendous depth perception. And my smoking grass at the time triggered even more of those innate sensations—I had all kinds of dimensional feelings, and I used to play with them all the time. When I drew, I was always trying to make things overlap and create internal spatial relationships. I liked giving my art a sort of internal distance. I think I communicated a lot of my feelings to Rick Griffin and Victor Moscoso, because they were playing with the same relationships in their own heads.

We used to draw together. Just hang out and draw, both in L.A. and in San Francisco. We'd draw over at my house, we'd draw in front of Griffin, then in front of each other. Then we'd draw together as one body. And there was a lot of other cross-pollinization besides—like R. Crumb, who drew the first ZAP comic, showing up one day at Victor's. And that was the day the two of them—both New Yorkers—decided they were going to continue doing underground comics, which led to the whole ZAP line.

My work at Pinnacle and at Capitol set me up with a reputation, and I went on to do more than three hundred album covers, working for all the record companies and for all the major bands. I've handled videos, t-shirts, advertising and campaign graphics, restaurant interiors, complete magazine designs, and even an Olympic mural, a 365-foot piece that hung alongside the Los Angeles Coliseum.

But I still see the Pinnacle posters around. I was up at UCLA, in their architectural school, on the second floor, and I came around to this one little room, happened to see the door open, and there was one of the "Indian" posters staring me in the face. It had been hanging in that room for almost seventeen years. I think it might have had the original push pins in place.

Woodstock and Others

Woodstock (August 15–17, 1969), the most talked-about festival in the history of rock music, attracted more than 400,000 people. The original plan had been to hold the festival in Wallkill, New York, but just four weeks before the event, the zoning board banned the concert. David Byrd, known for his Fillmore East work, had already created a poster (3.2). It gave very little information—nothing about who would be performing or where to buy tickets—and was probably intended as an eventual souvenir.

The forced relocation of the festival called for a new poster, fast. Arnold Skolnick's piece has since come to represent all that was positive about Woodstock (3.1). Unlike Byrd's effort, it listed the performers and drew attention to the planned

(continued on p. 258)

3.1
Final Woodstock Poster
Max Yasgur Farm, Bethel, New York, 1969
Artist: Arnold Skolnick

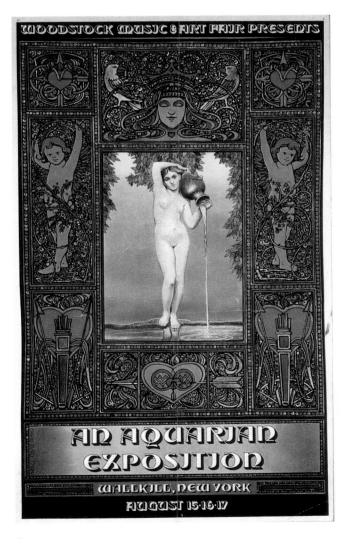

3.2
Original Woodstock Poster
Wallkill, New York, 1969
Artist: David Byrd

3.3
Backstage pass: Rolling Stones
Altamont Speedway, Livermore,
California, 1969

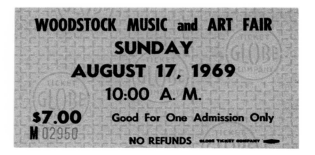

3.4
Ticket: Woodstock
Max Yasgur Farm, Bethel, New York, 1969

3.5

Monterey Pop Festival
Fairgrounds, Monterey, 1967
Artist: Tom Wilkes

3.6

First Seattle Pops Festival
Goldcreek Park, Woodinville, Washington, 1969
Artist: John Moehring

(continued from p. 257)
art show, crafts bazaar, campground, and food and drink concessions. It specifically gave ticket-purchasing information—ultimately superfluous, since Woodstock became a "free" festival the weekend it was held. Skolnick's poster actually was produced in several variations, since more performers were announced as Woodstock weekend drew closer.

The Monterey International Pop Festival (June 16–18, 1967) set off "festival fever" in the late 1960s (3.5). The poster came in large and small sizes, and the limited-edition large size is highly prized.

In stark contrast to the happy images evoked by Monterey Pop and Woodstock, Altamont calls up dark memories of violence—even death—and bad drugs. An impromptu production, Altamont generated no commemorative poster. Only one piece of "art" associated with it has come to light: a crude official backstage pass (3.3).

1967–70 saw many successful rock festivals, including one at West Palm Beach, Florida, December 1969 (3.7).

3.8

Sky River Rock Festival II
Black Culture Center, Tenino, Washington, 1969
Photographer: Ben Spicer

3.7

First Palm Beach Music and Art Festival
West Palm Beach, Florida, 1969
Artist: Royce Emley

Napa, Davis, and Sacramento

These cities of California's Upper Central Valley took a back seat to the Bay Area, but they did harbor clubs hosting rock music, most notably Sacramento's Sound Factory. The majority of the big concerts were held in civic auditoriums.

The University of California at Davis deserves special mention for consistently presenting the best of the up and coming bands as far back as the late 1960s (3.11, 3.17). Napa's citizens were less tolerant of the Dream Bowl events held there (3.20): one evening, Country Joe McDonald was assaulted onstage, a victim of conservative attitudes outside the Bay Area.

3.10
Cream; Grateful Dead
Memorial Auditorium, Sacramento, 1968
Artist: Art Print

3.9
H. P. Lovecraft; Kaleidoscope
Sound Factory, Sacramento, 1968
Artist: L. J. Pennington

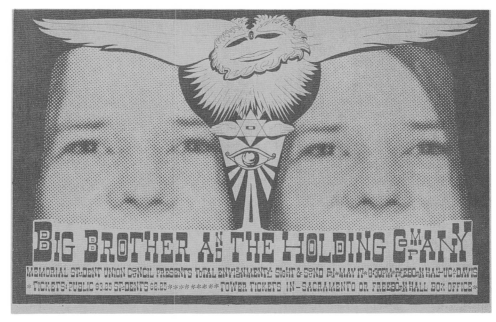

3.11
Big Brother and the Holding Company
University of California, Davis, 1968

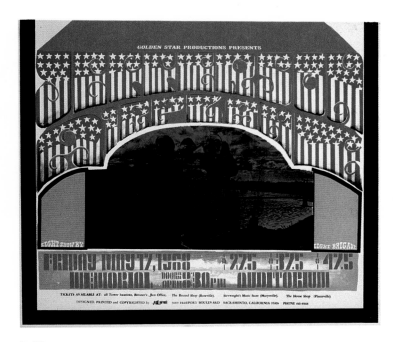

3.12
Jefferson Airplane
Memorial Auditorium, Sacramento, 1968
Artist: Art Print

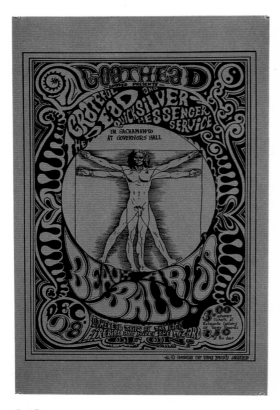

3.13
Beaux Arts Ball (version 1)
Governor's Hall, Sacramento, 1966
Artist: Yagé Firebird

3.14
Beaux Arts Ball (version 2)
Governor's Hall, Sacramento, 1966

3.15
Spirit; Pyewacket
Sound Factory, Sacramento, 1968
Artist: San Andreas Fault

3.16
Jimi Hendrix Experience; The Creators
Sacramento State College, Sacramento, 1968
Artists: Jim Ford, Steve Murphy/Art and Print

3.17
Jefferson Airplane; Steve Miller
University of California, Davis, ca. 1967
Artist: Tom Morris

3.18
Big Brother and the Holding Company
Sacramento State College, Sacramento, 1968
Artists: Jim Ford, Steve Murphy/Art and Print

3.19
Pink Floyd; A. B. Skhy
Sound Factory, Sacramento, 1968
Artist: San Andreas Fault

(left) **3.20**
Opening
New Dream Bowl, Napa, 1967
Artist: Wes Wilson

3.21
The Doors
Memorial Auditorium, Sacramento, 1968
Artist: Sam Sadofsky

Central Valley and Sierras

The Central Valley extends south from Sacramento to the desert areas inland from Los Angeles. Rock music has made an impact throughout this region, particularly in Stockton, Modesto, Fresno, and San Bernardino.

Just east of the Central Valley is the Sierra-Nevada mountain range, and atop the Sierras, Lake Tahoe. Although it is a famous resort, Tahoe is remembered only for a few appearances by the Grateful Dead and Boz Scaggs, among others. Tahoe and the neighboring Reno, Nevada, gambling casinos now host rock and pop acts aptly described as middle-of-the-road.

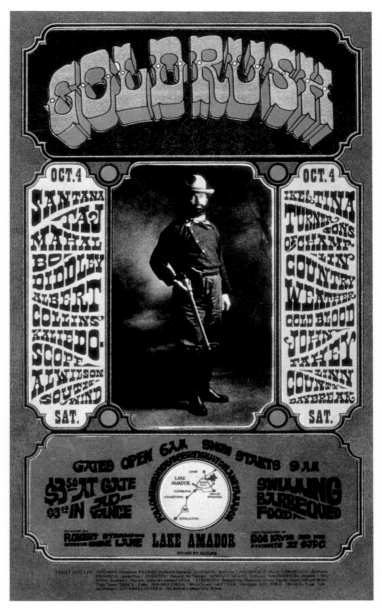

3.23
Goldrush
Lake Amador, 1969
Artist: Tom Morris

3.22
Big Brother and the Holding Company; New Breed
Civic Auditorium, Stockton, 1967
Artist: Stanley Mouse

3.24
Spirit and Time; The Hook
Swing Auditorium, San Bernadino, 1969
Artist: San Andreas Fault

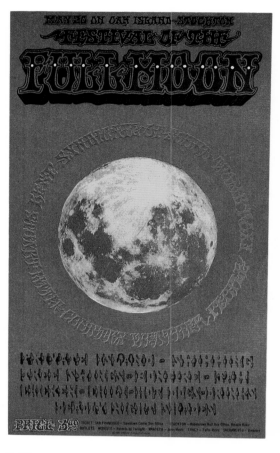

3.25

Festival of the Full Moon
Oak Island, Stockton, 1969
Artist: Carson-Morris Studios

3.26

Country Weather; Elastik Band
California Ballroom, Modesto, ca. 1968
Artist: Tom Morris

3.27

Grateful Dead; Country Joe and the Fish
Selland Arena, Fresno, 1968
Artist: Cheryl Rankin

3.28

Spirit; Peter and His Group
American Legion Hall, Truckee, California, 1967
Artist: Pascual

3.29

Grateful Dead; Morning Glory
Kings Beach Bowl, Lake Tahoe, 1968
Artist: Bob Fried

3.30

Big Brother and the Holding Company; Mint Tattoo
Selland Arena, Fresno, California, 1968

Northern California Coast

The coastline extending south from San Francisco is renowned for its beauty, and its larger towns have hosted rock music through the years. Santa Cruz is remembered as a laid-back center of hippie activity and the site of many outdoor events. Monterey, a popular tourist center, has an excellent fairgrounds site that has for decades featured jazz and folk music, as well as significant rock concerts, among them the 1966 appearance of Big Brother and the Holding Company (3.33) (one of their very first excursions out of San Francisco), and the historic Pop Festival of 1967 (3.5).

3.31

Moby Grape; Fields
Monterey Fairgrounds,
Monterey, 1969
Artist: Kelly Steels

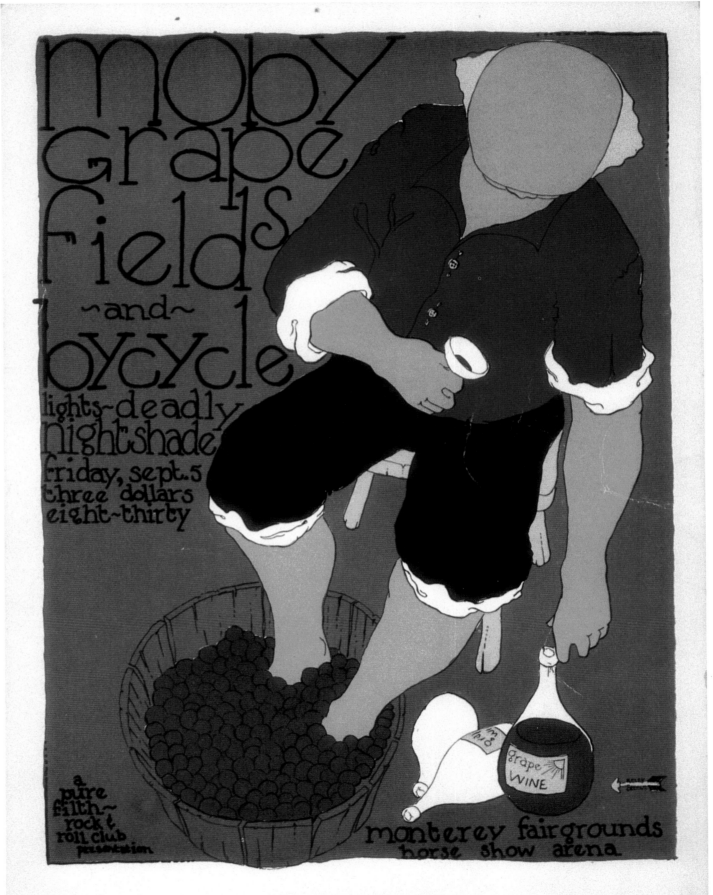

3.32
Magic Music
Cabrillo College, Santa Cruz, 1967

3.33
Big Brother and the Holding Company;
Quicksilver Messenger Service
Monterey Fairgrounds, Monterey, 1966

3.34
West Coast Love In and Watermelon Feed
Private Beach, Santa Cruz, 1968

3.35
Vernal Equinox Festival
Lime Kiln Creek, Big Sur, 1968
Artists: Kent Robertson, Cummings Walker

3.36
Jefferson Airplane
California Polytechnic State University
San Luis Obispo, 1967

Santa Barbara

The beach-front city of Santa Barbara has been the site of rock concerts since the late 1960s—partly because one of the campuses of the University of California is situated there and also because of the year-round sunny climate. Some of the most important shows, circa 1968, were presented by promoter Jim Salzer, often working in association with radio station KACY. Other events were organized by the University of California (Santa Barbara) Associated Students production board.

Los Angeles groups, including the Doors, the Byrds, and Buffalo Springfield; San Francisco groups like Jefferson Airplane, Grateful Dead, and Big Brother and the Holding Company; and such British groups as Traffic, Led Zeppelin, and Blind Faith, made Santa Barbara part of their touring schedule year after year. More recently, the Grateful Dead has staged outstanding mid-afternoon outdoor dances there.

3.37
Chambers Brothers; Steve Miller
Earl Warren Showgrounds, Santa Barbara, 1967

3.38
The Doors; Lavender Hill Mob
Earl Warren Showgrounds, Santa Barbara, 1967
Artist: R. Tolmach

3.39

Buffalo Springfield; Watts 103rd Street Band
Earl Warren Showgrounds, Santa Barbara, ca. 1968
Artist: R. Tolmach

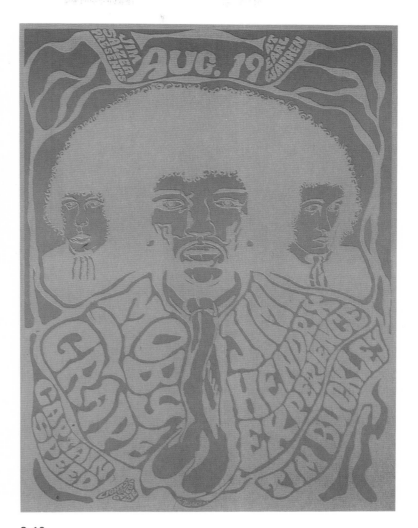

3.40

Jimi Hendrix; Moby Grape
Earl Warren Showgrounds, Santa Barbara, 1967
Artist: R. Tolmach

3.41

Led Zeppelin; Jethro Tull
Earl Warren Showgrounds, Santa Barbara, 1969
Artist: Frank Bettencourt

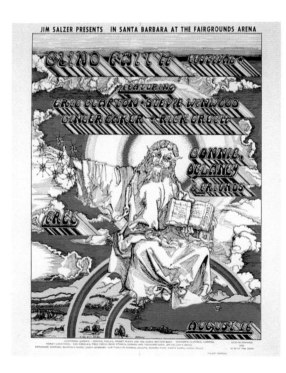

3.42

Blind Faith; Delaney and Bonnie
Earl Warren Showgrounds, Santa Barbara, 1969
Artist: Frank Bettencourt

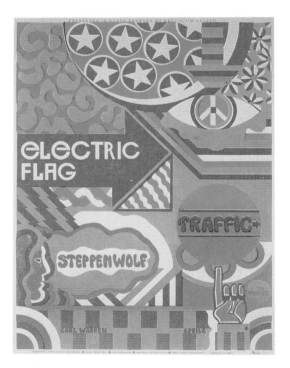

3.43

Electric Flag; Traffic
Earl Warren Showgrounds, Santa Barbara, 1968

3.44
Electric Flag; Cream
University of California, Santa Barbara, 1968
Artist: Chuck Miller

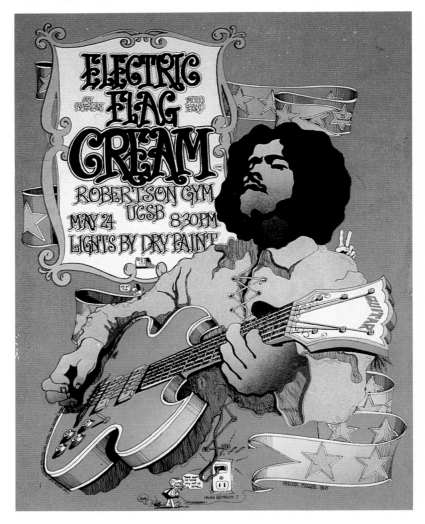

(above) **3.45**

Jefferson Airplane
Earl Warren Showgrounds, Santa Barbara, ca. 1968
Artist: R. Tolmach

(far left) **3.46**

Grateful Dead; The Doors
Earl Warren Showgrounds, Santa Barbara, 1967
Artist: J. Cushing

(left) **3.47**

Youngbloods; Canned Heat
Earl Warren Showgrounds, Santa Barbara, 1967
Artist: Frank Bettencourt

Los Angeles Area

Although San Francisco grabbed most of the headlines in the early psychedelic era, a great deal happened in Los Angeles and Southern California during 1965–70. Following the surfing movement, epitomized by groups like the Beach Boys, the Tornadoes, Jan and Dean, and the Ventures, the Byrds were hailed as the first real American challenge to the British Invasion. The Byrds' lyrical folk-rock was echoed and further developed by Buffalo Springfield, which itself yielded the first American "supergroup," Crosby, Stills, Nash (and Young). The most influential of the Los Angeles-based groups was the Doors, led by singer Jim Morrison.

Los Angeles boasted a vibrant club scene during the late '60s and early '70s. Places like the Troubador and the Whisky are now legendary venues, but larger halls, in particular the Shrine Auditorium, were also crucial. But except for art associated with the Pinnacle Production Company, only a handful of poster artists developed a presence on the Los Angeles scene.

3.48

Paul Butterfield Blues Band; Grateful Dead
Rose Palace, Pasadena, 1969

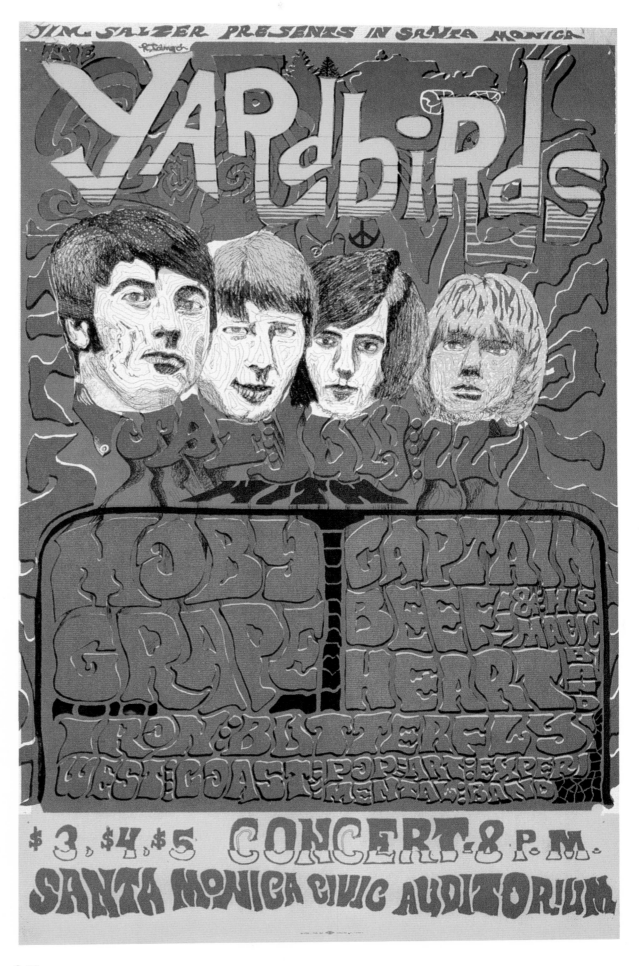

3.49

Yardbirds; Moby Grape
Civic Auditorium, Santa Monica, 1967
Artist: R. Tolmach

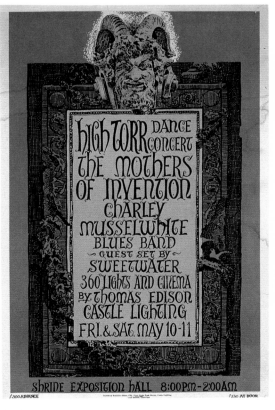

3.50

Mothers of Invention; Charlie Musselwhite
Shrine Auditorium, Los Angeles, 1968
Artist: R. L. Ramirez

3.51

Nomads; The Zoo
Zap Palace, Los Angeles, 1967
Artist: John Chamberlin

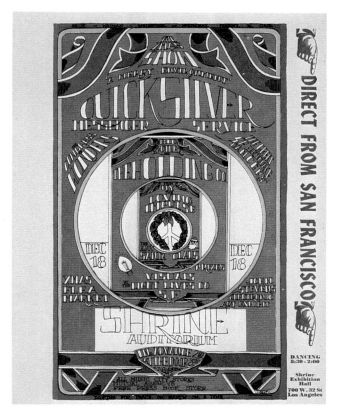

3.52

The Xmas Show
Shrine Auditorium, Los Angeles, 1967
Artist: Gut

3.54

Country Joe and the Fish; Grateful Dead
Shrine Auditorium, Los Angeles, 1968

3.53

Love-In
Elysian Park, Los Angeles, 1967
Artist: Gary Grimshaw

3.55
Mothers of Invention; Little Gary Ferguson
Shrine Exposition Hall, Los Angeles, 1966

3.56
Andy Warhol Presents the Plastic Inevitable Show
The Trip, Los Angeles, 1966

3.57
Turkey Blimp
Lynch Building, Santa Monica, 1966
Artist: Peter Leaf

3.58
Love; Sons of Adam
Whisky a Go-Go, Los Angeles, 1966
Artist: John H. Myers

3.59
Eric Burdon and the Animals
Whisky a Go-Go, Los Angeles, ca. 1968
Artist: armando

3.60

Led Zeppelin; Julie Driscoll and Brian Auger
Rose Palace, Pasadena, 1969

3.61

First Annual Newport Pop Festival
Orange County Fairgrounds, Costa Mesa, 1968

3.62

First Annual KTBT Freak Fair
International Raceway, Orange County, California, 1969
Artist: Lombard

3.63

Buffalo Springfield; The Seeds
Cheetah, Venice, 1967
Artist: Eugene Hawkins

ORANGE GROOVE

Since his death in 1975, Bob Fried has come to be regarded as among the most significant San Francisco-based artists. One of his most imaginative posters is known as "Orange Groove" (3.64), promoting a 1967 event at the Orange County Fairgrounds just south of Los Angeles. Like so many of Fried's best concert pieces, it was technically superior, reflecting his considerable art-school training.

3.64
Orange Groove
Orange County
Fairgrounds,
Costa Mesa, 1967
Artist: Bob Fried

RICK GRIFFIN

Although Griffin is deemed primarily a San Francisco poster artist, he began his career in Los Angeles, drawing highly amusing cartoons for *Surfer* magazine in the early 1960s—most notably creating the ''Murph the Surf'' series, a landmark in its time. Even after he moved to San Francisco in 1966, he periodically returned to execute commissions in Los Angeles.

Griffin's art is often characterized by insectlike imagery, used to great effect on a 1969 poster promoting the Who in concert at the Hollywood Palladium (3.65).

3.65

The Who; Poco
Hollywood Palladium,
Hollywood, 1969
Artist: Rick Griffin

PINNACLE CONCERTS / JOHN VAN HAMERSVELD

Los Angeles artist John Van Hamersveld was one of the people who helped establish the Southern California psychedelic community. He used his extensive art school education to great effect in posters for the Pinnacle Production Company, of which he was a founding partner.

Like Rick Griffin, Van Hamersveld was a major graphic artist of the early 1960s surfing movement. And as Griffin was hailed for the "Murph the Surf" cartoon character, Van Hamersveld gained renown for the emblematic poster heralding *The Endless Summer*, the definitive surfing movie.

The Pinnacle concert production company was the first hip organization to put on memorable rock concerts and dances in Los Angeles, primarily at the Shrine Auditorium. The posters Van Hamersveld designed for the first several Pinnacle events are now legendary works, prized for their bold graphics. His first, "Amazing Electric Wonders," advertised a 1967 Shrine concert by the Buffalo Springfield, Grateful Dead, and Blue Cheer (3.74). His next piece, known as "Indian," was for a 1968 Jefferson Airplane show and is the most widely circulated of all Van Hamersveld's posters (3.66). The artist used elements from his *(continued on p. 278)*

3.66

Jefferson Airplane; Charlie Musselwhite
Shrine Auditorium, Los Angeles, 1968
Artist: John Van Hamersveld

3.67

Traffic; Quicksilver Messenger Service
Shrine Auditorium, Los Angeles, 1968
Artist: John Van Hamersveld

3.68

Jimi Hendrix Experience
Shrine Auditorium, Los Angeles, 1968
Artist: Rick Griffin

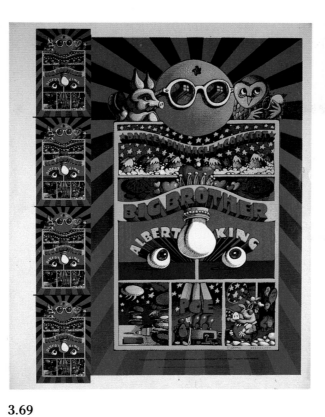

3.69

Uncut proof: Big Brother and the Holding Company
Shrine Auditorium, Los Angeles, 1968
Artists: Rick Griffin, Victor Moscoso

3.70

Butterfield Blues Band;
Sly and the Family Stone
Shrine Auditorium,
Los Angeles, 1968
Artist: Neon Park

3.71

An American Music Show
Rose Bowl, Pasadena, 1968
Artists: John Van Hamersveld,
Bob Schnepf

3.72

Jimi Hendrix; Electric Flag
Shrine Auditorium, Los Angeles, 1968
Artist: John Van Hamersveld

3.73

Cream; James Cotton
Shrine Auditorium, Los Angeles, 1968
Artist: John Van Hamersveld

(continued from p. 275)
"Indian" in his next poster, promoting the Cream's appearance at the Shrine (3.73), and then used elements of *that* poster in another, promoting Traffic (3.67). Both the "Indian" piece and his earlier Jimi Hendrix poster (3.72) were later distributed nationwide and were among the most consistently requested posters in their day.

By late 1968 other San Francisco artists, including Rick Griffin, Victor Moscoso, Bob Fried, and Bob Schnepf, contributed Pinnacle posters. Van Hamersveld went on to execute more than 300 album covers and, more recently, designed a giant outdoor mural for the Los Angeles summer Olympic games (1984); he is a major influence on Southern California commercial art.

3.74

Amazing Electric Wonders
Shrine Exposition Hall, Los Angeles, 1967
Artist: John Van Hamersveld

3.75

The Who; Fleetwood Mac
Shrine Auditorium, Los Angeles, 1968
Artist: Victor Moscoso

3.76

Pink Floyd; Blue Cheer
Shrine Auditorium, Los Angeles, 1968
Artists: John Van Hamersveld, Bob Fried

KALEIDOSCOPE

The series promoting musical events at the Los Angeles Kaleidoscope is thought to be the only complete poster run produced in the round. The individual designs vary in strength and imagination, but the series as a whole is most striking.

The Kaleidoscope was a state-of-the art venue, originally the site of the 1950s TV show "Queen for a Day." Like many top clubs emulating San Francisco, it featured a house-run lightshow.

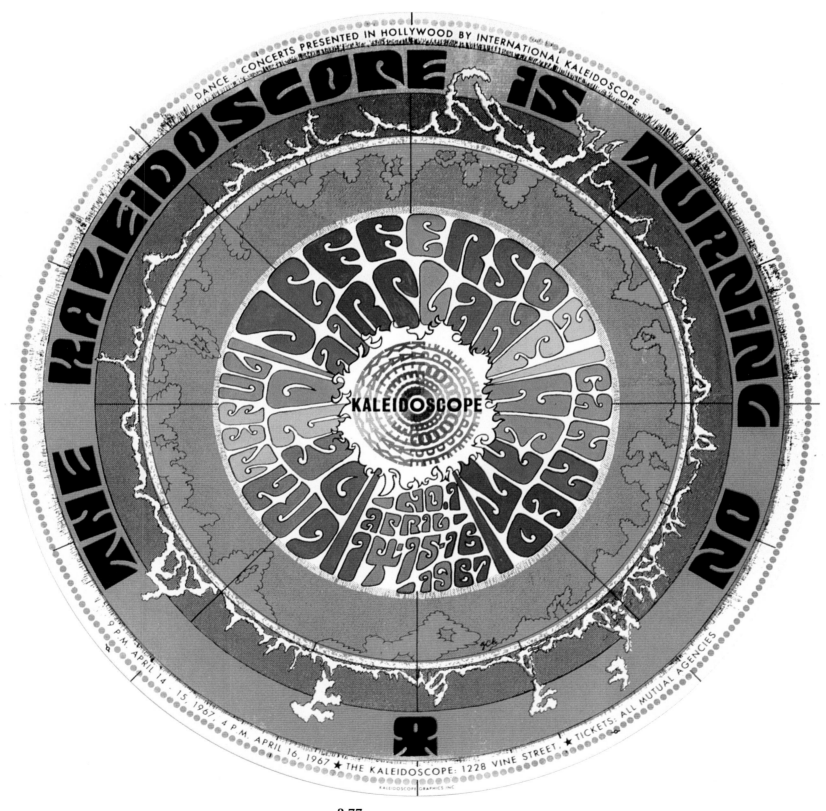

3.77

Jefferson Airplane; Grateful Dead
Kaleidoscope, Hollywood, 1967
Artist: Kaleidoscope Graphics

3.78

Moby Grape; Mt. Rushmore
Kaleidoscope, Hollywood, 1968
Artist: Mortimer

3.79

Jefferson Airplane; Buffalo Springfield
Kaleidoscope, Hollywood, 1968
Artist: Dahlgren

3.80

Independence Day Spectacular
Kaleidoscope, Hollywood, 1968
Artist: Lanning Stern

3.81

Them; Incredible String Band
Kaleidoscope, Hollywood, 1968

3.82
Easter Show
Kaleidoscope, Hollywood, 1968
Artist: Dahlgren

3.83
First Anniversary
Kaleidoscope, Hollywood, 1968
Artist: Dahlgren

3.84
Bo Diddley; Peanut Butter Conspiracy
Kaleidoscope, Hollywood, 1968
Artist: Dahlgren

3.85
Canned Heat; Sly and the Family Stone
Kaleidoscope, Hollywood, 1967
Artist: Farmer

THE BANK

Among the more obscure Los Angeles venues was The Bank, located in Torrance. The series of posters and handbills that have recently surfaced associated with the club demonstrate that top groups did play The Bank, but, like many clubs in the late 1960s, it suffered from police harassment. At one point, The Bank appealed to its patrons, asking them to "come clean, be safe, and be happy" and protest the club's imminent closing (3.92).

3.87

John Mayall; Chicago Transit Authority
The Bank, Torrance, California, 1968

3.86

Moby Grape; FairBeFall
The Bank, Torrance, California, 1968

3.88

Canned Heat; Harvey Mandel
The Bank, Torrance, California, 1968

3.89

Quicksilver Messenger Service; Sons of Champlin
The Bank, Torrance, California, 1968

3.90

Fugs; Mt. Rushmore
The Bank, Torrance, California, 1968

3.91

Grateful Dead; Cleveland Wrecking Company
The Bank, Torrance, California, 1968

3.92

Grateful Dead; Magic Sam
The Bank, Torrance, California, 1968

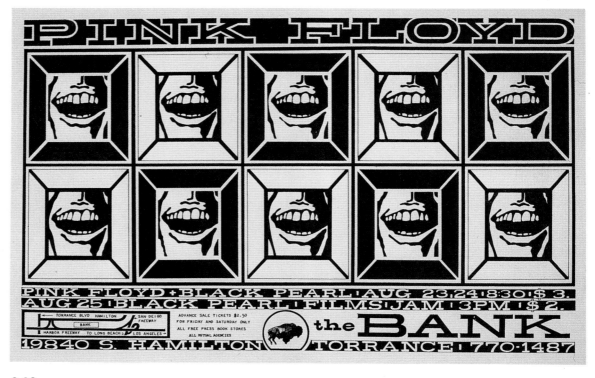

3.93

Pink Floyd; Black Pearl
The Bank, Torrance, California, 1968

San Diego

San Diego is the nucleus of the third largest metropolitan area in California, but it seems to operate in the shadow of Los Angeles to the north, in much the same way as San Jose bows to San Francisco. Like San Jose, San Diego did not develop its own musical style, but as in all California's large cities, there were a number of successful venues—particularly the Community Concourse and the Hippodrome—regularly visited by the top bands. Other events were produced in association with San Diego State University.

The Hippodrome was a communally run dance hall managed by Trans Love Airwaves Productions and, in spirit, modeled on the Avalon Ballroom in San Francisco. Its poster artist was Rebecca Galdeano, a transplanted San Fransciscan, who brought with her that city's psychedelic style.

3.94

Buffalo Springfield; Electric Flag
Community Concourse, San Diego,
1968
Artist: Don Kay

3.95

The Byrds; Brain Police
Community Concourse, San Diego, 1968
Artist: Don Kay

3.96

Palm Springs Pop Festival
Palm Springs, California, ca. 1968

3.97

Grateful Dead; Quicksilver Messenger Service
Del Mar Fairgrounds, San Diego, 1968

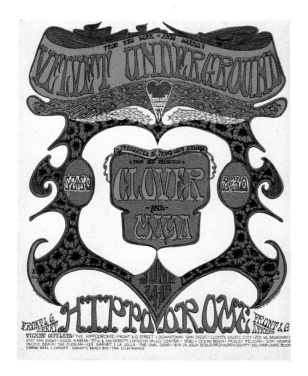

3.98

Velvet Underground; Clover
Hippodrome, San Diego, 1968
Artist: Rebecca Galdeano

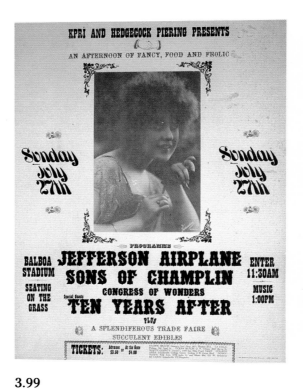

3.99

Jefferson Airplane; Ten Years After
Balboa Stadium, San Diego, 1969

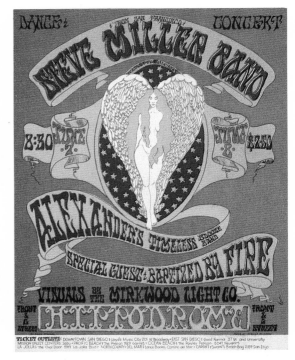

3.100

Steve Miller; Alexander's Timeless Blooze Band
Hippodrome, San Diego, 1968
Artist: Rebecca Galdeano

3.101

Grateful Dead; Curly Cooke's Hurdy Gurdy Band
Hippodrome, San Diego, 1968

3.102

Canned Heat; Grateful Dead
San Diego State University, San Diego, 1969

Pacific Northwest

The Grateful Dead was the California band that created the most lasting presence in this region, partly because their early compatriots, Ken Kesey and the Merry Pranksters, settled in the Eugene, Oregon, area and also because many of the Dead's crewmembers had come from Oregon.

The Dead's "Great Northwest Tour" (with the Quicksilver Messenger Service) took place in the winter of 1968. The distinctive, gothic-style posters and handbills announcing appearances in places like Seattle's Eagles Auditorium and Portland's Crystal Ballroom—where the Family Dog briefly established a Northwest operation—were the work of George Hunter, leader of the Charlatans. Each piece was made to look like a scuffed-up Wild West wanted poster. One stack of the posters was deliberately attacked with a blowtorch to create ragged, burned edges. This variant is among the most prized of all Grateful Dead posters.

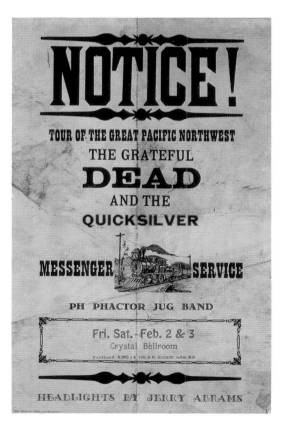

3.103
Handbill: Tour of the Great Pacific Northwest
Crystal Ballroom, Portland, Oregon, 1968
Artist: George Hunter

3.104
Tour of the Great Pacific Northwest
Eagles Auditorium, Seattle, 1968
Artist: George Hunter

3.106

Jethro Tull; MC 5
Eagles Auditorium, Seattle, 1969
Artist: John Moehring

3.105

Sky River Rock Festival II
Black Cultural Center, Tenino, Washington, 1969
Artist: J. Wood

3.107

Happy New Year
Seattle Ballroom, Seattle, ca. 1968

3.108

Piano Drop
Duvall, Washington, 1968
Artist: Shazam Society/Paul Heald

3.109

Jefferson Airplane; Byrds
Memorial Coliseum, Portland, Oregon, 1967

3.110

Grateful Dead; New Riders of the Purple Sage
Aqua Theater, Seattle, 1969
Artist: Porky Jake

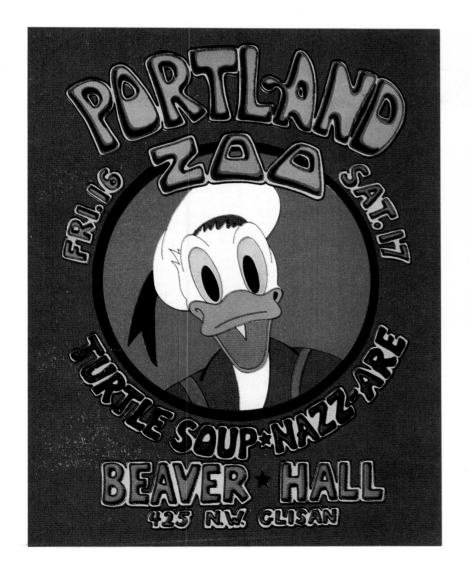

3.112

Magical Mystery Tour Film Showing
Beaver Hall, Portland, Oregon, 1969
Artist: Alton Kelley

3.111

Portland Zoo; Turtle Soup
Beaver Hall, Portland, Oregon, ca. 1968
Artist: Alton Kelley

Hawaii

The islands hosted fewer rock tours than did California or the Pacific Northwest, but Hawaiian events did unintentionally produce two of the most collectible Rick Griffin concert posters.

The 1969 Country Joe and the Fish poster (3.114), based on Griffin's renowned "Murph the Surf" cartoon character, is regarded as the rarest Griffin piece of all. Almost equally impossible to obtain is the original, large format version of the Grateful Dead/It's a Beautiful Day poster, executed for a 1969 concert in Honolulu. Why so scarce? The show was canceled, and the printer was unpaid; very few posters were released. But an even holier grail for collectors is the uncut proof of this poster (3.113). The piece is known as Griffin's "Hawaiian Aoxomoxoa" because of its resemblance to his Grateful Dead piece executed for the Soundproof show at the Avalon Ballroom earlier that year (2.39).

Several years after "Hawaiian Aoxomoxoa" was "buried," Griffin authorized the reissue of this design in a smaller format (3.116).

3.113

Uncut progressive proof: Grateful Dead
Honolulu International Center, Honolulu, 1969
Artist: Rick Griffin

3.114

Country Joe and the Fish; H. P. Lovecraft
Old Civic Auditorium, Honolulu, ca. 1969
Artist: Rick Griffin

3.115

Blue Cheer; The Wedge
Civic Auditorium, Honolulu, 1968
Artist: Hero Studios

3.116

Later Reprint: Grateful Dead,
It's a Beautiful Day
Honolulu International Center,
Honolulu, 1969
Artist: Rick Griffin

Texas

The link between San Francisco and the Lone Star State is surprisingly strong: Chet Helms, who became the head of Family Dog, and Janis Joplin, lead singer for Big Brother and the Holding Company, were among Texans who figured prominently in the West Coast psychedelic scene.

The local hotbed of psychedelic rock was the University of Texas at Austin. A group of students began a cooperative venture that resulted in Austin's Vulcan Gas Company, the state's first psychedelic dance hall. Texas groups played the Vulcan, but touring bands, including New York's Fugs and Velvet Underground, were—somehow—booked as well.

The Vulcan commissioned several posters from Gilbert Shelton, who was later among the artists responsible for the underground comix explosion (3.118, 3.119, 3.124).

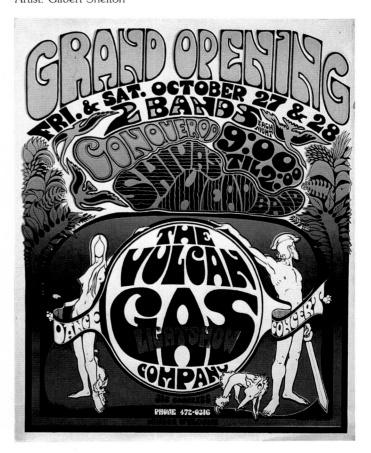

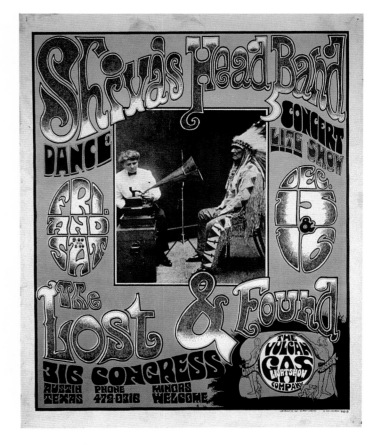

3.117

Uncut proof: Jefferson Airplane, Zachery Thaks
Municipal Auditorium, San Antonio, Texas, ca. 1968
Artist: Joe Moist

3.119

Shiva's Head Band; Lost & Found
Vulcan Gas Company, Austin, 1967
Artist: Gilbert Shelton

3.120

Mother Earth; Shiva's Head Band
Vulcan Gas Company, Austin, 1969
Artist: Jim Franklin

3.121

Muddy Waters
Vulcan Gas Company,
Austin, 1968

3.122

Joe Williams; Sky Blues
Vulcan Gas Company, Austin, 1968
Artist: Jim Franklin

3.123

Austin Love In
Zilker Park Bandstand, Austin, ca. 1968

3.124

13th Floor Elevator; Shiva's Head Band
Vulcan Gas Company, Austin, 1967
Artist: Gilbert Shelton

3.125

Fugs; Shiva's Head Band
Vulcan Gas Company, Austin, 1969
Artist: Jim Franklin

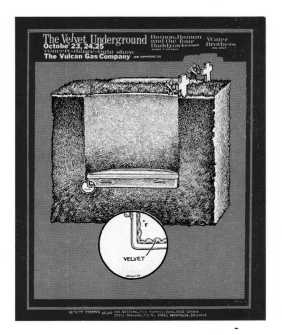

3.126

Velvet Underground; Ramon, Ramon and
the Four Daddyos. Vulcan Gas Company,
Austin, 1969. Artist: Jim Franklin

Chicago

Although Chicago appears to have developed little distinctive show poster art during the psychedelic period, the city did boast several notable dance halls, including the Kinetic Playground (better known to Chicagoans as the Electric Theater) and the Aragon Ballroom. Chicago is renowned as the home of the urban blues, but it also showcased all the rock music touring nationally.

Much of the Kinetic Playground's concert art was created by Mark Behrens (3.127–29), a Minnesota native who later moved to San Francisco and designed the Matrix's last posters and handbills along with art for Marin County's Pepperland.

3.127
May–June Calendar
Kinetic Playground, Chicago, 1969
Artist: Mark T. Behrens

3.128

January–March Calendar
Kinetic Playground, Chicago, 1969
Artist: Mark T. Behrens

3.130

SDS Concert: Grateful Dead; George Stavis
Purdue University, Lafayette, Indiana, 1969

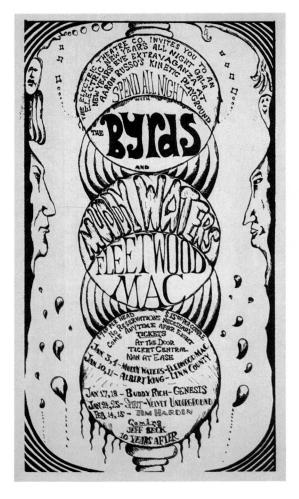

3.129

The Byrds; Muddy Waters
Kinetic Playground, Chicago, ca. 1969
Artist: Mark T. Behrens

Detroit

GARY GRIMSHAW

Except for Los Angeles, Detroit is the only city that rivaled San Francisco in poster design during the psychedelic years. Certainly the most significant Detroit artist was Gary Grimshaw, whose graphics helped establish rock music in his hometown. His work for the Grande Ballroom, Detroit's great rock dance hall, bears some resemblance to San Francisco art of the period—particularly in the lettering—but Grimshaw was not directly influenced by any single San Francisco poster artist. Few people outside of San Francisco have taken so thoroughly individualistic an approach to psychedelic art.

Many of Grimshaw's pieces appeared only as handbills because the Grande Ballroom's budget generally didn't allow for full-size posters. A complete set of Grande pieces, comprising posters as well as handbills, has recently achieved high value among collectors.

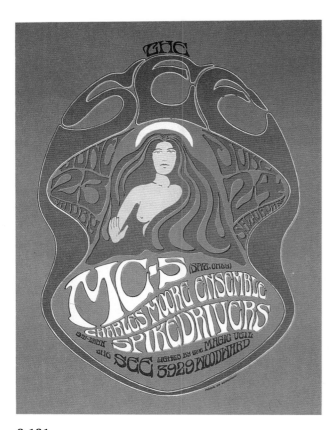

3.131
MC5; Spikedrivers
See Theater, Detroit, 1967
Artist: Gary Grimshaw

3.132
Cream; MC5
Grande Ballroom, Detroit, 1967
Artist: Gary Grimshaw

3.133

Mind-Zap
Grande Ballroom, Detroit, 1967
Artist: Gary Grimshaw

3.134

Sun Ra; MC5
Wayne State University, Detroit, 1967
Artist: Gary Grimshaw

3.135

MC5; Chosen Few
Grande Ballroom, Detroit, 1966
Artist: Gary Grimshaw

3.136

Eric Burdon and the Animals; Grateful Dead
Grande Ballroom, Detroit, 1968
Artist: Gary Grimshaw

3.137

Paupers; MC5
Grande Ballroom, Detroit, 1967
Artist: Gary Grimshaw

3.138

First Annual Detroit Rock & Roll Revival
Michigan State Fairgrounds, Detroit, 1969
Artist: Gary Grimshaw

3.139

Jimi Hendrix Experience; Soft Machine
Masonic Temple, Detroit, 1968
Artist: Gary Grimshaw

Chambers Brothers; MC5
Grande Ballroom, Detroit, 1967
Artist: Gary Grimshaw

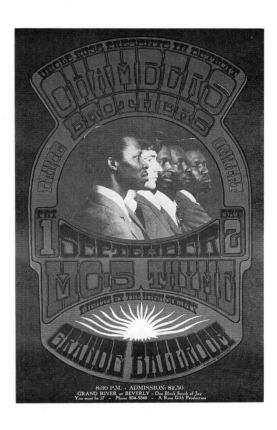

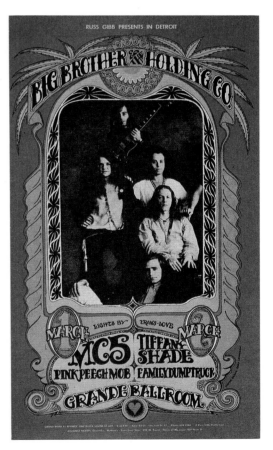

3.141

Big Brother and the Holding Company; MC5
Grande Ballroom, Detroit, 1968
Artist: Gary Grimshaw

3.142

Fugs; MC5
Grande Ballroom, Detroit, 1967
Artist: Gary Grimshaw

3.143

Southbound Freeway; Cowardly Thangs
Grande Ballroom, Detroit, 1967

3.144

The Pack; MC5
Grande Ballroom, Detroit, 1967
Artist: Gary Grimshaw

CARL LUNDGREN

Midway through 1968, Gary Grimshaw was joined in his work for the Grande Ballroom by Carl Lundgren. As Grimshaw became increasingly involved in political activity, through his association with local activist John Sinclair and the Detroit rock band called the MC5, he handed assignments over to Lundgren. Finally, Grimshaw was driven underground by the authorities, and Lundgren assumed responsibility for the Grande's weekly handbills.

His style was more florid than Grimshaw's but just as elegantly rendered, so that his work also holds up very well against the best efforts out of San Francisco.

3.145
James Cotton; MC5
Grande Ballroom, Detroit, 1967
Artist: Carl Lundgren. Photographer: V. Skreb

3.146
Canned Heat; Hamilton Face
Grande Ballroom, Detroit, 1968
Artist: Donnie Dope

3.147
Black Magic
Olympia Stadium, Detroit, 1969
Artist: Linz

3.148
Ten Years After; Dave Workman Band
Grande Ballroom, Detroit, 1968
Artists: Carl Lundgren, Donnie Dope

3.149
Spooky Tooth; McCoys
Grande Ballroom, Detroit, 1968
Artist: Carl Lundgren

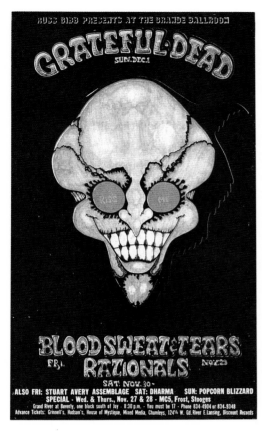

3.150

Grateful Dead; Blood, Sweat and Tears
Grande Ballroom, Detroit, 1968
Artist: Donnie Dope

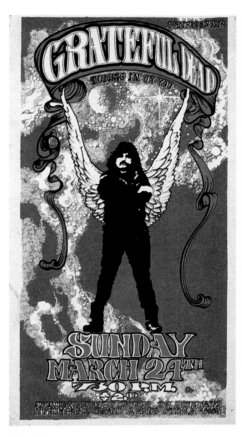

3.151

Grateful Dead
Fountain Church, Grand Rapids,
Michigan, 1968

3.152

Quicksilver Messenger Service; Frost
Grande Ballroom, Detroit, 1968
Artist: Carl Lundgren

3.153

Chambers Brothers
Grande Ballroom, Detroit, 1967
Artists: Carl Lundgren, Jerry Younkins

3.154

The Who; Joe Cocker
Grande Ballroom, Detroit, 1969
Artist: Carl Lundgren

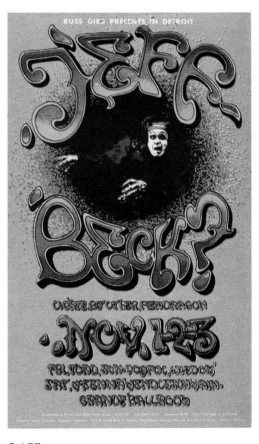

3.155

Jeff Beck; Toad
Grande Ballroom, Detroit, 1968
Artists: Carl Lundgren, Donnie Dope

3.156
Country Joe and the Fish; Muff
Grande Ballroom, Detroit, 1968
Artist: Carl Lundgren

Saugatuck Pop Festival
Potawatomi Beach, Saugatuck, Michigan, 1969
Artists: Carl Lundgren, David Baker

3.158
Jefferson Airplane; Tim Buckley
Grande Ballroom, Detroit, 1968
Artists: Carl Lundgren, Jerry Younkins, Donny Dope

East Coast

Baltimore, Washington, Pittsburgh, Philadelphia, and New York City, all major stops on the typical rock tour itinerary of the late 1960s, produced no distinctive school of rock poster art. Newspaper and radio ads largely supplanted poster promotion in these cities. Great venues abounded—New York's Madison Square Garden, Carnegie Hall, the Apollo Theatre; Philadelphia's Electric Circus—but only Bill Graham's New York-based Fillmore East produced anything like an identifiable *body* of poster art, which nevertheless paled by comparison with the work executed each week for his Fillmore West and Winterland shows in San Francisco.

3.159

Country Joe and the Fish; Iron Butterfly
Merriweather Post Pavilion, Columbia, Maryland, 1968
Artist: McNeill

3.160

Grateful Dead; Fugs
Stanley Theater, Pittsburgh, 1969
Artist: Gene King

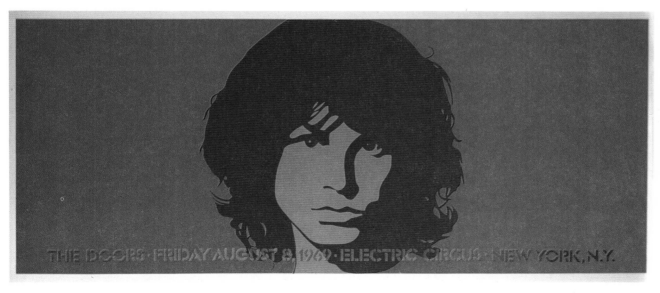

3.161

The Doors
Electric Circus, New York, 1969

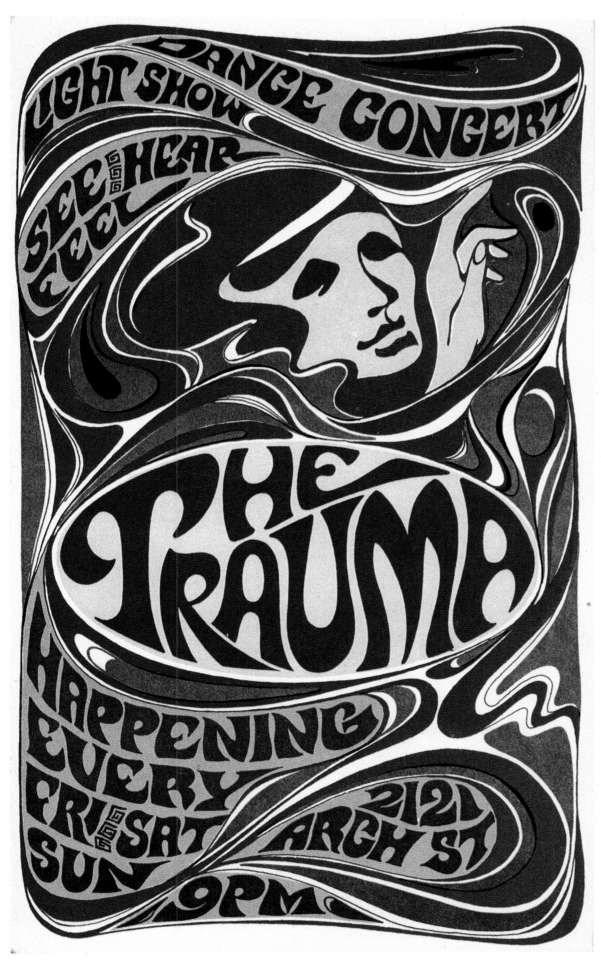

3.162

Promotional Handbill
The Trauma, Philadelphia, ca. 1967

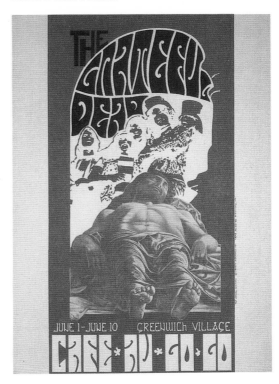

3.163

Grateful Dead
Café au Go-Go, New York, 1967
Artist: Daniel Fennell

3.164

Velvet Underground; The Wildflower
The Trauma, Philadelphia, 1967
Artist: Karen Fritz

3.165

Jimi Hendrix Experience; Soft Machine
Electric Factory, Philadelphia, 1969
Artist: Strange

3.166

Grateful Dead; Blues Image
Thee Image, Miami Beach, ca. 1967

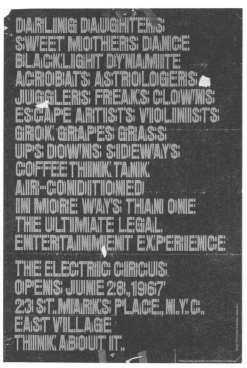

3.167

Opening
Electric Circus, New York, 1967
Artist: Chermayeff & Geismar Associates

3.168

Country Joe and the Fish
Yale University, New Haven, Connecticut, 1971

3.169

Janis Joplin; Butterfield Blues Band
Civic Center, Baltimore, 1969

BOSTON

Boston's many venues produced a surprising variety of poster art. Club 47 featured hybrid folk-rock, while the likes of the Grateful Dead and the Who performed at clubs like the Ark and the Boston Tea Party.

3.170

Jethro Tull
Boston Tea Party, Boston, 1969

3.171

New Year's Eve: Grateful Dead
Boston Tea Party, Boston, 1969

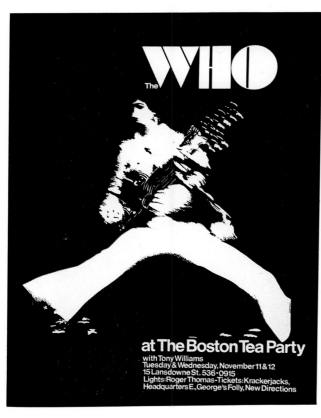

3.172

The Who; Tony Williams
Boston Tea Party, Boston, 1969
Artist: Engstrom

3.173

Allman Brothers; Big Boy Crudup
Boston Tea Party, Boston, 1971
Artist: Ravioli Graffiti

3.174
Lothar and the Hand People; Cloud
Boston Tea Party, Boston, 1968

3.175
Grateful Dead
The Ark, Boston, 1969

3.176
Staple Singers; Bo Grumpus
Boston Tea Party, Boston, ca. 1968

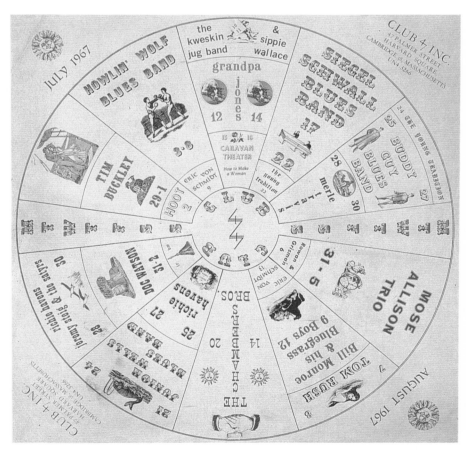

3.177
July–August Calendar
Club 47, Cambridge, Massachusetts, 1967
Artist: Jim Rooney

3.178
The Wildflower; The Bagatelle
Boston Tea Party, Boston, ca. 1967

Canada

Vancouver, British Columbia, just across the Washington border, was one of several Canadian cities—Toronto and Montreal were others—that featured American and English rock on a regular basis. San Francisco bands did very well in Canada, and the Jefferson Airplane made a particular impression. Vancouver's Retinal Circus commissioned from Canadian artists a number of unusual pieces.

3.179

Grateful Dead; Daily Flash Agradome/Dante's Inferno, Vancouver, Canada, 1967
Artist: Bob Masse

3.180

Promotional Poster:
Retinal Circus Light Show
Vancouver, Canada, ca. 1967
Artists: Wes Wilson, John Moehring

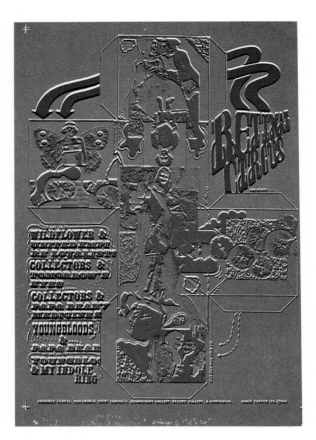

3.181

The Wildflower; Youngbloods
Retinal Circus, Vancouver, Canada, 1967
Artist: Fisher

3.182

Steve Miller Blues Band; The Collectors
Afterthought, Vancouver, Canada, 1967
Artist: Bob Masse

3.183

Jefferson Airplane; Tom Northcott Trio
Kitsilano Theater, Vancouver, Canada, 1966

Europe

Gunther Kieser, staff member of Germany's Lippmann and Rau production company, combined a slick, cool approach with an ad-agency technical bravura. Kieser's style contrasts greatly with Great Britain's Michael English, whose work at the time was whimsical and dreamlike, closer to San Francisco psychedelic art. English's work from this period—and later, as his scope and execution broadened—is greatly prized by European poster collectors.

3.184

Led Zeppelin
Earl's Court Exhibition Center, London, 1970
Artist: Peter Grainey

3.185

Jimi Hendrix
Beethovensall, Stuttgart, West Germany, 1969
Artist: Gunther Kieser

3.186

Jefferson Airplane
Falkoner Centret, Copenhagen, Denmark, ca. 1968

3.187

Country Joe and the Fish; Kaleidoscope
Concertgebouw, Amsterdam, Netherlands, ca. 1969

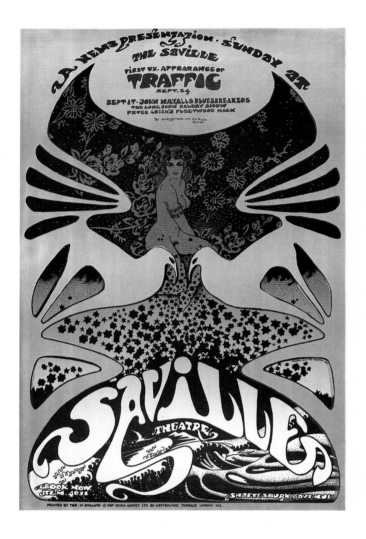

3.188 *(far left)*

Traffic; John Mayall
Saville Theatre, London, 1967
Artist: Michael English

3.189 *(left)*

UFO Coming
1967
Artist: Michael English,
Weymouth

3.190 *(far left)*

Fifth National Jazz and
Blues Festival
Athletic Association,
Richmond, England, 1965
Artist: Token Creative

3.191 *(left)*

Ninth National Jazz and
Blues Festival
Plumpton Race Course,
Sussex, England, 1969
Artist: Token Creative

4

The Mainstream: 1969–1987

Maybe it's what's been happening in California, but now it's just a step ahead of what's about to happen here in Oklahoma.

BRIAN JAMES THOMPSON in conversation
1985, Tulsa, Oklahoma

The 1970s were a time of fat cats and big bucks in rock music, and the successful exploitation of the music dramatically altered the course of rock 'n' roll. At first, the financial strength of 1970s rock was a joyous achievement; later, a reason for envy and suspicion; by the end of the decade, the occasion of such reactionary movements as punk and new wave.

A source of fulfillment and a target for derision, 1970s rock had very real power. In just a few years rock had risen from a counterculture movement to the dominant popular art form. Woodstock was the turning point in the economic destiny of rock. Everything about the late 1960s culminated in Woodstock. A triumph of communal will, talent, and ideals, it marked the peak of what could be accomplished by harnessing rock's musical power to a great massing of youth. And it also ushered in a new era of exploitation engineered by what had become rock's own powerful establishment and a host of outside interests.

For all its idealism, Woodstock represented the first *full* realization of rock's commercial potential, its marketability. The poster art created for Woodstock is an example of the rapid evolution of this realization.

Like much that surrounded Woodstock, the classic dove-and-guitar festival poster took on almost mythic proportions, becoming a sophisticated commercial emblem. Yet its mythic and commercial success were rooted in the same spontaneous, mostly unplanned evolution that characterized the genesis of the festival itself.

Woodstock was produced after much apprehension and collective tension. But Woodstock, held the weekend of August 15–17, 1969, just clicked—phenomenally. More than 400,000 fans made the trek to Max Yasgur's dairy farm outside Bethel, New York, jamming every freeway, county road, and dirt path. The journey became an epic pilgrimage.

The thought behind the initial poster design was innocent enough, since Woodstock, at its inception, was possessed of no more magic than any other rock festival of the late 1960s. But the event began to take on extraordinary stature just before it hit, and continued to increase in symbolic proportion years after it was held. The development of the second design for the Woodstock poster played into this process.

Woodstock was originally planned for a site outside the township of Wallkill in Sullivan County, New York. But just four weeks before the concert date, Wallkill's zoning board revoked the necessary licenses, and the promoters were forced to look for an entirely new location. The first Woodstock poster, which therefore became obsolete before it was used, was the work of David Byrd, known in New York City for his 1968 Fillmore East posters, which caught the eye of Michael Lang, one of the four promoter partners in Woodstock Ventures. Byrd's poster depicted a naked Aquarius—Woodstock was billed as the "Aquarian Exposition"—against a psychedelic background design.

When the Wallkill town fathers revoked permission for Woodstock, an eleventh-hour decision was made to relocate the festival. An intensive search for a new site led to the discovery of Max Yasgur's farm. New poster art was needed, and Woodstock Ventures hired artist Arnold Skolnick, who, unlike Byrd, was not known for any particular rock poster work. Nevertheless, his design has since become the classic graphic representation of Woodstock. It first appeared in newspaper, then in poster form.

Unlike Byrd's effort, which was intended more as a souvenir than an advertisement, the Skolnick poster described the event in detail. Just weeks before the target date, Woodstock purchasing agent Jim Mitchell ordered 35,000 copies of the second poster, most of which were placed in friendly storefront windows, tacked onto college bulletin boards, stapled to kiosks on campuses all along the Eastern seaboard, and glued to board-fence construction sites in towns and cities stretching from metropolitan New York through countryside that the audience would traverse in seeking out the concert. Prior to the Woodstock weekend, Skolnick's poster was reprinted to accommodate the expanding talent lineup. Thus the poster achieved an early circulation of tremendous proportions.

Its immediate appeal prompted subsequent adoption as a powerful commercial image. Perhaps only John Van Hamersveld's "Endless Summer" surf movie poster from the early 1960s or Stanley Mouse and Alton Kelley's "Skull and Roses" Grateful Dead poster from the Avalon Ballroom ever earned comparable iconic stature.

Three years after Woodstock, Bill Graham closed the Fillmore East (New York) and Fillmore West (San Francisco) concert halls. Graham understood that the new decade called for larger-size concert production and tour management. He acknowledged that the San Francisco psychedelic period was

a magical time . . . when people really believed in a new Utopia. While most of the people who went to the Fillmore were there just to have a good time, many also thought it was the beginning of a new world. But by 1971 I began to feel there was a sense of mass idolatry about rock bands, and what accompanied the work of making concerts happen was big, big business. The feelings that had first cast a spell over everybody—the musicians, the promoters, the audience—were now slipping away.

Graham's decision to close the Fillmore brought to an end a concert poster series that numbered almost three hundred works.

The task of creating a final Fillmore poster fell to David Singer, the accomplished collagist who handled the greatest number of Graham posters during the Fillmore era, between 1969 and 1971. Although Singer's culminating piece (#287 in the numbered

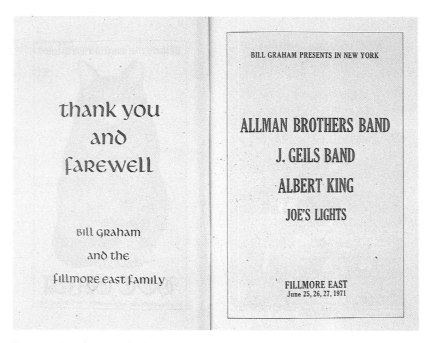

Program (inside spread): closing of Fillmore East, New York, 1971

David Singer, Oakland, California, with original art for the "Closing of Fillmore West"

series) is now regarded as a classic, it confused and even disappointed Graham at first:

I had envisioned some kind of Grand Finale *effort. Instead, what David did . . . he soft-toned the work. But I know now that he created a* beautiful *poster. After time went by, I ended up saying to myself, thank God he didn't do something Ta-Da-DAH! . . . It was every bit what it absolutely should have been. It was from the heart.*

David Singer remembers the task of wrapping up all the Fillmore years:

I'm glad Bill Graham finally liked the design. I never really had the chance to ask him how he felt. I just know I never really planned to follow a specific intellectual path in coming up with the end result; I just sort of did what was natural for me at the time. It was commissioned maybe not quite a month after the week of shows that closed the Fillmore West. All the noise about Bill's sudden decision to close the hall was finally beginning to die down. Keeva Crystal, then one of Bill's right-hand men, told me they wanted something right away—just like they'd always wanted everything right away. But I said to him, "Look, what's the rush? The closing week's already happened. So if it takes me a week or a month or three months, who cares? What's the difference?" I wanted to think about it for awhile, and I also wanted to do a large, double-size poster.

So I began to think about all the various relationships that would symbolize the Fillmore years. But there was a problem in being literal about it. The Fillmore experience was by now an entire structure that had hundreds of elements. And there was the matter of the final concerts themselves, along with the fact that everything had ended on July 4th. Was I to make a statement about the end of the Fillmore era, the last, final shows, and also do a July 4th thing? I think my first approach actually tried to tackle it all.

But then I began to go through all sorts of changes. I didn't want to be literal, and I really wanted to do something that was in essence my style of artwork—an evocation.

I used the relationship of my unconscious being to my conscious self. I never simply thought out intellectually what I would do. I felt I would be guided by a symbology that was part mine and part belonging to the outside world.

I needed to free myself, to make the project my own. By disconnecting from the burden of illustrating a particular Fillmore experience, the final celebrations, and so on, my own feelings about the previous few years began to take form. Using my extensive clip files, which have been indispensable for all my collages, I started to toy with the idea of a dream state, a reverie. This coalesced around an image I found of a sleeping dog, from a 1950s article entitled "Living the Dog's Life." This eventually led me to the two cat images, because a dog might dream of cats. The big dark cat came out of an October 1948 Fortune *magazine.*

The dog and cat combination was filled with suggestion. The images worked perfectly together. As my unconscious started to come into play, the symbolism expressed itself through the creative experience I was having, and this poster became a path of discovery for me.

I saw the dark cat as the expression of the unconscious and the white cat as symbolic of the conscious. The two images were very different; the one was light and playful while the other was mysterious and somewhat sinister. This interplay, I felt, was exactly right for what the mood and music of the time were all about. Then, to bring the dark and the light together, I chose the image of Saturn, with its halo of rings. Saturn is the "heavy" planet, associated with the metal lead. The presence of Saturn implies confrontation, especially in the material world. Saturn relates to that which is actual and made real, and to seedtime and the harvest. The Saturn photo came out of a January 1953 National Geographic.

As I worked with the design, I also began to make connections with my roots. I grew up in Pennsylvania Dutch country, an area where there is a tradition of folk art from colonial days. I was exposed to a lot of antiques, and one of the motifs that always intrigued me was the theme of two birds facing a central image, like guardians or protectors. So, I used this as a key element in my poster—two stylized birds flanking the central collage.

Let me explain something else. I became very interested in geometry, especially in those aspects that have to do with symbology and sacred art. As a child, I was taught how to use a compass to split a circle into parts and create the six-pointed star. This was known as the "hex" sign, and hexes were painted with many variations on barns, chests, documents, and were used generally for decoration. They were considered very potent protection, for they were an image of the order of the world.

The tulip is another central figure of this folk art. Tulips appear everywhere as decorations, and the Pennsylvania Dutch seem to have had a fascination with them. It is a beautiful flower, and if you bend back the petals it forms a six-pointed star. The tulip, therefore, represents the hex, and it has special significance. Much of the Pennsylvania Dutch folk art depicts two birds guarding a sacred tulip or tulip tree. So, not wanting to put the hex star in the center of my poster, I began to think of my collage as a form of hex, as my sacred tulip, flanked by the two birds.

All of this, of course, just evolved as I went along. I thought about it, but it also felt right. It all fit together, and that is what I was interested in. I wanted a design that was highly evocative rather than intellectual, but I also wanted it to have depth. It was a gift for Bill Graham, and it is the only one of the Fillmore series that is a commemorative piece, so far as I know. It is special because I was able to do a meditation, to linger over it, and that's why I think the lettering flows so smoothly into the overall design, and why the piece is so integrated.

"The Art of the Poster" exhibition San Francisco, 1972
Artist: David Singer

For me, the Fillmore always was a beautiful mystery—how it could work so well to bring so many people together, celebrating themselves. My poster doesn't try to explain the experience; I think it works because it leaves the interpretation of the Fillmore essentially open. The poster has a lot of pathways, but it leaves out the directions.

David Singer's work was a new style of poster for Bill Graham, an indication of what might be possible in the art of the 1970s.
Bill Graham:

By 1969 or so, I thought some of the artists were running a bit dry. Then David Singer came along with a whole portfolio of collage pieces. He takes his thousands of pictures—all the things that he's cut out and saved and distilled in his brain—and he comes up with something that really catches the spirit. Singer—as much as Wes Wilson or Rick Griffin—revolutionized concert-poster art.

David Singer:

I was delighted with the way Bill reacted to my work. He was the first publisher to take me seriously, and I had made the rounds of most of the publishing companies in the area at the time. My imagery was a departure from what was generally available, and I had not thought much about doing rock posters. I saw my collages as greeting cards or something. But life can be funny; here I am having designed all these posters, and I've never done any greeting cards at all.

One of the reasons I think Bill liked my work originally was that I presented him with a variety of images right from the start; I had a series all ready for him, and this had never happened before. He liked this because for the first time he could say, "Okay, we'll

David Singer: An Exhibition. The Poster, San Francisco, 1971
Artist: David Singer

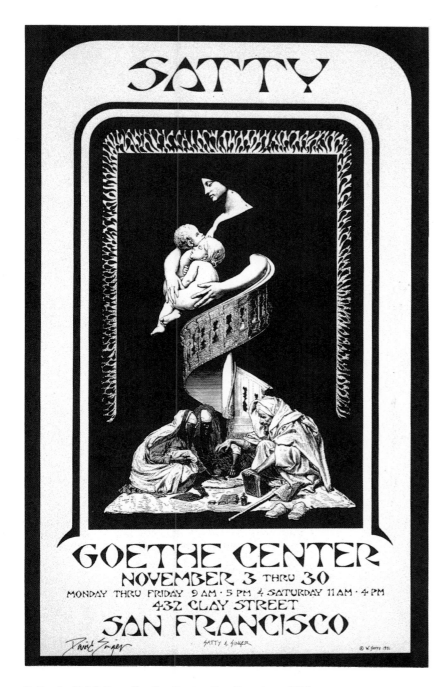

Satty: An Exhibition. Goethe Center, San Francisco, 1971
Artist: David Singer

do these first and these next." Actually, Graham was getting ready
for his summer series of shows at the Fillmore, so we immediately
picked twelve collages and had the color separations made.

I then designed my first "Fillmore West" heading, and then, as I
received each poster's billing, I'd pick the collage that seemed to
go best, and I'd finish the rest of the lettering. I was able to use
the same style for the entire first series, which was a fortunate
circumstance for me, as I knew very little about lettering. I had
assured Bill that I could handle this—and so I had to learn how.
The first series gave me the confidence I needed; after that, I was
able to find my own way. Many of my posters are essentially
borders, designed with lettering, which frame an art piece. I would
vary the lettering style and border colors to set off my images.
My alphabets developed well, but I was never comfortable with the
amount of lettering that needed to be worked out.

Everything was last minute. Usually by the time they put the bill

together, it was necessary to work round-the-clock for several days
to finish and deliver it to the printer. And speed was just part of
the reality. You lived with the pressure that at any moment you
were going to get a phone call saying the bill had changed. It
happened to me many times. Suddenly it was no longer the
Grateful Dead headlining. Well, shit, you might have spent half a
day designing the lettering for "Grateful Dead," and suddenly it
was taken away from you. This was doubly frustrating when the
imagery was also geared to a particular act that now was
cancelled. I tried to avoid getting into this bind by using a format
with interchangeable collages, which made me fairly flexible.

Printing was another matter. By the time I walked into the print
shop I had usually been up for a couple of days working on the
thing, and I was really out there in space. There were all kinds of
questions in my mind and insecurity about decisions I was making,
and then I was confronted with having to translate my thinking
into printing, and into relationships with people.

All my posters for Bill Graham were printed at Tea Lautrec
Litho, the shop of Levon Mosgofian. Eventually, I developed good
rapport with him and everyone there, but at the beginning I had
a lot of difficulty. It was very hard for me to let go and turn over
my work to others. Decisions over the final details were often killers
for me. I had labored so hard, and I would be thinking that this
really wasn't coming together quite right. I would hang out around
the press the whole time my posters were being run, and I would
sometimes get into hassles with Levon and his pressman, Monroe
Schwartz, because I wanted to fiddle with something. They wanted
it to be right, too, but they were removed from my delicate state
of mind and were busting ass to get the posters printed on time.
Levon even tossed me out of his shop once. He just ordered me
out and refused to continue work until I left, so I had to leave.
Levon was very strong, like a bull. He planted himself in front of
you, and that was it.

When possible, Levon would have Joe Buchwald, his other
pressman, work with me. Joe's son was Marty Balin of the
Jefferson Airplane, and because of that he had more patience with
my creative insecurities. Joe always seemed slightly amused while
he flowed along with my ups and downs. Later on, Levon gave
Joe and me permission to come in on weekends to run experimental work on the press. The hardest thing for me was color
choice and projecting in my imagination how a particular combination of colors would turn out in the final printing. I had almost
no formal art training. I did well with collage because I could see
the shapes and colors in front of me. I was very good with
balancing color when I could see it and make adjustments. But
when I had to decide on the colors for one of my posters, I would
get very nervous. I'd see it coming off the press, and I'd think,
oh boy, wait a minute—I should have put something else in there,
or I should have toned it down.

Levon used to say, "I can match any color you want," so I'd
give him a swatch of something and ask him to match it—but
sometimes the result looked very different to me. He'd show it to
me, and he'd have his own idea of how it looked, and he'd say,
"No, that's good. It's really very close." He'd be selling it to me,
you see. He was thinking of the 3,000 posters he had to produce
by tomorrow morning. Somehow, he'd always get them out on
time. Tea Lautrec wasn't a 9-to-5 shop. I was there with Levon
many times late at night, helping him strip-up my posters. I used
to hang out with him like that, if I could stay awake.

The Fillmore period was great training for me. There was the *opportunity as a developing artist to take risks, to make mistakes, and then to grow. I had the freedom to put it all out there, and I had to take responsibility for that. Looking back, I think most of my posters stand up pretty well. There was vitality in my work, which reflected the music and energy of the time. The posters were vehicles through which people plugged into this energy. Bill Graham certainly helped plug me in. He was saying, in effect, "Here, David, do your thing." And I did my thing, and it opened up a world for me. That was the beauty of it.*

"Doing your own thing" was still possible in 1968, when the Family Dog came to the end of their Avalon Ballroom era, and during the next three years, until Bill Graham closed Fillmores East and West in the summer of 1971. After that, rock entered a mainstream period in which the music took the broadest avenues to popular acclaim. Accordingly, the poster art took on a slick, commercial professionalism.

By the beginning of the 1970s, all the major touring rock bands were able to sell out most of the largest indoor arenas and many of the outdoor stadiums coast to coast. Rock opened up new possibilities for the use of civic arenas and sports stadiums, and the rock band—even more so now than the rock promoter— became firmly established as a fixture in the business of rock 'n' roll.

Satty and Singer: Visionary Graphics. The Poster, Los Angeles, ca. 1970
Artists: David Singer and Satty

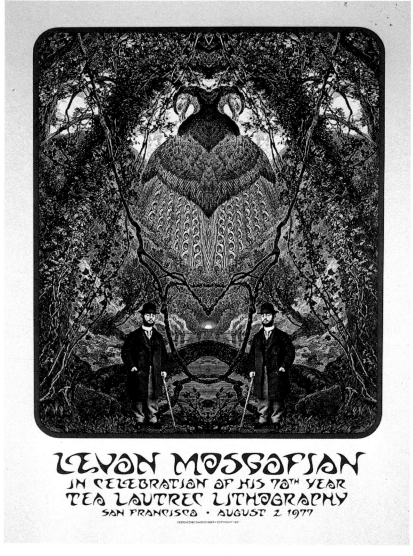

Levon Mosgofian: In Celebration of His 70th Year. Tea Lautrec Lithography, San Francisco, 1977 Artist: David Singer

The transformation out of the idealistic late 1960s saw the use of rock to sell a myriad of products, from cars to cosmetics to clothing. With all of this exploitation came a lessening of the social commitment that most of the great rock bands of the 1960s had demonstrated as an integral part of their music. As the new decade proceeded, a rock band's success was measured more and more by album sales. Popular appeal was easily reduced to numbers. And the creation of the intimate concert posters that just a few years before was seen as integral to rock drastically diminished. Radio and newspaper ads supplanted posters, which were relegated to a merely adjunct art form.

While most rock bands subscribed to the new mass-media advertising methods, several noteworthy exceptions continued to include poster commissions as part of promotional campaigns. As might be expected, the San Francisco bands were most reluctant to abandon concert posters. The Grateful Dead continued, throughout the new decade, to sustain an extremely personal relationship with its growing audience, still embodying a special energy well into the 1980s and still the cause of many concert posters.

Another San Francisco band, Journey, also continued to see the value of powerful posters. Journey was in many ways typical of the commercially savvy rock bands of the turn of the decade, but its management differed from others in finding new ways to develop the commercial potential of concert poster art, primarily by turning concert posters into album covers that helped sell out concert appearances.

Journey's manager was Walter "Herbie" Herbert, a man driven by a need for commercial success but also by personal ideals and a respect for tradition:

The Fillmore and Avalon dance posters stayed with me. It was their lingering impression that probably was the reason I turned to

Allman Brothers Band. Winterland, San Francisco, 1973
Artist: David Singer

Village Voice ad: Grateful Dead and the Band
Roosevelt Stadium, Jersey City, New Jersey, 1973

Mouse and Kelley to collaborate on Journey's third album cover. I respected what they had done in the past, and I had the feeling they had the vision and talent to do something new for me, something just as terrific as their best older work that would now say something about where we were today, in the midst of the 1970s.

I know it wasn't always easy for Mouse and Kelley to collaborate. I'm sure they were each feeling pulled in separate, new directions. Yet they were partners still, in a new time and place, and their Journey art reflected their personal growth and their greater technical mastery.

The transition from the easy-going—sometimes highly refined, sometimes funky and earthy—psychedelic poster art of the Avalon and Fillmore series to the now highly calculated and carefully polished productions of the 1970s affected those who had previously led the way—like Mouse, Kelley, Griffin, and the others—and also served to establish younger talents, like Randy Tuten and David Singer. Although the volume of poster art dropped off sharply, a tradition persisted, and many of the pieces executed in the mainstream 1970s are landmarks in the continuing evolution of the contemporary rock poster.

The experience of Stanley Mouse, whose achievements epitomize the San Francisco graphic tradition, is typical of what any artist of the period had to grapple with:

I remember it was toward the end of 1968, just after Kelley's San Francisco house was fire-bombed (burned down on top of my cherry 1934 Ford sedan!) with a considerable loss of artwork, that I began to spend more and more time by myself. I'd started reading books about Eastern religion, and I began meditating for the first time. My meditation books said, "Good things happen when you do it right . . . but, be careful about what you want, because you might get it!"

It was around then that an old friend of mine, photographer Bob Seidemann, who had left the Haight to live in London, gave me a call. Seidemann says hello, and hands the phone over to Eric Clapton, the guitarist in bands like Cream and Blind Faith, who asks me directly, "Stanley, how would you like to join us in London and flame my Rolls Royce?" "Sure," I said, "I'll leave right away." I went back to Detroit and did some airbrushing at

Newspaper ad: Bruce Springsteen
Madison Square Garden, New York, 1980

Newspaper ad: Ted Nugent; Rex
Madison Square Garden, New York, 1977

the Michigan State Fair, like I'd done so many times before in my high school days, doing t-shirts for the hot-rod crowd. I raised the money I needed and hopped on a plane.

I landed and immediately hooked up with Seidemann and Clapton. They took me to a totally mad birthday party up on King's Road, which is immortalized in one of the Beatles' songs. It was an unbelievable party. All the guys in Cream were there, all the British heavies. George Harrison played us some new Beatles songs, and there were tremendous goings-on in every room.

But, this was when Clapton was being hassled by the British police, and Seidemann was in a pretty precarious state himself. I would soon be, too, only I didn't know it. Finally, one day, Clapton's house was busted, and Seidemann was an unlucky victim through a bizarre set of circumstances. And then one of Clapton's friends totaled the Rolls I was supposed to flame. So the whole situation I was counting on to get me started in England was shot to hell. Bob and I suddenly had to fend for ourselves, strangers in a strange land.

With the gig off, I scrambled fast. Bob and I tried to score graphic work from Apple, the Beatles' company, but the assignments were few and far between. And my current forte—rock concert posters like the ones I'd done for the Avalon and Fillmore—wasn't happening either.

Britain was a tighter scene than what I knew in America. It didn't seem to be such a widespread community of heads. And now the British winter seemed just a few months away. I came back for Woodstock. Afterwards, I touched down again in Detroit, and then I made my way to Boston, searching for Kelley. There was a hip scene in Boston, not so big as back in San Francisco, and for awhile Kelley and I took on a sort of prominent role. But I couldn't take Boston forever, and I split for California after just a few months.

This was the early winter of 1970. It was when I did the art and design for the Grateful Dead's Workingman's LP jacket. When Workingman's Dead came out, the band was first beginning to sense a greater potential in marketing their position in the rock world. They had come into an image that was no bullshit, and they had the potential to control the direction of their image. What was important about their image—to me as a graphic artist working in and out of their sphere—was that it reflected a perspective on life in America and goals and aspirations that the band shared with a real audience of intelligent, caring people.

Just around the time Workingman's Dead came out, I was approached by Sam Wagstaff at the Detroit Museum of Art, who wanted to present two decades of "Graphic Works of Stanley Mouse." After that show ended, I went back to California and linked up again with Kelley, this time in Marin County. Two of the first pieces Kelley and I developed together were for the Dead, called "Ice Cream Kid" and "Rainbow Foot." In due course, the band used both pieces as front and back for their Europe '72 triple-record live album. Because of the demand for t-shirts based on these designs, Kelley and I formed in 1971 a new official partnership, a t-shirt company that we called Monster Corporation of America (and which was known more popularly as Monster Company).

Mouse Studios logo, ca. 1972.
Artist: Stanley Mouse

Europe '72 was one of the efforts Warner Brothers records made to market the Dead creatively to a mostly hip audience that had developed a self-identity as "Deadheads." I don't think any other audience ever was called by a special name. The term Deadheads actually came as a result of an appeal featured in the Dead's previous live album, titled Grateful Dead, and bearing as album cover art the classic skull-and-roses design Kelley and I had many years before discovered and drew into an early Avalon poster. Warner issued free t-shirts bearing this design—a massive release of promotional product at high-visibility record outlets in all the major markets.

Warner's t-shirt was part of a classic record promotion. Although the design was one we ourselves had borrowed from Edmund Sullivan, a prominent artist of the nineteenth century, the new focus on this symbol, which the Dead would later adopt as their personal image, somehow reflected a feeling the Dead's fans had about the band. The Warner's t-shirt spread the word that much farther, drawing in new fans and building an even stronger bond with the already ded-icated. This was not your usual t-shirt. It was a talisman.

Being in the t-shirt business myself since 1958, I took a close look at the success of Warner's skull-and-roses give-away, and Kelley and I decided we could print shirts of our own. So we started making color separations of our new designs, "Ice Cream

Stanley Mouse, San Francisco, 1968

Backstage pass; Grateful Dead
American University, Washington, D.C., 1972

T-shirt catalog: Monster Corp., 1974
Artists: Stanley Mouse and Alton Kelley

they were the best quality designs on the best quality cotton shirts—but soon nobody cared. But it's funny how things come around. Ten years later, people are coming up to me and asking, "Whatever happened to those great Monster shirts?" Everybody's Monster shirts were now in a drawer, they had holes in them, but they were the best. Now you couldn't get them; all you could get were tons of cheaply made, quickly designed, almost generic rock t-shirts.

While initially successful, the artists were unable to cope on their own with the growing complexity of producing and promoting massive runs of t-shirts. Monster Company folded, and new and much greater attention was given to Winterland Productions, also a home-grown Bay Area project. Named after the concert hall and ice-skating palace, Winterland was first just a small business within the Bill Graham concert operation (Winterland started out as a t-shirt and poster store at the concert hall itself). Within ten years, and aided by having its first major retail outlet as Bill Graham's rock shop, Winterland grew into a multimillion dollar operation. Poster sales were insignificant by comparison to t-shirt sales; but Winterland developed the art and science of marketing rock merchandise to unprecedented levels, handling items that featured logolike rock graphics commissioned by individual bands. This was a significant step in the evolution of rock art, and graphics quickly became the basis of almost every band's "line of product."

Joint Show II. The Postermat's '60s Poster Gallery, San Francisco, 1986
Artist: Wes Wilson

Kid" and "Rainbow Foot," and took the printing work over to our friends at Rip Off Press, a San Francisco publishing operation run by artist Gilbert Shelton, heavily involved in producing and distributing the underground "comix"—provocative new-style comic-book art being created by some of our poster friends like Rick Griffin and Victor Moscoso.

Seeing the new potential, we arranged to rent a whole building for ourselves, scored a loan from the Dead in order to get our own silk-screening equipment, and basically rolled up our sleeves and started having fun. You know, in just a little more than two weeks we actually had made enough money from our first run of shirts to pay off the Dead and begin thinking of an actual product line, a body of designs we thought would appeal to all the far-out people in the world—people like the Dead's audience, certainly, but also a lot of others. Our stuff was like the Mercedes-Benz of t-shirts—

The Five Joint Show Artists—Alton Kelley, Victor Moscoso, Rick Griffin, Wes Wilson, Stanley Mouse
Moore Gallery, San Francisco, 1967

The Five Joint Show II Artists—Victor Moscoso, Wes Wilson, Stanley Mouse, Alton Kelley, Rick Griffin
The Postermat's '60 s Poster Gallery, San Francisco, 1986

The slick new graphics had their origin in rock concert posters of the late 1960s but were marketed in a far more sophisticated manner.

Artists who had established themselves in the psychedelic sixties were faced with challenges and opportunities in the new world of commercial rock. For example, widespread distribution and sophisticated marketing meant that the art of Stanley Mouse and Alton Kelley received recognition far beyond what they had earned with their Fillmore and Avalon posters and even their Grateful Dead album graphics and t-shirts. But it also meant that the successful rock artist of the 1970s could no longer hold himself aloof from the concerns of commerce, including sophisticated marketing and prudent management. The demise of Monster Company showed how painful the transition from hippie poster artist to commercial graphic artist could be.

Mouse and Kelley did have tremendous success in designing album covers—as did Southern California artist John Van Hamersveld—in the mid 1970s. The most notable works were the Journey albums (done jointly and separately): *Infinity, Evolution, Departure, Captured,* and *Escape.* Mouse and Kelley also won a Grammy award in 1977 for their Pegasus cover art for Steve Miller's *Book of Dreams.*

Despite the rewards and perils of their commercial work in various graphic media—including t-shirts and album covers—and despite the reduced demand for rock posters in the 1970s, Mouse and Kelley jointly and separately did create some of the decade's classic posters. Most notable is the "Blue Rose" image commissioned for the closing of Winterland Arena on New Year's Eve, 1978, a concert featuring the Blues Brothers and (who else?) the Grateful Dead. While for many years "Blue Rose" was easily obtainable, Winterland ran out of stock in 1986 and did not reprint the poster, thereby instantly conferring collectible status on it. Kelley's "Egypt" poster, commissioned in 1978 by the Grateful Dead themselves, has even greater collectible value since its print run numbered a mere thousand. No other rock poster is more valued than this one, which commemorates the Dead's epic concerts at the foot of the Great Pyramid in Egypt.

Except for the occasional appearance of such classics, most of the graphic work mainstream concert promoters commissioned was for display ads in the Sunday entertainment sections of major newspapers—*almost* a distinctive genre of rock art, one limited by the instantly disposable nature of the medium.

For a number of years in Bill Graham's organization, it was staff artist Randy Tuten who handled the ad designs. Tuten had created several dozen Fillmore posters in the numbered series beginning in 1969 as well as handbills and posters for the Family Dog late in 1968. His ad graphics were often clever and engaging, and he was particularly skilled as a letterer. But the ads exhibited a certain sameness. Fortunately, Graham also commissioned from Tuten a number of special-event posters, notably pieces commemorating concerts by Led Zeppelin, the Rolling Stones, and Pink Floyd. Like the rest of Graham's concert posters during the 1970s, these were strictly one-time efforts, very different from the pieces included in the glory days of the numbered series.

What Tuten didn't handle for Graham, David Singer did, and while the two artists had Bill Graham in common, they generally steered their own courses, having found collaboration difficult. Nevertheless, their styles reflected equally a growing technical maturity: their 1970s-era posters reflect a crisper, more refined

Original art for newspaper ad: The Who; Grateful Dead
Oakland Stadium, Oakland, 1976
Artist: Randy Tuten

execution. Indeed, the 1970s proved that the majority of the psychedelic-era poster artists were capable of evolving as illustrators, painters, designers, and collagists—well beyond what was evidenced in their earlier work. David Singer, for example, had many trepidations about his lettering abilities, but soon found himself capable of developing whole alphabets by the time the Fillmore series ended. He also developed the strength to act in very bold fashion during the mainstream period, as is evidenced by his simple but extremely powerful "Tumbling Dice" image for the poster that heralded the Rolling Stones 1972 appearance at Winterland. Like all of Singer's work, this effort was the result of collage and imaginative lettering, an approach that was a design breakthrough in rock posters. Collages of a different sort would come to mark a subsequent era in rock, in the handbills of punkers and devotees of the new wave, whose collaged works were much less sophisticated than Singer's but linked to the earlier creations nonetheless.

However infrequently it appeared in the 1970s, the rock poster was still a useful promotional tool for smaller concert operations in less-traveled areas of the country. In such places, the rock poster also continued to represent new opportunities for local artists. This smaller-town sensibility is well illustrated by the experience of a group of rock 'n' roll fans in Tulsa, Oklahoma—not a small town, really, but far from being a leading rock music center. Brian James Thompson tells the story:

Original art for newspaper ad and poster: The Eagles
The Forum, Los Angeles, 1977. Artist: Randy Tuten

Rick Griffin: An Exhibition. Roundhouse, London, 1976
Artist: Rick Griffin

Newspaper ad: 4th of July All American Rock & Roll Show
Oakland Stadium, Oakland, 1979. Artist: Randy Tuten

I was born in Tulsa in 1953. My interest in art actually started when I was five years old, doing drawings inspired by a guy I saw on TV, John Gnagy, who had a syndicated Saturday morning show teaching people how to draw elephants and all kinds of neat stuff. I got started because art seemed to me like fun.

I attended Cascia Hall Preparatory School, where the emphasis was on law and medicine, and not at all on art. But my feelings about art were still pretty intense, and at prep school I started reading about art history. I discovered Toulouse-Lautrec, one of the greatest poster makers of them all. I got a tremendous hit seeing his dancing girl posters, and I began to feel that doing poster art like his would be a whole lot of fun.

When I was around fourteen or fifteen, I discovered the Grateful Dead. This was music that really knocked me out. I feel like I have this incredible knack of tripping over powerful art—in this case, music—that's ahead of its time. Of course, maybe it's what's been happening in California, but now it's just a step ahead of what's about to happen in Oklahoma.

What also happened to me was meeting bunches of people who'd moved away from New York and Northern California to rediscover their roots. They decided to move to places like Oklahoma—Indian territory, places that signified a back-to-the-land kind of thing. Mostly these were people five to ten years older than me, with a lot more living under their belt. I started growing my hair long for the first time and listened to the Grateful Dead more and more.

Around 1968 I did some of my first serious, "way out" posters. The first was done in a moiré type of pattern, what I thought of as multidimensional psychedelic. I did these posters for my own enjoyment, to put up on my own walls. But then a few bits of real

Cain's Ballroom, Tulsa, Oklahoma, 1983

psychedelic art began to surface around town. One place that
had some of these posters was called the Etcetera House, and I
vividly remember the day I stopped over there when they just got
in two hundred Bill Graham posters from the Fillmore, that myth-
ical auditorium in San Francisco. The posters sold for a dollar
apiece, and I came home with an armful.

After seeing that art, I started to realize what I was shooting for.
The artistry of the San Francisco posters was outrageous. I particularly liked Rick Griffin's work, and Victor Moscoso's posters were
some of my other favorites. I also liked Greg Irons's work a lot,
Wes Wilson's stuff, and the tremendous drawings by Mouse and
Kelley. My whole reaction to this outrageousness could be summed
up in one word: Wow! It made me think a lot about traveling to
the West Coast. I wanted to see what surfing was all about and
what it must be like going to all the dances. But the visit just never
came about. I had to remain at home. There's no surf in Oklahoma.

After prep school, I briefly tried the University of Tulsa and lasted
in the commercial art program for one year. Then I went to work
for a couple of local typesetting shops, places that handled
production for things like law briefs and Coleman gas stove
pamphlets. I was given assignments like illustrating in diagram
form the assembly sequence for all the nuts and bolts of a particular small piece of equipment. It was a gig. It gave me a start and
a paycheck. I'm sure lots of young commercial artists have had
to start out in a similar manner.

All the while, my real attention was focused on music. I began
to see the stirrings of a new scene over at the Cain's Ballroom.
It is a historic place, a dance hall that began as a parking garage

in 1924 until Madison "Daddy" Cain turned it into the Cain's
Academy of Dance. For the next several years, maybe up until
1934, the Cain's was where parents took their children for ballroom
dance lessons. Then, by the mid 1930s, O. W. Mayo began to
book appearances by traditional Western swing bands, like the
great Bob Wills and His Texas Playboys. I think around the early
1960s there might have been a few appearances by some rock 'n'
roll groups, the ones that had strong country roots, like Ronnie
Hawkins and the Hawks (later known as the Band). But rock
didn't make much of an impact back then on the City of Tulsa.

By the end of the 1950s and well into the 1960s, the scene at
the Cain's was well into decline. People weren't going, in part
because the Cain's was in a rough part of town and also because
Western swing had faded in popularity. The Cain's was showing its
age. It lacked some basic modern amenities, like air conditioning,
which meant the place sweltered on Saturday nights in the summer.

At the time when younger people started looking at the Cain's
as a place to do gigs, it was owned by Mrs. Marie Meyers. She
was eighty-five years old and lived in the building, with little business coming her way. Then things suddenly changed. Robert C.
Bradley, Jr., known to all as R. C., graduated from Duke University,
after having grown up locally. While he was in college, he assisted
an East Coast promoter who booked groups like Deep Purple,
the Dead, and the Allman Brothers. R. C. knew the ins and outs of
concert production, and now had returned home. This was in the
fall and winter of 1974—75. It was the time when Leon Russell was
the main attraction in Oklahoma. Russell had written a song about
a "Streakers Ball," so R. C. and his friends decided to throw a
Halloween "Freakers Ball" at the Cain's. Naturally, it went like
gangbusters. Here was this old ballroom that looked like time had
stopped for it somewhere in the 1940s and hadn't been the place
for anything of consequence in over fifteen years. R. C. wanted to
rent the ballroom from Mrs. Meyers for a three month period. I
thought, no way was Mrs. Meyers going to let R. C. have the
Cain's, but she signed with him and his partners, and the first
show of the planned series happened in January 1975.

The Cain's is a wonderful place, but one of its limitations is size.
Total capacity for a dance event is 1,100 people, sufficient to book
bands like Asleep at the Wheel, Commander Cody, Hot Tuna,
Tracy Nelson, the Nitty Gritty Dirt Band, Elvin Bishop, and so on,
but more popular acts like the Grateful Dead had to pass, even
after Jerry Garcia himself came down to take a look.

At the beginning it was the hottest thing going. People were
coming from all over to experience the historic atmosphere, the
feeling of camaraderie among those who knew how wonderful it
was to get together, dance, and have a good time. It was like
people were really trying to capture what they'd missed by not
being in San Francisco during the Avalon/Fillmore era.

I felt much more at home doing rock music graphics than
instruction booklets for camp stoves. Doing posters was a contin-
uous, evolving process of evoking the muse several times a month,
trying to top myself, if I could. There were no client considerations
placed on what I did, except that each poster had to serve a
promotional purpose and attract as many customers for each event
as we could from a surprisingly large community of interested,
aware people in the area.

Much of what I've done as a poster artist was self-taught and
influenced by Bauhaus artists, as well as Rick Griffin. You only
really learn through experience, and I was being handed a new
experience nearly every week for many months running. Of

Brian James Thompson, Tulsa, Oklahoma, 1986

course, I had to learn how to create very rapidly, because the schedule for each show allowed like ten days for me to design the piece, get it over to the printer, get the printer to complete his end, and then deliver the posters as far in advance of each show as possible.

What I was aiming to achieve with all my posters was recognition and appreciation by people driving the streets. I felt flattered to think that my best art was something that caused someone to take home a poster, something that someone would consider worth saving.

What was kind of funny about doing rock posters in Tulsa was that, after awhile, the city utility companies wouldn't allow the Cain's people to put them up on telephone poles and such. Finally, the electric company began sending the Cain's people nasty cease-and-desist letters. I remember one poster that particularly upset some citizens. I used a picture treatment of a seminude woman—although no critical parts were showing. I recall that on 15th Street, runners from the Cain's had put a dozen or so posters straight up the street on all the poles. But each of the posters had a part torn off, just the picture portion. There they were, twelve posters in a line, each edited by some unknown guardian of public morality.

But in the best instances of the regular postering all around town, my phone would start ringing. Friends would be calling up and laughing, going "B. T., I can't believe you! You're really a wild and crazy guy! How can you do this in Tulsa!?" Response like that really made my day. And what would be even better was

when I'd be driving by myself, going to pick up bread at the grocery store, and I'd see somebody parked by the curb, motor running, trying to unstaple one of my posters from a construction-site fence.

Chris Frayne was another regional artist of the period. He usually worked under the name of "Ozone," a nom de guerre associated with Commander Cody and the Lost Planet Airmen, the quintessential bar band. Commander Cody's real name is George Frayne, who is Chris's older brother.

Joe Kerr, now an investment banker in Marin County, California, was manager of the Commander Cody band during its ten years of notoriety. Kerr recalls:

The term ozone goes back to the earliest roots of the band. "Ozone art," along with "ozone music," is really a prank concept, reflecting the eccentricities of the band. Chris and George, along with their friend John Copley, conceived of ozone art as an attempt to articulate the upright craziness associated with the Cody experience.

The band formed in Ann Arbor, home of the University of Michigan. What's interesting is that, initially, art—painting, sculpture, graphic design—was a whole lot more important to George Frayne than music, and a lot of who he is comes out of his art school years at the university.

The Cody band was sort of like the Charlatans in San Francisco. Weird. Couldn't quite say what they were up to. But, without a

Business card: Joe Kerr, manager, Commander Cody and His Lost Planet Airmen, ca. 1972 Artist: Chris Frayne

Promotional bumper sticker:
Commander Cody and His Lost Planet Airmen, ca. 1972

doubt, one hell of a good time. Both Frayne brothers were big on mechanical things: biplanes, train sets, huge freight-hauling trucks. They always liked metal that moved. And you see a whole lot of this in Chris's art—the handbills and posters that went along with Cody gigs, first in Ann Arbor and then in Berkeley and then all across the country. Chris had a real passion for large-scale machinery that displayed personality traits. I think there's a sort of basic universality in what he dug. Chris likes poking fun at big trucks. He also likes to honor the essential spirit of the trucks—things like bulk, power, and what you'd have to call facial characteristics. Chris sees trucks as having faces. I think Chris always thought trucks worked well on posters because nobody is a stranger to a truck. Of course, the whole Cody band loved trucks. Many of their trademark songs had to do with truckers and their eighteen wheelers sailing down the highway.

The Cody band always was a people's band. We took a street-level approach to almost everything we did. That's why we put a lot of stock in fliers to promote gigs.

What the Cody band wasn't was psychedelic. We consciously avoided all the psychedelic stuff, and we scoffed at all the psychedelic bands. We took our cue from John Copley and the Frayne brothers and did something that combined the American way with things that were absurd, off the wall, clearly a bit out of control, but in an okay way. We liked rope lettering, we liked trucks, planes, and trains. We liked cowboys and truckers and dancing musical notes.

Our poster art followed right along with the music, and wherever we turned up, Chris's graphics got as good a reception as the band's songs. The art worked because it was extremely friendly. There wasn't any place we went where it would have been out of step.

Chris Frayne:

What a scene! Big beer blasts. Total party atmosphere. And that, of course, was the original roots of the Cody band—the frat blasts. Early on I ran a sort of lightshow while they made the music. Sometimes we had more people onstage or doing things like the lightshow than there were at the actual party. This was your basic ozone in action. It's when ozone music began taking on a form of its own. And ozone art, the stuff I specialized in, was not even a step behind. We were making everything up all at once.

George was always into airplanes. My dad was into trains, and I dug trucks. I got a huge hit, as a kid, from truck ads. Like, the best truck ads, for my money, are the ones in the old Saturday Evening Post. *Particularly the ads for International trucks. These ads must have spoken some kind of secret language to me. I guess it's because I think trucks have tons of charisma. They have a real boss look about them. So, I always used trucks for my fliers and posters. What could be better than a big ol' friendly truck grinning right out at you? I guess the only thing better would be a truly bizarre-looking truck, of which there are many. You have to be into trucks to know what I'm talking about. There are trucks out there you can't hardly believe real human beings designed them to look like that.*

All my poster art came naturally. Ozone art, ozone music, the whole ozone thing was basically a combined vision—mine and George's and John Copley's and then everyone else's. Ozone was all our adventures. Ozone was the crazy cars and vans we painted up and took cross country.

One experience Chris Frayne had while in Ann Arbor was working for the radical underground newspaper, the *Ann Arbor Sun*, the local version of the *Berkeley Barb*. The *Sun* was itself part of another operation called Rainbow Graphics, run by several radical women leaders associated with John Sinclair and his original White Panther Party, which later became the Rainbow Peoples Party. Gary Grimshaw, the highly regarded Detroit poster artist, a close associate of John Sinclair, was himself part of Rainbow Graphics:

If you want to get a capsule chronology of what I was involved in, there's a chapter in John Sinclair's Guitar Army *called "The*

Business card: Joe Kerr, manager, Asleep at the Wheel, ca. 1972
Artist: Chris Frayne

Gary Grimshaw, Detroit, ca. 1980

Lessons of July 23." In that chapter, John goes over the whole thing quite succinctly, and it's quite a lot to go through, too! Because starting around 1966 I was working with John very closely; he was sort of my mentor, and he taught me about a whole lot of things. How to deal with who I was, with what I was doing, with what was going on in the real world. I collaborated with John before my marijuana bust, but especially beginning in 1970, the year I returned to Michigan after being underground for about three years, and through 1974 we had a bond that almost can't be described. John was released from jail in December 1971—I worked pretty much full-and-a-half-time trying to get him out of prison. His brother, David, and his wife, Leni, and I were the only ones outside of his parents authorized to go into jail and see him.

I had a marijuana charge in Michigan, too. The warrant came out in 1968. Some friends of mine and I had gone up to Traverse City after the Detroit riots to kind of collect our thoughts, and while I was up there I was at a party where some joints were being rolled. The next thing I know, there's a warrant out for my arrest for possession with attempt to sell. I was just in no position to fight this thing, so I left the state. I went to Boston first, worked as a messenger and studied macrobiotics, and I stayed there through the end of 1968. In 1969 I went to California and stayed there for about eighteen months.

I lived in Marin County, in San Francisco, in Berkeley, and I moved around a lot. While I was living in Marin, I did a poster for

an MC 5 (the band associated with Sinclair) appearance at the Straight Theater in San Francisco, a piece that a lot of people seem to remember. The design was of a charging white panther, a pretty powerful thing. And I worked as production manager for the Berkeley Tribe, a street newspaper. I did a poster for a poetry reading in Berkeley and another for a big radical street fair. But my main thing in the Bay Area was doing comic book art—the new-style "comix"—and I did some things with Carl Lundgren, who'd followed me out to San Francisco.

I came back to Michigan early in 1970. The same people who were trying to get John out of jail also lined up a lawyer and bail bondsman for me, and I came back on a train, drove up to Traverse City in the bondsman's limousine, surrendered, posted bond, and then later went through a pre-trial hearing where my lawyer basically shot down the state's case. The charge was later dropped after the "Sinclair" decision of the State Supreme Court lowered penalties for marijuana possession from a maximum of ten years down to a six-month maximum.

When I got back in 1970, I began living in a commune in Ann Arbor with about twenty-five other people who were all very well organized—very centralized around the goal of getting John Sinclair out of jail. And things were set up for me so I could just do artwork constantly. The details of doing the business and running the household were all handled communally. I mean, the scene was organized.

I did quite a number of "Free John" concert posters, and we were also publishing a newspaper, the Ann Arbor Sun, and running Rainbow Graphics. Finally getting John out in 1971 led to our producing the Ann Arbor Blues and Jazz Festival. The promoter who made the festival possible—and the final "Free John" concert with Yoko Ono and John Lennon—was Pete Andrews. By the time we finally sprung John, Pete had become very knowledgeable about promoting, staging, and everything else involved in producing concert events. And John had the connections and the savvy to book the right acts for the festival. Pete and John and I worked together as a team. I art directed the event and got all the promotional material together as a production of Rainbow Graphics. We were so organized from our "Free John" work that the moment he got out, we just knocked things off, no sweat. We felt we could produce anything.

I think when I lived in Ann Arbor during the 1970s I did some of my best posters. That's when things were really humming for me, from a technical point of view. I had a lot more time to do my work—I wasn't on such a rushed schedule like I'd been with the earlier Grande Ballroom pieces. And I did a lot of oversize, colorful posters for Pete Andrews, who in due course started promoting shows at the University of Michigan and at Eastern Michigan University. I was getting paid well, and I had the time to do my best.

Pete Andrews ultimately got out of promoting—he's living up at Ann Arbor and working for a satellite communications company. John and I, along with Frank Bach, went on to become partners in Music Services Associates. We've done some concerts ourselves, but the main things we do are manage, book, and promote bands and clubs. The thing about the Detroit scene now is that most of the local bands play a circuit of clubs rather than one primary venue like the Grande. St. Andrews is one of the larger clubs, holding around eight hundred people. I've done a lot of posters and handbills for gigs there.

I've seen a lot of changes happen in graphic design since the 1960s. In the 1970s, things got a lot more ordered, more

Urbations; Cuppa Joe. New Motor City Showcase, Detroit, 1984
Artist: Gary Grimshaw

road manager for the Starship (successor to the Jefferson Airplane), nothing much in the way of backstage or crew passes was needed in the early days

because there were so few of us. The band was a small unit, the crew was myself and a few other guys, and we didn't need to identify ourselves all that much.

For a long time, the backstage pass was a rubber stamp on the hand, if you were that lucky—usually you were just a name on a list. Then came stamps and ink pads that you could change from night to night. Then it got to the point where fluorescent ink was used, so that the stamp could be identified under black light.

Sometime around Woodstock and all those festivals, you could see the whole scene changing and getting a lot larger, a lot more intricate. Identity was an important thing now. You wanted to know who the people were running around backstage. I had a laminated ID card from the days I worked at a Sylvania electronics lab. I was thinking of this laminated pass when I started developing our first internal Jefferson Starship IDs. I was thinking that some-

geometric, more symmetrical. The punk/new wave style of the late 1970s was a reaction against this too-perfect flash and gloss. Here in the mid 1980s all of the graphic styles—going back to the 1920s—are being recycled and updated. Personally, I've been rediscovering the art and music that turned me on in the first place—the great originators of rhythm and blues in the late 1940s and early 1950s. This isn't "nostalgia," it's more like ancestor worship. I love the emotional power of the music and the fun look of the graphics. There's even been a revival of the old "boxing-style" poster, particularly for blues events and black music. But it's new wave that's turning on all the graphic artists. I know it's what I've been feeling myself. It's like I want to get into something modern, something a little bit crazy. I don't want to be doing what's safe and predictable, or too comfortable. Nothing about art or music ever should be too comfortable.

As artists like Gary Grimshaw were adjusting to the changing times in the early 1970s, a new genre of graphic art was becoming associated with the rock concert industry: the backstage pass and laminated pass.

It is true that, from the beginning, rock used some form of backstage pass—Elvis Presley's backstage passes looked like award ribbons from a county fair—but it was the volume of concert work that now necessitated a whole genre of rock art, which became known as "the pass." According to Bill Laudner,

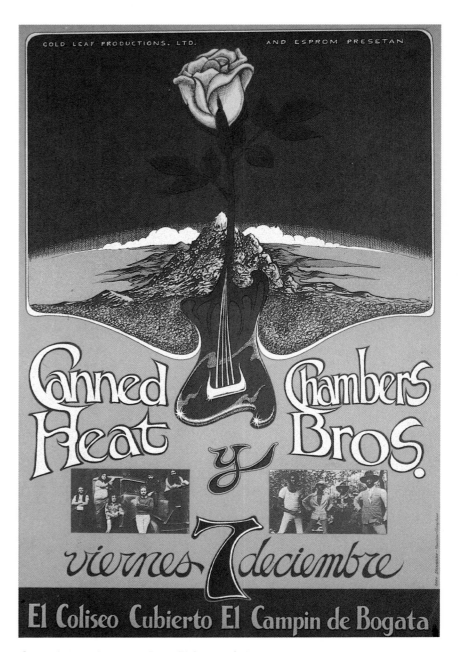

Canned Heat, Chambers Bros. El Coliseo Cubierto, Bogota, Columbia, 1973. Artist: Gary Grimshaw

Muddy Waters; John Lee Hooker. Hill Auditorium, Ann Arbor, Michigan, 1971
Artist: Gary Grimshaw

thing ought to have your picture on it, it ought to tell basically who you were, when the event or tour was taking place, and how long the pass was valid, all that sort of thing. The first ones I did for the band were really very crude, a kind of experiment to see if they would help clear up the backstage mystery. I guess they did, because within just a couple of years, backstage passes were absolutely mandatory. You just couldn't get around a rock 'n' roll stage without a laminated picture pass. And now there are one- and two-sided laminates, special stick-on passes for guests, things with some status, things with a great deal more status, things that give you Godlike status. And it's all very regularized. It's also a form of concert poster in itself.

Most backstage and laminated passes are farmed out to special printers, in particular Jack Otto & Sons, Inc., of Cincinnati, Ohio. Mark Alger is one of the company's vice presidents in charge of marketing this service:

Otto's reputation rests on a foundation of work that began with Bruce Springsteen's "River" tour and continued through the massive U.S. Festival and Live Aid concerts. It all started when we first picked up the "River" tour, about three months along. The Springsteen people were having problems with their cheaply produced passes being counterfeited. Otto came along with what must have been a life-saving offer. In exchange for total artistic license and the unlimited use of the publicity value, Otto would

produce three new passes for each show. This tied in well with Bruce's "every night is something special" credo. Among the first were the passes that netted us our first national press—the passes for the Christmas concerts at Madison Square Garden that featured a die-cut apple. In the July 1981 issue of Oui magazine there was an item noting that our apple was going for more than $20 at collectors' conventions. What a nice stroke for us!

The artist responsible for much of the three-a-day passes—and for a good deal of Otto's subsequent design standards—is Carole Winters, who was Art Director at Otto during 1979–1981. She left for calmer seas after having established the pattern for the Stones 1981 tour. For the year and a half of the "River" tour, she lived daily with the need to come up with three different but interrelated designs that tied into the day, date, city, or special occasion of a given Springsteen show.

As the Springsteen tour wore on, we all got tired of the daily grind and started engaging in slap-happy humor, in an attempt to avoid staleness and predictability (which is easy to counterfeit). Most of the visual jokes were of an "inside" nature and are long

Laminated crew pass: Bill Laudner, road manager, Jefferson Starship, 1974
Artist: Bill Laudner

Laminated all-access pass: Simon & Garfunkel, 1983
Artist: Otto Printing

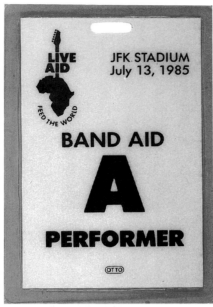

Laminated guest pass:
USA for Africa (recording benefit),
1984

Laminated performer's pass: Live Aid
JFK Stadium, Philadelphia, 1985
Artist: Otto Printing

special *After Show Only* pass for a Stevie Nicks run of shows in Los Angeles at the Wilshire Theater. Being a big fan of the lady, I wanted to do it pretty for her. One problem: we had to turn the job around in less than sixty hours.

My wife was at home that day. I sent the company driver to our apartment to get her copy of the album *Bella Donna,* and I turned it over to Denny Kiel, who shot a fast screen PMT of the back jacket, did a wild outline, and set the special type. By the end of the day we had art at the big camera and were shooting line film. Plates were made that evening, and the job was on the press the next morning. It was printed as four passes, one for each color: red, blue, green, and purple. It went out the door the following evening, and Harry had his passes in Los Angeles forty-eight hours after he picked up the phone. Even today, with thousands of other passes gone by, most everyone agrees it is one of the prettiest one-color passes we have ever done.

Most of our creative moments—the ones that please us the most—are either the ones that let us rise above even our norm and create something of exceptional beauty, or when we exercise a rather twisted sense of humor and blend in some exceptional satire. For the rest, we are fans, like anyone else, and we enjoy the ego boost that comes with working with the biggest names in popular music.

And that's life in the mainstream.

forgotten now, but the prurient contrast of the phallic Washington Monument and the virginal W.W. II female figure done for the Washington, D.C., shows is an example.

That same series of Bruce Springsteen passes also marked a first in the industry—one of many Otto firsts, which includes the printing of four-color process on fabric badges. We used hot-stamp foil on satin passes because passes were again being counterfeited. The element of unpredictability was no longer enough. Someone within the Springsteen organization was revealing pass designs, and they were being duplicated. We had to add an element that could not be duplicated, an element of randomness that no one could predict. The foil was hit upon as one part of a solution that included a high level of secrecy. Randomness was added by the use of loose specifications: the foil press operators were not told what color leaf to use or where to position the dies. The passes were not finish-cut at Otto's shop until after hours, and samples were not kept in the normal files.

By the time the Rolling Stones 1981 North American tour was well under way, the Otto of today had pretty much taken shape. New customers were coming aboard daily, and by the beginning of 1982 we could legitimately claim that there was no major tour with which we did not have something to do. We take a lot of pride in noting those artists who got their first backstage passes from us, including Joan Jett, the Police, the Eurythmics, Asia, Julian Lennon, Robert Plant, and Pat Benatar.

Every once in awhile, we get handed a challenge that we enjoy. It will come at the right time—when we are not too busy to rise to the occasion—and from the right source, who will give the proper input for rare inspiration and allow us to use the right source art.

One such occasion came along when Harry Sandler called for a

It's Only Rock & Roll (retail store). Greenwich Village,
New York City, ca. 1984. Artist: Rick Griffin

San Francisco Bay Area

MAINSTREAM ART

Rock's dominance as an art form became a fact of life in the 1970s. Poster art was transformed by rock's broad acceptance in the marketplace and home. Emulating the music and the times, the art was "safer" and more technically proficient. The art and the artists—like the musicians—had settled into a comfortable niche.

As the decade began, San Francisco continued to lead in volume production of concert art. At least through the first half of the 1970s, many shows—in particular club bookings—were heralded by great numbers of handbills. In the Bay Area, Bill Graham now made greater use of larger venues, like the Cow Palace and Oakland Stadium. Occasionally, other concert producers made brief inroads into Graham's territory (4.12). On the club front, various operations, like the Boarding House (4.9) and the Great American Music Hall, carved out identities separate from Graham. *BAM Magazine* hosted a number of free "Summer in the City" outdoor events (4.8), and the Hells Angels continued to produce gatherings (4.13).

4.2

Tennessee Farm Band
Vancouver, Portland, San Francisco,
ca. 1976

4.1

Duane Eddy; Mud Dogs
Wolfgang's, San Francisco, 1984

4.3

Second North Beach Photo Fair
Washington Square Park, San Francisco, 1972
Artist: Gilbert Johnson

4.4

Marijuana Legalization Benefit
The Village, San Francisco, 1971
Artist: A. Funcke

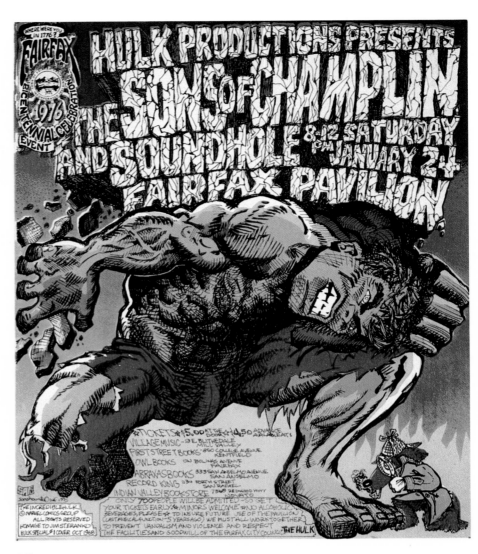

4.5

Bicentennial Celebration
Fairfax Pavilion, Fairfax, 1976
Artist: San Andreas Fault

4.6

Taj Mahal; Journey
Stanford Music Hall, Palo Alto, 1975
Artist: Jake Pierre

4.7

Camp Meeker Benefit
Santa Rosa High School,
Santa Rosa, 1977
Artist: S. Margolin

4.8

Summer in the City
Civic Center Plaza,
Vaillancourt Plaza,
San Francisco, 1979

4.9

Barry Melton; Swami from Miami
Boarding House, San Francisco, 1978
Artist: Monte Dolack

4.10

Cow Rock Show
Cow Palace, San Francisco, 1969
Artist: Loren Rehbock

4.11

A Party for Mother Earth
Friends and Relations Hall, San Francisco, 1971
Artist: Alton Kelley

4.12

Jackson Browne; Jimmy Buffett
Spartan Stadium, San Jose, 1978

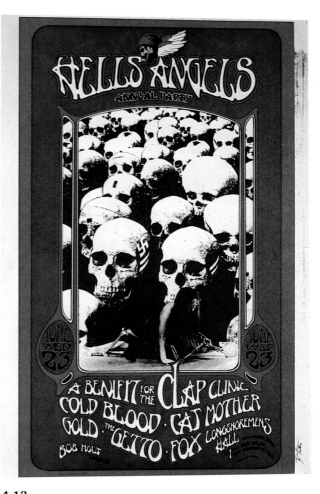

4.13

Hells Angels Annual Party
Longshoremen's Hall, San Francisco, 1971
Artist: Randy Tuten

4.14

Tubes' Talent Hunt
The Boarding House, San Francisco, ca. 1976
Artists: Prairie Prince, Edwin Heaven

4.15

The Tubes in "Mondo Bondage"
The Village, San Francisco, ca. 1979
Artist: Minnie O. Pain

4.16

New York Dolls; The Tubes
The Matrix, San Francisco, 1973
Artist: Airamid

4.17

The Tubes; Pointer Sisters
The Village, San Francisco, ca. 1974
Artist: A. Mebicks

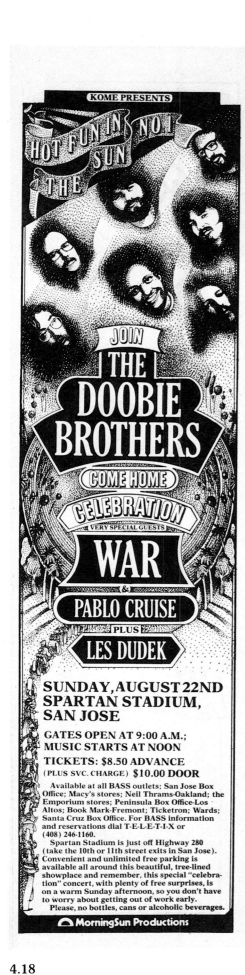

4.18

Doobie Brothers; War
Spartan Stadium, San Jose, 1976

4.19

Joan Jett
Civic Auditorium, San Jose, 1982
Artist: Mick Rock

4.20
Reality House West Benefit
Friends and Relations Hall, San Francisco, 1971
Artist. Dennis Nolan

4.21
Sylvester
Poor Richard's, San Francisco, 1970

4.22
Jerry Garcia and Mickey Hart
Palace of Fine Arts,
San Francisco, 1973

4.23
Kate and Anna McGarrigle
Wolfgang's, San Francisco, 1984

4.24
Ned Lagin and Phil Lesh
Palace of Fine Arts, San Francisco, 1975

4.25
Pisces Party
Bimbo's, San Francisco, 1973
Artist: David Singer

ETHNIC MUSIC

Handbill art was essential in promoting ethnic music to rock audiences. Among the cheapest and most effective forms of public announcement, handbills were a fact of life on Berkeley's Telegraph Avenue and in San Francisco's Haight Ashbury and North Beach during the 1970s. Club promoters arranged for hand-to-hand distribution by the thousands the week before each show, and hundreds more were affixed to every conceivable street-front space: stapled to telephone poles, taped to lampposts, and pasted—with utter disregard for private property—to the sides of commercial buildings.

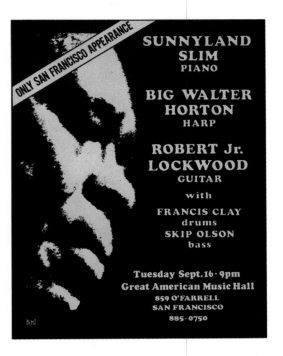

4.26
Third World
California Hall, San Francisco, 1976
Artist: JB / Rastagrafix

4.27 *(top right)*
Sunnyland Slim; Big Walter Horton
Great American Music Hall, San Francisco, 1975
Artist: SK

4.28
Toots and the Maytals
Longbranch, Berkeley, 1974

4.29

Mardi Gras Bacchanal Carnival
Longshoremen's Hall, San Francisco, 1976
Artist: JB / Rastagrafix

4.31

Mardi Gras Mambo
Boarding House, San Francisco, 1977
Artist: Randy Tuten

4.30

Mardi Gras Mambo. Coconut Grove, Santa Cruz, 1979
Artist: James McCaffry

BLUES

The first major American folk festivals, including those held at Newport, Rhode Island, and on the University of California (Berkeley) campus, included blues performers on their bills. Musicians like Lightning Hopkins, Mississippi John Hurt, and Bukka White made a tremendous impression on white folksingers and on those who would later lead electric rock bands. By 1963–64, Chicago-based electric blues bands led by black musicians like Muddy Waters became part of the typical festival lineup. But, beginning around 1966, rock displaced blues music, which now was mostly relegated to hometown club appearances, college-town coffee houses, and tours on the black "chitlin' circuit." A notable exception to this trend was Bill Graham, who continued to present blues acts on top bills at his Fillmore and Winterland dance halls.

More recently there has been a revival of interest in blues, and the San Francisco Blues Festival has played a prominent role in showcasing the genre annually. The Festival commissioned a different poster every year, in the manner of the equally renowned New Orleans Jazz and Heritage Festival (4.178).

4.32
Tenth Annual San Francisco
Blues Festival
Fort Mason, San Francisco, 1982
Artist: NAP Graphics

4.33
Eighth Annual San Francisco Blues Festival
Golden Gate Park Bandshell, San Francisco, 1980
Artist: Jim Shumaker

4.34
Sixth Annual San Francisco Blues Festival
Golden Gate Park Bandshell, San Francisco, 1978
Artist: Andrew Woodd

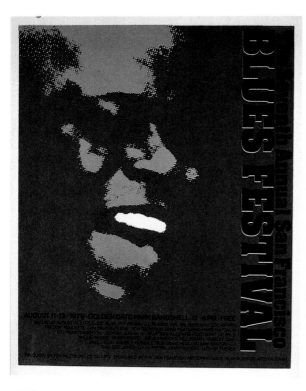

4.35
Seventh Annual San Francisco Blues Festival
Golden Gate Park Bandshell, San Francisco, 1979
Artist: Andrew Woodd

4.36
The San Francisco Blues Festival in Japan
La Caveau, Nagasaki, 1984

4.37
Third Annual San Francisco Blues Festival
McLaren Park, San Francisco, 1975
Artist / Photographer: Paul Kohl

Bill Graham Presents

In July 1971 Bill Graham closed the Fillmore East, in New York, and the Fillmore West, in San Francisco. From that point on, his productions were distributed among a large number of halls throughout the Bay Area. Winterland, however, continued to serve as a focal venue until Graham closed it on New Year's Eve, 1978.

With the closing of Fillmore West, Graham's numbered poster series came to an end. In the years that followed, however, he did commission posters—generally larger than those in the numbered set—for special events. These were commemorative rather than pre-show promotions. (Like other promoters in the mid 1970s, Graham relied on newspaper ads and radio spots to sell out events.) A number of these commissions went to David Singer (4.42, 4.48), who had executed the last poster in the numbered series. Many other important posters were the work of Randy Tuten (4.47, 4.49, 4.50), then Graham's in-house artist, who designed the weekly display ads for the Bay Area papers.

(continued on p. 345)

4.38

New Year's Eve Closing
Winterland, San Francisco, 1978
Artists: Stanley Mouse, Alton Kelley

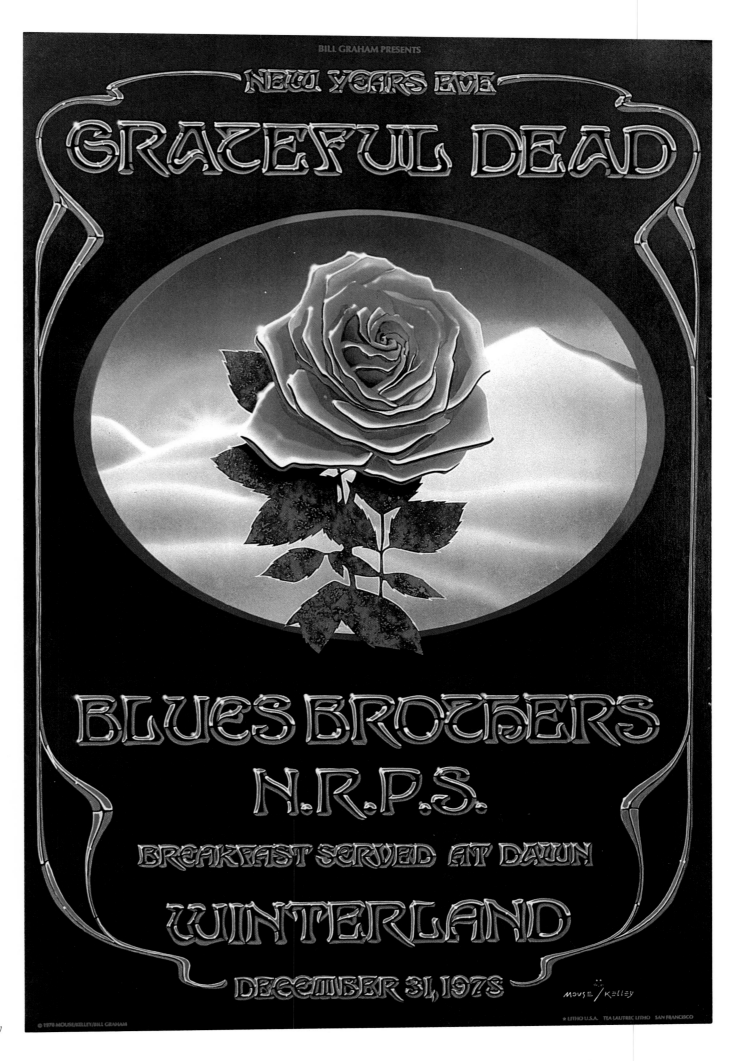

4.39

Rolling Stones
Candlestick Park, San Francisco, 1981
Artist: Kaz

4.40

Fillmore: The Movie
1972

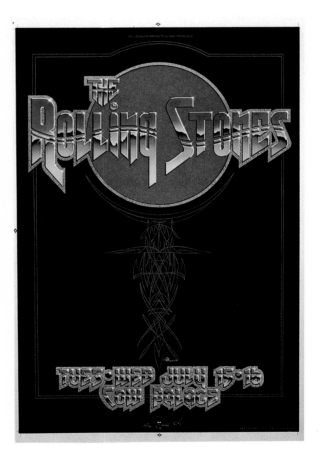

4.41

Rolling Stones
Cow Palace, San Francisco, 1975. Artists: Alton Kelley,
Stanley Mouse, Randy Tuten, Crazy Arab

(continued from p. 343)
One particularly historic and artistically triumphant Graham production was the ''Last Waltz'' extravaganza, the 1974 final concert appearance by the Band. To Graham's disappointment, the two posters honoring the event did not live up to the show's brilliance (4.46). In contrast to the ''Last Waltz'' pieces, the most graphically inspired among the 1970s Graham posters was ''Blue Rose,'' a poster honoring the Grateful Dead's New Year's Eve concert that closed Winterland in 1978 (4.38). The work of Stanley Mouse and Alton Kelley, it was a pinnacle effort in a partnership dating back to 1966.

4.42

The Who
Cow Palace, San Francisco, 1973
Artist: David Singer

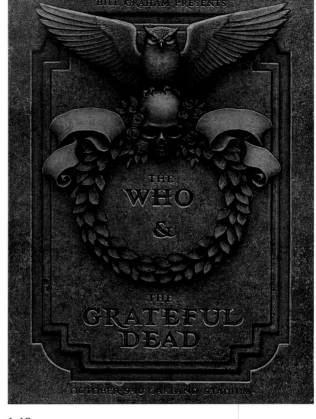

4.43

Grateful Dead; The Who
Oakland Stadium, Oakland, 1976
Artist: Philip Garris

4.44

Kantner/Balin/Casady
Fillmore Auditorium, San Francisco, 1986
Artist: Alton Kelley

4.45

Grateful Dead
Warfield Theater, San Francisco, 1980
Artists: Dennis Larkins, Peter Barsotti

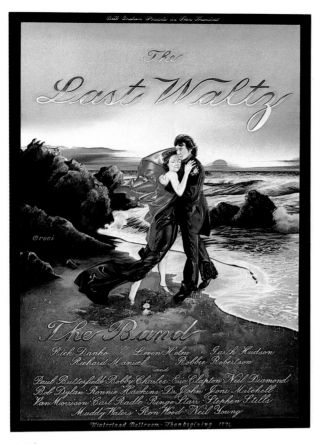

4.46

The Last Waltz
Winterland, San Francisco, 1976
Artist: Croci

4.47

Pink Floyd
Oakland Coliseum, Oakland, 1977
Artists: Randy Tuten, William Bostedt

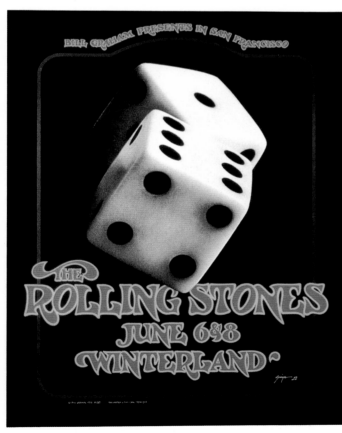

4.48

Tumbling Dice; Rolling Stones
Winterland, San Francisco, 1972
Artist: David Singer

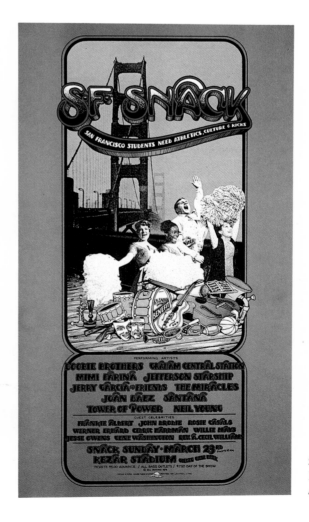

4.49

SNACK Benefit
Kezar Stadium, San Francisco, 1975
Artist: Randy Tuten

4.50

Led Zeppelin
Oakland Stadium,
Oakland, 1977
Artists: Randy Tuten,
William Bostedt

WINTERLAND
AND FILLMORE
SHOWS

Winterland Arena, long the site of ice skating shows and boxing matches, was chiefly the domain of Bill Graham beginning around 1968. But others did use the hall occasionally, and for a brief period in 1970 one of Graham's former associates attempted to book shows into Winterland on a regular basis. Randy Tuten lettered the posters in this series, but disclaims responsibility for the choice of photographic images that form their backgrounds (4.52–54).

In 1968, Graham ended the run of shows that began at the original Fillmore Auditorium in 1966 and shifted operations to the Fillmore West, previously the Carousel Ballroom. For some years the original Fillmore was vacant, opening only occasionally under other promoters (4.56–59). In 1986, Graham again began using the original Fillmore, on a spot basis.

4.51

Grateful Dead; New Riders of the Purple
Sage. Winterland, San Francisco, 1972
Artist: TH

4.52

Ike and Tina Turner; Spirit
Winterland, San Francisco, 1970
Artist: Randy Tuten

4.53

Steve Miller; Country Joe and the Fish
Winterland, San Francisco, 1970
Artist: Randy Tuten

4.54

Sly and the Family Stone; Pacific Gas & Electric
Winterland, San Francisco, 1970
Artist: Randy Tuten

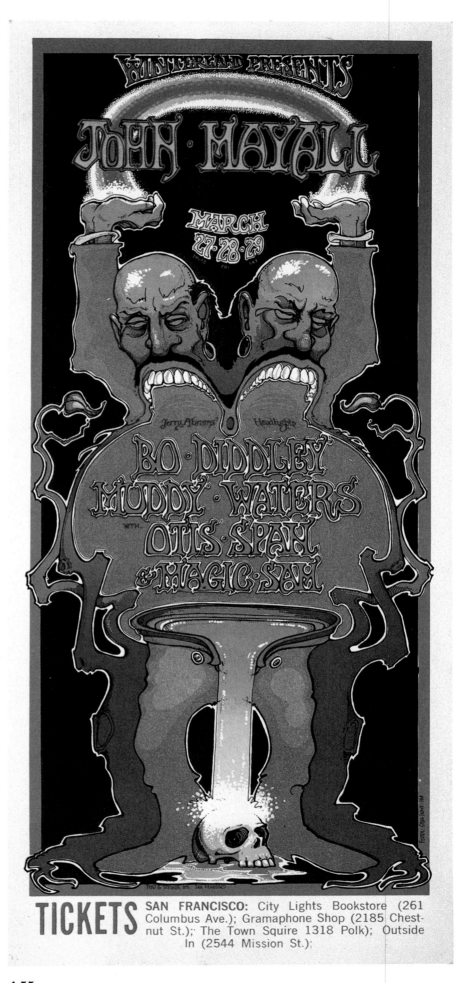

4.55

John Mayall; Muddy Waters
Winterland, San Francisco, 1969
Artist: Greg Irons

4.56

Boogie-Man Halloween Ball
Fillmore Auditorium, San Francisco, 1969
Artist: Cab Covay

4.57

Grateful Dead; Crimson Madness
Fillmore Auditorium, San Francisco, 1969
Artist: Cab Covay

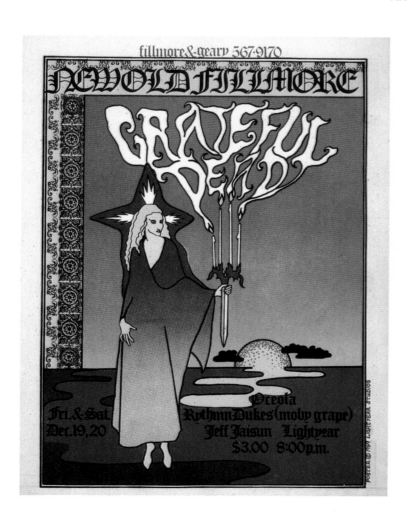

4.58

Grateful Dead; Oceola
Fillmore Auditorium, San Francisco, 1969
Artist: Lightyear Studio

4.59

Iggy Pop; Flamin' Groovies
Fillmore Auditorium,
San Francisco, 1970
Artists: Mark T. Behrens,
Burke

Hookers' Ball

Feminist crusader Margo St. James's COYOTE organization produced the several years' worth of events known variously as the "Queen of Hearts Ball," the "Masquerade Ball," and—more commonly—the "Hookers' Ball," all intended to raise funds for the legalization of prostitution. Several excellent posters were produced, one drawn by David Goines, now a world-renowned fine artist and printer (4.61). Others were impressive collaborations led by Randy Tuten (4.60).

4.61
Queen of Hearts Ball
Galleria, San Francisco, 1977
Artist: David Goines

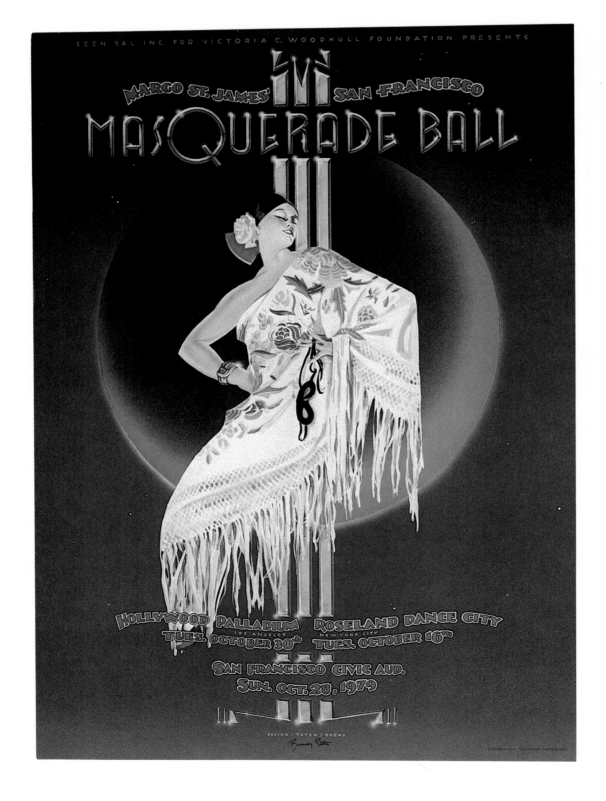

4.60
Hookers' Masquerade Ball
San Francisco, New York, Hollywood, 1979
Artists: Randy Tuten, D. Bread

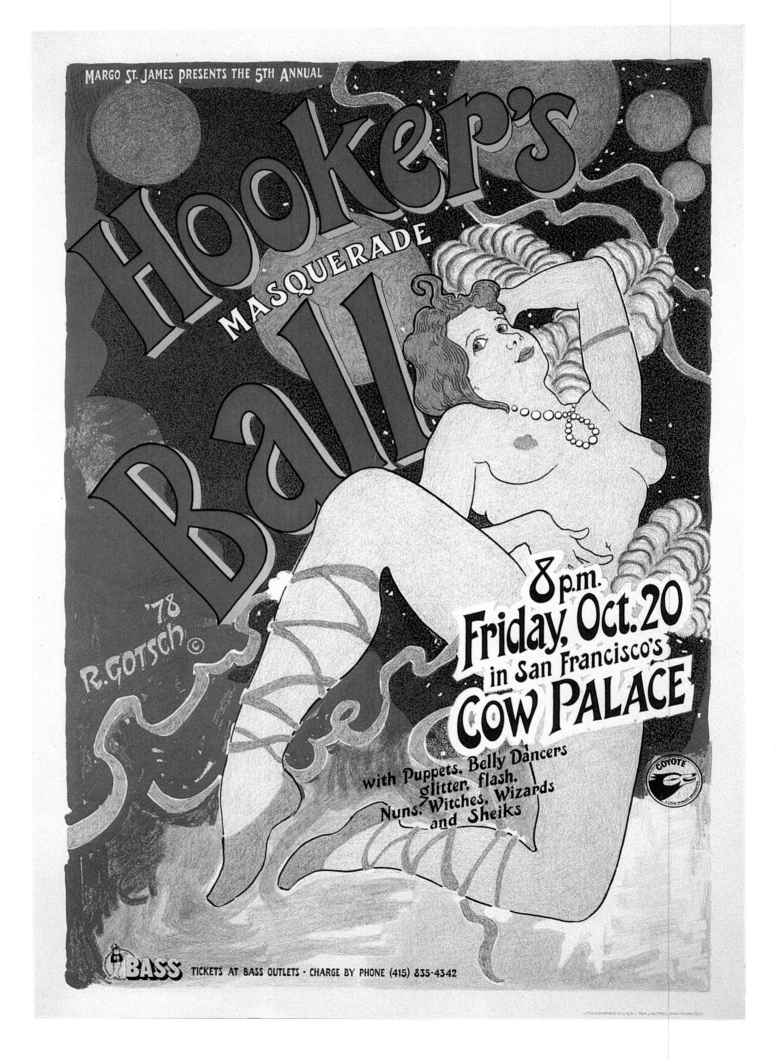

4.62
Fifth Annual Hookers' Ball
Cow Palace, San Francisco,
1978. Artist: Robert Gotsch

Dinosaur Series

Alton Kelley, one of several pioneer artists of the late 1960s psychedelic period, has continued to design posters without pause. Some of his latest creations were executed for the Dinosaurs, a band of musicians formerly associated with major San Francisco bands, including Big Brother and the Holding Company, Quicksilver Messenger Service, and the Grateful Dead. For these "dinosaurs," Kelley decided to revive the concert poster series. As the examples reproduced here demonstrate, the series is unified by some form of dinosaur image, whether a heroic 1930s gasoline tanker (4.63), a scientific illustration (4.64), or a toy Godzilla monster (4.66).

4.63 *(top)*

Dinosaurs
Wolfgang's, San Francisco, 1983
Artists: Alton Kelley, Randy Tuten

4.65 *(above)*

Dinosaurs
Corte Madera Center, Corte Madera, California, 1983
Artist: Alton Kelley

4.64

Dinosaurs
Marin Veterans Auditorium, San Rafael, 1984
Artist: Alton Kelley

4.66
Dinosaurs
Kabuki Theatre,
San Francisco, 1984
Artist: Alton Kelley

East Bay

Boz Scaggs's uniquely styled rhythm-and-rock shows at the Oakland Paramount Theatre in the mid 1970s yielded several excellent commemorative posters, the best known of which, "Slow Dancer" (4.67), became the cover of an album by the same name. Scaggs's wife at the time, Carmella, posed for all the Paramount Theatre pieces.

East Bay clubs like the Longbranch, West Dakota, and Mandrakes (later renamed Keystone Berkeley) issued hundreds—if not thousands—of handbills promoting appearances by Commander Cody and his Lost Planet Airmen and Asleep at the Wheel, among many others. Greg Irons, who created some excellent posters for the Fillmore and Avalon and who went on to even greater renown as a tattoo artist, executed some of these pieces (4.70–71). Others were the work of Chris Frayne, whose nom de plume was "Ozone." Frayne was responsible for much of the Commander Cody concert art (4.72, 4.81).

One of the most unusual East Bay pieces is the Grateful Dead poster for an appearance at the Black Panther Party's 1971 "Revolutionary Intercommunal Day of Solidarity." Only one copy is known to exist, rescued from a telephone pole outside the Oakland Auditorium, where the event took place.

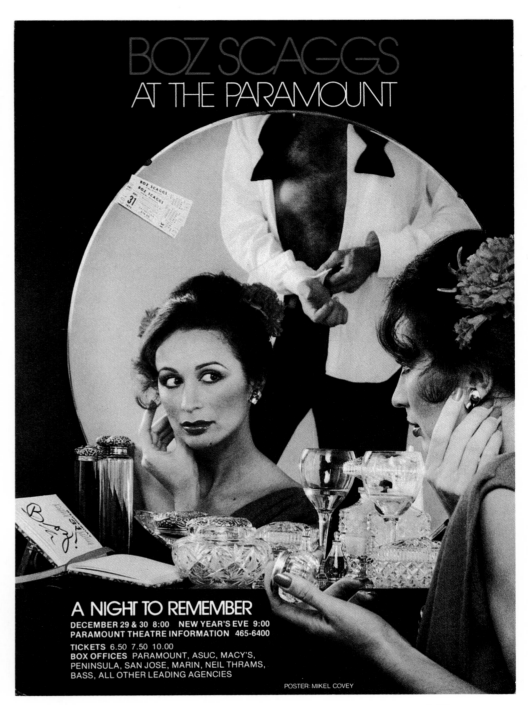

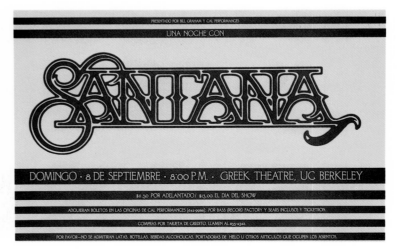

4.68

A Night to Remember—Boz Scaggs
Paramount Theatre, Oakland, 1975
Artist: Mikel Covey

4.67

Slow Dancer—Boz Scaggs
Paramount Theatre, Oakland, 1974
Artist: Tony Lane

4.69

Santana
Greek Theater, Berkeley, ca. 1979
Artist: Arlene Owseichik

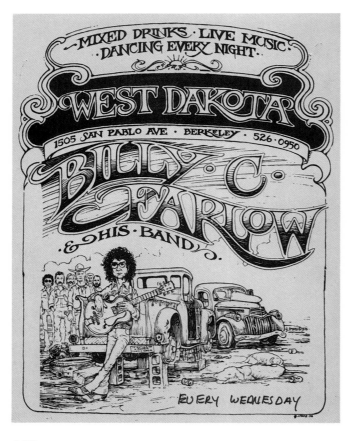

4.70

Billy C. Farlow
West Dakota, Berkeley, 1976
Artist: Greg Irons

Norton Buffalo
West Dakota, Berkeley, 1976
Artist: Greg Irons

4.71

4.72

Asleep at the Wheel;
Commander Cody
Longbranch / Mandrakes,
Berkeley, 1972
Artist: Chris Frayne / Ozone

4.73

New Riders of the Purple Sage
Keystone, Berkeley; Great American Music Hall,
San Francisco, 1979. Artist: Pat Ryan

4.74

Wavy Gravy
Fiftieth Birthday Celebration
Berkeley Community Theater, 1986
Artists: Ruby Lee and Alton Kelley

4.75

Berkeley Centennial
Provo Park, Berkeley, 1972
Artist: Tom Morris

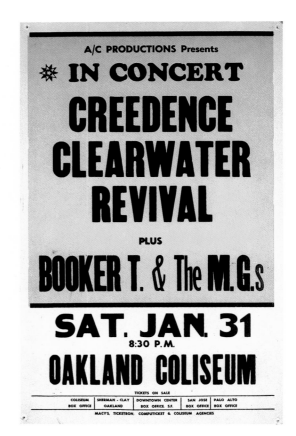

4.76

Creedence Clearwater Revival; Booker T.
and The M.G.'s
Oakland Coliseum, Oakland, 1976

4.77

Earthquake; The Rockets
University of California, Berkeley, 1973
Artist: Garmen

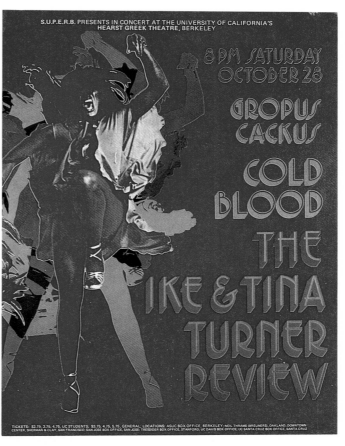

4.78

Ike and Tina Turner; Cold Blood
Greek Theater, Berkeley, 1972
Artist: Tom Morris

4.79
Black Panther Party Rally
Oakland Auditorium, Oakland, 1971

4.80
Dan Hicks and His Hot Licks; Richard Greene
University of California, Berkeley, 1969

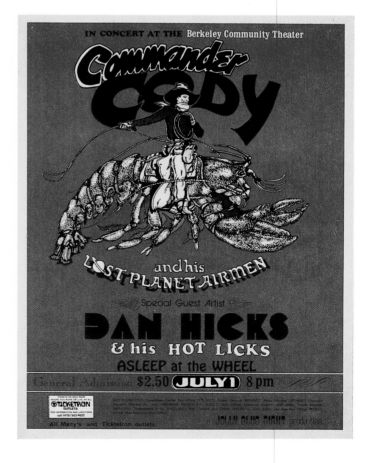

4.81
Commander Cody; Dan Hicks and His Hot Licks
Berkeley Community Theater, Berkeley, 1972
Artist: Chris Frayne / Ozone

BREAD AND ROSES

The annual (now defunct) Bread and Roses outdoor festival, held for six years at the University of California's Berkeley Greek Theater, was a remarkable showcase of talent. Proceeds went to Bread and Roses, which presents music and entertainment in prisons, hospitals, old age homes, youth facilities, and similar sites.

The three-day event was originally conceived as an all-acoustic festival. Few events ever have boasted such impressive lineups of acoustic talent, and it was always a great surprise to hear electric rock musicians change instruments just for the festival. By the final year of the benefit, electric bands did become part of the roster, inevitable but disheartening to the festival's founders.

Bread and Roses posters were widely distributed, the art also used on t-shirts and other merchandise. One of the most graphically successful posters was the work of Stanley Mouse (4.85), who by this time had gained a wide reputation for drawing similar rose images in connection with poster and t-shirt art commissioned by the Grateful Dead.

4.82
Fourth Bread and Roses Festival
Greek Theater, Berkeley, 1980
Artist: Stanley Mouse

Second Bread and Roses Festival
Greek Theater, Berkeley, 1978
Artist: Daniel Ziegler

4.84

First Bread and Roses Festival
Greek Theater, Berkeley, 1977

4.85

Third Bread and Roses Festival
Greek Theater, Berkeley, 1979
Artist: Stanley Mouse

Marin County and Points North

During the early 1970s, a Marin County club, Pepperland, was an important venue featuring Bay Area bands. The club also was called Euphoria, and the Grateful Dead played at least one important show there (4.93).

Many of the best Pepperland posters and handbills were the work of Mark Behrens, (4.86, 4.88) who in 1969 left his first poster-creating base in Chicago to make a new home in the Bay Area. Behrens also drew many important handbills for the Matrix during that club's last few years.

A band known as Clover, based in Marin County, along with another Marin band, Soundhole, appeared often at Pepperland. While otherwise unsuccessful, the two groups did yield harmonica player and vocalist Huey Lewis, along with the bandmembers comprising the group he now leads, Huey Lewis and the News, which achieved worldwide recognition in the 1980s.

4.86

Frank Zappa; Tim Buckley
Pepperland, San Rafael, 1970
Artist: Mark T. Behrens

4.87

Tower of Power; Cold Blood
Pepperland, San Rafael, 1971
Artist: Tom Morris

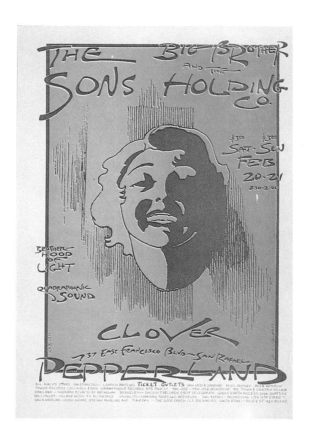

4.88

The Sons; Big Brother and the Holding Company
Pepperland, San Rafael, 1971
Artist: Mark T. Behrens

4.89

Elvin Bishop; Cold Blood
Pepperland, San Rafael, California, 1973

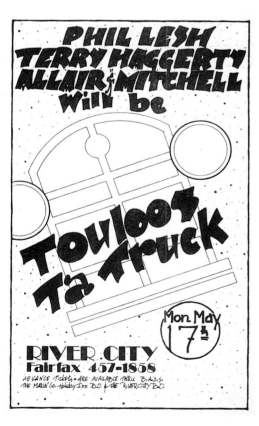

4.90

Touloos Ta Truck
River City, Fairfax, California, 1976

4.91

Tam Jam
Mt. Tamalpais Amphitheater, Marin County,
California, 1982
Artist: Alton Kelley

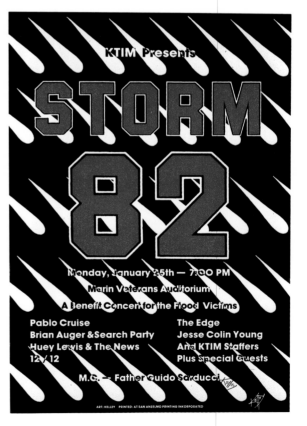

4.92

Storm '82 Benefit
Marin Veterans Auditorium, San Rafael, 1982
Artist: Alton Kelley

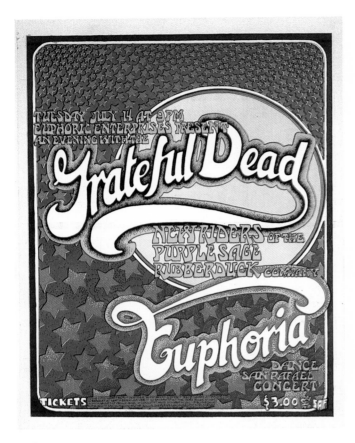

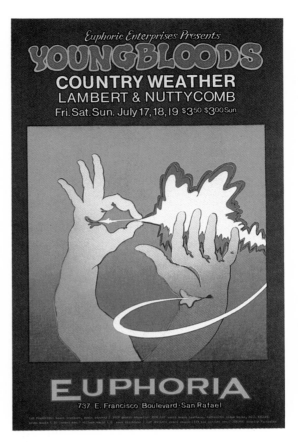

4.93

Grateful Dead; New Riders of the Purple Sage
Euphoria, San Rafael, 1970
Artist: San Andreas Fault

4.94

Youngbloods; Country Weather
Euphoria, San Rafael, 1970
Artist: Bob Fried

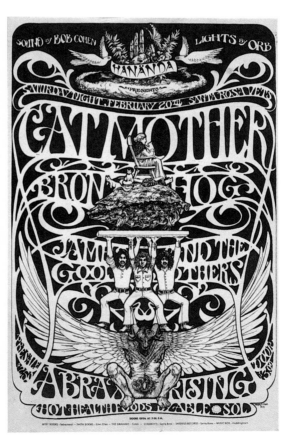

4.95

Grateful Dead; New Riders of the Purple Sage
Santa Rosa Fairgrounds, Santa Rosa, 1970
Artist: Stanley Mouse (portraits)

4.96

Cat Mother; Bronze Hog
Veterans Memorial Auditorium, Santa Rosa, 1971
Artist: Timothy Dixon

Mountain Aire

Mountain Aire, an annual festival-style event held at the Calaveras County Fairgrounds (also the site of California's frog-jumping championships), has featured a variety of top bands. Each of the concerts has also included a between-sets airshow presented by top-ranked stunt pilots.

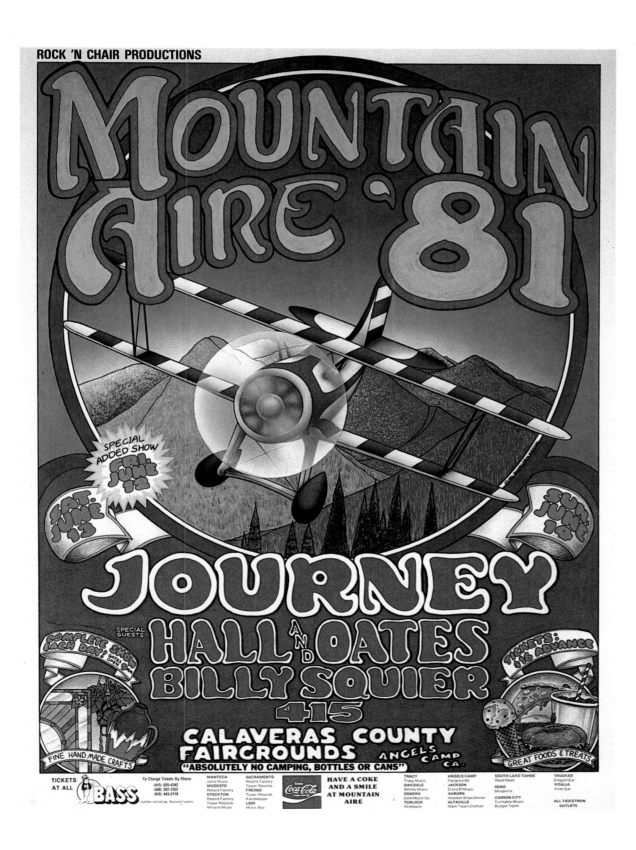

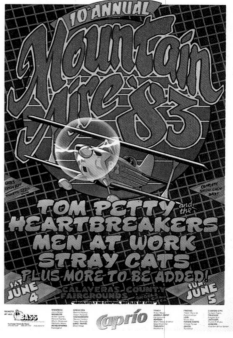

4.98

Mountain Aire '83
Calaveras County Fairgrounds,
Angels Camp, California, 1983
Artist: Roger Labon Jackson

4.97

Mountain Aire '81
Calaveras County Fairgrounds,
Angels Camp, California, 1981
Artist: Roger Labon Jackson

Northern California

Throughout California, a number of regionally based poster artists created works in a variety of identifiable personal styles. One such artist was Sacramento's Roger Shepherd (4.99, 4.101), who also did some of the first Mountain Aire posters. Another was Jim Phillips, who made his home near Santa Cruz, on the coast south of San Francisco. His graphic work garnered local acclaim; it appeared frequently on concert posters, in newspaper ads, and on magazine covers. His cartoon-style drawings were always distinctive, and many believe Phillips is one of a number of obscure artists deserving much wider recognition.

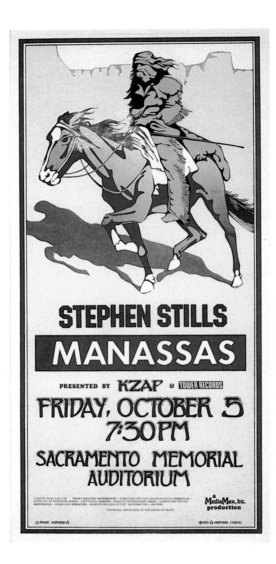

4.99

Stephen Stills; Manassas
Memorial Auditorium, Sacramento, 1973
Artist: Roger Shepherd

4.100

Old and in the Way; Ramblin' Jack Elliott
Sonoma State University, Rohnert Park, California, 1973
Artist: Earth Signs

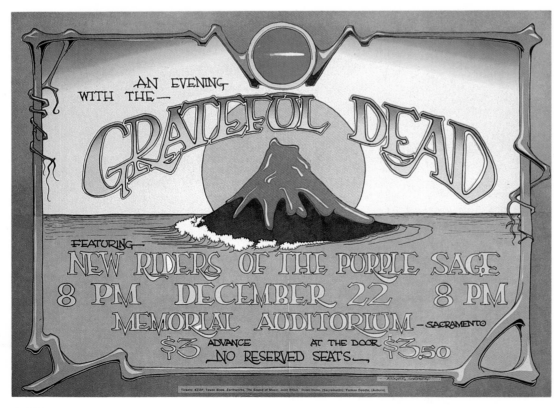

4.101

Grateful Dead; New Riders of the Purple Sage
Memorial Auditorium, Sacramento, 1970
Artist: Roger Shepherd

4.102

Beach Boys; Three Man Army
Memorial Auditorium, Sacramento, 1973
Artist: Roger Shepherd

4.103

Second KFAT Halloween Party
Boulder Creek Theater, Boulder Creek, California, 1977
Artist: Jim Phillips

4.104

Boulder Creek Theater Benefit
Boulder Creek, California, 1977
Artist: Jim Phillips

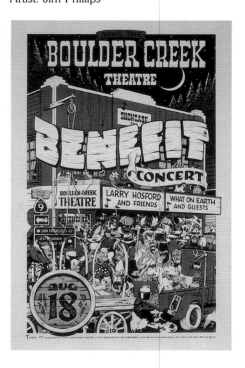

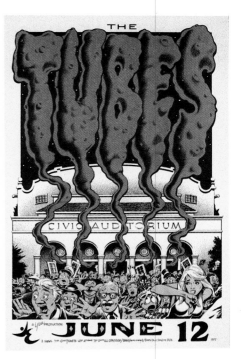

4.105

The Tubes
Civic Auditorium, Santa Cruz, 1977
Artist: Jim Phillips

4.106

Farmworkers Benefit
Spartan Stadium, San Jose, 1971

4.107

Country Joe and the Fish; Joy of Cooking
Shasta College, Redding, California, 1970
Artist: Peerless Graphics

4.108

Grateful Dead; New Riders of the Purple Sage
University of California, Davis, 1971
Artist: James Pierce

4.111

It's a Beautiful Day; The Byrds
University of the Pacific, Stockton, California, 1970
Artist: Bourret / McAllister Photography

4.109

Grateful Dead
University of California, Davis, 1982
Artist: Jim Pinkoski

4.110

Elvin Bishop; Crazy Horse
California Ballroom, Modesto, 1975
Artist: Tom Morris

Santa Barbara

Beginning with the heyday of surf music, and then during the late 1960s psychedelic era, Santa Barbara has served as the site of many memorable rock concerts. The Grateful Dead may well have made the greatest impression there during the 1970s. Certainly the Dead's several appearances at the University of California's Santa Barbara campus stadium were among the sunniest, most thoroughly pleasurable events of their kind.

4.113

Grateful Dead
University of California, Santa Barbara, 1978
Artist: Maas

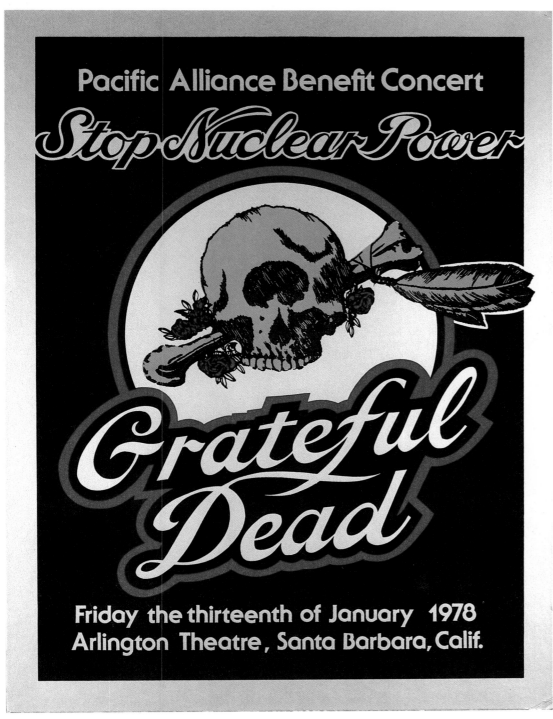

4.112

Pacific Alliance Benefit
Arlington Theatre, Santa Barbara, 1978

4.114

Grateful Dead; New Riders of the Purple Sage
University of California, Santa Barbara, 1973

4.115

Grateful Dead; Maria Muldaur
University of California, Santa Barbara, 1974

4.116

Memorial Day Ball
University of California,
Santa Barbara, 1969

Southern California

Southern California poster art of the 1970s was frequently the work of San Francisco artists. A few, such as Randy Tuten and Rick Griffin, actually grew up in Southern California and migrated their way up to San Francisco after high school. By the mid 1970s, less work was available—particularly after Graham's numbered poster series ceased production in 1971—and artists had to go farther afield to obtain commissions.

One Bay Area artist, "San Andreas Fault," did his strongest work during this period, handling pieces promoting events throughout the entire state. Rick Griffin also did some of his strongest work at this time, in an updated but nonetheless characteristic style (4.123–25), promoting rock events in and around Los Angeles. Shortly after these pieces were drawn, Griffin began a study of Christian imagery, which led to a religious conversion that affected the content and meaning of his art for many years afterwards. Only recently has he again drawn posters and t-shirt art for bands like the Grateful Dead.

4.118
The Sons; Elvin Bishop
University of San Diego, San Diego, 1969
Artist: San Andreas Fault

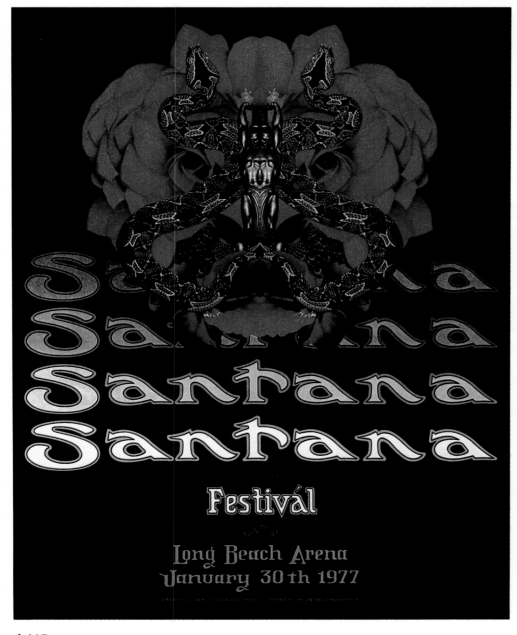

4.117
Santana
Long Beach Arena, Long Beach, 1977
Artists: Randy Tuten, David Singer

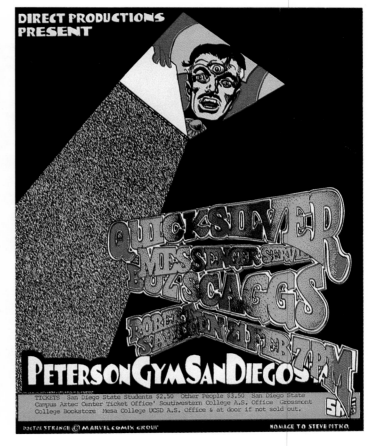

4.119
Quicksilver Messenger Service; Boz Scaggs
San Diego State University, San Diego, 1969
Artist: San Andreas Fault

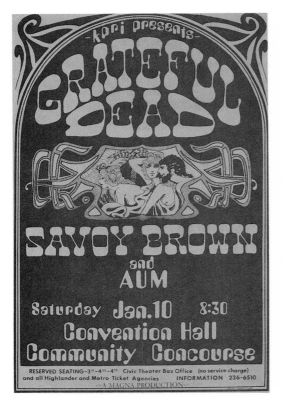

4.120

Grateful Dead; Savoy Brown
Community Concourse, San Diego, 1970
Artist: Dennis Friga

4.121

Electric Flag; Moby Grape
Civic Auditorium, Santa Monica, 1974
Artist: Roger Shepherd

4.122

Grateful Dead; New Riders of the Purple Sage
Hollywood Bowl, Hollywood, 1972

4.123

Orange County Jam
Anaheim Convention Center, Anaheim, 1975
Artist: Rick Griffin

4.124

Frank Zappa; Alice Cooper
California State College, Fullerton, ca. 1972
Artist: Rick Griffin

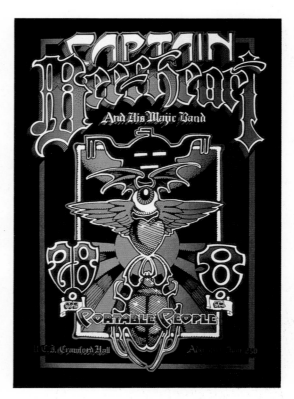

4.125

Captain Beefheart; Portable People
University of California, Davis, ca. 1972
Artist: Rick Griffin

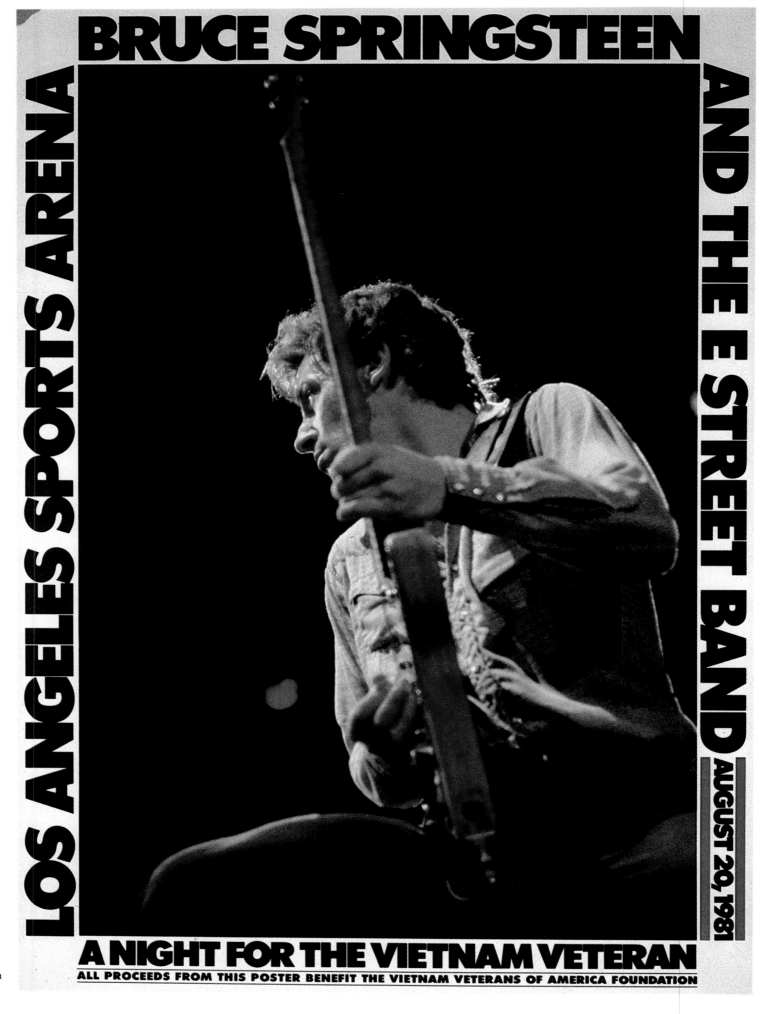

BRUCE SPRINGSTEEN

AND THE E STREET BAND

AUGUST 29, 1981

LOS ANGELES SPORTS ARENA

A NIGHT FOR THE VIETNAM VETERAN

ALL PROCEEDS FROM THIS POSTER BENEFIT THE VIETNAM VETERANS OF AMERICA FOUNDATION

4.126

A Night for the Vietnam
Veteran
Los Angeles Sports Arena
Los Angeles, 1981

4.127

Crosby, Stills, Nash and Young
University of California, Los Angeles, 1969

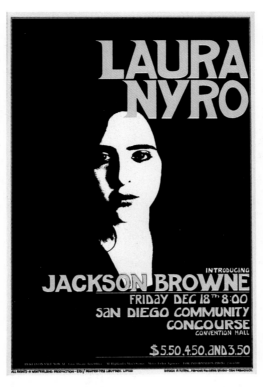

4.128

Laura Nyro; Jackson Browne
Community Concourse, San Diego, 1970
Artist: Randy Tuten

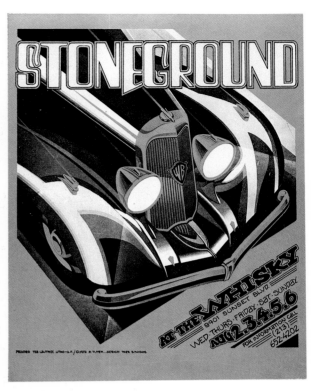

4.129

Stoneground
The Whisky, Los Angeles, 1972
Artist: Randy Tuten

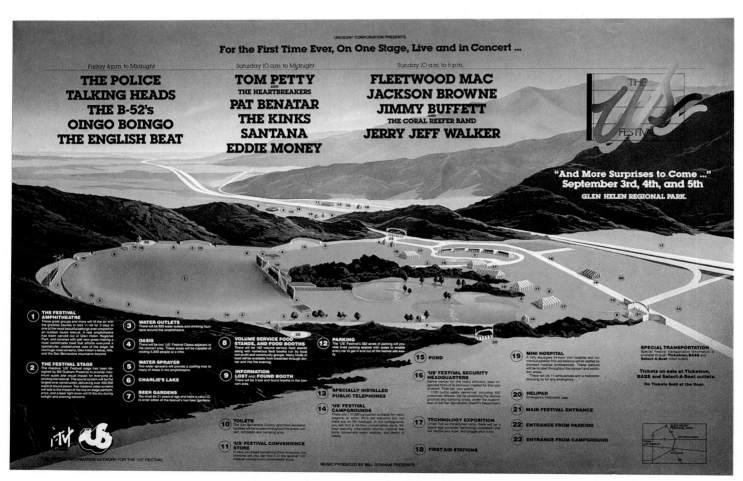

4.130

The US Festival
Glen Helen Park, San Bernardino, 1982

Pacific Northwest

With some exceptions, 1970s posters from the Pacific Northwest are a stodgy lot. But as the end of the decade approached, excellent work began to emerge from the burgeoning new wave and punk scene. Indeed, relatively isolated from the rest of the country, Seattle developed its own indigenous punk aesthetic.

Art Chantry is currently one of the best poster designers working in the Pacific Northwest. Not only an excellent illustrator and draftsman, he has chronicled the popular aesthetics of his region with a book on the Seattle punk and new wave poster art, called *Instant Litter* (1985).

4.131

Tina Turner; Annie Rose
University of Washington,
Seattle, 1983
Artist: Art Chantry

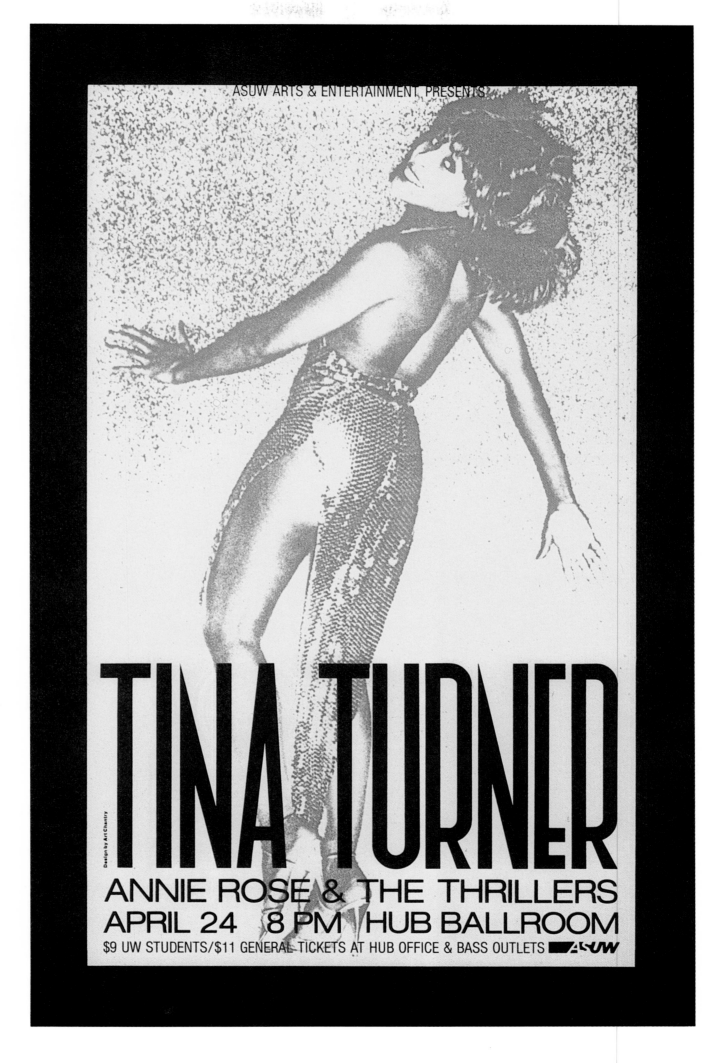

4.132

Trans Continental Pop Festival
Canadian National Expo Grandstand, Toronto, 1970
Artists: Ken Walker, John H. Lown

4.133

B. B. King; Joy of Cooking
The Gardens, Vancouver, British Columbia,
Canada, 1973
Artist: Mark T. Behrens

4.134

Stoneground
Gold Hill Depot, Gold Hill, Nevada, 1977
Artist: Dan O'Neill

4.135

Trips Festival—13 Year Reunion
Odd Fellows Hall, Seattle, 1979
Artist: Doug Fast

4.136

Grateful Dead; River
Springers Ballroom, Portland, Oregon, 1970
Artist: Jim Blashfield

4.137

Second Decadenal Field Trip
Oregon Country Fair, Veneta, Oregon, 1982

SOUND SPECTRUM PRESENTS
FIRST ANNUAL CARSON CITY LABOR DAY MUSIC & ART FESTIVAL

Cold Blood   Boz Scaggs   Joy of Cooking

Stoneground   Elvin Bishop   Doobie Brothers

Sunday September 3

A Thousand Wonders and Over 10 Hours of Beautiful Music

TICKETS: $4.00 ADVANCE; $5.00 AT THE GATE (OPEN 2:00 PM); OUTLETS: ALL TICKETRON, INCLUDING ALL SEARS, EMPORIUM AND MONTGOMERY WARDS. SAN JOSE BOX, SAN FRANCISCO BOX, SACRAMENTO BOX, DISCOUNT RECORDS IN BERKELEY. NORTH SHORE TAHOE: BIPLANE, JANET'S JUICE BAR. SOUTH SHORE TAHOE: DUSTY'S. DEAD HEAD, RENO NEVADA: DISCOUNT RECORDS, SNEED HEARNS LTD., NEVADA AUTO SOUND, IMPORT TRADING POST. CARSON CITY NEVADA: THE T-CAR SPEEDWAY

ARTS & CRAFTS DISPLAYS, POSTER BOOTHS, MOD FASHION SHOW, SKY DIVERS, WANDERING MINSTRELS, BODY PAINTING, JEFFERY, THE GREAT ESCAPE ARTIST

T - CAR SPEEDWAY, CARSON CITY, NEVADA *(HIGHWAY 50 BETWEEN SOUTH SHORE AND RENO)*

4.138

First Carson City Labor Day Music and Art Festival
T-Car Speedway, Carson City, Nevada, 1972
Artist: Rainbow Zenith

4.139

Sly and the Family Stone
Idaho State University, Pocatello,
Idaho, ca. 1972

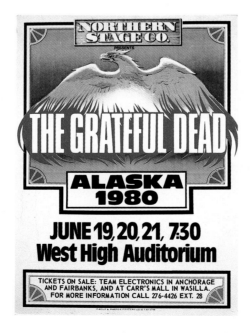

4.140

Grateful Dead
West High Auditorium, Anchorage,
Alaska, 1980

4.141

Grateful Dead
Paramount Northwest, Seattle, 1972

Hawaii

Perhaps reflecting growing affluence on the rock scene, Hawaii in the 1970s became a popular place for major bands to play concerts and vacation. The annual Sunshine Festival was the Hawaiian equivalent of California's Mountain Aire.

One of the most eagerly anticipated pairings of talent was the collaboration of David Singer, who handled more Bill Graham posters in the numbered series than any other artist, and Satty, an accomplished San Francisco collage artist whose artistic vision was similar to Singer's. An eccentric, Satty loved both extravagant hedonism and life in the underground. Singer led a much quieter life. For the 1973 Rolling Stones concert in Honolulu, Singer and Satty produced a strong piece that was sabotaged by Satty's strange indifference to completing it on time (4.147).

4.143

Grateful Dead; Quicksilver Messenger Service
Civic Auditorium, Honolulu, 1970

4.142

Sixth Annual Sunshine Festival
Diamond Head Crater, Hawaii, 1974
Artist: Tom Sellers

4.144

It's a Beautiful Day; Aum
Bandshell, Waikiki, 1969
Artist: Lee Conklin

4.145

Spring Crater Celebration
Diamond Head Crater, Hawaii, 1972
Artist: Jim Evans

4.146

Komo Mai
Diamond Head Crater, Hawaii, 1974
Artist: John Tsara

4.147

Rolling Stones
International Center, Honolulu, 1973
Artists: David Singer, Satty

4.148

Ninth Annual Sunshine Festival
Diamond Head Crater, Hawaii, 1977

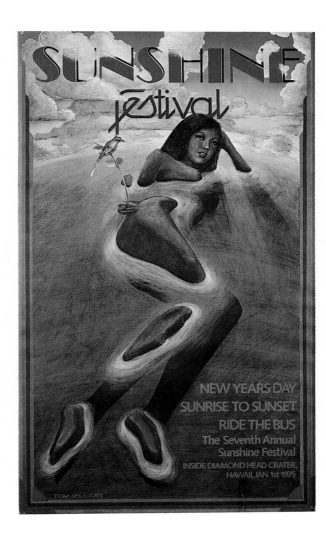

4.149

Seventh Annual
Sunshine Festival
Diamond Head Crater,
Hawaii, 1975
Artist: Tom Sellers

Oklahoma and the Southwest

Rick Griffin, attending a 1981 religious convention in Tulsa, Oklahoma, discovered the work of Brian Thompson, who was creating posters for Tulsa's historic Cains Ballroom. Griffin became Thompson's champion, among other things making it possible for this book to include some of Thompson's work.

Dennis Larkins, who designed various Grateful Dead-related poster, t-shirt, and album cover art, has been praised for his imaginative poster promoting one of the Dead's frequent late 1970s Southwestern appearances (4.153). Larkins, working in association with stage manager Peter Barsotti, was previously a set designer for Bill Graham. Larkins and Barsotti created the posters for the Dead's fifteen-night run

(continued on next page)

4.151

Elvin Bishop
Cains Ballroom, Tulsa, 1982
Artist: Brian Thompson

4.152

Pat Travers; Rainbow. The Old Lady of Brady, Tulsa, 1981. Artist: Brian Thompson

4.150

The Pretenders; The Bureau. Cains Ballroom, Tulsa, 1981. Artist: Brian Thompson

(continued from preceding page)

at San Francisco's Warfield Theater in 1980 (4.45) as well as the eight-night stint at New York's Radio City Music Hall a few weeks later. The latter poster caused the Dead some trouble: Radio City objected to a design that featured skeletons leaning up against its building. A lawsuit was filed, and the band recalled the poster, much to the dismay of the Dead's large following, long a major consumer of group-related graphic art.

4.154

Brian Auger; Aspen
Cains Ballroom, Tulsa, 1981
Artist: Brian Thompson

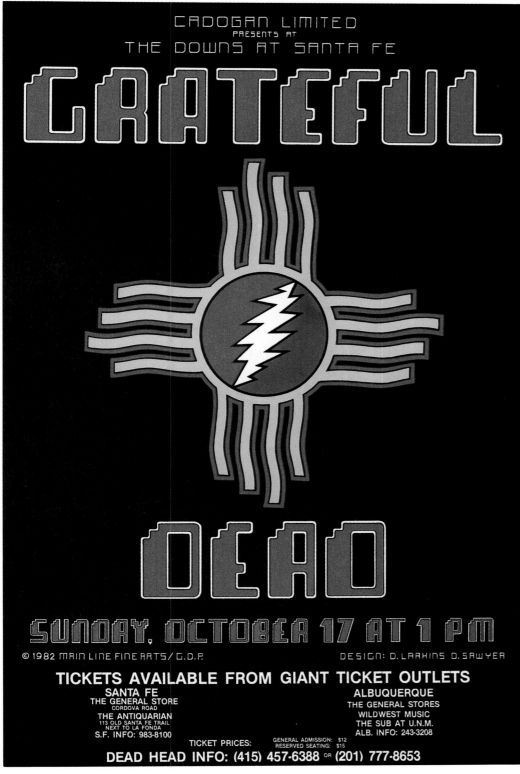

4.153

Grateful Dead
Santa Fe Downs, Santa Fe, 1982
Artist: Dennis Larkins, D. Sawyer

4.155

Utopia
Cains Ballroom, Tulsa, 1981
Artist: Brian Thompson

Texas, Utah, Colorado

With his hugely successful Fourth of July "picnics" held near Austin, Texas, beginning in 1973, singer-songwriter Willie Nelson demonstrated that country music had a large component audience of rock fans. He became the leader of country music's self-styled "outlaw" movement. Nelson's strong Texas base and his rise to national prominence opened the way for other fresh, exciting country music songwriters and performers. Thus country-rock became a major musical force in the 1970s.

4.156
SDS Ball
University of Utah. Salt Lake City. 1969
Artist: Richard Taylor

4.157
Third Willie Nelson 4th of July Picnic
Liberty Hill, Texas, 1975
Artist: Jim Franklin

4.158

Guess Who; Albert King
Tarrant County Convention Center, Fort Worth, 1970
Artist: Randy Tuten

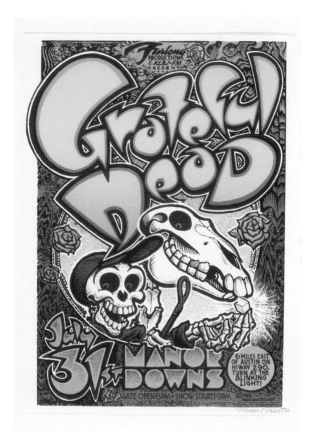

4.159

Grateful Dead
Manor Downs, Texas, 1982
Artist: Michael Priest

4.160

Benefit for Rubin "Hurricane" Carter
Astrodome, Houston, 1976
Artist: Carson

4.161

Grateful Dead; Quicksilver Messenger Service
Panther Hall, Fort Worth, 1970

4.162

Led Zeppelin
Arizona Coliseum, ca. 1972
Artist: Richard Taylor

ARMADILLO WORLD HEADQUARTERS

Beginning in 1969, this Austin dance hall gave Texas a major place in rock history—although the city was already the locus of the original Texas psychedelic movement, which had emerged as early as 1963–64 from peyote-culture experiments among some University of Texas students. Their activity led to the 1967 opening of Austin's first psychedelic dance hall, the Vulcan Gas Company.

Following the Vulcan's closure in 1969, the Armadillo developed Austin into a center of rock energy that held its own against any other American city. During the peak of its success, around 1974, the club earned the distinction of becoming the second largest retail beer outlet in Texas, bested only by the Houston Astrodome.

Much of the Armadillo's success had to do with two key people, owner Eddie Wilson and poster artist and frequent emcee Jim Franklin. Franklin's graphics often portrayed armadillos in fantastic situations. Few clubs anywhere have benefited so much from such an enduring, immediately identifiable image.

4.163

Tracy Nelson and Mother Earth; Shiva's Head Band
Armadillo World Headquarters, Austin, 1971
Artist: Jim Franklin

4.164

30th Annual Art Students Exhibition
University of Texas Art Museum, Austin, 1969
Artist: Jim Franklin

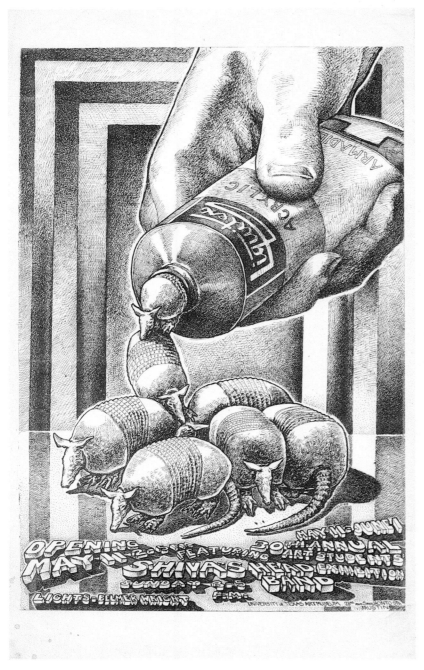

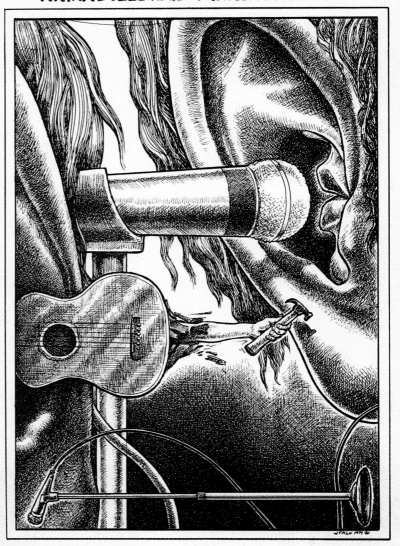

4.165

Bruce Springsteen
Armadillo World Headquarters, Austin, 1974
Artist: Jim Franklin

4.166

Taj Mahal; Lightning Hopkins
Armadillo World Headquarters, Austin, 1971
Artist: Jim Franklin

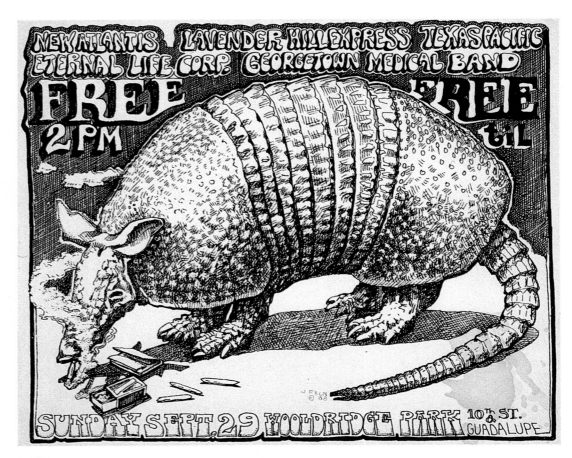

4.167

Armadillo in the Park
Wooldridge Park, Austin, 1968
Artist: Jim Franklin

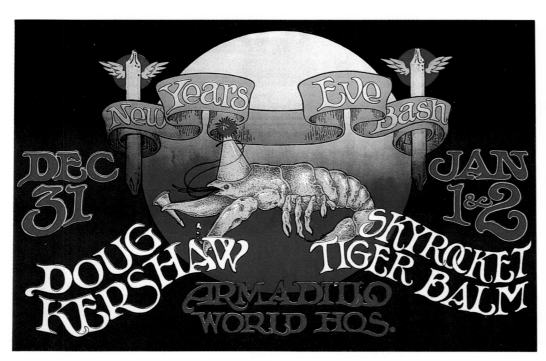

4.168

New Year's Eve Bash
Armadillo World Headquarters, Austin, 1970
Artist: J. Doumey

4.169

Ramon-Ramon and the 4 Daddyos; T. Thelonious Troll
Armadillo World Headquarters, Austin, 1970
Artist: J. Shelton

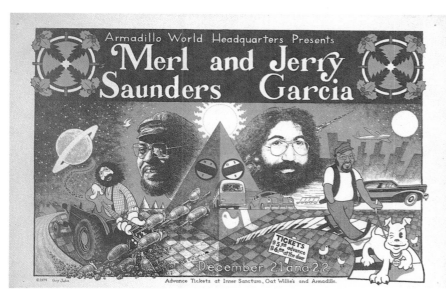

4.170

Jerry Garcia and Merl Saunders
Armadillo World Headquarters, Austin, 1974
Artist: Guy Juke

4.171

Freddie King; Mance Lipscomb
Armadillo World Headquarters, Austin, 1970
Artist: Jim Franklin

4.172

Earl Scruggs Revue; Rat Creek
Armadillo World Headquarters, Austin, 1971
Artist: J. Harter

4.173

U.S. Armydillo
Fort Hood, Kileen, Texas, 1971
Artist: Jim Franklin

The South

NEW ORLEANS

As far back as the turn of the century, New Orleans has been a major influence on American popular music, especially jazz. Beginning in the mid 1950s, New Orleans rhythm-and-blues musicians like Fats Domino imparted an exotic touch to early rock, the spice of a cosmopolitan, Carribean-flavored city. The late Professor Longhair (4.177), composer Allen Toussaint, and the Neville Brothers Band have all contributed to a New Orleans renaissance.

The Neville Brothers (some of whose members were earlier part of the fondly remembered Meters) are celebrated as the premier New Orleans rhythm-and-rock band. They have merged the city's distinctive rhythm and blues with progressive rock stylings, and in some circles are compared to the Grateful Dead. Like all New Orleans musicians, the Nevilles draw on the New Orleans tradition of public music making. They also are members of the Wild Tchoupitoulas ''Indian-style'' performing troupe (4.174, 4.176), whose music, based on ritual, is successfully reworked for modern ears.

4.174

Wild Tchoupitoulas; Neville Brothers
Austin Opry House, Austin, 1978
Artist: Wilkins

4.175

New Orleans Jazz and Heritage Festival
Multiple venues, New Orleans, 1983
Artist: St. Germain

4.176

Film: *Always for Pleasure*
1980
Artists: Michael Smith, Mischa Phillippott

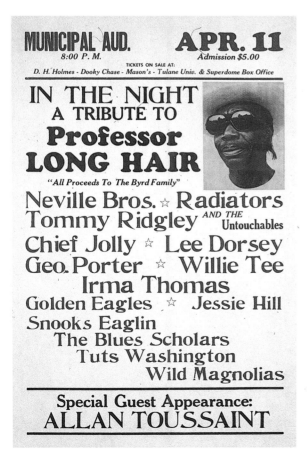

4.177

A Tribute to Professor Longhair
Municipal Auditorium, New Orleans, ca. 1984

OTHER SOUTHERN LOCATIONS

Southern-based rock came into its own at the start of the 1970s. The Allman Brothers, followed by Lynyrd Skynyrd, the Charlie Daniels Band, the Marshall Tucker Band, and more recently Z. Z. Top, developed a regional audience that, in turn, earned national respect for its recognition and appreciation of the Southern sound.

The success of large-scale festivals, like the two Atlanta International Pop Festivals (4.178), helped create a new image for Southern rock. By the early 1970s, all touring bands, American and European, made regular forays into every corner of the region, opening, as never before, civic centers, municipal halls, theaters, and county coliseums to mainstream rock music.

4.178

Second Atlanta International Pop Festival
Middle Georgia Raceway, Atlanta, 1970

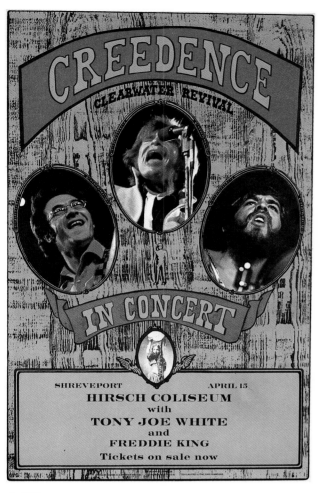

4.179

Creedence Clearwater Revival; Tony Joe White
Hirsch Coliseum, Shreveport, Louisiana, 1972
Artist: D. Grace

4.180

Doobie Brothers
Memphis Showboat, Memphis, 1975
Artist: Palombi

4.181

Mar Y Sol Pop Festival
Vega Baja, Puerto Rico, 1972

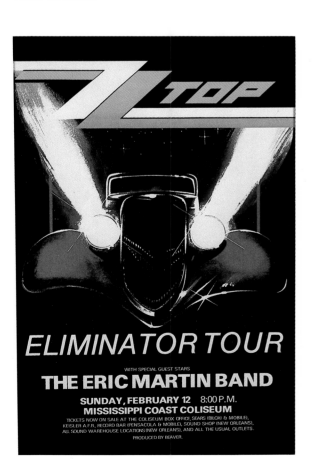

4.182 *(left)*

Z. Z. Top; Eric Martin Band
Mississippi Coast Coliseum,
Biloxi, Mississippi, 1984

4.183

First Atlanta International Pop Festival
Middle Georgia Raceway, Atlanta, 1969

Michigan: Gary Grimshaw

Gary Grimshaw was the most celebrated Detroit-area poster artist. His career, which began in the late 1960s, was interrupted when he fled Michigan in 1968 to escape prosecution on unjust drug charges. Grimshaw returned to Detroit and Ann Arbor in 1971, successfully beat the charges, and resumed regular poster and newspaper work.

Grimshaw's second period of work shows great maturity; the posters from the early

(continued on next page)

4.185

James Gang; SRC
Central Michigan University, Mount Pleasant, Michigan, 1971
Artist: Gary Grimshaw

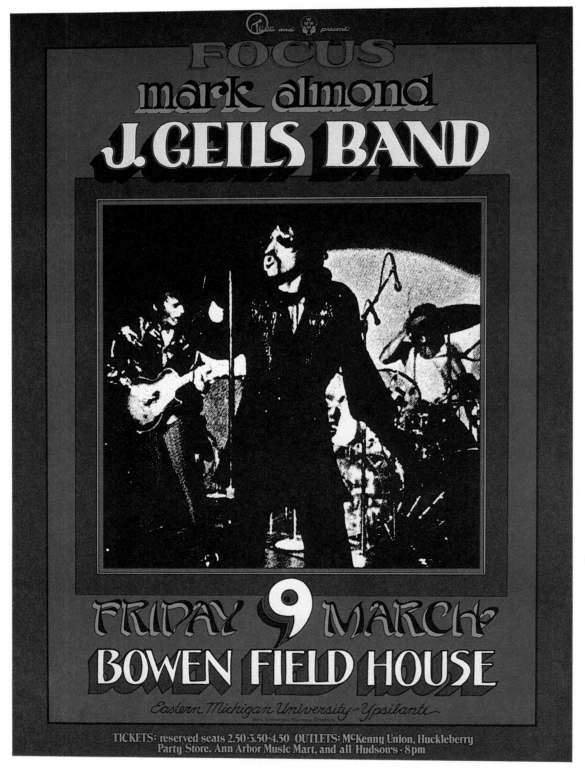

4.184

J. Geils Band; Focus
Eastern Michigan University, Ypsilanti, 1973
Artist: Gary Grimshaw

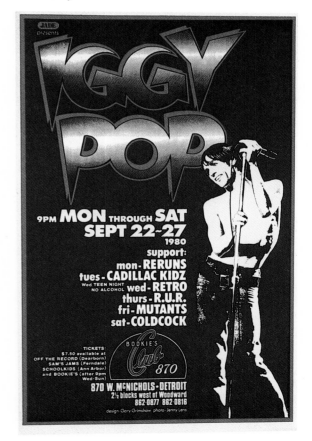

4.186

Iggy Pop; Reruns
Bookie's Club, Detroit, 1980
Artist: Gary Grimshaw

(continued from preceding page) 1970s are among his most imaginative. His return to Michigan was made not only to clear his own name, but to aid his friend John Sinclair, an outspoken social activist who in 1969 was given an extremely harsh prison sentence for a minor drug offense.

During the several years it took to win Sinclair's parole, Grimshaw designed *Guitar Army* (1972), his friend's radical commentaries in book form. He also drew many celebrated posters promoting rock events benefiting Sinclair's legal defense fund (4.193).

Perhaps the most important poster of this period in Grimshaw's career was produced for the 1970 Freedom Rally held at the University of Michigan's large Crisler Arena. John Lennon and Yoko Ono were prominent among the performers. The outcry the event raised helped hasten Sinclair's release (4.194).

4.187

Grateful Dead; New Riders of the Purple Sage
University of Michigan, Ann Arbor, 1971
Artist: Gary Grimshaw

4.188

Alice Coltrane; Leon Thomas
University of Michigan, Ann Arbor, 1967
Artist: Gary Grimshaw

4.189

Ike and Tina Turner; Blue Scepter
IMA Auditorium, Flint, Michigan, 1972
Artist: Gary Grimshaw

4.190

Buddy Guy; Fred McDowell
The Park, North Baltimore, Ohio, 1971
Artist: Gary Grimshaw

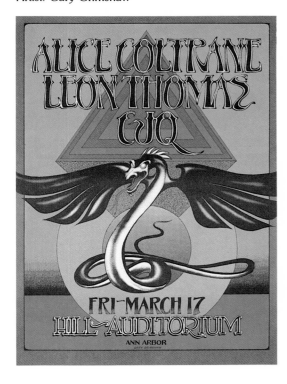

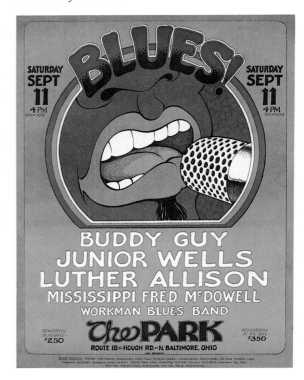

4.191

Sound of Detroit '83
Saint Andrews Hall, Detroit, 1983
Artist: Gary Grimshaw

4.192

Allman Brothers; Dr. John
University of Michigan, Ann Arbor, 1972
Artist: Gary Grimshaw

THE SINCLAIR POSTERS

4.193
Free John Sinclair Rally
Grande Ballroom / Eastowne Ballroom, Detroit, 1970
Artist: Gary Grimshaw

4.194
John Sinclair Freedom Rally
University of Michigan, Ann Arbor, 1971
Artist: Gary Grimshaw

4.195
Jefferson Airplane; Commander Cody
Cobo Hall, Detroit, 1972
Artist: Gary Grimshaw

Commander Cody in the Midwest

Commander Cody and his band, the Lost Planet Airmen, came together in the late 1960s at the University of Michigan, Ann Arbor, where Cody (real name George Frayne) was a graduate student. Most Cody band appearances were promoted by distinctive, stylistically inter-related posters and handbills, primarily the work of Chris Frayne, George's brother. Chris signed the posters "Ozone," a reference to the lost-in-the-ozone state of mind the Cody band identified themselves with. A notable feature of Frayne's designs are old trucks, especially the semi-truck rigs referred to in many Cody songs (4.196–197, 4.227–28).

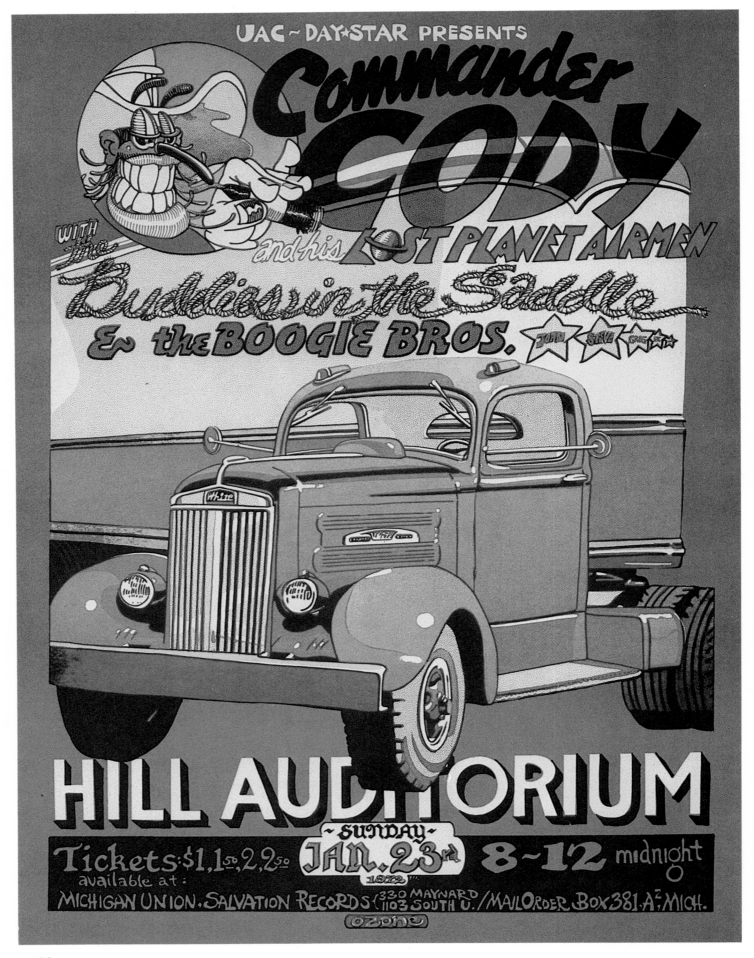

4.196

Commander Cody; Buddies in the Saddle
University of Michigan, Ann Arbor, 1972
Artist: Chris Frayne / Ozone

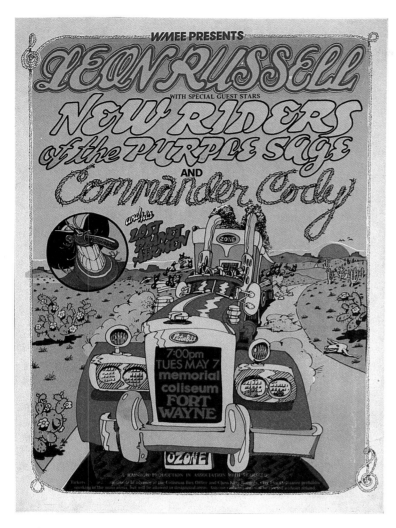

4.197

Leon Russell; Commander Cody
Memorial Coliseum, Fort Wayne, Indiana, 1974
Artist: Chris Frayne / Ozone

4.198

Evansville Freedom Celebration
Roberts Stadium, Evansville, Indiana, 1973

4.199

Ann Arbor Blues and Jazz Festival in Exile
St. Clair College, Windsor, Canada, 1974
Artist: Gary Kell

4.200

Grateful Dead
University of Michigan, Ann Arbor, 1981

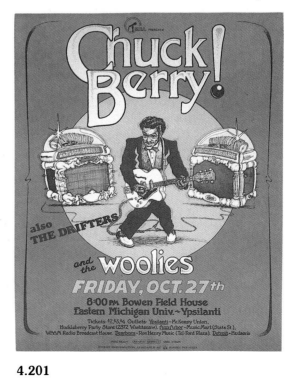

4.201

Chuck Berry; The Drifters
Eastern Michigan University, Ypsilanti, 1972
Artists: Mike Brady, Greg Sobran /
Rainbow Graphics

Chicago and the Midwest

There was little noteworthy poster art developed in Chicago during the early psychedelic years, but a small, distinctive series appeared several years later promoting shows at the Aragon Ballroom, the work of American Tribal Productions.

At the time of the classic Aragon dances, Hugh Hefner's *Playboy* magazine operation was still based in Chicago, and a number of the artists who drew rock posters for the Aragon events also free-lanced for *Playboy*.

4.203

Grateful Dead
Memorial Hall, Kansas City, Kansas, 1979

4.202

Grateful Dead; It's a Beautiful Day
Aragon Ballroom, Chicago, 1970
Artist: Daniel Clyne

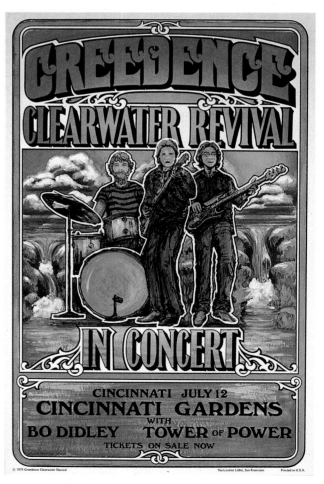

4.204

Creedence Clearwater Revival; Bo Diddley
Cincinnati Gardens, Cincinnati, 1971
Artist: Walker-Parkinson Design

4.205

Traffic; SRC
Aragon Ballroom, Chicago, 1970
Artist: Daniel Clyne

4.206

Ten Years After; B. B. King
Aragon Ballroom, Chicago, 1970
Artists: Wandroo, Linda Borstrom

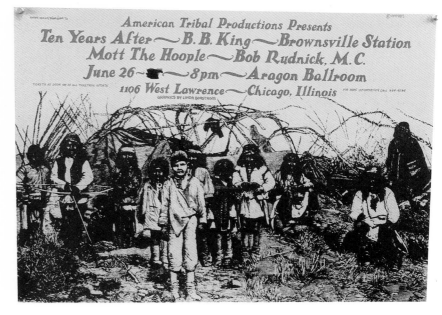

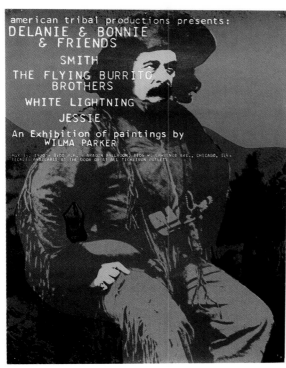

4.207

Delaney and Bonnie; Flying Burrito Brothers
Aragon Ballroom, Chicago, 1970

4.208

Country Joe and the Fish; Amboy Dukes
Aragon Ballroom, Chicago, 1970
Artist: Laura Green

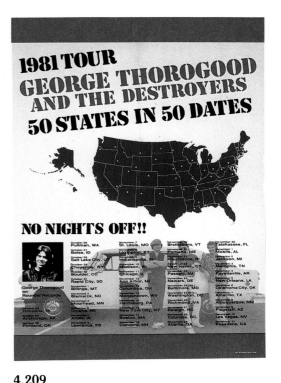

4.209

50 States in 50 Dates—George Thorogood
1981

Philadelphia and Other Pennsylvania Cities

As rock entered the 1970s mainstream, Philadelphia, Pittsburgh, and other Pennsylvania cities and college campuses hosted important appearances. Philadelphia's Electric Factory, an outgrowth of a club operation, handled shows in Philadelphia and numerous East Coast cities other than New York.

The Electric Factory did not place particular emphasis on posters for promotion, but nevertheless produced a series of graphically strong pieces, most executed by their principal artist, Spencer Zahn.

4.210

Traffic; Cat Stevens
Academy of Music, Philadelphia, 1970
Artist: Spencer Zahn

4.211

Jethro Tull; Bob Seger System
Comerford Theater, Wilkes-Barre, Pennsylvania, 1970

4.212

Grateful Dead; New Riders of the Purple Sage
Franklin and Marshall College, Lancaster, Pennsylvania, 1971
Artist: Spencer Zahn

4.213

Three Dog Night
Spectrum, Philadelphia, 1971
Artist: Spencer Zahn

4.214

Delaney and Bonnie; B. B. King
Electric Factory, Philadelphia, 1970

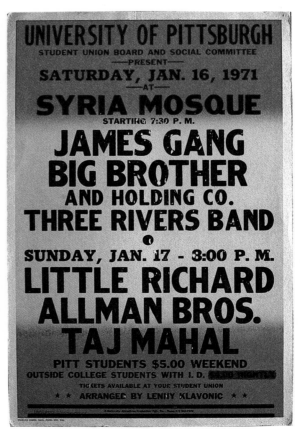

4.215

Little Richard; Big Brother and the Holding Company
Syria Mosque, Pittsburgh, 1971

New York City and the East Coast

Like most East Coast cities, New York produced relatively few concert posters during the 1970s. Promoters in the New York area relied on impressive newspaper display ads and calendar listings in such popular weeklies as the *Village Voice*.

However, Bill Graham did commission a number of special-issue posters, including pieces for the Who's Lincoln Center performances of the rock-opera *Tommy* in 1970 (4.221), and the Grateful Dead's first appearance at Long Island's Nassau Coliseum in 1973 (4.220). Drawn by Graham's primary New York artist, David Byrd, "A Swell Dance Concert" is one of the promoter's personal favorites—perhaps in part because Graham himself helped choose the distinctive "He's truckin', she's posin'" motif.

(continued on p. 405)

4.217

Ozzy Osbourne
Multiple venues, New York and New Jersey, 1982

4.216

Iron Maiden; Quiet Riot
Madison Square Garden, New York, 1983

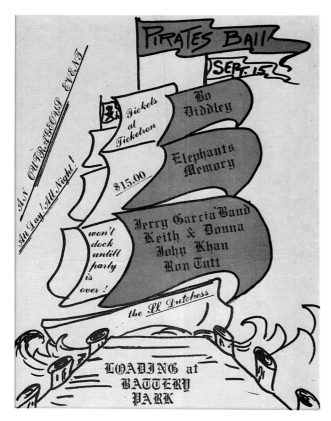

4.218

Pirates Ball
S.S. Dutchess, New York–New Jersey, 1976

4.219

Record promotion—Hot Tuna
New York, 1976
Artist: Kenny Pisani

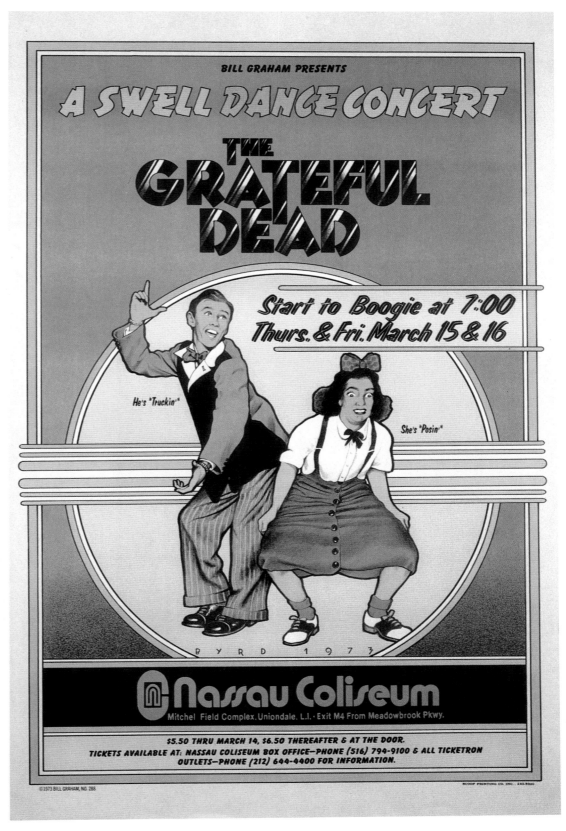

4.220

A Swell Dance Concert
Nassau Coliseum, Uniondale, Long Island, 1973
Artist: David Byrd

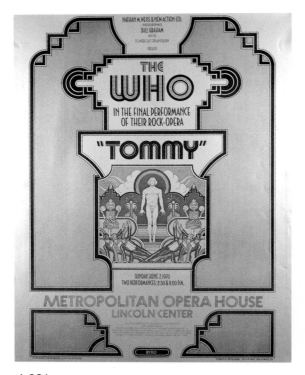

4.221

Final performance—*Tommy*
Lincoln Center, New York, 1970
Artist: David Byrd

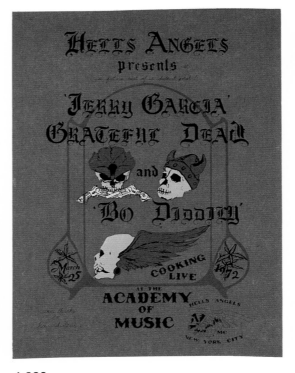

4.222

Grateful Dead; Bo Diddley
Academy of Music, New York, 1972

4.223

Bruce Springsteen
Bottom Line, New York, 1975

4.224

Stiff Records Tour
Bottom Line, New York, ca. 1981

4.225

Cockettes; Sylvester
Anderson Theater, New York, ca. 1977
Artist: Todd Trexler

(continued from p. 402)

Many East Coast college campuses and middle-size cities were sites for memorable rock concerts in the 1970s. Of particular note: the rising fortunes of the Grateful Dead and the gradual disappearance of other late 1960s mainstay San Francisco bands. Bands from the South, like the Allman Brothers, and new bands from England, like Jethro Tull, were part of a new mainstream movement.

The largest gathering of rock fans in history took place in 1973 at the Watkins Glen grand prix raceway (4.231): over 600,000 fans—200,000 more than had attended Woodstock in 1969.

It was also during the early 1970s that Bruce Springsteen began the work destined to make him a superstar by the 1980s. One of his first New Jersey-based bands was called Steel Mill, and another called Child (4.236). Springsteen and his young E-Street Band played the Jersey shore extensively. His 1975 appearance at New York's Bottom Line nightclub was a break-through for him (4.223).

4.226

Final U.S. Appearance—Cream
Rhode Island Auditorium, Providence, 1969
Artist: Mad Peck Studios

4.227
Commander Cody; Asleep at the Wheel
Mount Holyoke College, South Hadley,
Massachusetts, 1978
Artist: Chris Frayne / Ozone

4.228
Commander Cody; Buzzy Linhart
University of New Haven, New Haven,
Connecticut, ca. 1973
Artist: Chris Frayne / Ozone

4.229
Quicksilver Messenger Service
Boston Tea Party, 1970
Artist: Alton Kelley

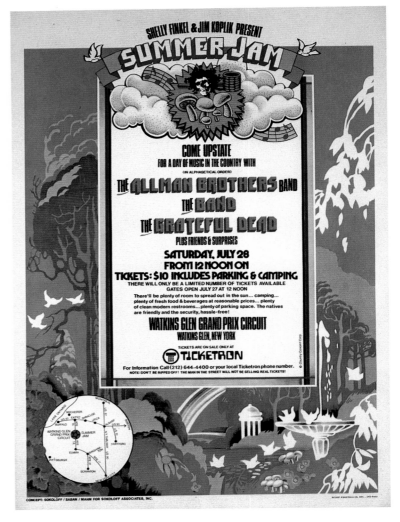

4.230
Grateful Dead
Shea's, Buffalo, New York, 1979
Artist: Andrew Elias

4.231
Summer Jam
Grand Prix Circuit, Watkins Glen, New York, 1973
Artists: Sokoloff, Sabin, Mahn

4.232

Grateful Dead
Massachusetts Institute of Technology, Boston, 1970
Artist: Jureurez

4.233

Twenty Years of Rock & Roll—Grateful Dead
1985
Artist: Gary Kroman

4.234

Spring Weekend
Brown University,
Providence, 1970

4.235

Brooklyn Rock
46th Street Rock Palace,
Brooklyn, 1970
Artist: Corey Graphics

4.236

Child (with Bruce Springsteen)
Shore Motel, New Jersey, 1970

Europe
(and Egypt)

GRATEFUL DEAD

The Dead made a few British appearances in 1970, but their first real European exposure was a 1972 tour of England and the Continent. The group returned to England and Germany on a number of occasions. One such appearance—Munich, 1974—yielded an especially striking poster by Gunther Kieser, whose work goes back to the mid 1960s (4.237).

Perhaps the most famous overseas Dead poster is the Alton Kelley piece for the band's 1978 concerts at the foot of Egypt's Great Pyramid. Run in an edition of 1,000, it is now a valuable collectible (4.239).

4.237

Grateful Dead
Olympiahalle, Munich,
West Germany, 1974
Artist: Gunther Kieser

4.238

Grateful Dead
Sports Palace, Barcelona, Spain, 1981
Artist: J. R. Brusi

4.239

Grateful Dead in Egypt
Great Pyramid, Giza, Egypt, 1978
Artist: Alton Kelley

4.240

Grateful Dead
Multiple venues, West Germany, 1981
Artists: Dennis Larkins, Peter Barsotti

4.241

Jamaica World Music Festival
Bob Marley Memorial Performance Center, Kingston,
Jamaica, 1982

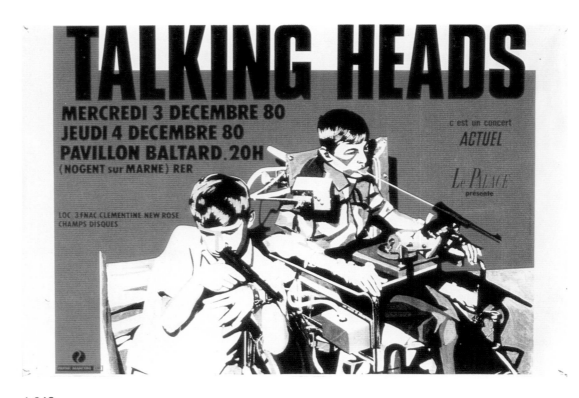

4.242

Fête de l'Humanité
Paris, 1972

4.243

Talking Heads
Baltard Pavilion, Paris, France, 1980
Artist: S. Chaprion

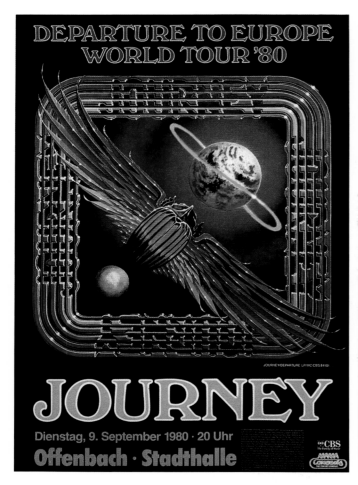

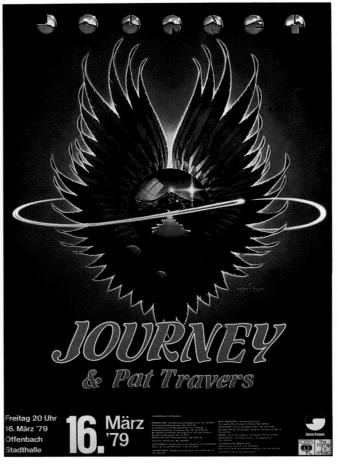

4.244

Journey
Stadthalle, Offenbach, West Germany, 1980
Artist: Alton Kelley

4.245

Journey; Pat Travers
Stadthalle, Offenbach, West Germany, 1979
Artists: Alton Kelley, Stanley Mouse

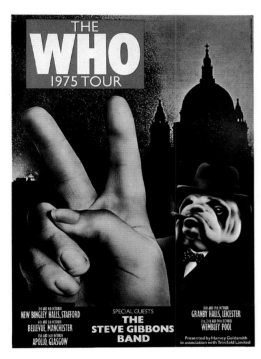

4.246
1975 Tour—The Who
Multiple venues, United Kingdom, 1975
Artist: John Pasche

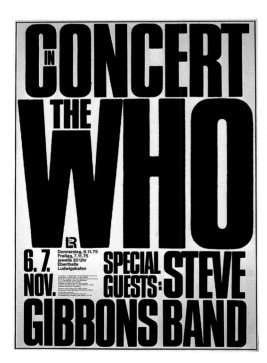

4.247
The Who; Steve Gibbons
Eberthalle, Ludwigshafen, West Germany, 1975

4.248
The Who
Olympiahalle, Munich, West Germany, 1976
Artist: Gunther Kieser

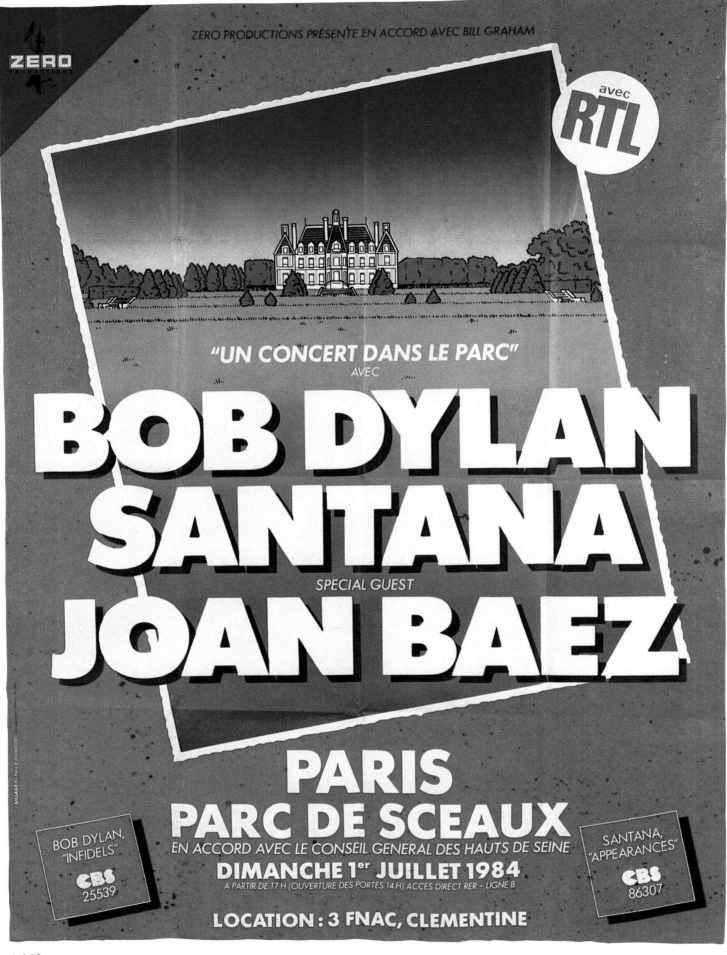

Plate 4.249 is a good example of the oversize kiosk poster very common on the Continent. This piece is about six feet tall by four feet wide.

4.249

Bob Dylan; Santana
Parc des Sceaux, Paris, 1984

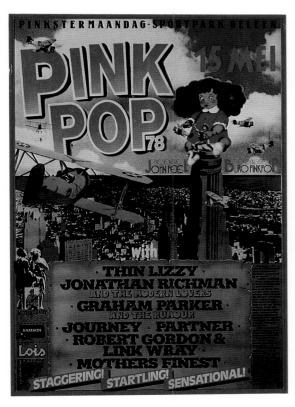

4.250

Pink Pop Festival
Sportpark Geleen, Netherlands, 1978

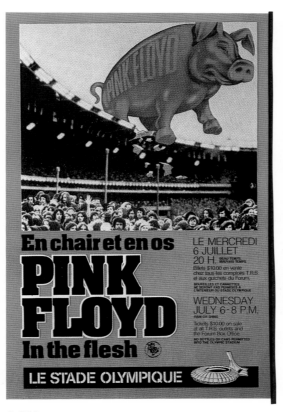

4.251

Pink Floyd
Le Stade Olympique, Paris, 1977

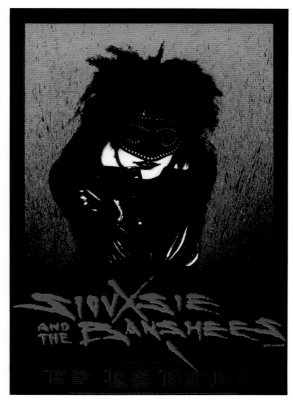

4.252

Siouxie and the Banshees
Multiple venues, 1986
Artist: Stanley Mouse

4.253

Fleetwood Mac
Deutsches Museum, Munich, West Germany, 1970
Artist: Gunther Kieser

4.254

Traffic; Sutherland Brothers
Jahrhunderthalle, Frankfurt, West Germany, 1974
Artists: Gunther Kieser, Hartmann

ROLLING STONES
AND OTHERS

Just as the Grateful Dead used the skull and roses design as something of a trademark, the Rolling Stones adopted the red lips symbol, which first made an appearance on their *Sticky Fingers* album inner sleeve.

While the Grateful Dead has been featured on more posters than any other band, the Rolling Stones and the Dead run neck and neck so far as quantity of *high-quality* posters is concerned. Many of the Stones' best were created by English artist John Pasche. (4.259, 4.263, 4.267, 4.272).

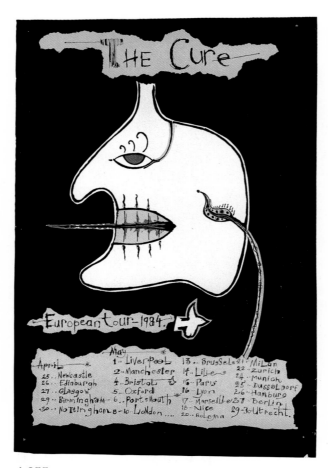

4.255

European Tour—The Cure
Multiple venues, Europe, 1984

4.256

Joe Jackson
The Zenith, Paris, 1984

4.257

Journey; Pat Travers
Volkshaus, Zurich, Switzerland, 1978

4.258

Rock Explosion New Year Special—The Rolling Stones
Budokan Large Hall, Tokyo, Japan, 1973

4.259

Rolling Stones
European Tour, 1970
Artist: John Pasche

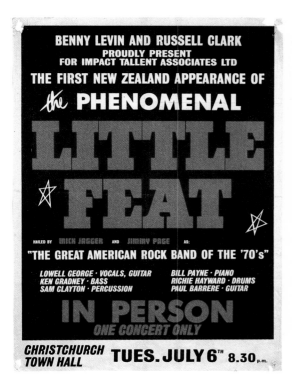

4.260
Little Feat
Town Hall, Christchurch, New Zealand, 1976

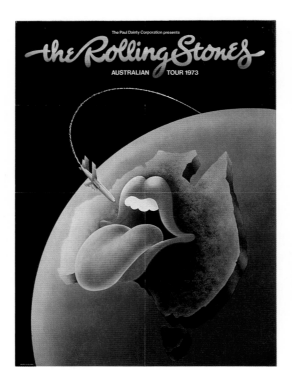

4.261
Rolling Stones
Australian Tour, 1973
Artist: Ian McCausland

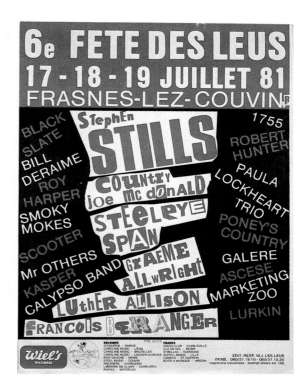

4.262
Stephen Stills; Country Joe
Frasnes-Lez-Couvin, Belgium, 1981

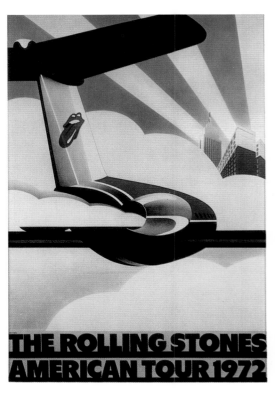

4.263
Rolling Stones
American Tour, 1972
Artist: John Pasche

4.264
Bob Marley and the Wailers
Plaza de Toros, Ibiza, Spain, 1978

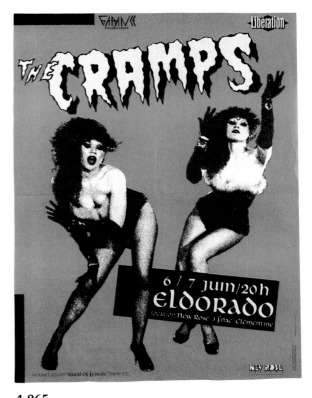

4.265
The Cramps
Eldorado, Paris, 1984

(left)
4.266
Rolling Stones; 10cc
Knebworth Park,
Stevenage, England,
1976

(right)
4.267
United Kingdom Tour—
Rolling Stones
Multiple venues, 1971
Artist: John Pasche

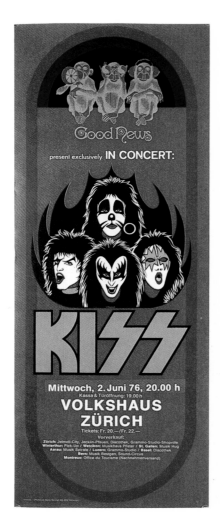

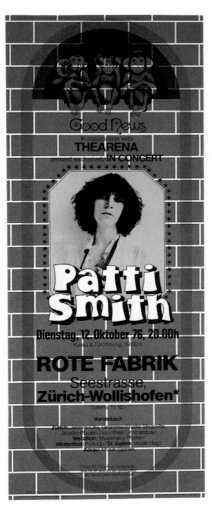

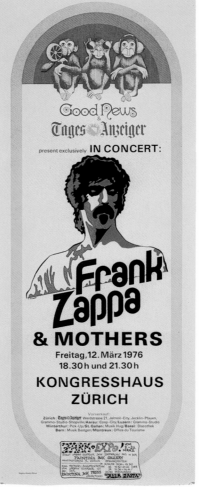

4.268
Kiss
Volkshaus, Zurich,
Switzerland, 1976

4.269
Patti Smith
Rote Fabrik, Zurich,
Switzerland, 1976

4.270
Rick Wakeman
Eulachhalle, Winterthur,
Switzerland, 1974

4.271
Frank Zappa
Kongresshaus, Zurich,
Switzerland, 1973

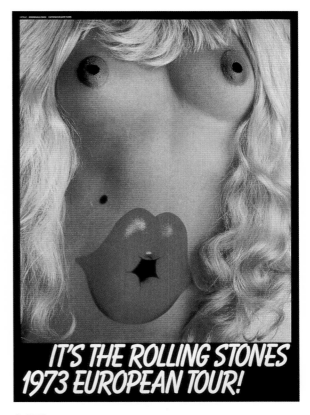

4.272

European Tour—Rolling Stones, 1973
Artists: John Pasche, David Thorpe

4.273

Rolling Stones
Cardiff Castle, Cardiff, Wales, 1973
Artist: J. Purness

4.274

Rolling Stones Tour, 1978
Artist: Raindrop Productions

Unusual Ephemera

Many leading San Francisco artists created non-concert posters during the 1970s, just as they had in the late 1960s. Before their working partnership dissolved around 1980, Stanley Mouse and Alton Kelley designed several platinum-selling Journey album covers (4.244–45), for Steve Miller's *Book of Dreams* (4.278) and Grateful Dead songwriter Robert Hunter's *Tiger Rose* (4.277). David Singer concentrated on abstract collages based on classical mythology (4.281).

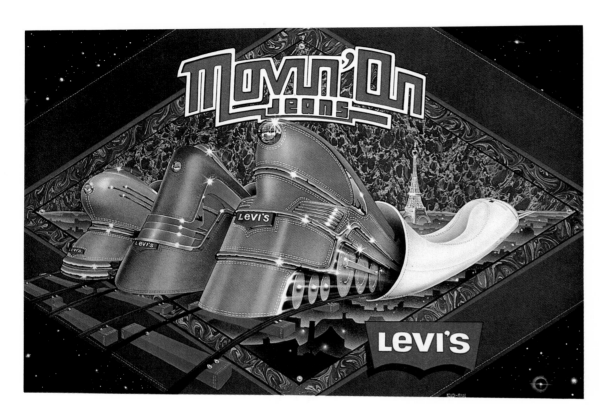

4.275
Advertisement: Levi's Movin' On Jeans
San Francisco, ca. 1972
Artists: Alton Kelley, Stanley Mouse

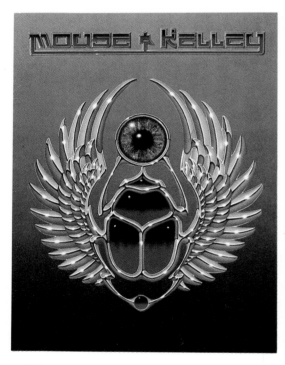

4.276
Mouse / Kelley packet cover, 1976
Artists: Alton Kelley, Stanley Mouse

4.277
Tiger Rose—Robert Hunter, 1976
Artists: Alton Kelley, Stanley Mouse

4.278
Book of Dreams—Steve Miller, 1976
Artists: Alton Kelley, Stanley Mouse

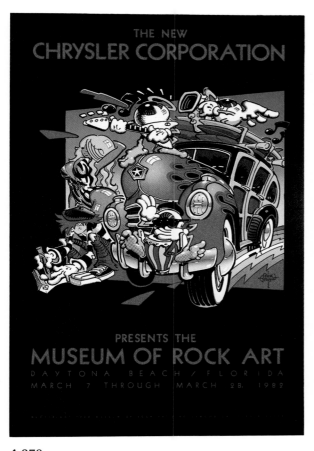

4.279

Traveling exhibit: Museum of Rock Art
Daytona Beach, Florida, 1982
Artist: Rick Griffin

4.280

Concrete Foundation of Fine Arts Show. Peanut Gallery, San Rafael, California, 1978
Artists: Dave Sheridan, Stanley Mouse, Alton Kelley, Victor Moscoso, Pat Ryan, Tim Harris

4.281

Khepr-Ra, 1978
Artist: David Singer

Record Company Promotions

One of the best of the early 1970s newspaper ads was for Grateful Dead guitarist Jerry Garcia's first solo album (4.283). Garcia lost part of one finger on his picking hand—chopped off by his brother in a childhood accident—and his distinctive handprint became part of the Grateful Dead symbology.

4.282

Newspaper record promotion:
Madness, 1981
Artist: Ian Wright

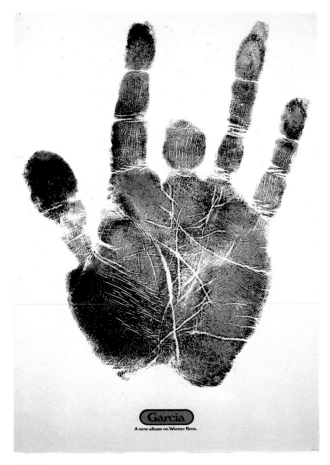

4.283

Album promotion: Jerry Garcia
1972

4.284

Newspaper record promotion:
The Who, 1981

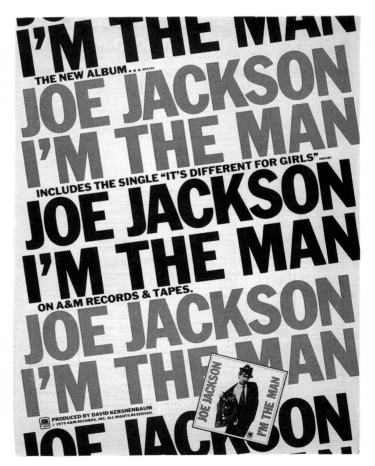

4.285

Newspaper record promotion: Joe Jackson
1979

Backstage and Laminated Passes

Fewer major concert posters were made by the late 1970s, but a great body of new music-related art began to emerge in the form of backstage passes and laminated crew passes issued by bands and promoters to identify authorized guests, crew, and production personnel.

These passes served as mini-posters. Sometimes the same design was printed in different colors for multiple appearances at the same venue or to avoid the necessity of new backstage art for every gig on a tour.

4.286
Laminated all-access pass:
Bob Dylan and Santana,
Wembley Stadium, London, 1984

4.287
Special seating pass: Rolling Stones
Candlestick Park, San Francisco, 1981
Artist: Randy Tuten

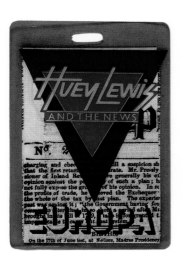

4.288
Laminated tour pass:
Huey Lewis and the News
Europe, 1975
Artist: Su. Suttle

4.289
Special laminated
tour pass: Herbie Herbert (Journey), ca. 1983

4.290
Laminated tour pass:
ARMS Benefit for Ronnie Lane
Dallas, Los Angeles,
San Francisco, 1983

4.291
Laminated tour pass:
Bootsy Collins
1978

4.292
Laminated crew pass: Santana
1986
Artist: Su. Suttle

4.293
Backstage pass: Bruce Springsteen
Madison Square Garden, New York, 1980
Artist: Otto Printing

4.294
Laminated staff pass:
Grateful Dead, 1985
Artist: Tim Harris

4.295
Backstage tour pass:
Adrian Belew. 1983

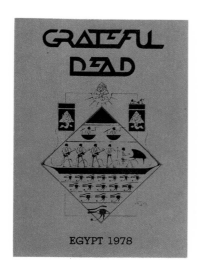

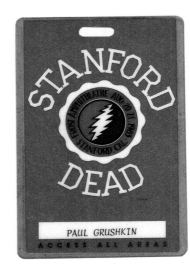

4.296

Laminated all-access pass (front):
Grateful Dead. Great Pyramid,
Giza, Egypt, 1978
Artist: Stanley Mouse

4.297

Laminated all-access pass (back):
Grateful Dead
Great Pyramid, Giza, Egypt, 1978

4.298

Laminated all-access
tour pass: Pat Benatar
1982

4.299

Laminated all-access pass:
Grateful Dead. Stanford University,
Palo Alto, 1983. Artist: Randy Tuten

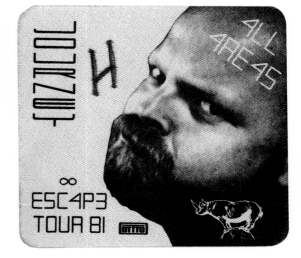

4.300

Backstage tour pass: Santana
ca. 1981
Artist: Su. Suttle

4.301

Backstage tour pass:
Cyndi Lauper
1984

4.302

Backstage tour pass: Journey
1981
Artist: Otto Printing

4.303

Laminated staff pass:
US Festival
Glen Helen Park,
San Bernardino, 1982

4.304

Backstage event pass:
Elvis Presley
Pittsburgh, 1975

4.305

Backstage tour pass: Iron Maiden
1983

4.306

Laminated crew pass:
Prince
1984–1985

4.307

Backstage pass: David Grisman Quintet
Commodore Ballroom, Vancouver,
British Columbia, Canada, 1981

4.308

Laminated backstage
tour pass: U2
1985

4.309

Press pass: Alice Cooper
ca. 1978

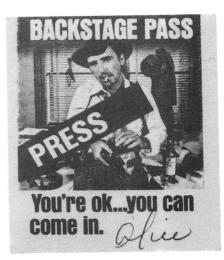

4.310

Backstage guest pass:
Fleetwood Mac
1982

4.311

Laminated all-access pass:
Sammy Hagar
ca. 1983

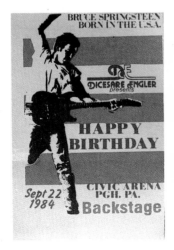

4.312

Backstage pass:
Bruce Springsteen
Civic Arena, Pittsburgh, 1984

4.313

Laminated backstage tour pass: Jefferson Starship
1976. Artist: Bill Laudner

4.314

Huey Lewis and the News
European Tour, 1986
Artist: Su. Suttle

4.315

Backstage tour pass: Allman Brothers
ca. 1973

4.316

Guest tour pass: Queen
South America and Japan,
1981

4.317

Laminated backstage
tour pass: Stray Cats
1984

4.318

Backstage crew pass: Frank Zappa
1981

4.319
Backstage pass: Santana Pacific Tour
1976
Artist: Randy Tuten

4.320
Backstage after-show pass:
Bruce Springsteen
Capital Center, Washington, D.C.,
1981   Artist: Otto Printing

4.321
Backstage pass: Grateful Dead
Civic Auditorium, San Francisco, 1984
Artist: Susie Reed

4.322
Laminated performer's tour pass: Grateful Dead
1983

4.323
Laminated limited-access tour
pass: Doobie Brothers. 1979
Artist: Stanley Mouse

4.324
Crew tour pass: The Who
1979

4.325
Laminated tour pass:
The Rolling Stones
1981

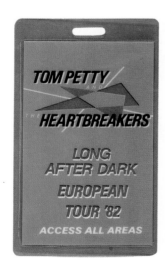

4.326
Laminated backstage tour
pass: Tom Petty
European Tour, 1982

4.327
Backstage pass: Grateful Dead
Marin Veterans Auditorium, San Rafael, 1984

4.328
Laminated backstage event pass:
MUSE Concert
1979

5

The New Music: 1976–1987

I've never gotten the same thrill out of having one of my cartoons printed in a magazine as much as seeing one of my old fliers—something I did for a punk gig the week before—laying in the gutter. Seeing it all mashed and dirty *thrilled* me, because that was how I was living, too. It looked exactly like my life.

SHAWN KERRI in conversation, 1986

New wave and punk poster art evolved over the past decade, and although it has slowed down, it is still evolving. While it reached back to the postering traditions of rock's first era, the 1950s, the new-style art of the 1970s and 1980s rapidly developed a strength of its own that justified flaunting all convention. The rise of punk and new wave was as much a challenge to the rock music establishment as were the psychedelic developments of the late 1960s. Mainstream rock of the 1970s had become big business, slick, professional, and removed from its audience. It had become *safe*. Punk and new wave offered anything but safety and predictability. It was music—as well as fashion and graphic art—for people who flaunted their outrageousness. Punk and new wave seemed the first indication of some new, unsuspected *NOW*. Brusque, angular, sarcastic, trashy, and disgusting, it was rock in its most innocent form. It was also a whole lot of fun.

Punk and new wave—originally interchangeable descriptions of the artistically deviant—first surfaced in "garage band" activity beginning in the late 1960s, contemporary with the later phases of the more successful psychedelic movement. Crude bands, like San Jose's Count Five (which had the underground hit "Psychotic Reaction"), were rough foils to the virtuosity that finally peaked in the mid 1970s. Garage-band rock was the fulfillment of the common man's rock consciousness, the desire to kick out the jams—however limited one's talent. Punk persisted in this attitude, while new wave came to represent artier aspirations.

As the 1960s came to a close, a number of art-rock bands, led by Lou Reed's Velvet Underground and the New York Dolls, appeared in various urban centers, bands that embodied elements of punk as well as new wave. These trendy new explorations accelerated with the emergence of British rocker David Bowie and led to producer Malcolm McLaren's founding the Sex Pistols. A small audience developed for the first art-rock bands—never a national upsurge of interest or commitment until, in the early 1970s, a real American provocateur appeared and took up the sort of mesmerizing, disquieting presence that Jim Morrison of the Doors had earlier personified. This was Iggy Pop, out of Detroit, backed by the appropriately named Stooges. Iggy, the most out-of-control presence that had been seen on a stage for a decade, had no regard for conventional limits. The instant debauchery he could whip up suggested new possibilities for uncontrolled excess in rock 'n' roll. Everything Iggy stood for was rude, crude, and *alive*.

By the mid 1970s, bands like Talking Heads, Blondie, Television, and the Heartbreakers appeared on the scene, often performing at CBGB, a club in Manhattan's seedy Bowery. Then came the Ramones, from the upper-middle-class enclave of Forest Hills, Queens. Clad in leather and pushing rock to breakneck speeds, they touched off the punk revolution, which now began to become distinct from the new wave. According to Legs McNeil, writing in *Spin* magazine, it was the Ramones who inspired the punk groups destined to be identified as the genre's prototypes: the Clash, the Pretenders, the Damned, and the Sex Pistols.

Poster art accompanied every phase of punk and new wave development. It was produced in greater and greater profusion—and with an evolving degree of sophistication—as the music gathered momentum. If punk and new wave music sounded very different from the mainstream, its graphic art looked and felt different as well. The louder the posters spoke, the weirder they looked, the more funny the inside jokes they conveyed, the more they partook of the new sensibility. But for all the noise it made—

and making noise was one of its basic intentions—punk and new wave art had the seductive appeal of the mischief that formed an unspoken bond among punks and new wavers.

If punk and new wave art owed something to anything, it was to the "boxing-style" art of the 1950s and early 1960s. The new posters shared the bold and relentless nature of the original black music posters. Certainly, there is a tremendous difference in graphic style between the old and the new work, just as there is between black music of the 1950s and early 1960s and punk and new wave rock. Yet both poster styles tend toward the loud and uncomplicated. They are designed to be noticed and intended to have a repetitive effect. In their overkill manner, they promise music that is appealing as well as low down and dirty.

Like the black music poster, the punk and new wave poster was shaped by the street. From the moment it is posted, this art becomes part of the neighborhood, its message gaining strength from repetition of sheer numbers—though the effective life of a single poster is perhaps only a week.

The Clash. The Roxy, London, 1977
Artist: Jamie Reid

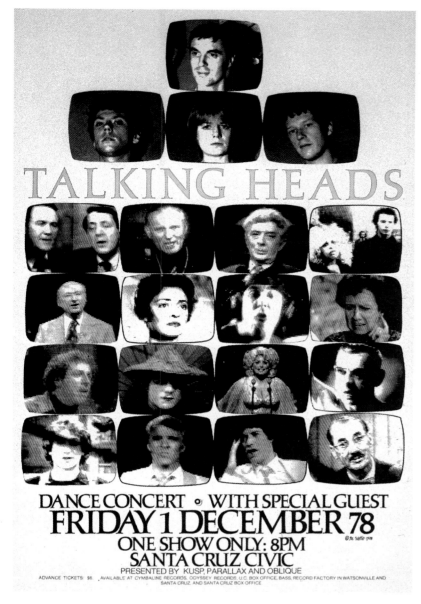

Talking Heads. Civic Auditorium, Santa Cruz, California, 1978
Artist: Su. Suttle

up. I went to an all-boy Catholic high school, and the heavy stuff was AC/DC, Ted Nugent, and Cheap Trick, and I was into those bands at the time, too, except that I started hearing about new stuff, like the first Clash album out on import and the first Generation-X album, stuff like that. I started hearing it and going nuts. And I'd go back to my school and tell the guys, "Hey, listen to this." And they'd go, "You pansy, you faggot." It was like I was the first person at my school to wear earrings. And I suffered for it.

Anyway, I was really into it, and I started going to as many shows as I could, and I would go all by myself because I didn't know anybody. I was still too square for the real punks to even talk to me, and too weird for my old friends. But I was having a good time; I didn't care. And then me and my brother Michael went to this Gang of Four show at the American Indian Center, and we saw a lot going on, and we thought: we want to get into this. We found out what it cost to rent the place, and we did some shows. We did gigs with the B-Team, Jars, and Translator. We were some of the first people to bring the Blasters to San Francisco.

I worked the door; my brother supervised everything and did the sound. We got friends to help us put up posters, and friends to do security. It was like everybody that worked on our gigs was a volunteer. The thing was, we never made any money because we were real idealistic about paying the bands. My brother and I literally were working our 9-to-5's just to support our doing shows, but we were having so much fun we didn't care we were losing money hand over foot.

How did I get involved with Defeatist Attitude? My brother had a band called Chill Factor, and it was partially because of Chill Factor that I got into posters. I remember they had some great posters, like their first one, bright purple on white, with a graphic of a guy in a long coat out in the cold. It was drawn by Michael Hall, a buddy of mine who played guitar in the band. After Chill Factor broke up, Mike was one of the guys who started Defeatist Attitude. And soon they started getting serious about practicing all the time and wanting to get gigs. I had been poking around Chill Factor, and then I started going to Defeatist Attitude practices, and I said, "Ok, I'll start doing your posters and getting you gigs."

Black music posters were almost never more than big pieces of cardboard bearing plain, oversize type and simple publicity photos. Punk and new wave pieces were often just slap-dash graphic configurations of the cut-and-paste variety. Both drew a sort of obnoxious attention to themselves during their brief period of street life. They were not the carefully wrought statements offered in the psychedelic posters, which were finally less for the street and more for indoor contemplative postings. Punk and new wave art was never more than the acting out of basic desire. It was not artfully planned or calculated. Like the music itself, the art is rock 'n' roll in its most basic form.

Anyone can do it, that was the key. Anyone can play it, anyone can manage it, anyone can do the artwork. You just have to put yourself out there. Such was the experience of Mark Barbeau, who managed the San Francisco bands Defeatist Attitude and My Sin, and who handled much of the street art, from the graphics and printing right to the actual posting:

The way I started out was I began going to shows in 1978 and 1979, a few years after the initial punk and new wave thing started

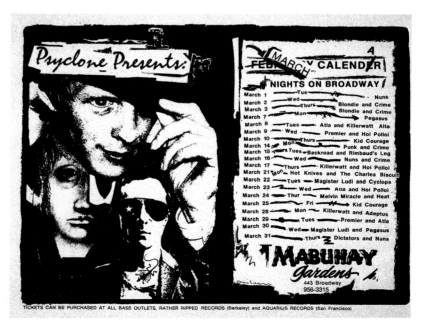

March calendar: Psyclone Productions. Mabuhay Gardens, San Francisco, 1977. Artist: Jerry Paulsen

Devo. Mabuhay Gardens
San Francisco, 1978

And it went on from there. I would call up clubs and say I managed
Defeatist Attitude, because it was like being manager wasn't
something you had to have a degree or anything to do. It was
more just like "get it done." And I always gave good phone. While
I was with Defeatist Attitude I did about 90 percent of their fliers;
the only ones I didn't do were sketched by my buddy Mike Hall.

It was an interesting coincidence that my day job was at a
printing company. I did almost all the fliers on the sly, while the
owner was gone. I handled the design myself and the prep work,
and some of the fliers I actually printed myself, because I knew
how to run a press by then.

Normally, three hundred fliers were enough. I could cover all the
important parts of San Francisco with three hundred. The basic
idea was to get out on the street a week or so before the gig and
put the fliers in places where they'd be noticed and where they
wouldn't be instantly covered up. You had to make an effort to get
the postering done right, and I found it was like a whole gig in
itself. Almost an art in itself.

We'd be out on the street putting up posters, and people would
come up to us and say, "Hey, what's that? Another Defeatist
Attitude poster? Can I have one? I've got all your posters." And

I'd say to them, "Well, have you ever been to one of our shows?"
And most of the time I'd hear them say, "No, I never have. But
I've got all your posters on my wall. Can I have this one?"

If you wanted to cut down some on poster snatching, and if you
wanted your posters to last very long at all, sometimes you had
to do more than just staple them up. You really wanted to paste
them on. We found that evaporated milk was the best thing. It was
so great! You'd pour undiluted evaporated milk into a spray bottle
and you'd spray the back of a poster, stick it up somewhere, and
it was up for good. It took hold like it would never come down,
unless somebody sandblasted it off.

Along the way we'd tried wheat paste, but it was so much more
messy. You'd be out there with a big bucket of wheat paste and a
roller, and pretty soon you'd be totally encrusted with the stuff.
It looked like you had some weird scaly disease all over your arms
and hands. Pet Milk was a lot easier.

But postering could be a pretty dangerous business. I remember
one night we were out there doing posters, and we had our cans
of Pet Milk, and we were hunched down behind some car, opening
them with a screwdriver and getting ready to pour them into our
spray bottles. All of a sudden a bunch of cops come up, flashlights
out—it felt like they had their guns drawn—and they were asking
us just what in hell we were doing down there. Because we were
all bent over, I guess they flashed we were making bombs or
something. And so we had to put them off from what we were
really doing, because that could have gotten us busted real quickly.
And the cops listened and told us that if we had already postered
on anything except legitimate street kiosks, we were in deep
trouble. The funny thing was, all you had to do was look back
over your shoulder five feet away, and there was half a side of a
building already covered.

Usually, the way we did postering was to find a stretch of territory, a whole line of telephone poles and lampposts, for instance,
put a couple on each pole, and then if we could find a good wall,
put up a whole block. We got busted only twice doing this.

Postering is like having a sixth sense. When you get into it in a
big way, you begin to feel out all the "must hit" situations. It's
all about working the angles. You always keep a mental map of
the logistics, like taxi drivers do. Like, Haight Street didn't used to
be a "must hit" situation early on, but now it's so trendy you have
to poster nearly the whole way down.

Looking back to the really active days of the late 1970s and
early 1980s, it seems to me that postering now is something of a
dead art. It was really thriving when punk was the most exciting
thing in the city, and it really picked up fast in just a few years.
There were a tremendous number of fantastic posters during that
time, and they were all over. You couldn't miss them if you had
any eyes at all. Nowadays, you only occasionally see a great
poster.

I think the high point for poster art in San Francisco came
around the time punks were running shows at the Temple, the old
synagogue out on Geary, next to Bill Graham's first Fillmore (and
right next to Jim Jones's Peoples Temple, also). There has to be a
lot of current energy in the music scene for poster artists to do
their thing in a big way. When the music is tight, everything along
with it is tight and intense, too. Posters take the same sort of
energy to produce.

A good flier is kinda warped and doesn't take itself too seriously.
The best punk pieces are the least complex, the most careless.
The most memorable are the ones that shock, that really offend.

You can't underestimate the value of a really nasty flier. Like, you'd see one that was basically a big close-up photo of anal sex, and it'd say, "so-and-so at the Temple." It was a chance to make a truly despicable statement about the world—in the guise of promoting a rock band.

Even the pieces that didn't go all the way could provoke a lot of bizarre reactions. Our fliers, for instance, were not as overtly kinky or disturbing as some others, but we would get stares and comments from people watching our posters go up. There was one old guy who literally did nothing but walk up and down Polk Street ripping off fliers he saw posted. I would get really pissed seeing him do that to us, and I was determined not to be beaten by this old guy. So I'd get my buddy Mike to start down the street postering, and when this guy would start up behind him, scraping away, I'd start to follow behind, replacing everything.

You had to feel a sense of mission while you were out postering. Belief in what you were doing was the only thing that mattered.

B People. Old Waldorf, San Francisco, 1981

Putting up your posters was a righteous act—you had to know that. And if you want to know the truth, nothing could be simpler than an armful of posters and a whole night to yourself.

In dealing with the music and in doing a lot of the poster work on my own, I managed to develop a feeling of what it's like to be a collector. It's an art in itself just getting a collection going. If the posters are glued to a wall—as they often are—it's a particularly tricky business. But if I want a poster bad enough, I find a way to get up there and start pulling it off. Sometimes it's incredibly frustrating because, just when I have a neat poster almost three-quarters off, and just when I'm about to make a final pull, it suddenly tears in half. I collected enough so that when I was living in a place out on Second Avenue—a total party household where Toxic Reasons lived for months along with some other bands—I was holed up in a little room of my own, covered top to bottom with posters. Not a painted piece of wall showed! A lot were posters I had done myself, but I reserved space for all the other great stuff that was just pouring out of the community.

While Mark Barbeau may have felt himself living very much in the present, he was also participating in San Francisco's great poster tradition. What distinguished the Bay Area from other urban centers was that it consistently sustained interest in rock poster art and over the years was home to the greatest number of graphic artists who worked on rock posters.

The output of other cities pales by comparison. In San Francisco, graphic art was linked with musical developments. While history deemed New York and London the focal points of the new music, it was San Francisco that produced the greatest volume of punk and new wave poster art.

What is most surprising about the development of new wave and punk in New York was how little excellent poster art was produced. New York never placed as high a premium on concert poster art as did other cities—particularly San Francisco, but also Los Angeles, Austin, and Seattle. Most of the New York announcements were made in display ads featured in the *Village Voice*. When posters, fliers, and handbills were issued, the effort was half-hearted at best. New York just moved too fast for lingering fascination over poster art.

But San Francisco continued to nurture a poster tradition. Among Barbeau's new wave counterparts is Tim Barrett, who designed many posters for his band No Sisters (composed entirely of the Barrett *brothers*):

I was initially inspired by psychedelic poster- and album-cover art. I was fascinated by the attempt to make images and messages—especially the lettering—incomprehensible to outsiders. If you weren't tuned in, forget it—you couldn't even read it.

New wave art is more aggressive than psychedelic art, but falls a bit short of pushing everybody's buttons, like punk. Unlike psychedelic art, it's more fundamentally street art, and the idea, most of the time, is to fill up space with large type and bold, simple images. There's often not so much a need to spend the attention working out a complex, individualized design. The idea, rather, is to jam a lot of things very quickly into the available space— quickly, but with a lot of wit and humor. Even though I turned on originally to psychedelic art and grew up during the psychedelic years, I really like the new style. I like it because it likes me.

At the time the psychedelic thing was beginning to happen, I was going to school in Ohio. We were so turned on by what was happening in San Francisco; we talked about it all the time. We used to go down to the travel agency just to stare at the airfares to San Francisco and wonder if we could make it on Easter vacation. Finally, in 1970, I quit school, got a Volkswagen bus, painted it in bright colors, and drove out to the West Coast. It took a month to make the trip—it *was* mind-expanding.

As soon as I got to San Francisco, I went right to the Haight; I was with this guy who insisted on taking acid his first day there. But the scene I had envisioned was gone—stores were boarded up, and there was heroin on the street and junkies in the doorways. Lots of unexpected tension in the air. Reality began to take over, and then Altamont happened, which resulted in free outdoor concerts being banned. From there through the next several years—1972, 1973, till about the mid 1970s—there was a definite

Ad: Patti Smith; Television
Max's Kansas City, New York, 1978

lull; nothing of any significance was happening. I felt I was on the wrong coast, because one of my brothers was in a band back East, and by 1976 they were part of the new CBGB scene. So, I flew back with some of my first attempts at song writing.

It was a gas for all of us. Even though I had studied art and had done it for most of my life, music was something I always wanted to do. But I never felt I had the talent or aptitude to become a professional musician. Then I heard the Ramones, Patti Smith, and Television, and I went, wait a minute! These guys were just like me! I saw a picture of Richard Hell and thought he looked exactly like me—a skinny, geeky guy with glasses—and here he was getting major press in New York and he still didn't know how to play his guitar.

I wasn't ready to abandon California, and before I flew back to San Francisco I convinced my brothers to think about coming out themselves. When I got off the plane, things were happening all around. I saw the Nuns play for the first time, and they were hilarious, they were just so terrible. They were so crude and yet so great. Primal, urgent, wonderful—that's what it felt like. They were really quite inspiring to me, and I actually designed a logo for them—a swastika entwined on a Roman cross—but their manager never called. Maybe that's when I knew I had to start my own group—so I could hire myself to do the art!

Some things I did resulted from very little effort; other pieces I labored on for a long time. I couldn't say one method was better than the other. At one point I was fixated on the idea of depicting

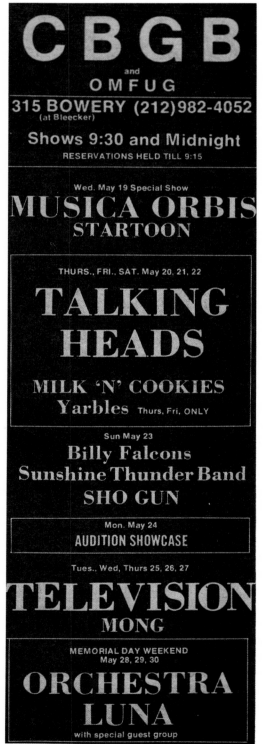

Ad, *Village Voice*, 1976

our band—the brothers—as "picto-men," because I had the idea that the 1980s were highly mechanized. But the art didn't meet with a lot of enthusiasm on the part of the No Sisters fans, because they never thought of us as "picto-men." They thought of us as loose, goofy guys, at home in the 1980s, in tune with the times, but also just a wee bit out of sync. We didn't have to be trendy.

Of course, in such a fluid scene as new wave, there were a lot of trashy pieces of poster art out on the streets. There was a lot of terrible stuff, in part because the nature of the thing was that anybody could do it. There was free license, the materials were available to all, and the cause was something anybody could take up. So, any art that came out of it could be either highly skilled or completely clumsy—totally bozo—or worse. To do punk and new wave art, you didn't have to be an artist at all, just like to play the new music you didn't have to be a musician, not really. You just did it, out of some sort of instinct.

Sometimes I'd consciously strive for my art to be sophisticated and articulate on some intellectual level; other times I just wanted a certain energy to come out. A lot of the poster art from this period wasn't really thought up in advance. No one really first made a sketch of their idea—they just went ahead and roughed it out in final form and pasted it up. Sometimes nothing changed—nothing was really altered—from beginning to end.

I wanted my artwork to have a longer life than most of what was being posted. I know I was very aware of street art and the manner in which it got posted. You'd see some amazing things on

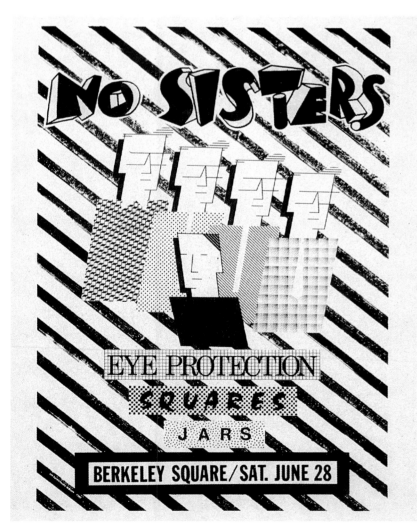

No Sisters; Eye Protection. Berkeley Square, Berkeley, 1980. Artist: Tim Barrett

your corner telephone pole. The only problem was that it got posted over within hours. The next guy down the line doesn't care about your particular piece—he just wants his to be seen, too. That's the nature of this kind of art; it appears out of the blue and disappears within seconds.

The San Francisco band that most exemplified new wave—in contrast to punk's harder core—was SVT. Its poster graphics and newspaper advertisements were created by the band's resident artist, Richard Stutting, who also designed more mainstream work for bands like Santana. Stutting's art bears a truly individual stamp that helped define the new wave school of art. Most of his work was done under the name of Artbreakers:

My idea was to keep a kind of continuity between the pieces coming out. I don't know whether it was intentional in the beginning, but a definite continuity developed, which I really liked. Sometimes what tied the pieces together were similar graphic devices or maybe a certain coloring or just an underlying feeling. A lot of the time I reacted to what was needed on instinct alone. Something would zap me, would go click inside my head, and that would be the direction I'd follow. Some things were premeditated, others were quick moves that just happened, presto, right on the spot.

What fascinates me about new wave art is that it moves so quickly through time and space. It's almost like you're just supposed to get a quick hit, then move on to the next poster, whether you're doing it in the studio or seeing it on the street. So the trick is to get people to see your art—your thinking—the very first time. If you see it, you get it. That's the way it should work. It's not something you can take a camera to and preserve forever. My kind of art doesn't work that way, or at least I don't think it should work that way.

All the work I did for SVT—the dozens of posters and fliers, the advertisements in all the new weeklies—really got me going, and I felt while I was doing it that, finally, I'd become established as an artist. While it lasted, it was very real. It was exciting.

I got my inspiration from a thousand different places. One was the Sears catalog, because it has some of the strangest stuff! It has everything you want for posters—buzz saws, dinosaurs, weird everyday kind of things. The trick, again, was keeping loose, keeping open to whatever you might see, in a Sears catalog or whatever. So there wasn't anything I didn't feel open to building off of, using as some totally new inspiration, ripping off for my own artistic recreation. Encyclopedias—especially the really old ones—were great food for thought. And picture magazines from the 1930s and 1940s. They would catch your eye and really make you think what could be done with some of that material.

One piece of mine that seems to be remembered very well was the one I built using a piece from a Korean newspaper. It gave me the right feeling. It was totally abstract, but also humorous, and it caused a whole lot of confusion. Confusion never hurt, you know.

I guess you could call all my work new wave, for lack of any better term. Punk has a harder edge, while new wave is slicker in style. I think the word for it is "stylized." Style works best for me, but I'm also aware of the good punk stuff. Punk always conveys to me feelings of anarchy, of antisocial behavior. Punk art makes the harshest visual statements, because the more bitter it is, the more harsh it is, the stronger the piece. Tension is what it's all about, really. Punk is like a skateboard ride over everything.

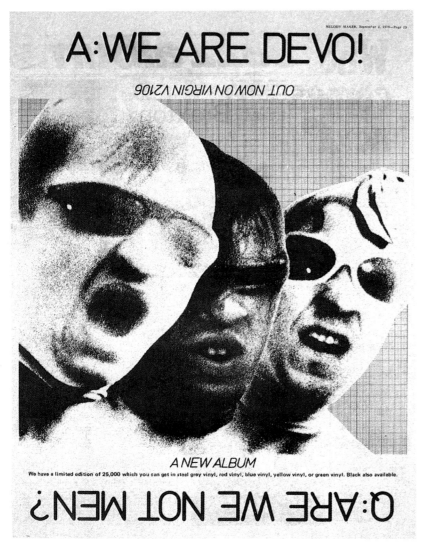

A NEW ALBUM
We have a limited edition of 25,000 which you can get in steel grey vinyl, red vinyl, blue vinyl, yellow vinyl, or green vinyl. Black also available.

Newspaper ad: Devo; 1978

One of the things I like doing the most is using the Xerox machine. Things done on the Xerox are never the same. It's an adventure. It's like you go to one shop and use their machine, then go to another across the street, and the whole tone of the piece changes. Sometimes you want a particular machine, sometimes another, and sometimes both machines act differently from what you were expecting. A lot of times I wasn't able to go back and recreate something. Sometimes I forgot where or how I got a particular result. That's a really marvelous surprise factor, because you never know exactly the effect you'll be getting, whether it's something you want, or whether it'll be totally different from what you were anticipating.

What's interesting to me about using the Xerox is not having to deal with the traditional printing process in order to turn out your fliers. You don't have to relate to some guy who's been twenty-five years on his press and the day you happen to walk in he's bored or got a backache. Because sometimes I'm after some radical effect; sometimes what I want to do is Xerox a piece ten times, then reduce it or enlarge it, then stick it back in the machine ten more times. Maybe your average printer wouldn't go this far to get a particular effect. I like the feeling of modern technology, having the chance to push it and extend its limits. That's when I get some of my most creative sensations.

I've found there's a whole lot of electricity that comes out of

working quickly. A great deal of my art reflects quick decisions—quick positioning, quick work with the scissors. Sudden moves are really inspiring to me. Suddenly, you know just what to do. It's like a flash. And it feels just like the music.

There were many other bands whose graphic art felt just like their music. One such was the idiosyncratically spelled Psycotic Pineapple, based in Berkeley and regarded locally more as a garage band than as new wave or even punk. But it was a band with both new wave and punk tendencies, and it produced some of the wittiest art seen on either coast. It featured a cartoon character known as the "Pineapple Man"—or "Pyno Man." John Seabury was the artist for Psycotic Pineapple:

I did the posters for all our gigs, even the very first ones. The Pyno Man didn't show up until after two or three posters. I originally did him as a joke, but, as it turned out, he became more popular than the band ever did. The problem with the Pyno Man series was that he became too popular. We had to start putting up more and more pieces because people were taking them down to keep. And a lot of these poster snatchers didn't know us as a band at all—just as a particular poster series that kept appearing on the street. We weren't known so much for what we really did, which was making music, but for being a huge success at making posters.

Our posters were the most exciting thing about us. Nobody had anything remotely like the Pyno Man out in the streets, cutting

SVT. Mabuhay Gardens, San Francisco, ca. 1979
Artist: Richard Stutting

Psycotic Pineapple; Mondellos. International Cafe
Berkeley, 1979. Artist: John Seabury

Pyno Jam. Ashkenaz, Berkeley, 1982. Artist: John Seabury

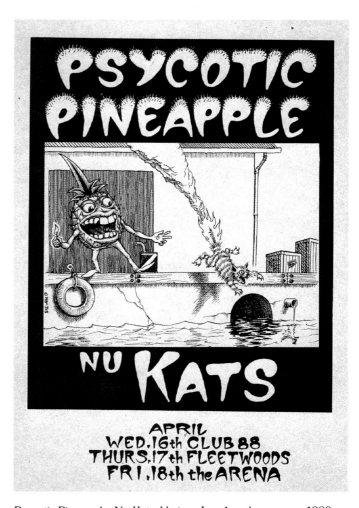

Psycotic Pineapple; Nu Kats. Various Los Angeles venues, 1980
Artist: John Seabury

up and wisecracking. It was like street theater, being as smartass as
you'd like, all on the basis of a lot of posters. Posters really were
our image. We were the Pyno Man, except he existed only in
poster form, not in real life. Maybe that was the disappointment
we were always living with. We could never get to be as good as
our posters.

While the punk ethos—and, to a diminishing extent, that of the
new wave—fostered art among the untrained, people like John
Seabury were very talented artists. Indeed, there was a significant
connection between a number of art students and the new music.
Photographer Stanley Greene chronicled the scene:

*I was living in Paris when everything began, and I ran into friends
of mine who had seen this whole movement kick itself off in the
United States and then really get itself together in San Francisco.
When I got back to San Francisco from Europe, I went over to the
Art Institute, of which I was still a member, and I saw all these
old friends of mine, whom I'd last seen standing on line to enroll,
now having grown their hair into weird shapes and starting bands
with weird names, like the Mutants. All sorts of people came out
of the Art Institute, like Penelope Houston, Jonathan Postal, and
Deborah Iyall. They even took over one of the studios at the
school, and all of these punks were living there. You would go
down there, and they had their instruments there, their motorcycles
there, and the school was going crazy because the punks had*

*changed all the locks. They were making art and poetry and
music. That's where Penelope Houston got her influence to start
the Avengers; she'd always be going down to the studios to listen
to those guys rap.*

*I think a lot of punk stuff was influenced by dada, plain and
simple. There was a resurgence of dada that came out of the Art*

Institute, and I think it's one of the most important things about the punk scene in San Francisco. New Yorkers will argue about it until the day they die, but San Francisco kept the true spirit of punk alive longer than any other city because of that art anger.

If you look at dada art and dada posters, or if you look at any anarchy movement's posters, you can see it's all a passion thing, it's about slinging on the paint. The posters are pretty incredible because of the anger, the angst. And the moments in the music that got to me most were the loudest, most discordant, most incoherent, most way out there—moments when I was thinking very clearly, moments in which everybody's up and dancing in that strange flow. It's out of control and in control, and it takes a lot of human being to perceive that laughing and cheering means throwing your body against someone else's and dancing means leaping up and down. The only other experience I can relate it to is antiwar demonstrations. Being chased down the street by the cops and everything, with my girlfriend alongside me, being maced and beaten on, and then going home and fucking like rabbits . . . it was so real because we'd be just so psyched up, it was a total adrenaline rush. In fact, it was addictive, which is what punk represented to a lot of kids: a chance to be drunk and out of control and say something.

The Mutants definitely said something. So did the Avengers, the

Avengers. Mabuhay Gardens, San Francisco, 1977
Artist: Penelope Houston

Dils, the Dead Kennedys. The Nuns probably said it first, Howie Klein, president of 415 Records recalls:

The Nuns really captured the imagination of San Francisco. I can remember the lines outside the Mabuhay, down Broadway, down around the hill. I don't think it could ever happen again like that. There is an argument over who was first—Mary Monday or the Nuns—but it didn't matter, it was the Nuns. They were really the first band that came along and made San Francisco look up, and they quickly became identified as part of the national scene, what was happening back East at CBGB and elsewhere. Because of the Nuns, San Francisco became recognized as the second city of new wave and punk, after New York.

And the Mabuhay was very important, too. For a long time it was the key club in the middle of the whole scene, but then things began to break into some fantastic shapes, with clubs like the Sound of Music, the Deaf Club, Temple 1839, and things on the most street of street level. You could say the scene just continued rotting over. The first batch of bands were those like the Nuns, and then came a second batch close on their heels. These were the Dils, who were very political, and the Avengers, who were very strange. They were more like the Sex Pistols than any other San Francisco band—they really looked to England for their inspiration. They actually became friends with the Sex Pistols, and when the Pistols played what turned out to be their last show on earth, at Winterland Arena, in San Francisco, December 1978, the Pistols insisted that the Avengers open for them. However, Bill Graham had booked the Nuns, and reluctantly added the Avengers. Then Malcolm McLaren, who managed the Sex Pistols, came up to me asking, "Beyond the Avengers, who's the worst band on the whole scene?" And I told him Negative Trend, because they made the most horrible, disgusting, mindless kind of noise. And he said, "I want them on the show." When he told Bill Graham, Bill didn't want anything to do with it, but finally said, "Okay, here's a compromise. We'll put the Avengers on the bill, and if you want Negative Trend, let them close the show."

So the Pistols did their thing—which turned out to be the last thing they ever did, because they broke up the next day—and in those days at Winterland, at the close of all the Winterland shows, Graham would play a tape of "Greensleeves." So the Sex Pistols go off, the audience is roaring, and "Greensleeves" comes on immediately. And here comes Negative Trend, the biggest chance any band could ever get, at the biggest punk show in America. And they ran to try to get it on, except that everybody was filing out. There were like twenty people left in the whole place listening to Negative Trend.

Negative Trend disappeared from the scene immediately, but what the Avengers had going for them was great poster art. It was the bands mostly—not clubs like the Mab and the others—which did the bulk of the posters. Edwin Heaven handled most of the Nuns posters, which were very slick, unlike the posters a guy named Rico did for the Avengers, posters that had to do with sex, S & M, foul play, that sort of thing. He never did a normal poster— nor did the Avengers' Penelope Houston. She did a lot of weird posters. Some of the Mutants' bandmembers did posters for themselves, too, which were sick and depraved like all the best ones.

The band generally acknowledged to have the best posters was Crime. Responsible for nearly all of them was James Stark, whose given name was William Glover:

Sex Pistols; Clash. 100 Club, London, 1976
Artist: Jamie Reid

Everybody changed their name during that time, but I didn't pick the name Stark consciously for any graphic style; it was just all of a sudden there.

Stark was born in Visalia, a small farming community in California's central valley. He started with early rhythm and blues and Elvis and graduated from high school in 1959, then he went into the service and didn't come out until 1966. During that time he met a lot of artists who, like him, had been drafted. When Stark got out of the Army, he lived in New York on the Lower East Side. He went to see the Velvet Underground (''all the time''), and took some classes at the School of Visual Arts, mostly in photography. Stark got a particularly heavy hit of New York sensibility, but in 1968 returned to the Bay Area in time to catch the Avalon and Fillmore in full swing:

I had a definite preference. I went to the Avalon a lot. If you wanted to have a good time, you went to the Avalon. If you wanted to get pushed around, you went to the Fillmore. I also hung out at the Carousel, the old El Patio ballroom that Bill Graham subsequently renamed the Fillmore West. The Carousel had those Tuesday Night Jams, which involved bands like Santana before people made them big. Some of the best music in San Francisco came out of those nights. All that great music had an influence on

me, and I also had enough interest in art and photography to do one Avalon poster, late in the numbered series (credited to photographer Billy Glover). But things deteriorated after the Family Dog left the Avalon, and it was not until the onset of the punk and new wave era that I had a lot of new interest in the music scene.

Posters played a large part in what began to happen. Before the whole scene got together, there were very few posters like those we see today all around us on every city block. The poster thing, in fact, had greatly diminished by the time we got it started up again. It was a whole new discovery for those of us with Crime—that we could put up our art all over the walls. And it was because of our posters that people came to the first Crime show. We got fifty or a hundred people to see a band that no one had ever heard of before. The posters had actually compelled them to come! This was surprising to us, because everything was pretty raw in those days. Bands like Crime and the Nuns pretty much evolved all on their own. When you went to see them, you were assaulted, especially your hearing. The whole idea was assault; the idea was to go out and get visually and aurally assaulted. And it was assault, I can tell you that. People would run out holding their ears.

I don't know exactly how I started doing Crime's posters on such a regular basis. Someone did their first one, and I did the second and third ones. It went on from there. Like my development of the Crime logo—I don't think I was consciously aware it would turn into something. I guess my basic instinct was to get as far away from 1960s psychedelic art as possible, to be different from all that complex, hard-to-read, intricate kind of stuff, and instead do things that were much more slam!

A lot of my things were crude in the beginning—everyone's were. It was meant to be like that. I think I had to work harder at getting into crudeness than some people, especially the young ones. First of all, I'm much older, second, I've already had fifteen to twenty years of background in art, whereas a lot of punk artists had never done any art before.

People all over the art community were borrowing images and sticking them up on posters. I did, too. One time I took a photo out of a French fashion magazine, and—incredibly—the guy who took the photo, this French guy, shows up at the next Crime gig. He just happened to see my poster, of which I had made no more than a hundred or a hundred fifty copies. He thought it was great. I thought he was going to sue me.

James Stark in his studio

Crime; Pearl Harbor & The Explosions
Mabuhay Gardens, San Francisco, 1978

Posters went along with all the new magazines popping up. Jean Caffeine, who did a few posters herself right out of high school, started New Diseases. Then there was Search and Destroy, No Exit, and Damage. I photographed for a lot of them.

One of the guys I thought was very brave was Patrick Miller. He's a painter and a printer, and he came through the San Francisco Art Institute. He's the guy who goes around stenciling Minimal Man images. He started out originally as a roadie for Crime, and then at some point he decided to let someone else carry the equipment because what he was really interested in doing was going around with his skull images and spray painting them on walls. He once had a show where he had fifty or sixty skull images, so he had a lot to draw from. He spray painted everywhere. You can still go around town and see Minimal Man skulls. Patrick did a lot of his work under freeway overpasses, on sidewalks, and on the backs of street signs. I think Patrick really became Minimal Man.

Accolades for new wave and punk art were not confined to a mutual admiration society among the artists. Three books publi-

cized the otherwise fugitive posters and fliers. *STREETART* (1981) grew out of a poster exhibition held in conjunction with the Western Front punk music festival in San Francisco. It was the work of Tool & Die club owner Peter Belsito and performance artist Bob Davis, who recalls that

Susan Pedrick, Peter, and I put up about five hundred posters at the show, having chosen from six to eight times that number. There were a lot of arguments about the exhibit and about the content of the book—arguments about what everybody would agree to include and what didn't qualify to be included. We set ourselves up as the critical panel, because it was the only way to get the exhibit done; it was mostly a system of, "Okay, we'll take the one you like if you take the one I like."

There was a supreme amount of difficulty in tracking poster artists down. I still have these massive telephone logs. Like, to

Minimal Man; Mark Pauline. Eureka Theatre, San Francisco. ca. 1980. Artist: Patrick Miller

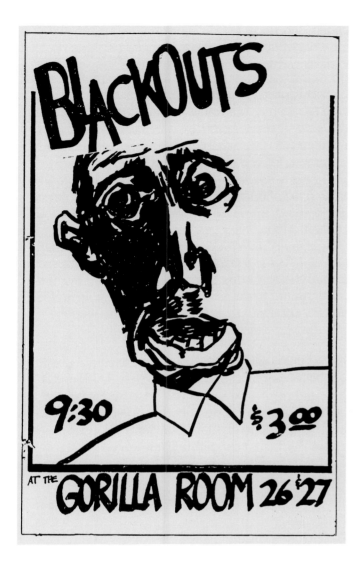

Blackouts. Gorilla Room, Seattle, 1981
Artist: Erich Werner

Blackouts; The U-Men. 913 East Pine, Seattle, 1982
Artist: Erich Werner

credit some of the Nuns posters, we had to first find Alejandro, who was in the band, and to do that we had to phone his brother, and then someone who knew his brother, and then finally we found Alejandro, and Alejandro tracked through his memory as to who was the poster artist involved, and then we had to find the poster artist.

Most of the punk artists in STREETART were astounded that their posters were remembered. So much of this stuff was just meant to be thrown out on the street—not hung in a gallery or celebrated later on. Even getting decent reproductions was a hassle. There was one guy—I think his name was Jimmy Wilsey—whose band I don't even remember now. We were looking for a better copy of one of his posters, and we were hoping he still had his Xerox master, like a lot of people did. Well, he had made up his poster by taking an arm band off his jean jacket and throwing it on a Xerox machine. Apart from that, he told us, there never was an original. A lot of times we had to reconstruct posters, which is why our book versions look better than the actual street posters—and why so many artists are amazed when they open up STREETART. Astonished I think is even a better word.

According to Ron Turner, publisher of STREETART and its companion, Hard Core California (1984):

It was indeed a nightmare shooting off of old tattered handbills and trying to recreate posters. But we were on a mission! It had to be done. I was getting sick of seeing books on the beatniks and

Art Chantry, Seattle, ca. 1984

books on hippies written by people who weren't part of those cultures. I thought, well, here's a real new phenomenon, and its story can be told by the people who are directly involved in it. I suppose it was a gamble for us, thinking we could sell books to punks. But I saw punks as being more like the beatnik era—more aware of themselves in literary and art terms than hippies. The hippie era was kind of pandemic, whereas the beatnik and punk eras were more concise. I'm not a punk myself, but punk was something you could be-up-front about; you either liked it or you didn't, you were either part of it or you weren't.

The feeling of intimacy and the sharing of secrets was a special part of being punk and new wave. The facilitation of communication among punks seemed to be as much the intent of street art as was the promotion of particular gigs. Art Chantry is a highly regarded art director and poster designer in the Seattle region and author-editor of *Instant Litter* (1985), an excellent pictorial book about Seattle punk poster art:

Much of punk art was commercially unnecessary, even commercially suicidal. Major-league concert promoters proved time after time that all one needed to sell out a show was a poster facing the street (not the sidewalk) with big type declaring who, where, and when. But the artists in my book weren't trying to attract people who drove cars. They didn't even want to attract average pedestrians. They preferred to post in very specific neighborhoods, where the images scared off the common folk and caught the

attention of those who understood. The result was more of a community primal scream than advertising. The message haunted us all, but acted as communication (communion?) to an underground elite. It mostly seemed the right thing to do at the time.

I wish my book were five hundred pages long—then maybe I might have managed to include—just maybe—one third of the posters I researched. Even at that, I only scratched the surface. Largely, I couldn't locate all the samples. It seems that nobody, not even the artists, bothered to save copies—this was truly disposable art. I once saw the original pasted-up artwork for one poster stapled to a telephone pole! Many of the poster makers were totally anonymous, some changed names at a whim, and almost half of them moved away to New York, Los Angeles, or San Francisco. Others couldn't recognize their work when they saw it; in one case I had four different people claiming sole credit for a single poster. Keep in mind that this was not the "normal" world here, but a murky place where reality was flexible and image/attitude was everything. Legends make better stories anyway.

Seattle, with Austin, Texas, was one of the few cities beyond San Francisco, New York, and Los Angeles, that developed a significant punk and new wave presence and attendant poster art. While many of the posters were done by bandmembers, artists like Helena Rogers (Student Nurse), Gary Minkler (Red Dress), and Erich Werner (the Blackouts) created brilliant works, which, despite constant police harrassment, were posted throughout the city.

The Fags. Danceland USA, Seattle, 1981. Artist: Barb Ireland

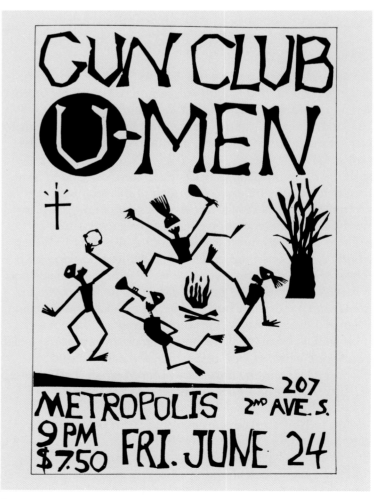

Gun Club; The U-Men. Metropolis, Seattle, 1983. Artist: John Bigley

The punk scene in Austin grew out of the demise of the legendary dance hall known as the Armadillo. Richard Dorsett, resident historian of Austin's musical culture, recalls:

Austin always represented a midway point between the coasts, and a lot of people would come down here, nut it out, and fly back to their coast with all these weird new ideas. Or they would come back here with weird new ideas acquired on the coasts. Austin sent a lot of people (Chet Helms and Janis Joplin were two) to San Francisco, and the other parts of the country gave us tours by the Ramones, the Talking Heads, and Elvis Costello. I saw Elvis Costello at the Armadillo just before the doors closed, and if the place had gone on, it would definitely have featured all of the new stuff coming around.

The first punks in Austin were just rough rock 'n' rollers. By the mid 1970s, we had our share of local bands that would play fraternity houses. No one was doing original material except for the country bands. There were no really great big-time bands in Austin then, and so things began to concentrate on a much more grass-roots level. A band called the Skunks formed, and they were the very first of what we knew as punk bands. They started playing in a dive on Guadaloupe Street, the main drag in Austin, right across from the University. This was Raul's, a Mexican bar, as much an important site in Austin as the Mabuhay was in San Francisco. The next band to come was the Huns, influenced by the English and New York sound, and they were all art students at U.T. They knew what was happening, and they wanted to be part of it, and they were that much ahead of everybody else. They were outrageous. They were a slap in the face. And what happened to them was a mixture of luck and chutzpah, being in the right place at the right time. One night at Raul's—their first gig in public, their first paying gig—a cop answered a noise complaint. The place was packed because there'd been a lot of posters put up. The cop walked into the front of the club—the stage was right next to the front door—and the Huns' lead singer, Phil Halstead, pointed to the cop and started screaming "eat death, scum." So the cop walked on stage, handcuffed him, and started a riot. I was one of the people who got arrested in the melee, for being part of starting a riot, resisting arrest, and using fighting words—"I'll have your badge, motherfucker asshole!"—and this was all big news for days, all over the front pages. So that assured punk's place in local music annals.

Because of nights like that, the Raul's crowd became like a big family. I mean, I was at Raul's every night of the week for a year. Literally, I would go there and hang out until the small hours of the morning, work be damned. It was my life, my friends. My girlfriend was in a band—the F-Systems—which I managed. I took tickets at the door. It was a real communal kind of thing. It was wonderful.

There was a clan of people who did the posters, and there was another clan of people who showed them to each other. We collected the damn things for years, just because we thought they were interesting, not because we thought they'd be worth anything. We loved the art as much as we loved the music. And people postered all over the main drag. There were even people who doctored billboards in the punk style, getting up there in the dead of night with spray paint.

Mike Nott, who often worked under the name of Noxx, was the most influential artist on the scene. His stuff was derivative as hell, but it was still good. No one in Austin had seen anything like it

Punk Symphony Orchestra
Antone's, Austin, Texas, ca. 1980

before. Then there were the Art Maggots. Paul Sabal was the main Maggot, a very talented draftsman, and, interestingly, a major collector of punk and new wave art. Paul's an architect who moonlights doing posters. People think he's the most innovative. Andy Blackwood collaborated with Paul on many occasions. Rick Turner was one of the most talented of the artists in that period, but his output was somewhat limited. Randy Turner, known as "Biscuit," was also the lead singer for the Big Boys, which came to be Austin's leading punk band. To people here on the scene, Randy's a scenemaker, skateboarder, and father confessor. He's both an artist and a collector, and a lot of his work dates from the early Raul's era. Shirley Staples is another artist and collector who doubled (tripled?) as a band manager. One of the most devoted collectors was the doorman at Raul's, Rudy Hyde, known to one and all as "Mr. Rudy," a major counterculture historian and font of local color. All these people really loved the posters.

While the punk rebellion in Austin, as in San Francisco and Seattle, was finally suffused with the kind of good feelings that

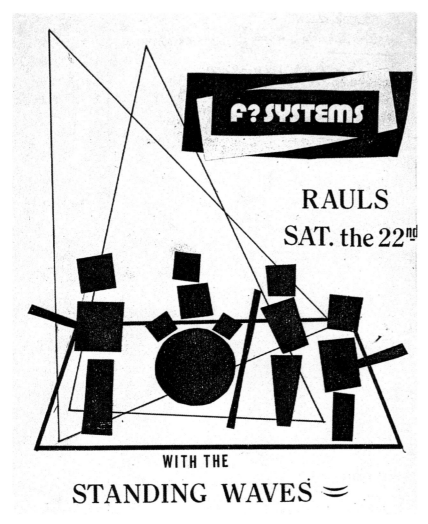

F Systems; Standing Waves. Raul's, Austin, Texas, ca. 1980
Artist: Mike Nott

had characterized much of the psychedelic era, the scene developed more ominously in Los Angeles.

Howie Klein:

At first there was something a little precious, a little intellectual, a little arty about the punk/new wave scene, and even in L.A. it started out that way, except that the people in L.A. immediately started trying to get it out, get it out as fast as they could. They spread it a lot faster. I mean, everyone wanted to spread it, but in L.A. it went too fast, much too fast, and suddenly the collective IQ of the people involved in new wave/punk dropped down below 100. The new wave IQ was higher at first, because there were more intellectual people involved at first, but in L.A. it all went down a lot faster, and before long there were surfers, drug users, rowdy people, kooks, and everybody jumped in at once. It was very, very barroom. It even brought in hard-core right-wing attitudes, which caught on very quickly in L.A.

In some respects, Los Angeles punk was the most hard core of all, since it came to embody fewer and fewer artistic pretensions— aside from those of the nationally known group, X. According to Club 88 owner Wayne Mayotte, interviewed in a film, *The Decline of Western Civilization,* hard-core L.A. punk was characterized by speed, "the fuzz"—what's cranked into it, high volume, monotone vocals, and protest lyrics. Brendan Mullen, manager of the Masque Club, also interviewed in *Decline,* explained:

Punk music gets out of hand because the speed of the music is well above the normal rhythm of the dance. Most dance music— disco, for example—is done to a 4/4 beat, a time signature that is comfortable and easy to dance to. It usually runs at about 126– 132 heartbeats per minute. Punk, on the other hand, or at least the kind of punk put out by the Germs or Black Flag, is played at 250–300 heartbeats per minute. It's not normal or comfortable to dance to it. You can only pogo dance to it, by jumping up and down or bouncing off walls, or bouncing off people. There's an abnormal level of energy and adrenaline, and sometimes violence breaks out, especially if the kids are bored or desperate.

But even the anarchic Los Angeles scene produced provocative posters and highly imaginative artists, among them Gary Panter (who handled work for the Screamers) and Shawn Kerri, a cartoonist whose work appeared (under a nom de plume) in *Hustler,* and who enjoyed a close relationship with L.A.'s notorious Circle Jerks:

The Jerks were great. I've been a Keith Morris fan for a long time. And nobody could beat Lucky; he is one of the best drummers that ever lived. The Circle Jerks stayed at my house in San Diego, when they were down there. It's my parents' house, actually. From about late 1978 to early '79, I was staying at my parents', and one time the Germs stayed at the house when they came here to play. My folks were very patient about putting a lot of bands up.

Screamers. The Whisky, Los Angeles, ca. 1977

My dad used to drive a Greyhound bus—just imagine a cross between Ralph Kramden and Fred Flintstone! My dad didn't understand the punk scene, but I guess he didn't really mind it too much, either. My mom's the same way; she's a little more cool, but then older ladies usually are. One time I walked with the Circle Jerks down to a pizza place near my home in San Diego. Before we even ordered, the police came in and told us to leave and literally ran the Circle Jerks out of town.

Punk was a bad scene. They'd never seen anything like it in San Diego. Thirty people walking down the street in leather jackets . . . well, San Diego's pretty straight. In fact, San Diego's boring beyond belief. The only good thing you can say about this place is the beach. There's never been anything to do. It's not a Navy town like everyone thinks; it's just really dead. And it's not because there aren't nightclubs and things to do; it's because a lot of the people who came here really want a life-style that is peaceful and perfectly bland. I think it was a writer for Slash magazine who said that "S.D." stood for "slow death."

I started listening to music pretty early. I remember always hearing rock 'n' roll, because I was brought up at the beach. I can remember my babysitters and the older kids hanging out at the beach, always with radios blasting. That was like in the mid 1960s. When I was just a kid, when I was real little, I heard Motown, and I loved that stuff because that's when it was hot.

Unfortunately, I was forced to be in junior high and high school in the mid to late 1970s, which will probably go down in history as the most boring time on the whole face of the earth—and that's why when punk came along it was like a light from heaven. I went to a Catholic school for seven years, so I don't know what a public school's like, but I've always felt like an outsider and misfit. The nuns used to think I was weird because I preferred to be off by myself drawing all the time. I was always in trouble for drawing in class, constantly. I used to love drawing ancient battle scenes—Romans vs. Barbarians, Crusaders vs. Moslems, etc. Those Bible stories they told us in Catholic school really fired up the imagination!

I went to the Whisky for the first time on New Year's Eve, 1977. A Sex Pistols imitation band called the Wildcats came onto the stage, and I was absolutely awestruck. They were the most thrilling sight and sound I had ever seen! Then the headliner came out . . . a brand new band called VAN HALEN. While I've never liked heavy metal bands like that, normally I would have just ignored them. But after having my first taste of punk, Roth and his boys sent me out of the place retching violently.

All of a sudden I found hundreds of other kids that grew up feeling exactly the same way. They had always been a little bit different—the outcasts—and never had a lot of friends, because they just never understood each other. It was like finally fitting in someplace. There were really two punk movements in L.A. I don't think it's right to call the second one more hardcore, but it was with different kids. I moved to L.A. in late 1977, started hanging out, and the people who were in the first movement were a little older; they were like 20 years old or so. Then the second wave—hardcore describes it perfectly—came washing in, and the kids were a lot younger. They were 15, and it was a lot more physical scene.

I thought the whole physical thing was so funny. When you're standing there drunk and you're watching all that—well, I thought it was the funniest thing I'd ever seen. It's like when people do chicken fights in swimming pools, sitting on people's shoulders

Shawn Kerri, San Diego, 1986

trying to knock each other off. Things could get pretty violent. Jello Biafra of the Dead Kennedys knocked me out cold one night. This was at the Skeleton Club in San Diego. He did one of those flying leaps off the stage, and his boot caught me right in the temple, and I just went right down on my back. I remember thinking about trying to get up, and I said, "No way," and blacked out. I woke up next somewhere backstage.

I was also arrested at the Elks Club show. It was pretty famous in L.A.—a sort of St. Paddy's Day Massacre—and the L.A.P.D. swarmed in. I was one of the seven arrested. I had managed to find some loose masonry and tossed it in the direction of the cops; well, you don't ever get away from the L.A.P.D. I didn't quite make it to my car.

One of my favorite places was Blackies, in Hollywood. It was such a strange little hole in the wall, really like our very own place. It was more like the old Masque, the original Masque, which closed not long after I moved to L.A. I hung out there as long as it was open. It was in a basement alley off Cherokee and Hollywood Boulevard, and it was the most exciting of all the punk clubs because it was the first. Later, they opened another Masque down the street, off Santa Monica and LaBrea. It was just an old warehouse, but it had a wide-open alley to party in and a huge dirt lot that saw a lot of spirited games of kick the can and (after rainy days) mud wrestling.

On the other end of the spectrum, the Fleetwood, which was in Redondo Beach, was real bad news. I hardly ever went there and had a good time. It was always trouble and fights, plus a lot of

X; Big Boys. Club Foot, Austin, Texas, ca. 1980

been more rude and lewd than I was. I'm basically a cartoonist. I was doing cartoons to amuse my friends. I never thought the rest of the world was looking. If I had known, the art would have been designed to really piss them off!

I was proud as hell of my handbills. I'd see them all over the place. And you know, I've never gotten the same thrill out of having one of my cartoons printed in a magazine as much as seeing one of my old fliers—something I did for a gig the week before—laying in the gutter. Seeing it all mashed and dirty thrilled me, because that was how I was living, too. It looked exactly like my life.

There are a lot of my handbills that I think became classics in their day. Like the one with the mohawked skull breaking through the Germs' "coat of arms"—a blue circle, either worn on a black armband or spray-painted wherever you found a flat surface. The true initiates had a cigarette burn on their left wrist, and quite a few people had it tattooed on themselves. The "Germs Return" flier had quite an impact on people. It was done for the show they performed shortly before Darby Crash, their lead singer, killed himself with an overdose. He didn't know what I was going to do—he didn't tell me that's what he wanted—he only said, "do a flier." I did it, and when I showed him the art, he was strangely excited by it. It was like a pre-post-mortem. I wondered later if he liked the Death's Head motif (the skull and the hairdo are undoubtedly him) because he had suicide on his mind at the time. It was very spooky.

A personal favorite of mine is a Circle Jerks flier that shows a classroom scene with an enraged nun shaking her fist at whoever

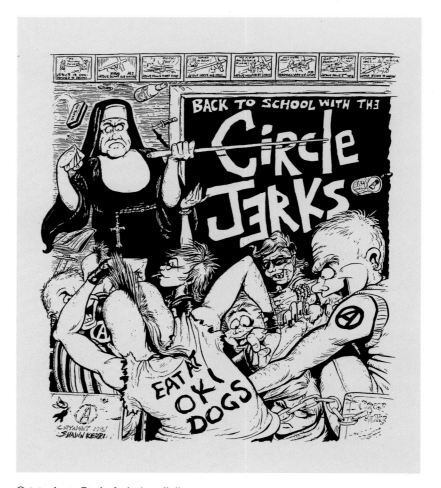

Original art; Circle Jerks handbill
Los Angeles, 1981. Artist: Shawn Kerri

non-converted surfers hanging around just to beat up on isolated groups of punks. And the bouncers were bad, too.

I think there was a difference in attitude between the initial punk and the hardcore that followed. Poseurs could hang out more in the earlier days because they weren't automatically chased off with physical harm. The "beach punks" of the second generation could get so bad about who was "in" and who wasn't that it eventually led to real fighting among people who should all have been on the same side. What it comes down to is that some of the people who hung out in the old days were a little bit snobbish and a little artsy, whereas in the later scene it was a little more physical and violent, and it weeded a lot of the older people out. But I feel I earned my stripes and put in my time, and I have the scars to prove it.

The thing I liked about punk was the anonymity. The only people I cared to impress were the people going to the shows, and the bands; and I couldn't care less about impressing anybody else. What I was doing with my poster art was more like illustrating the scene as it was happening, chronicling it, so to speak. I was doing cartoons of punks in action, and it was all so frenetic, all these flailing arms and legs. It was wild. Sometimes I wish I had

(top left)
"Skull Hall of Fame," ca. 1980
Artist: Shawn Kerri

(top right)
Germs. Starwood, Hollywood, 1980
Artist: Shawn Kerri

(left)
"The Skank Kid," 1981
Artist: Shawn Kerri

wrote "Circle Jerks" on the blackboard. It was looking from the back of a classroom, and it was kind of the typical insane scene I do in that kind of cartoon with kids jumping around in mohawks and chains and boots, and everyone's looking toward the chalk board that has "Circle Jerks" written in big letters. And the nun is up there pointing to it with a pointer, which they often use as a weapon, and she's shaking her fist at the class. Of course, the nun is the principal of the school I went to. What a lot of people also enjoyed was that the flier had the stations of the cross cartooned just above the chalkboard. It was just extremely rude—my version of the stations of the cross—and everybody got a kick out of it because they knew what it was. If you were Catholic, you knew it. So if I wasn't struck down at my drawing board doing that one, I guess I'm okay.

I think everyone raves the most about my "Skank Kid." What he was, was a composite—the reason he has sort of a bland face was because I wanted everyone of those kids to think they were him. He was supposed to be all of them lumped into one. He was everyone of those little beach brats. I was terrified of them, but they were a lot of fun to watch. The Skank Kid appeared first on a flier for a Fleetwood show. Then I put him on the Circle Jerks' Group Sex record, inside the sleeve on the lyrics sheet, and also on a yellow bumper sticker. He evolved out of doodles that were "slam-dance instructions" used to fill up space on the lyrics sheet. Everyone went crazy over the little creep. He started out as space filler, and now everyone has made a character out of him. From that sheet, the boys in the band picked out the swastika-shaped Skank Kid, and the rest is history. The Skank Kid was finally done in full color on one of their albums, and it was artwork eventually stolen by the record company. We also made it into a ten-foot-tall dropcloth to hang up behind the band when they played. They displayed it at only one show, and they had a big fight about it with their manager, who stole it or destroyed it or something. I finally signed the copyright over to Keith Morris, the lead singer. It was turning into a terrible legal brawl—that was the reason I signed it away. Believe me, I'm very fierce about protecting my copyright when it comes to work for a magazine, but I deliberately signed the Skank Kid away so no one could ever blame me for any of that foolishness. I saw it coming.

I'm really sorry I didn't save more of my art. I have quite a bit, but not like some people, people with photo albums of it, with pages and pages. These are the people who weren't the hardcore, but were on the fringes, who dug the scene—and who realized, more than "we" ever did, how impressive all this artwork really was. I didn't meet too many of my fellow punk poster artists— I never met Pushead, or Ray (from Black Flag)—and Mad Marc Rude is the only one I know well, but that's because we went together for a couple of years. But I also know I'm part of a much larger artistic community than just punk, a community including hot rod artists like Ed "Big Daddy" Roth, artists from a lot of eras who had a glint in their eye and a whole lot of sarcasm. A lot of people have told me that I'm working in a tradition. And the thing is, I'm working for Cracked magazine now. Talk about going full circle and coming back to the 1950s and early 1960s. Some of my all-time favorite artists I was impressed with as a kid were Jack Davis and Bill Elder, who worked for Mad in the 1950s. So for me to be working for Cracked, a real early imitator of Mad (Cracked was born in 1958, the same year I was), is very strange. Cartoons magazine has been my bread-and-butter job for eight years. I've had comic stories in Cocaine Comics #3 and in the last two and

"God Damn It! We Want a Drummer and We Want 1 Now!": flier for X, ca. 1978

an upcoming Commies from Mars. I've also sold gags of pornographic artwork under the pen name of Dee Lawdid to Hustler, Chic, and Velvet, and wrote Donald Duck stories for the Disney comics they send to Europe.

I think it worries straight people when young kids take matters into their own hands, especially kids that look as weird as punks. Straight people can see there's definitely a lot of work involved in the punk scene, and that punks are putting their own money into it. People would rather think kids just want to be stupid and get drunk and go to the high school dances and screw around. And there's a lot of that in the punk world, too. But there's a surprising amount of punks who are putting their energy into things that are thoughtful. That scares a lot of people.

I always thought the late 1970s and early 1980s were just like the 1950s. Hardcore punk seems just like the beatnik movement. And the times are much like the 1950s, with a conservative government, a real right-wing attitude from a lot of our elders, and a lot of exasperating bullshit. I think something real big is coming up in the next couple of years, something as socially important as what went down in the late 1960s, which I really wasn't part of.

But that'll work out just perfect, then. Whenever the next movement comes along, I can start charging money for my work. Just like Peter Max! I was young and idealistic once, too, and all I ever wanted for my posters were a few beers and a spot on the guest list. But when the new movement comes along, guess what, I'm going to be one of the old timers!

New Wave

In contrast to the music of the late 1960s, mainstream rock of the mid 1970s yielded rather little poster art; newspaper ads and radio spots were the favored means of promoting concert events. But just as the new music bucks the rock establishment, so its promotion runs counter to prevailing trends.

The new poster and handbill art is a throwback to early psychedelic art in that it announces a new music *and* a new community. But the major difference between the new art and the psychedelic works is that the earlier artists created full-size, multicolored pieces, while the new wave artists mainly issue handbills, generally in black and white. While the psychedelic artists aspired to work with creative printers and sophisticated printing machinery, new music artists are often content to produce their work in the cheapest, most commonplace job printing establishments, even on Xerox and other office-style copiers. New music posters are usually street art, in this sense recalling the letterpress concert posters of the 1950s.

(continued on page 448)

5.1
Mondellos
International Cafe, Berkeley, 1979

5.2 *(above right)*
The Police; The Knack
Zellerbach Auditorium, Berkeley, 1979
Artist: Hugh Brown

5.3
Natives
Starry Plough, Berkeley, 1980

5.4

Translator
Old Waldorf, San Francisco, 1983
Artist: Al Gordon

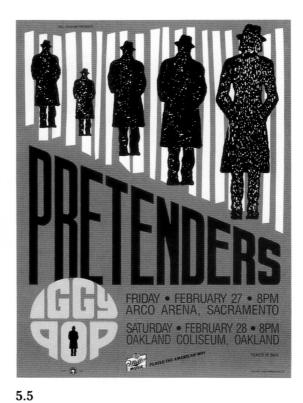

5.5

Pretenders; Iggy Pop
Henry J. Kaiser Auditorium, Oakland, 1987
Artist: Arlene Owseichik

5.6

Hostages
181 Club, San Francisco, 1983

5.7

Pajama Party
Bench & Bar, Oakland, 1979
Artists: Tim Barrett, John Seabury

5.8

Aries Party
The Stone, San Francisco, 1982

5.9

Ronnie Spector; Elements of Style
The Stone, San Francisco, 1983
Artist: David Barker

5.10

Rank and File; C. F. Players
I Beam, San Francisco, 1982

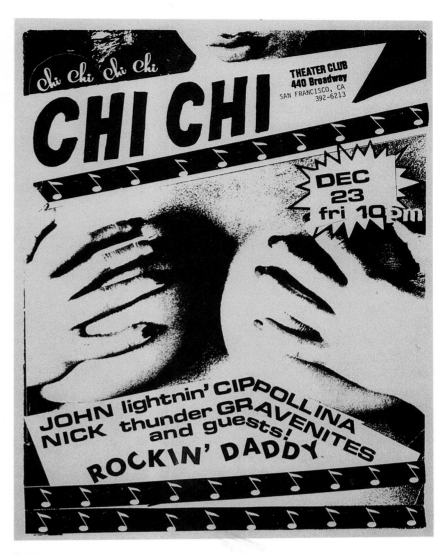

5.11

John Cipollina and Nick Gravenites; Rockin' Daddy
Chi Chi Club, San Francisco, 1983

5.12

Squares Fan Night
Keystone Berkeley, Berkeley, 1982

5.13

Violent Femmes
I Beam, San Francisco, 1984

(continued from page 445)

As the music divides into punk and new wave, a distinctive graphic style has come to be associated with each. Far less refined than mainstream rock art, new wave work is nevertheless more controlled than punk. New wave art tends to be witty rather than deliberately offensive, as the best punk pieces are. New wave posters are most often the product of educated sensibilities at the cutting edge of music and fashion, not so blunt a protest as punk.

Emerging Bay area bands of the late 1970s like Eye Protection (5.14, 5.15), the Defectors (5.18), Indoor Life (5.23), and No Sisters (5.21) offered up trendy versions of basic garage rock. The engaging spirit of No Sisters was particularly admired, and the band's spunky character was aptly reflected in cheery promotional art created by one of the band members.

No Sisters guitarist Tim Barrett from the beginning doubled as the group's own poster artist. (After the demise of the band, he went on to create a design firm called Studio DeBoom.) Barrett's designs were conspicuously new wave, emphasizing angular, stylized silhouette figures and modernesque lettering. No Sisters achieved recognition as much for their widely distributed handbill art as for their music.

5.14 *(above)*

Eye Protection; Cha Cha Billy
Rose and Thistle / Back D.O.R.,
San Francisco, 1980
Artist: Joseph Prieboy

5.15 *(right)*

Eye Protection; Jim Carroll
Back D.O.R. / Old Waldorf,
San Francisco, 1981
Artist: Joseph Prieboy

5.16

"Dance Dance: Winter 1986–1987"
Wolfgang's, San Francisco, 1986
Artist: Tim Barrett

5.17

Rock Justice
Old Waldorf, San Francisco, ca. 1980

5.18

Defectors
Le Disque, San Francisco, 1981

5.19

March Calendar
Berkeley Square, Berkeley, 1981

5.20
The Mutants; The Aliens
Back D.O.R., San Francisco, 1980
Artist: Brenda Shahan

5.21
No Sisters; Contractions
Berkeley Square, Berkeley, 1980
Artist: Tim Barrett

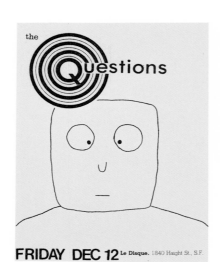

5.22
The Questions
Le Disque, San Francisco, 1981

5.23
Indoor Life
Back D.O.R., San Francisco, 1980

5.24
Bow Wow Wow
Kabuki Theater, San Francisco, 1983

5.25
The Motels; Kid Courage
Old Waldorf, San Francisco, 1980

PSYCOTIC PINEAPPLE

This deliberately misspelled band was one of the Bay Area's best-known garage-style new wave groups. Like many similar American bands of the late 1970s, this Berkeley-based group enjoyed a rowdy local following that built for a time and then faded. During its heyday, roughly 1978–83, Psycotic Pineapple became very familiar as a name and even as a kind of East Bay concept—largely because of a long series of cartoon-style handbills executed by one of the group's members, John Seabury.

Psycotic Pineapple's weekly postings were classic bits of street culture, particularly in Berkeley, along Telegraph Avenue near the University of California campus. The cartoons were witty and sarcastic; their key element the "Pineapple Man," who mocked and taunted passersby from kiosks and lampposts. The Pineapple Man series provided an insightful portrait of Berkeley street life in the post-hippie period.

5.26

Pineapple Jam
Keystone Berkeley, Berkeley, 1980
Artist: John Seabury

5.27

Psycotic Pineapple; Sudden Fun
Keystone Berkeley, Berkeley, 1979
Artist: John Seabury

5.28

Pyno Jam
Ashkenaz, Berkeley, 1983
Artist: John Seabury

SVT

This, one of San Francisco's better "second wave" bands of the late 1970s new wave period, was led by writer-guitarist Brian Marnell and featured bassist Jack Casady, formerly with the Jefferson Airplane and Hot Tuna. SVT generated a fine body of stylistically linked concert art executed by Richard Stutting.

SVT bandmembers and management recognized the need for a savvy promotional image and commissioned highly stylized art employing a host of trendy, but very effective, touches. Stutting's SVT poster art, credited to his own Artbreakers design firm, stands out because of its currency and graphic wit. Not only did his designs make for distinctive street pieces, they were easily adapted to print ads, particularly in such new wave weeklies as *Boulevards*.

A few of Stutting's SVT pieces became underground hits, like the one that rains chainsaws (5.32), and have come to mark a new fashion and new music that began to turn San Francisco heads in new directions.

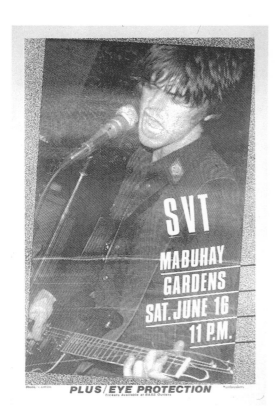

5.29
SVT; Eye Protection. Mabuhay Gardens, San Francisco, 1979. Artist: Richard Stutting / Artbreakers. Photographer: Vince Anton

5.30
SVT; Jim Carroll. Old Waldorf, San Francisco, 1979
Artist: Richard Stutting / Artbreakers. Photographer: Steve Gruver

5.31
SVT
Multiple venues, Los Angeles, 1979
Artist: Richard Stutting / Artbreakers
Photographer: Steve Gruver

5.32
SVT
The Palms, San Francisco, 1979
Artist: Richard Stutting / Artbreakers

5.33
SVT; Aliens
Rio Theater, Rodeo, California, 1979
Artist: Richard Stutting / Artbreakers

ELEMENTS OF STYLE

This local band, which appeared frequently in San Francisco during the late stages of the new wave period, copped its name from the famous writer's handbook by Strunk and White, which, according to the *New Yorker*, is distinguished by "brevity, clarity, and prickly good sense"—a good description of the band, which was closer to Talking Heads than to the Sex Pistols.

The Elements of Style was promoted creatively through concert handbills designed by guitar player and bandleader David Barker. The economy and precision of his poster work was very much in the mode of Barker's legendary shortstopping for his softball team: crisp, efficient, dramatic as the occasion warranted.

5.34
Elements of Style; Jack Face
Le Disque, San Francisco, 1982
Artist: David Barker

5.35
Elements of Style
Multiple venues, San Francisco, 1983
Artist: David Barker

drawings by Doc Boehland

5.36
Elements of Style; Early Man
Chi Chi Club, San Francisco, 1983
Artists: David Barker, Bo Richardson

with **EARLY MAN** at the fabulous **CHI CHI CLUB**, 440 Broadway! Saturday, September 3rd at 9:30pm.

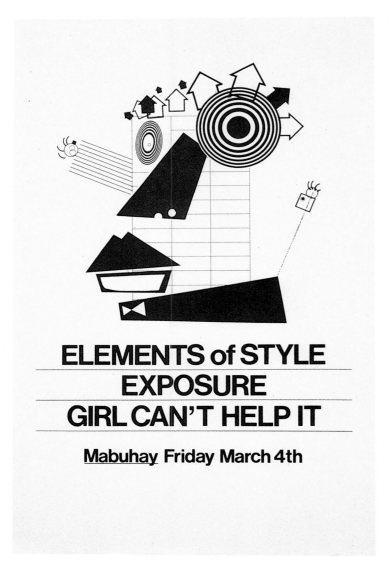

5.37
Elements of Style; Exposure
Mabuhay Gardens, San Francisco, 1983
Artist: David Barker

5.38
Elements of Style; Times Beach
Berkeley Square, Berkeley, 1983
Artists: David Barker, Jad King

SU. SUTTLE

The creators of new wave posters generally did not develop the name recognition of the psychedelic artists, but their achievements are just as deserving of celebration. One of the best working on the West Coast goes by the name of Su. Suttle. Born Sue Taggart, she became well known for her lighting and set designs, and was given her *nom de guerre* in 1971 by a friend after seeing some costumes she created for a play. With no formal training in graphics during her years at the University of California at Davis and at UC Santa Cruz, she began designing posters for the schools' drama and music departments, and subsequently for local music promoters.

Suttle lays claim to no personal design style—if pressed, she calls herself ''neo-psychedelic''—and prefers to let the nature of the performance dictate the style of her graphics. In recent years, she has become widely recognized for expanding the artistic possibilities of laminated and backstage passes, and she has done excellent work for bands like Huey Lewis and the News and Santana.

5.40
Talking Heads; The B-52's
Cocoanut Grove, Santa Cruz, 1979
Artist: Su. Suttle

5.39
Talking Heads; The B-52's
University of California, Davis, 1979
Artist: Su. Suttle

5.42

Humans; No Sisters
Catalyst, Santa Cruz, 1980
Artist: Su. Suttle

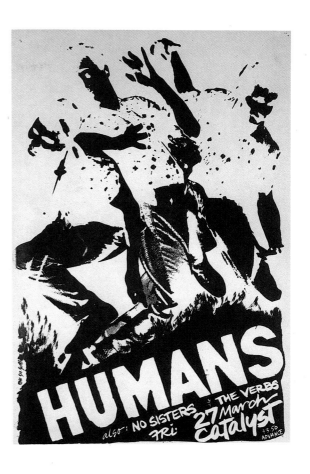

5.41

The Ramones
Civic Auditorium, Santa Cruz, 1980
Artist: Su. Suttle

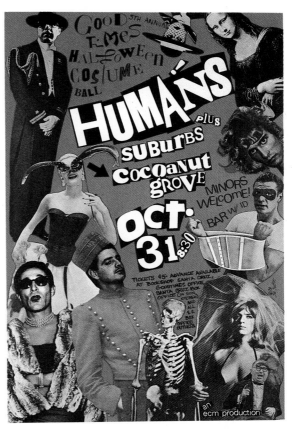

5.43

Fifth Annual Good Times Halloween Ball
Cocoanut Grove, Santa Cruz, 1979
Artist: Su. Suttle

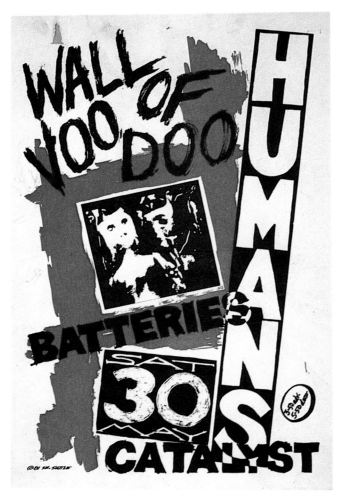

5.44
Wall of Voodoo; Humans
Catalyst, Santa Cruz, 1981
Artist: Su. Suttle

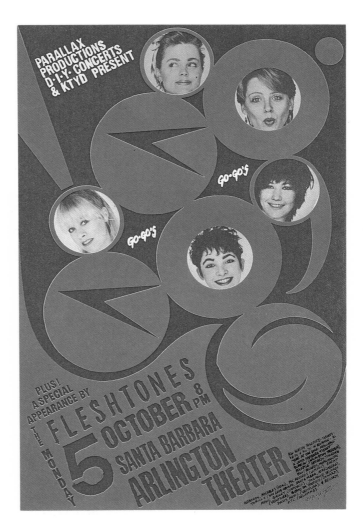

5.45
Go-Gos; Fleshtones
Arlington Theater, Santa Barbara, 1981
Artist: Su. Suttle

5.47
Brian Eno
University of California, Santa Cruz, 1980
Artist: Su. Suttle

5.46
Humans
Catalyst, Santa Cruz, 1981
Artist: Su. Suttle

SEATTLE: ART CHANTRY

The new wave and punk music that pervaded the country by the late 1970s influenced local graphic artists, who in turn affected the direction of ad agencies and regional print media. Chantry is one such artist, who earned a fine arts degree but is self-taught as a designer. Creator of more than 400 posters and 60 record album jackets, Chantry is also art director of Seattle's monthly arts newspaper, *The Rocket*. He is adept at creating logos and other consumer-oriented material, but his first love is music.

Chantry, in fact, is a music fanatic. He is also an authority on the subject of punk and new wave poster art, a passion developed from his interest in dada and Expressionism and that resulted in the 1985 book, *Instant Litter: Concert Posters from Seattle Punk Culture*. Chantry's own art has been influenced by underground graphics, which he credits with sharpening his wit and emboldening his approach.

5.49
Thomas Dolby; Modern English
University of Washington, Seattle, 1984
Artist: Art Chantry

5.48
Romeo Void; Visible Targets
University of Washington, Seattle, 1982
Artist: Art Chantry

5.50
Gang of Four; 3 Swimmers
Showbox, Seattle, 1982
Artist: Art Chantry

Punk

SAN FRANCISCO BAY AREA

If new wave was a challenge to the mainstream, then punk was total provocation. While new wave was a logical, inevitable step beyond mainstream music, punk outrageously assaulted any and every community sensibility.

Punk style first developed in England out of earlier mod, rocker, and skinhead movements. It was exported to America by word-of-mouth and through late-night TV documentaries, exploding like a mushroom cloud in New York, San Francisco, and Los Angeles during 1975–83, spawning a punk street culture that in turn spawned punk poster art.

Punk art is the essence of street art, not designed for leisurely enjoyment or careful hoarding, but for the moment. Yet, so many punk pieces are of such strong design that quite a number were taken down from the lampposts and telephone poles and saved. These pieces are almost exclusively of handbill size, either printed at neighborhood "instant printers" or on Xerox machines by the dozens.

Thanks to its decades-old poster tradition, San Francisco's punk art is among the most creative of the period, featuring recognizable series, such as Jo Jo Planteen's posters for the Alter Boys (5.52–54), and the free use of newspaper images and headline type in collage form—a more spontaneous process than methods favored by new wave artists.

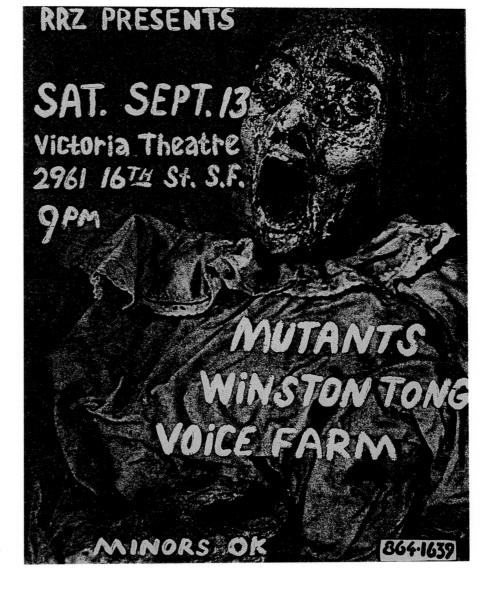

5.51
Mutants; Winston Tong. Victoria Theatre, San Francisco, 1980. Artist: Paul Rat

5.52
Alter Boys
Deaf Club, San Francisco, 1979
Artist: Jo Jo Planteen

5.53
Alter Boys; Pink Section
Savoy Tivoli, San Francisco, 1979
Artist: Jo Jo Planteen

5.54
Alter Boys; Plugz
Mabuhay Gardens, San Francisco, 1979

5.55

X; No Alternative
Russian Center,
San Francisco, 1981

5.56

Second KSAN Heretics Party
Mabuhay Gardens, San Francisco, 1979
Artists: Pete Thorpe, Bob Zimmerman

5.57

"Keyboardist Wanted"
San Francisco, ca. 1981

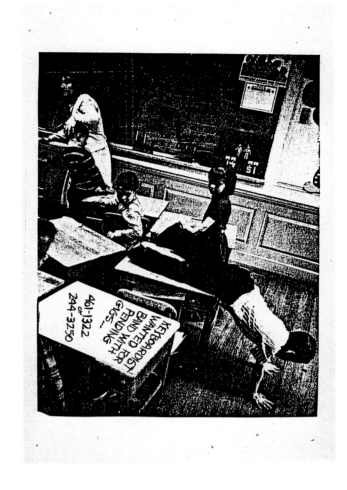

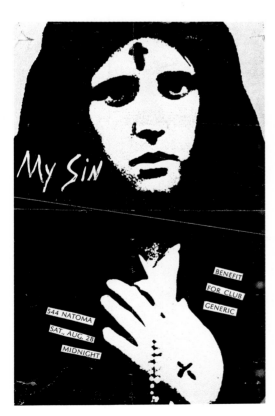

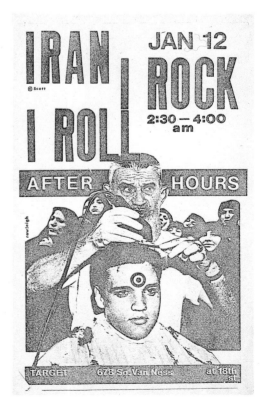

5.58

My Sin
544 Natoma Street, San Francisco, 1982
Artist: Mark Barbeau

5.59

Dennis Lee and the Living Daylights; Shitheads
330 Grove Street, San Francisco, 1978
Artist: Dennis Lee

5.60

Iran Irock Iroll
Target Video, San Francisco, 1980
Artist: Rawleigh Pardun

5.61
Girls on Drugs; Wolverines
Day's, San Francisco, 1982
Artist: C. LaPlante

5.62
Amputee and the Eunichs
2431 Ellsworth Street, Berkeley, 1978

5.63
Target Video Benefit
Savoy Tivoli, San Francisco, 1980

5.64
ssi
Deaf Club, San Francisco, ca. 1980

5.65
The Young Adults
International Cafe, Berkeley, 1979

5.66
The Lewd; Fartz
Oakland Auditorium, Oakland, 1982

5.67
Eastern Front Festival
Aquatic Park, Berkeley, 1981

5.68

Eastern Front Festival
Aquatic Park, Berkeley, 1981
Artist: Pepe Moreno

5.69
Nuns
Mabuhay Gardens, San Francisco, 1977
Artist: Edwin Heaven

5.70
Social Unrest; Sleeping Dogs
Club Foot, San Francisco, 1983
Artist: Eric Snowconehead

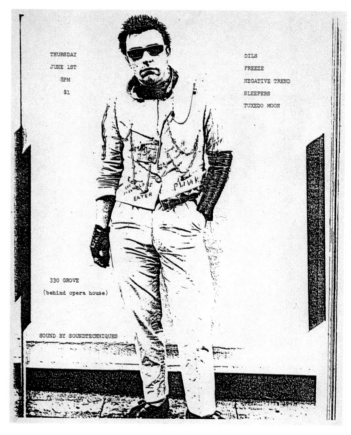

5.71
Dils; Freeze
330 Grove Street, San Francisco, 1978

MABUHAY GARDENS

Mabuhay Gardens, a Filipino night spot in North Beach, was the most important San Francisco punk rock club. The first real punk group to appear there, in the fall of 1976, was Mary Monday and the Britches, followed by the Nuns.

During its heyday, Mabuhay produced some of the most street-effective punk art of the period. Various artists were responsible for these pieces, but, in punk tradition, most are uncredited. With few exceptions, the posters were all black-and-white handbills, and most were collages. The Mabuhay was one of the few punk clubs to feature a distinctive logo on its concert art.

This oversize handbill promoting the Suicide Hotline benefit at Mabuhay Gardens (nicknamed "Fab Mab") features a thematic unity rare in punk work. The artist took great pains to link the nature of the event to the name of the featured band—the Golden Gate Jumpers—and with the central graphic, the Creature from the Black Lagoon walking out of the water, holding a—suicide?—victim.

5.72
Screamers; Middleclass
Mabuhay Gardens, San Francisco, 1978
Artist: Gary Panter

5.73
VOM; Nuclear Valdez
Mabuhay Gardens, San Francisco, 1978
Photographers: M. Kohoe, D. Evenson

5.74
Mutants; Fleshapoids
Mabuhay Gardens, San Francisco, 1979

5.75
Toiling Midgets; Mutants
Mabuhay Gardens, San Francisco, 1980

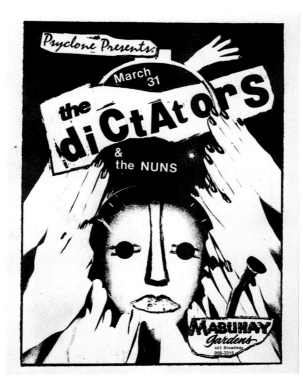

5.76
Ulna and Femurs
Mabuhay Gardens, San Francisco, 1980

5.77
The Dictators; The Nuns
Mabuhay Gardens, San Francisco, 1979

5.78
Vauxhall; The Dimes
Mabuhay Gardens, San Francisco, 1983

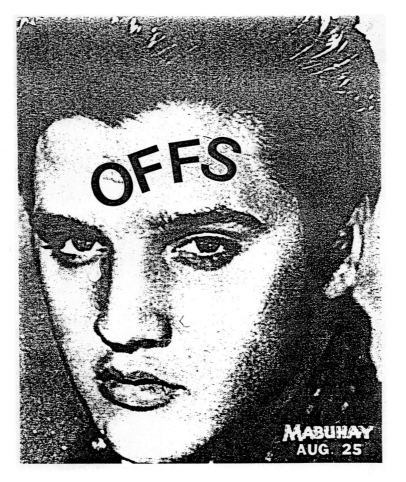

5.79
Blondie; Crime
Mabuhay Gardens, San Francisco, 1977
Artist: Jerry Paulsen

5.80
Offs
Mabuhay Gardens, San Francisco, 1979

5.81
Folsom Street Night with Ruby Zebra
Mabuhay Gardens, San Francisco, ca. 1979

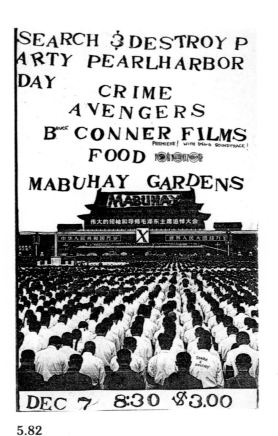

5.82
Pearl Harbor Day Party
Mabuhay Gardens, San Francisco, ca. 1978
Artist: Penelope Houston

5.83
Black Flag; Dead Kennedys
Mabuhay Gardens, San Francisco, 1979
Artist: Raymond Pettibone

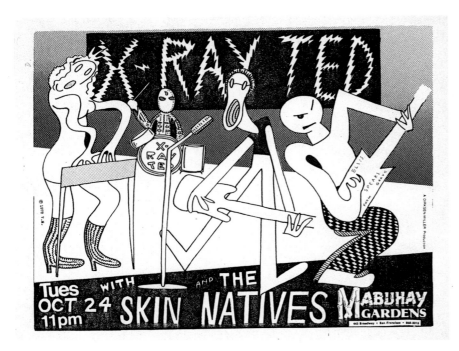

5.84
X-Ray Ted; The Natives
Mabuhay Gardens, San Francisco, 1978
Artist: Victor Moan

5.85
Voice Farm; Pink Section
Mabuhay Gardens, San Francisco, ca. 1978
Artist: Patrick Miller

5.86
Suicide Hotline Benefit
Mabuhay Gardens, San Francisco, 1981

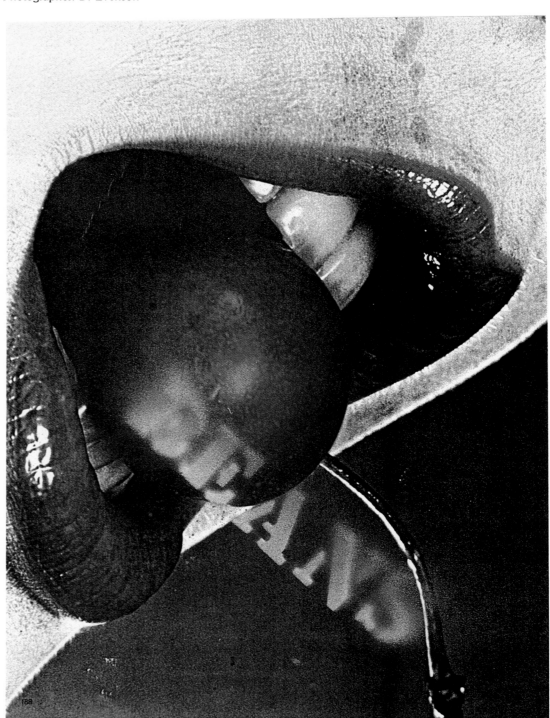

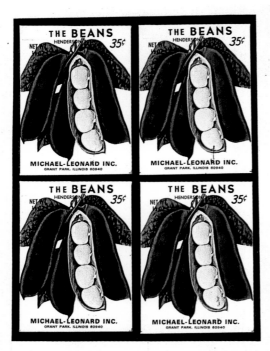

5.88
The Beans
Mabuhay Gardens, San Francisco, 1978
Artist: Edward Bachmann

5.89
The Beans
Mabuhay Gardens, San Francisco, 1978
Artist: Judy Tampa

SOUND OF MUSIC

During punk's best years—roughly 1976–82—San Francisco boasted a slew of noteworthy, if only-for-the-moment, punk rock clubs. By the early 1980s, following the success of the first Western Front festival, the mayoral campaign of the Dead Kennedys' Jello Biafra, and a host of independent punk record releases, the scene supported clubs that booked punk exclusively, heavily, or just frequently.

Among the clubs that opened in the winter of 1980 was the Sound of Music, located in the seedy Tenderloin district. Its musical activity was almost completely hardcore, in contrast to the more varied booking schedule of clubs like X's, Le Disque, the Keystone, the Palms, Savoy Tivoli, the Old Waldorf, the Back D.O.R., and Rock City. The Sound of Music was more likely to feature nasty bands like the Fuck-Ups, or groups with a particular cult following among punks, like Flipper.

The handbill art associated with Sound of Music shows was more bizarre and confrontive than many, although the Sound of Music was by no means the most notorious club outside of Mabuhay. Other punk havens included Project One, Temple 1839, Hotel Utah, Tool & Die, the A-Hole, Club Foot, and Club Generic. Probably the most celebrated—due to its utter novelty—was the Deaf Club, where deaf people were among the patrons.

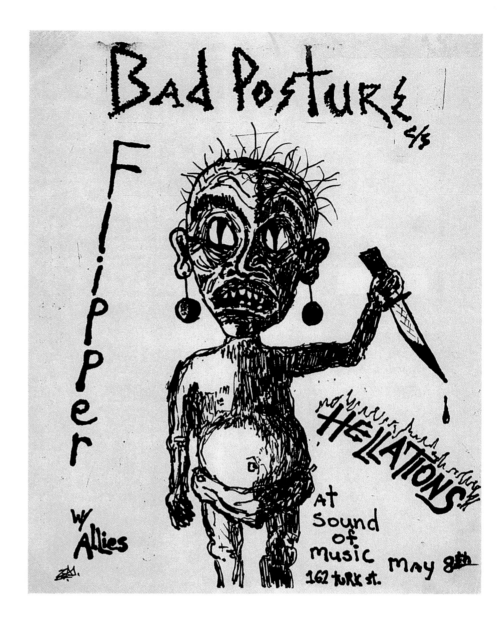

5.90

Bad Posture; Flipper
Sound of Music, San Francisco, 1982

5.91

The Fuck Ups
Mabuhay Gardens, Sound of Music,
San Francisco, 1981
Artist: Bob Noxious

5.92

Fuck Ups; Infidels
Sound of Music, San Francisco, 1983

5.93

Geeks
Sound of Music, San Francisco, 1982

TOOL & DIE

With Target Video, a radical punk-style independent television documentary company, Mabuhay, the Deaf Club, and Tool & Die brought San Francisco punk culture to whatever maturity it managed to achieve. Established in 1980 in the city's Latino Mission District (home of several other mid-era punk establishments), Tool & Die also hosted punk art exhibitions and multimedia presentations.

The founder of the club, Peter Belsito, helped to publicize punk art, co-editing *Damage* magazine and co-authoring two punk art books —*Streetart* (1981) and *Hardcore California* (1983). He also organized a traveling exhibition of punk posters.

5.94

Barry Beam; Los Microwaves
Tool & Die, San Francisco, 1981
Artists: Peter Belsito, Lisa Fredenthal

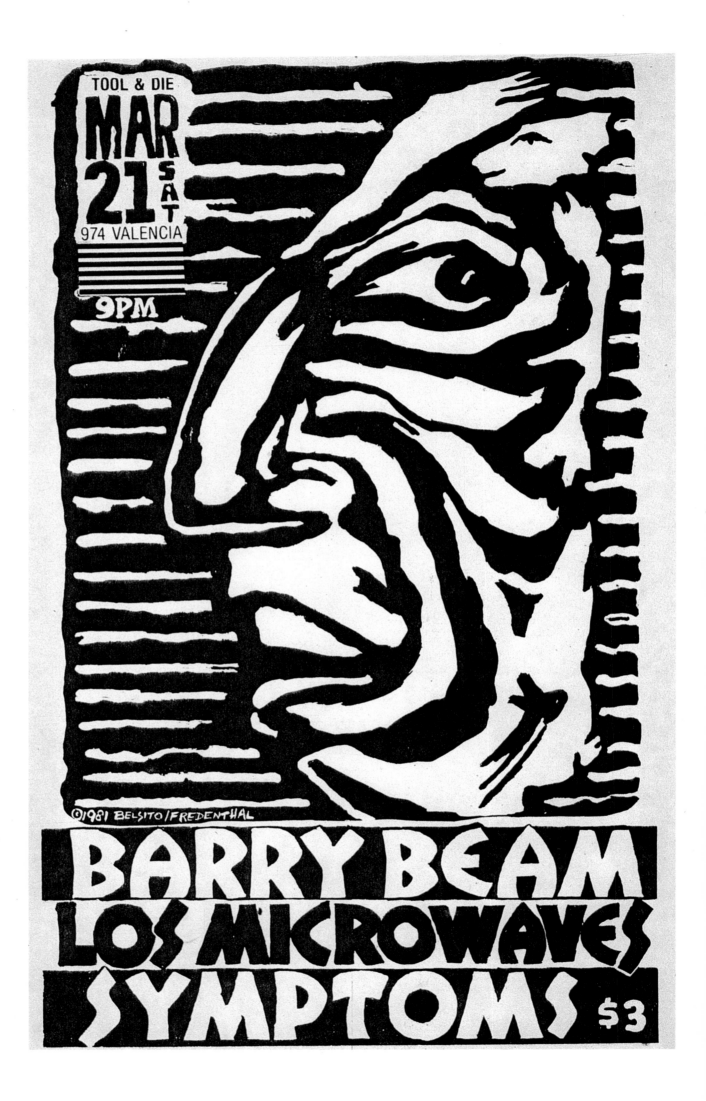

5.95
You Can Run But You Can't Hide
Tool & Die, San Francisco, 1982
Artist: Mark Barbeau

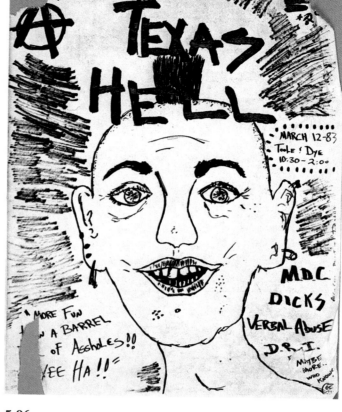

5.96
A Texas Hell
Tool & Die, San Francisco, 1983

5.97
Units; Indoor Life
Tool & Die, San Francisco, 1980
Artist: Peter Belsito

5.98
Crucifix; Social Unrest
Tool & Die, San Francisco, 1977
Artist: Chris Douglass

TEMPLE 1839

The name merged the street location, 1839 Geary Boulevard, with the building's former function as a synagogue—Temple Beth Israel. Curiously—or ominously—Temple 1839 was located between the original Fillmore Auditorium and the People's Temple, headed by the Rev. Jim Jones, who led his flock to mass suicide in the jungles of Guyana.

On the fringe of a rundown and dangerous neighborhood, Temple 1839 had some trouble drawing a crowd, except when such groups as Dead Kennedys appeared.

By the early 1980s, punk audiences were often violent, and at many shows crowd members climbed onstage and dived back into the audience with reckless abandon. Slam-dancing was now part of punk behavior, and the old temple rocked and rolled beyond the imagination of the most extreme religious enthusiast.

Temple 1839 and venues like the Deaf Club provided independently run alternatives to Dirk Dirksen's "establishment" Mabuhay operation downtown.

5.99

Flamin' Groovies; Minimal Man
Theater 1839, San Francisco, 1980

5.100

Urge; Dead Kennedys
Theater 1839, San Francisco, 1979
Artist: Jean Caffeine

5.101

X; Dils
1839 Geary, San Francisco, 1979

5.103

Buzzcocks; Dead Kennedys
1839 Geary, San Francisco, 1979

5.102

Crime; Dead Kennedys
1839 Geary, San Francisco, 1979

THE CLASH
AND OTHER
BRITISH VISITORS

The Sex Pistols and the Clash symbolize punk youth culture as it had developed in England by 1977.

The Clash was hard pressed to top the sensation of the Sex Pistols (whose first American tour was also its last, the group disbanding in San Francisco), but ultimately the sincerity of the Clash's political and social commitment was more compelling. They sang about real issues affecting youth in England, but they made their point on the strength of basic rock 'n' roll, which was easier to get behind than the aimless flailing of the Sex Pistols.

Early in 1979, the Clash made an important appearance at a San Francisco benefit for New Youth Productions, held at Temple (here called ''Theater'') 1839 (5.105). Later that year, the band appeared in an unusual show held at the old Kezar Pavilion (5.106), and at

(continued on next page)

5.104

The Clash; Negative Trend
Theater 1839, San Francisco, 1979
Artist: Alexis Scott

5.105

A Night of Treason
England, ca. 1976

(continued from preceding page) the Family Dog's Tribal Stomp festival at the Monterey Fairgrounds.

A host of British bands like the Gang of Four, the Pretenders, Graham Parker and the Rumor, Elvis Costello and the Attractions, and more recently U2, all influenced by new wave and punk movements, found great favor in the Bay area.

5.106
The Clash
Kezar Pavilion,
San Francisco, 1979
Artist: Hugh Brown

5.107
Gang of Four; B People
American Indian Center, San Francisco, 1980

5.108
Gang of Four; B People
American Indian Center, San Francisco, 1980

5.109
Gang of Four; B People
American Indian Center, San Francisco, 1980

MINIMAL MAN
AND OTHERS

As might be expected, tempestuous punk bands were short-lived. But, on occasion, memorable groups like Minimal Man survived long enough to be associated with the release of extraordinary poster art. In a few cases the posters were linked to the performance art itself. The key figure in Minimal Man, also responsible for the posters, was Patrick Miller. He became recognized all along the West Coast for a variety of artistic street pranks, including (allegedly) stenciling Minimal Man skull designs on sidewalks, street signs, and freeway overpasses.

Sometimes, punk posters, like those for Minimal Man and Arkansaw Man, developed into a vaguely coherent series, usually executed in skillful collage, but occasionally in pen-and-ink cartooning, of which the Mr. E pieces are excellent examples (5.117–119).

5.110

Minimal Man; Pink Section
Back D.O.R., San Francisco, 1980
Artist: Patrick Miller

5.111

Tuxedomoon; Minimal Man
Victoria Theater, San Francisco, 1981
Artist: Patrick Miller

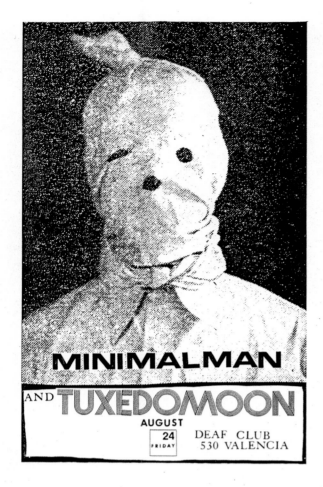

5.112

Minimal Man; Tuxedomoon
Deaf Club, San Francisco, 1979
Artist: Patrick Miller

5.113

Minimal Man; Toiling Midgets
On Broadway, San Francisco, 1982
Artist: Patrick Miller

5.114

Arkansaw Man
On Broadway, San Francisco, 1982

5.115

Arkansaw Man
974 Valencia Street, San Francisco, 1982

5.116

Arkansaw Man
Hotel Utah, San Francisco, 1982

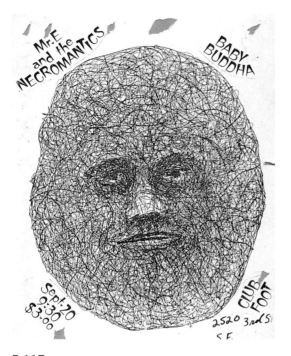

5.117

Mr. E and the Necromatics; Baby Buddha
Club Foot, San Francisco, 1980
Artist: Dennis C. Lee

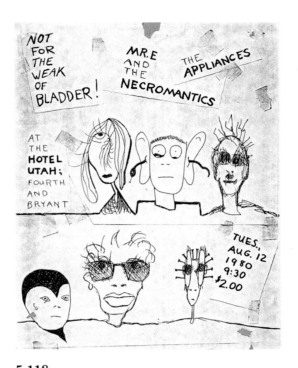

5.118

Mr. E and the Necromantics; Appliances
Hotel Utah, San Francisco, 1980

5.119

Mr. E and the Necromantics; Men in Black
Hotel Utah, San Francisco, 1980

5.120

Repeat Offenders
Hotel Utah, San Francisco, 1982
Artist: B. Tagrin

5.121

Repeat Offenders; Aural Canvas
Heaven's Gate, San Francisco, 1982
Artist: B. Tagrin

CRIME

Another punk band that managed to establish more than a transient identity was Crime, whose performance style was altogether original. Often they wore police uniforms on stage, their shows introduced with sirens and searchlights.

Like Crime, which hacked out its own musical identity, a handful of punk poster artists earned particular respect and recognition during the height of the period. James Stark, responsible for most of Crime's promotional art, gave great clarity and immediacy to the Crime series of posters by focusing on dominant images and by incorporating into each piece the group's distinctively lettered logo. The band name and the simple images made Stark's posters the most visible on the street. They are also tinged with a refined sarcasm that makes them the more enduring.

5.122
Crime; Dils
Mabuhay Gardens, San Francisco, 1977
Artist: James Stark

5.123
Crime
San Quentin, Marin County, California, 1978
Artist: James Stark

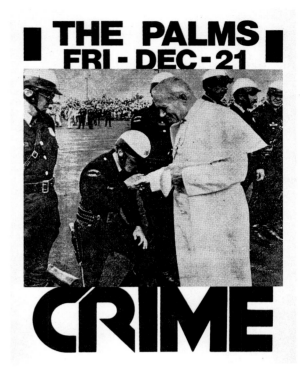

5.124

Crime; The Mutants
Mabuhay Gardens, San Francisco, 1979
Artist: James Stark

5.125

Crime
Civic Center, San Francisco, 1978
Artist: James Stark

5.126

Crime
The Palms, San Francisco, 1979
Artist: James Stark

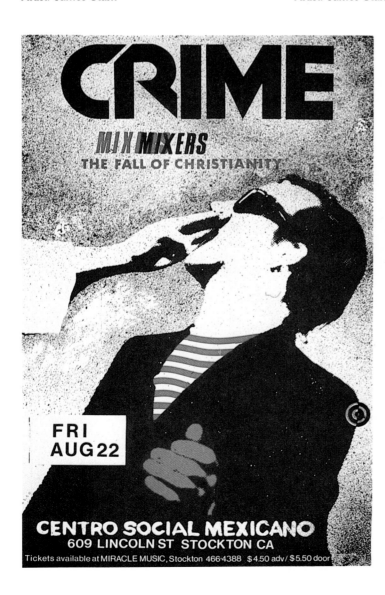

5.128

Crime; Vktms
Mabuhay Gardens, San Francisco, 1979

5.127

Crime
Centro Social Mexicano, Stockton, 1980
Artist: Ratto

DEAD KENNEDYS

At first, their name provided much of their allure, since it conveyed all the offensive posturing the punks so loved. But much of the Dead Kennedys' success was due to the substance of their performances.

Obviously their name alone does set them apart, and every poster on which it appears elicits a certain shock. Even so, most Dead Kennedys posters are no more offensive than hundreds of other punk pieces. Yet they are somehow more *classically* offensive, such as the one depicting a slain Mafia chieftain lying in a pool of blood (5.130). Truly vulgar street art like this bestows distinction on a hardcore punk band, especially when the vulgarity is incongruously tempered with well-thought-out black humor.

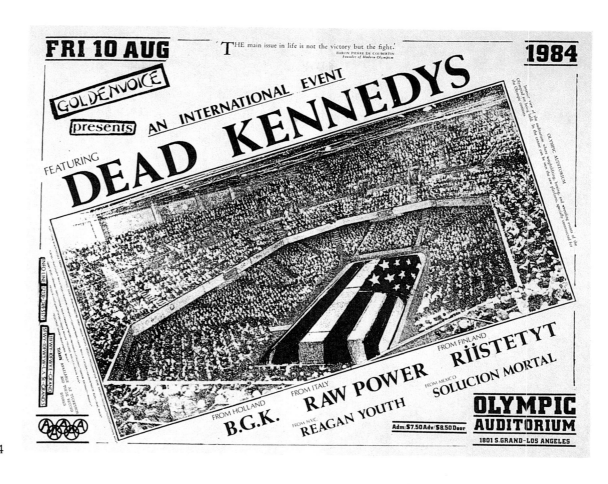

5.129

Dead Kennedys; Raw Power
Olympic Auditorium, Los Angeles, 1984

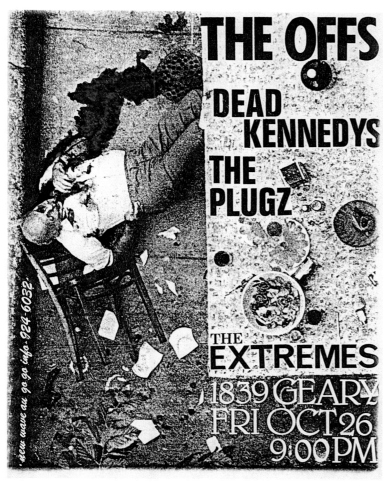

5.130

Offs; Dead Kennedys
1839 Geary, San Francisco, 1979

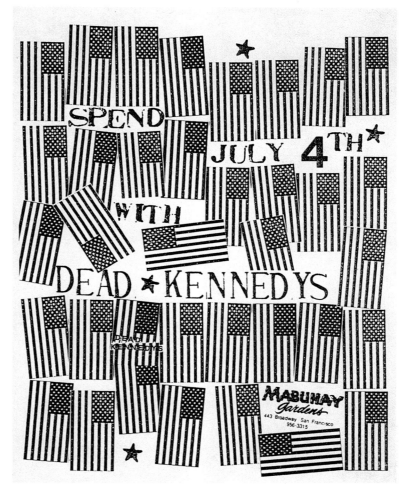

5.131

Dead Kennedys
Mabuhay Gardens, San Francisco, ca. 1981

5.132

Biafra for Mayor
1839 Geary, San Francisco, 1980

SAN FRANCISCO HARDCORE

If there is no limit to the extent to which punk music can offend, there is also no self-restriction on the offensiveness of poster imagery. In San Francisco, the Dils and the Avengers have been responsible for some of the most provocative art, including two Avengers posters that feature photographs depicting women in sexual bondage (5.138, 5.140). Outraged citizens brought the posters to the police and then to the attention of San Francisco Mayor Dianne Feinstein, whose angry response closed down some punk clubs.

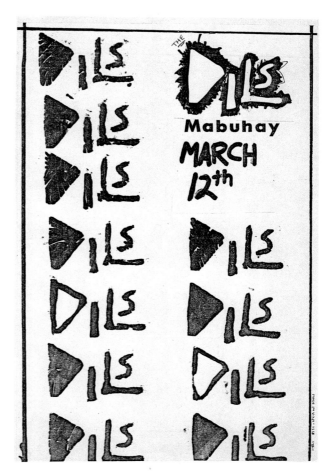

5.134
Dils
Mabuhay Gardens, San Francisco, 1978
Artist: Penelope Houston

5.133
Dils; Crime
Mabuhay Gardens, San Francisco, 1978
Artist: Jean Caffeine

5.135
Dils
Mabuhay Gardens, San Francisco, 1978

5.136
The Avengers; X-Ray Ted
Mabuhay Gardens, San Francisco, 1977
Artist: Penelope Houston

5.137
Avengers; Liars
Mabuhay Gardens, San Francisco, ca. 1978
Artist: Penelope Houston

5.138
KSAN Outcaste Party
Mabuhay Gardens, San Francisco, 1977
Artist: Rico

5.139
The Avengers; Dils
Mabuhay Gardens, San Francisco, 1978
Artist: Penelope Houston

5.140
The Mutants; The Avengers
800 Chestnut Street, San Francisco, 1979
Artist: Bruce Pollack

5.141
The Avengers
Mabuhay Gardens, San Francisco, 1977
Artist: Penelope Houston

LOS ANGELES

Pioneer Los Angeles punk bands included the Nerves, Germs, Screamers, and Weirdos. The Screamers established a strong presence in part through distinctive poster art, the work of Gary Panter, who created the screaming head logo (5.72).

Early 1978 saw the beginning of a second punk wave, dominated by young suburban punks reckless in their deportment: instead of pogoing, they slam-danced. Their heroes were bands without any art-rock pretensions, including Black Flag, Circle Jerks, 45 Grave, China White, Fear, and many more.

Some of the most humorous hardcore punk handbill art was drawn for the Circle Jerks by cartoonist Shawn Kerri, an active participant in punk concert life.

Clubs have always played an important role in Los Angeles music. Their proliferation is in part due to the city's geography, which sprawls over a vast area. And geography was one reason why clubs issued handbills every week, posted along whole city blocks to attract the attention of the ubiquitous Los Angeles motorist.

As in other cities with punk communities, bands often used handbills for their own solicitations. Sometimes the handbills they posted sought out new musicians (5.57) and created informal fan clubs (5.145).

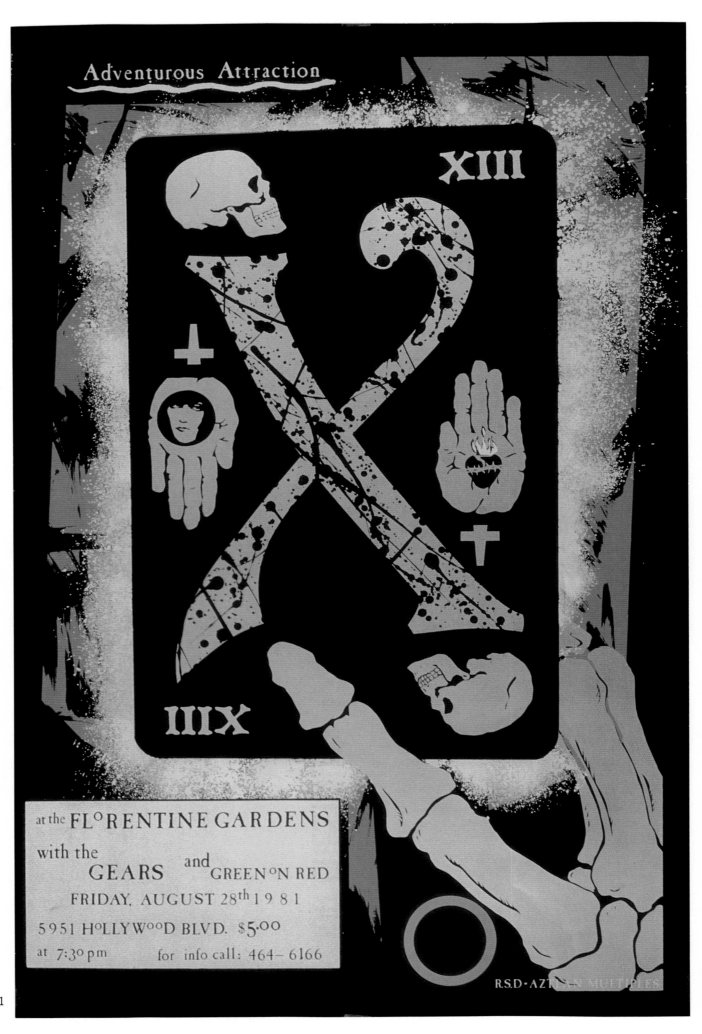

5.142

X; Gears
Florentine Gardens, Los Angeles, 1981
Artist: Richard Duarte

5.143

Fear; Angry Samoans
Blackies, Los Angeles, 1980

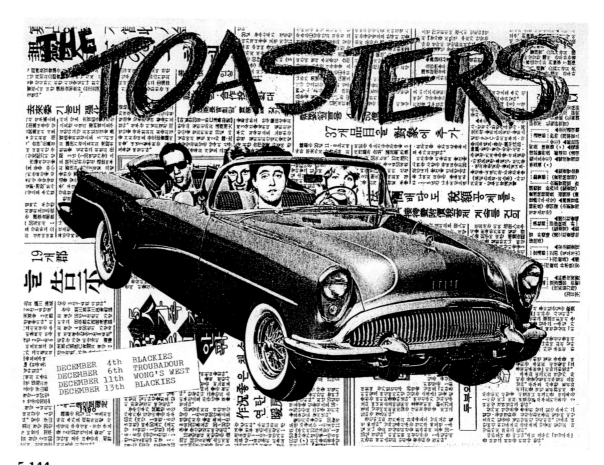

5.144

The Toasters
Blackies, Los Angeles, ca. 1979

5.145

Mumps Fan Club
Los Angeles, 1979

5.146

The M-80's
Blackies, Santa Monica, ca. 1980
Artist: Fotie

5.147
Circle Jerks; Bad Brains
California State University, Northridge, 1981
Artist: Shawn Kerri

5.148

Up Yer Bum
Olympic Auditorium, Los Angeles, ca. 1979

5.149

Weirdos; Plugz
Baces Hall, Hollywood, 1980

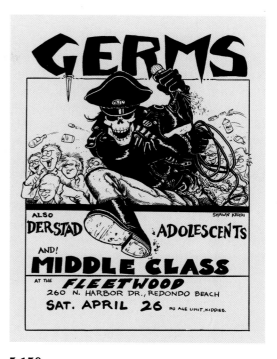

5.150

Germs; Middle Class
Fleetwood, Redondo Beach, 1980
Artist: Shawn Kerri

5.151

True Sounds of Liberty; Flipper
Ukranian Center, Hollywood, 1983
Artist: Shawn Kerri

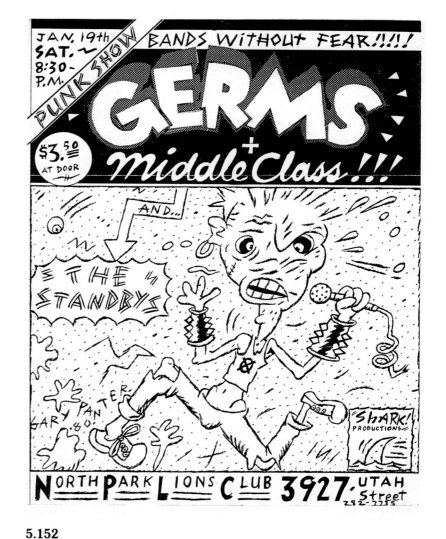

5.152

Germs; Middle Class
North Park Lions Club, Los Angeles, 1980
Artist: Gary Panter

BLACK FLAG

Along with Fear, led by Lee Ving, and the Circle Jerks, led by Keith Morris, Black Flag, headed by Henry Rollins, was in the vanguard of Los Angeles's second-stage punk movement. Its audience was tougher, angrier, and less civil than any other. As one observer put it, "Black Flag always seemed to be at the skinned head of LA punk."

Black Flag's stylistically integrated concert art was drawn by one of their associates, Raymond Pettibone. He worked in pen and ink, creating mostly dark-humored cartoons. His poster art—mostly black-and-white handbills—was strangely introspective, in contrast to Black Flag's stage excesses. Pettibone helped create the group's four-bar logo.

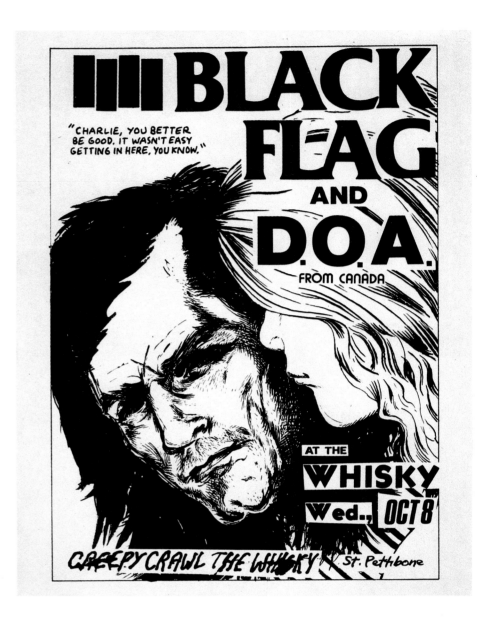

5.154
Black Flag; D. O. A.
The Whisky, Los Angeles, 1980
Artist: Raymond Pettibone

5.153
Black Flag; Fear
Stardust Ballroom, Los Angeles, 1981
Artist: Raymond Pettibone

5.155
Black Flag; Circle One
Dancing Waters, San Pedro, 1982
Artist: Raymond Pettibone

NEW YORK: CBGB

The Ramones, New York's first true punk band, came along in 1976. Owing nothing to the mainstream conventions of the day, its band-members were musically unschooled, but loved noise and made many ear-shattering appearances at CBGB, the key club site for New York punk rock. Originally a Bowery biker bar, CBGB featured weekly punk lineups in the late 1970s. Certain bands came to the forefront, including Television, the Patti Smith Group, Blondie, and—most importantly—Talking Heads. The latter became the most artistically well received of American punk and new wave groups.

The New York punk scene relied heavily on display and calendar ads in hip weeklies like the *Village Voice*. There was handbill and poster art, but on the whole it was less imaginative than similar art developed on the West Coast. Occasionally, CBGB shows were heralded by colorful silkscreen posters very often pasted to wooden fences surrounding construction sites.

5.156

Dead Boys
CBGB, New York, 1977

5.157

Big Fat Clams from Outer Space
CBGB, New York, ca. 1980

5.158

Active Ingredients; Bloodless Pharaohs
CBGB, New York, 1980

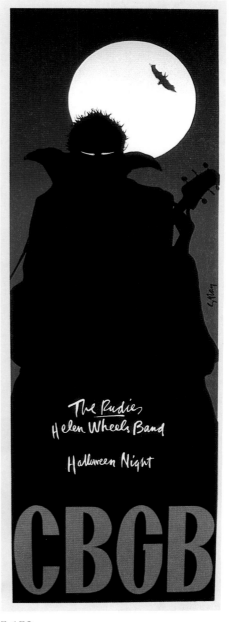

5.159

Rudies; Helen Wheels
CBGB, New York, ca. 1980

AUSTIN, TEXAS

Austin, home of the University of Texas, always responded to popular music trends: psychedelic rock of the late 1960s, "outlaw" country music of the early and mid 1970s, and finally punk and new wave, as the 1970s drew to a close.

Popular music in Austin is largely symbolized by the Armadillo, a fondly remembered dance hall that mixed progressive rock and country, and, in its last days, featured bands like the Ramones and Elvis Costello. Raul's, formerly a Mexican bar, was the first punk club. Austin's first punk band was the Skunks. Next came the Huns, whose appearances galvanized municipal repression due to their outrageous behavior. But in due course a host of additional punk clubs opened, including most importantly, Club Foot, where out-of-state bands like X, from Los Angeles, appeared (5.160).

Quite a bit of street poster art accompanied the new music, much of it the product of a loose-knit collective called the Art Maggots, led by Paul Sabal, an architect moonlighting as a

(continued on next page)

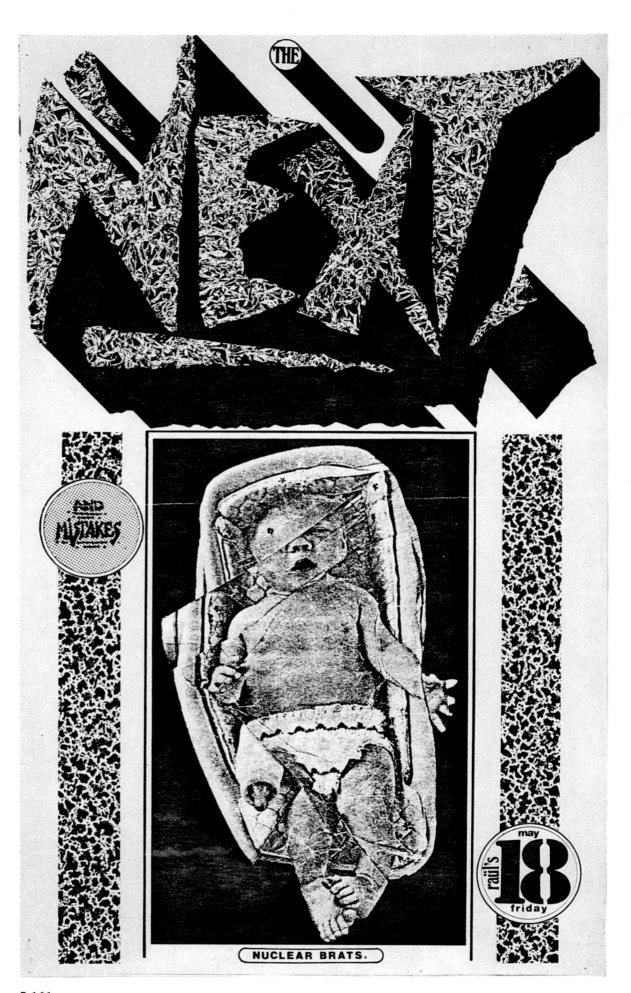

5.160

X; Club Foot, Austin, 1982
Artists: Paul Sabal, Andy Blackwood, Carbonee

5.161

Next: Mistakes
Raul's, Austin, 1984

(continued from preceding page) punk poster artist. Sabal was joined by Mike Nott and others, spearheading a clan of new music adherents that also included collectors—who ripped Art Maggot pieces down from telephone poles nearly as quickly as they were posted.

5.162

F-Systems; d-day
Raul's, Austin, 1980
Artist: Mike Nott

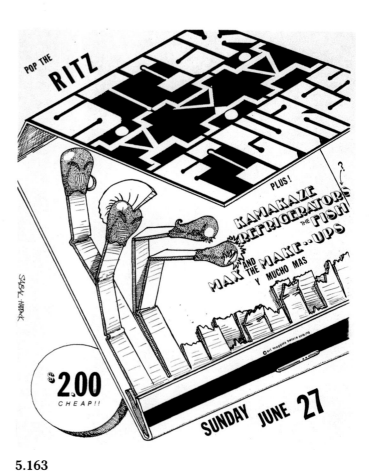

5.163

Stick Figures; Kamakaze
The Ritz, Austin, 1982
Artists: Paul Sabal, Haddock / Art Maggots

5.164

Bow Wow Wow; Chinanine
Opry House, Austin, 1983
Artists: Paul Sabal,
Andy Blackwood / Art Maggots

5.165

Black Flag; Saccharine Trust
Ritz, Austin, 1982
Artist: Randy Turner

SEATTLE

Punk rock was a Seattle subculture by 1977, the new music generating much new street art, an outpouring equal to or greater than what was produced locally during the psychedelic period.

Seattle punk posters were grass-roots, street-level communication that symbolized a new community bond.

Many of Seattle's punk poster artists were members of punk bands, including Helena Rogers of Student Nurse, Gary Minkler of Red Dress, and Erich Warner of the Blackouts (5.168).

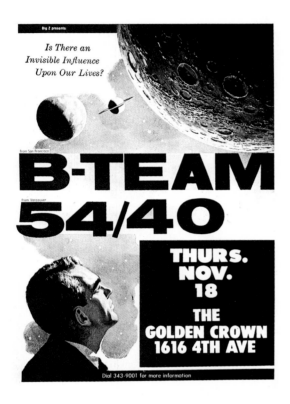

5.166
B-Team; 54/40
The Golden Crown, Seattle, 1982
Artist: Dennis White

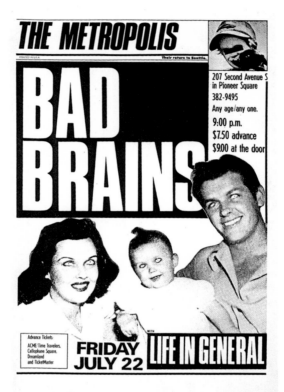

5.167
Bad Brains; Life in General
The Metropolis, Seattle, 1983
Artist: Dennis White

5.168
Units; Blackouts
Baby O's, Seattle, ca. 1980
Artist: Erich Warner

5.169
The Lewd; Wraith
The Golden Crown, Seattle, 1979
Artist: Robert Bennett

ACKNOWLEDGMENTS

First and foremost, I am grateful to Philip Grushkin for making this beautiful book possible. It is a rare honor for a son to have his book designed by his father, and I thank you, Dad, for all your patience, wisdom, and artistic sensibility.

The Art of Rock would never have seen the light of day without Robert E. Abrams, president of Abbeville Press. It was Bob who suggested I climb this particular mountain, and I thank you, Bob, for keeping the faith during the arduous process.

The book owes much to Abbeville editor Alan Axelrod, who goaded me into finishing the damn thing, and to rights director Sharon Gallagher, who handled many delicate negotiations.

Many others made vital contributions: Art Chantry, Nick Clainos (of Bill Graham Presents), Phil Cushway, Harold Feiger, Ben Friedman, Lori Gates, Paul Getchell, John Goddard, Rick Griffin, Gary Grimshaw, Alton Kelley, Shawn Kerri, Dennis King, Eric King, Gil Levey, Walter Medeiros, Levon Mosgofian, Stanley Mouse, Michael Ochs, Lynn Pedigo (of *Deadline*), Ron Schaeffer, Bill Schuessler, Joel Selvin, David Singer, Warwick Stone (of the Hard Rock Cafe), Brian Thompson, the Charles F. Tilghman family, Randy Tuten, John Van Hamersveld, Cummings Walker, and Wes Wilson. I thank you all.

I am also indebted to Nancy Achilles, Nancy Aimola, Peter Albin, Mark Alger (of Jack Otto & Sons), Ray, Joan, and Sunny Andersen, Gene Anthony, Zohn Artman, Stevanne Auerbach, Tom Ballantyne, Mark Barbeau, David Barker, Tim Barrett, Bob Barsotti, Peter Barsotti, the Bay Area Music Archives, Mark Behrens, Bill and Janice Belmont, Peter Belsito, Jeff Berger, John Berns, Judy Bickford, Les Blank, Susan Blond, Inc., Dave Bowman, Bill Bradt, Stephen Braitman, Jerilyn Brandelius, Don Bratman, Steve Brown, Toni Brown, Joe Buchwald, Nick Buck, David Byrd, Bob Carillo (of Tea Lautrec Litho), Mike Casey, Sean Casey, Luria Castell, Frank Cicero (of Globe Printing Co.), Evelyn Cipollina, Hank Clark, Roger Clark, Bob Cohen, Lee Conklin, Copymat, the Country Music Foundation Museum and Archives, Chris Coyle, Greg Davidson, Bob Davis, Richard Dorsett, Harry Duncan, M. Dung, Trent Dunphy, Michael English, Tom Eskilson, Ray Etzler, Blandina Farley, Michael Ferguson, Robert Fletcher, Chris Frayne, Bob Fried, Del Furano (of Winterland), Rita Gentry-Turrini, Marlene Getchell, David Getz, Jean and Ralph J. Gleason, David Graham, the Grateful Dead, Herbie Greene, Stanley Greene, Manny Greenhill, Jean Grushkin, Peter Guralnick, Dorothy Gutterman, John Hartmann, Ned Hearn, Chet Helms, Herbie Herbert, Barry Herman, Lee Hildebrand, Eleanore Hockabout, Lee Houskeeper, Glenn Howard, George Hunter, Tad Hunter, Bill Hurst, Don Hyde, Greg Irons, Blair Jackson, Jack Jackson, Pat Jacobsen, Debi Jacobson, Robert Jacobson, Steve Jefferson, Jacaeber Kastor, Ken Kelley, Joe Kerr, Steve Kingsley, Les Kippel, Howie Klein, Bill Koch, John Kuzich, Dennis Larkins, Bill Laudner, Anne Rene LaVasseur, Steve LaVere, Don Law Company, Eileen Law, Steve Lawson, Steve Levitt, Barbara Lewitt, Andy Levison, Brian Linse, Carl Lundgren, Country Joe Macdonald, Bonnie MacLean, Dennis McNally, Suzanne McNary, Steve Marcus, Jim Marshall, Russell Maylone (of Northwestern University Library Special Collections), Tom Mazzolini, George Michalski, John Moehring, Tony Mongeluzzi, Victor Moscoso, Mimi Moungovan, Paul Natkin, the Neville Brothers, Dennis Nolan, Jane Oliver, Barry Olivier, James Olness, John Olsson, Jim and Amy O'Neal, Arlene Owseichik, Richard Panken, Gary Panter, Jerry Paulsen, Susan Pedrick, Charles Perry, Raymond Pettibone, Jim Phillips, Steve Pincus, John Platt, Positively 4th Street, Bill Quarry, Wes Race, Otis Redding, Hillel Resner, Bob and Peggy Rita, Sally Robertson, Howard Sachs, Danny Scher, Don and Alice Schenker, Bob Schnepf, Gene Sculatti, John Seabury, Davin Seay, Bob Seidemann, Selectric Rental Service, Jim Sherraden (of Hatch Show Print), Wendy Sievert, Bob Simmons, Bonnie Simmons, Jan Simmons, Jimmy Simmons, Kent Simmons, John Sinclair, Deborah Sloan, Michael Valentine Smith, Mary Smotrys (of Electric Factory), Ed Spiro, Bruce Springsteen, James Stark, Karen Stern, Chris Strachwitz, Richard Stutting, Su. Suttle, Rick Swig, Roselyne Swig, Lou Tambakos, Berigan Taylor, Queenie Taylor, Terré, Alan Trist, Ron Turner, Michele Vignes, John Villanueva, Jim Wageman, Ed Ward, Steve Welkom, Tom Weller, Serena Wilkie, Clyde Williams, Terry Wilmott, Baron Wolman, Clyde Woodward, Heather Zahl, and Marc Zakarin.

I apologize for leaving anyone out.

Jon Sievert, editor and chief photographer at *Guitar Player*, did a magnificent job photographing over five thousand pieces of art, of which more than fifteen hundred are reproduced here. Jon also served as research assistant for the *Art of Rock*. It took a big man of extreme patience and great good nature to put up with my madness.

Tim Patterson and I went down many a sunlit street and bloody alley in search of posters, and our treks almost always paid off in gems or, at least, *amazing* experiences.

My wife, Jane Eskilson, saw this book through as surely as I did. It has been another member of our household, and not always a welcome one. So now we have lived through another book, and I thank you, love, for your constancy and strength. And may our daughter, Jessica, come to enjoy the miracle of rock 'n' roll herself.

Ultimately, this book is for Bill Graham. Everything that is important to me about rock 'n' roll is bound up in the strength I've gotten working for Bill and with his staff. You just have to *believe*—believe in what's possible and even what's impossible. If it means enough to you, do it. That's Bill's message. So now I've done it, and I'd like to think this book is worthy of Bill, and that I can rest easy.

Paul Grushkin
Pinole, California
1987

BIBLIOGRAPHY

Abdy, Jane. *The French Poster*. New York: Crown, 1969.

Ades, Dawn. *Posters*. New York: Abbeville Press, 1983.

Albright, Thomas. "Visuals: One Panel Is Worth a Thousand Balloons." *Rolling Stone*, September 14, 1968.

———. "Wilson's Giant Step Forward." *San Francisco Chronicle*, March 3, 1973.

Allner, Walter H. *Posters: Fifty Artists and Designers Analyze Their Approach, Their Methods, and Their Solutions to Poster Design and Poster Advertising*. New York: Reinhold, 1952.

Amaya, Mario. *Art Nouveau*. New York: E. P. Dutton, 1966.

Anthony, Gene. *The Summer of Love*. Millbrae, Calif.: Celestial Arts, 1980.

Arnold, Thomas K. "Rick Griffin: A Long, Strange Trip." Brooklyn: *Relix* 8, no. 4 (August 1981).

Bangs, Lester. "Peter Laughner: He Was a Friend of Mine." *New York Rocker*, September–October 1977.

———. "Punk Roots." San Francisco: *New Wave*, 1977.

Barnes, Pete, and Townshend, Pete. *The Story of* Tommy. London: Eel Pie, 1977.

Barnes, Richard. *The Who: Maximum R & B*. New York: St. Martin's Press, 1982.

Barnicoat, John. *A Concise History of Posters: 1870–1970*. New York: Harry N. Abrams, 1972.

Belsito, Peter; Davis, Bob; and Kester, Marian. *STREETART: The Punk Poster in San Francisco*. San Francisco: Last Gasp, 1981.

Belsito, Peter, and Davis, Bob. *Hardcore California*. San Francisco: Last Gasp, 1983.

Berckenhagen, Ekhart. *Art Nouveau and Jugendstil: A Catalog for the Exhibition*. Berlin, West Germany: Staatlichen Museen, 1970.

Berry, Jason; Foose, Jonathan; and Jones, Tad. *Up from the Cradle of Jazz*. Athens, Ga.: University of Georgia Press, 1986.

Bessy, Claude. "Weirdos and Dils at the Whisky." Los Angeles: *Slash*, August 1978.

———. "Middle Class, Negative Trend, Weirdos, and Dils at the Azteca." Los Angeles: *Slash*, September 1978.

———. "Screamers at the Whisky." Los Angeles: *Slash*, August 1979.

———. "U.X.A. and the Plugz at the Hong Kong Cafe." Los Angeles: *Slash*, August 1979.

———. "Hot Bands for a Hot Summer, Part II." Los Angeles: *Slash*, October 1979.

———. "Wall of Voodoo and X at the Hong Kong." Los Angeles: *Slash*, December 1979.

———. "The Decedents, the Screwz, Vicious Circle, the Chiefs, the Mau Mau's, and Black Flag at the Fleetwood." Los Angeles: *Slash*, April 1980.

"Bill Graham Presents in San Francisco: A Poster Checklist." San Francisco: Winterland Productions, ca. 1978.

"Blues and Jazz Festival Program," Ann Arbor, Mich.: *Sun*, September 4–20, 1974.

Bonds, Ray. *The Illustrated Encyclopedia of Rock*. New York: Harmony Books, 1982.

Booth, Stanley. *Dance with the Devil: The Rolling Stones and Their Times*. New York: Random House, 1984.

Boston, Virginia. *Punk Rock*. New York: Penguin, 1978.

Breitenbach, Edgar, and Cogswell, Margaret. *The American Poster*. New York: The American Federation of Arts/October House, 1967.

Bronson, Fred. *The Billboard Book of Number One Hits*. New York: Billboard Publications, 1985.

Broven, John. *Walking to New Orleans*. Bexhill-on-Sea, Sussex, Great Britain: Blues Unlimited, 1974.

Cantillon, Jane. "Brendan Mullen of the Masque." San Francisco: *Damage*, August–September 1979.

Carr, Roy, and Tyler, Tony. *The Beatles: An Illustrated Record*. New York: Harmony Books, 1975.

Carr, Roy. *Rolling Stones: An Illustrated Record*. New York: Harmony Books, 1976.

Carr, Roy, and Murray, Charles Shaar. *Bowie: An Illustrated Record*. New York: Avon Books, 1981.

Carr, Roy, and Farren, Mick. *Elvis: The Illustrated Record*. New York: Harmony Books, 1982.

Carr, Roy; Case, Brian; and Dellar, Fred. *The Hip*. New York: Faber & Faber, 1986.

Carson, Tom. "Talking Heads." *New York Rocker*, September–October 1977.

Chantry, Art. *Instant Litter*. Seattle: Real Comet Press, 1985.

Christgau, Robert. *Christgau's Record Guide*. New York: Ticknor & Fields, 1981.

Cirker, Hayward and Blanche. *The Golden Age of the Poster*. New York: Dover Publications, 1971.

Clayton, Peter, and Gammond, Peter. *The Guinness Jazz: A–Z*. London: Guinness Books, 1986.

Clifford, Mike, ed. *The Illustrated Encyclopedia of Black Music*. New York: Harmony Books, 1980.

Cohn, Nik. *Pop from the Beginning*. London: Weidenfeld and Nicolson, 1969.

Coleman, Ray. *Lennon*. New York: McGraw-Hill, 1985.

Collins, Tom. "Wes Wilson: Rock and Roll Posters as Art." Berkeley: *The Daily Californian*, November 30, 1966.

Coon, Caroline. *1988: The New Wave Punk Rock Explosion*. New York: Hawthorne Books, 1978.

Corcoran, Michael. "Sincerity: The Scene Behind the Scene in Austin, Texas." New York: *Spin*, 1985.

Cott, Jonathan. *Dylan*. New York: Rolling Stone Press/Doubleday, 1985.

Craig, Pat. "Bill Quarry Remembers '60s Rock Scene." Richmond, Calif.: *West County Times*, August 21, 1985.

Cranor, Rosalind. *Elvis Collectibles*. Paducah, Ky.: Collector Books, 1983.

"Crime Time." San Francisco: *Search & Destroy* 1, 1977.

D., Chris. "X, Plugz at Bace's Hall." Los Angeles: *Slash*, June 1979.

Dalton, David. *Janis*. New York: Simon and Schuster, 1971.

———. *Rolling Stones*. New York: Amsco Music Publishing, 1972.

———. *The Rolling Stones: The First Twenty Years*. New York: Knopf, 1981.

Davies, Hunter. *The Beatles*. New York: McGraw-Hill, 1968.

Davis, Jerome. *Talking Heads*. New York: Vintage/Random House/Musician: 1986.

Davis, Stephen. *Hammer of the Gods: The Led Zeppelin Story*. New York: William Morrow, 1984.

Dean, Roger; Thorgerson, Storm; and Howells, David. *Album Cover Album: The Second Volume*. New York: Dragon's World/A & W Visual Library, 1982.

———. *Album Cover Album: The Third Volume*. New York: Dragon's World/A & W Visual Library, 1985.

"The Decline of Western Civilization." A Film by Penelope Spheeris (1982).

Dellar, Fred. *The New Musical Express Guide to Rock Cinema*. London: Hamlyn, 1981.

Doukas, James N. *Electric Tibet*. New York: Dominion Publishing, 1969.

Dylan, Bob. *Lyrics: 1962–1985*. New York: Knopf, 1985.

Edwards, Henry, and Story, Bruce. *Stardust: The David Bowie Story*. New York: McGraw-Hill, 1986.

Ehrenstein, David, and Reed, Bill. *Rock on Film*. New York: Delilah, 1982.

Eisen, Jonathan. *Altamont*. New York: Avon Books, 1970.

Eisen, Jonathan, ed. *The Age of Rock: Sounds of the American Cultural Revolution*. New York: Random House, 1969.

Eliot, Marc. *Death of a Rebel: Starring Phil Ochs*. New York: Anchor Press/Doubleday, 1979.

English, Michael. *3-D Eye*. New York: Paper Tiger/Perigee/Putnam, 1980.

Epstein, Brian. *A Cellarful of Noise*. New York: Doubleday, 1964.

Escott, Colin, and Hawkins, Martin. *Sun Records*. New York: Quick Fox, 1980.

Farren, Mick, ed. *Get On Down: A Decade of Rock & Roll Posters*. London: Big O Publishing, 1976.

Felton, Dave. "What Happens When the Psychedelic Ball Ends?" *Los Angeles Times*, April 13, 1967.

———. "Hippies Get Charged Up on Electric Rock Music." *Long Island Press*, April 28, 1967.

Ferris, William. *Blues from the Delta*. New York: Doubleday, 1978.

Fitzgerald, f Stop, and Kester, Marian. *Dead Kennedys*. San Francisco: Last Gasp, 1983.

Flippo, Chet. "Scene or Mirage? Austin: The Hucksters Are Coming." *Rolling Stone*, April 11, 1974.

Flippo, Chet; O'Regan, Denis; Suares, J.C.; and Haggerty, Mick. *David Bowie's Serious Moonlight*. New York: Dolphin/Doubleday, 1984.

Fong-Torres, Ben, ed. *The Rolling Stone Rock & Roll Reader*. New York: Bantam Books, 1974.

———. *What's That Sound?* New York: Anchor Press/Doubleday, 1976.

Formula, Jonathan. "Welcome to the War Zone." San Francisco: *Damage*, December 1980.

———. "Kickboy (Claude Bessy): Face the Audience." San Francisco: *Damage*, December 1980.

Fox, Ted. *Showtime at the Apollo*. New York: Holt, Rinehart and Winston, 1983.

———. *In the Groove*. New York: St. Martin's Press, 1986.

Frame, Pete. *Rock Family Trees*. New York: Quick Fox, 1980.

Friedlich, Jim. "The Business of Bruce Booming for S.F. Firm" (article on Winterland). *San Francisco Chronicle*, September 20, 1985.

Friedman, Ben. "A Guide to the Numbered Family Dog Posters." San Francisco: The Postermat, ca. 1970.

Friedman, Myra. *Buried Alive*. New York: William Morrow, 1973.

Fullington, Greg. "The Poster Art of David Goines." San Francisco: *California Living*, March 15, 1981.

"Further! Ken Kesey's American Dreams." A Television Special Produced by Joan Saffa and Stephen Talbot for KQED (San Francisco), 1987.

"Furthermore: More About Ken Kesey's American Dreams." A Television Special Produced by Joan Saffa and Stephen Talbot for KQED (San Francisco), 1987.

Gaines, Steven. *Heroes and Villains: The Story of the Beach Boys*. New York: NAL Books, 1986.

Gallo, Max. *The Poster in History*. New York: American Heritage/McGraw-Hill, 1974.

Gans, David, and Simon, Peter. *Playing in the Band*. New York: St. Martin's Press, 1985.

Garland, Phyl. *The Sound of Soul*. Chicago: Henry Regnery, 1969.

George, Nelson. *Where Did Our Love Go?* New York: St. Martin's Press, 1985.

Gholson, Craig. "Max's Easter Rock." New York: *New York Rocker*, May 1976.

Gillett, Charlie. *Making Tracks*. New York: Dutton, 1975.

———. *The Sound of the City*. New York: Pantheon, 1983.

Gleason, Ralph J. *The Jefferson Airplane and the San Francisco Sound*. New York: Ballantine Books, 1969.

Goddard, Peter. *Rolling Stones Live in America*. Toronto, Canada: Beaufort Books, 1982.

———. *Rolling Stones Live in Europe*. Toronto, Canada: Beaufort Books, 1983.

———. *The Who: Farewell Tour*. Toronto, Canada: Beaufort Books, 1984.

Godden, Jean. "A Radical Turn of Events for a Former Protester: Walt Crowley." *Seattle Post-Intelligencer*, September 4, 1986.

Goldman, David. "Doing the Convention Rock: Griffin & Kelley at the Rock Ages Convention." Brooklyn: *Relix* 8, no. 3, June 1981.

Goldrosen, John. *Buddy Holly*. Bowling Green, Ohio: Popular Press, 1975.

"Graphics: Nouveau Frisco." New York: *Time*, April 7, 1967.

"The Great Poster Wave: Expendable Graphic Art Becomes America's Biggest Hang-Up," *Life*, September 1, 1967.

Green, Blake. "Poster Pals Gather Again: Artists of the '60s Relive Their Psychedelic Successes." *San Francisco Chronicle*, October 1, 1985.

Greenfield, Robert. *S.T.P.: A Journey Through America with the Rolling Stones*. New York: Dutton, 1974.

Greer, Jon. "T-Shirt Firm Targets Corporate Market." *San Francisco Chronicle*, February 12, 1987.

Griffin, Rick, and McClelland, Gordon. *Rick Griffin*. Perigee/Putnam, 1980.

Groia, Philip. *They All Sang on the Corner*. Setauket, N.Y.: Edmond Publishing, 1974.

Gross, Michael. *Bob Dylan: An Illustrated History*. New York: Grosset and Dunlap, 1978.

Grushkin, Paul; Bassett, Cynthia; and Grushkin, Jonas. *Grateful Dead: The Official Book of the Dead Heads*. New York: William Morrow, 1983.

Grushkin, Paul, ed. "A Tribute to Bill Graham, September 29, 1984" (program booklet). Mill Valley, Calif.: Mill Valley Film Festival.

Guralnick, Peter. *Feel Like Going Home*. New York: Outerbridge & Dienstfrey, 1971.

———. *Lost Highway*. Boston: David R. Godine, 1979.

———. *Sweet Soul Music*. New York: Harper & Row, 1986.

Hall, Douglas Kent, and Clark, Sue C. *Rock: A World as Bold as Love*. New York: Cowles, 1970.

Hammond, John. *On Record*. New York: Summit Books, 1977.

Hannusch, Jeff. *I Hear You Knockin'*. Villeplatte, La.: Swallow Publications, 1985.

Harris, David, and Shaw, Greg. "Interview with the Grateful Dead." San Francisco: *Mojo Navigator Rock & Roll News* 1, no. 4, August 1966, and no. 5, September 1966.

———. "Interview with Big Brother and the Holding Company." San Francisco: *Mojo Navigator Rock & Roll News* 1, no. 9, October 1966.

———. "Interview with Country Joe and the Fish." San Francisco: *Mojo Navigator Rock & Roll News* 1, no. 11, December 1966, and no. 12, January 1967.

Harrison, Hank. *The Dead Book*. New York: Links, 1973.

Harter, Jim. *Die Gretchen*. Austin, Texas: Speleo Press, 1973.

Hedges, Dan. *Yes: The Authorized Biography*. London: Sidgwick & Jackson, 1981.

Heilbut, Tony. *The Gospel Sound*. New York: Simon & Schuster, 1971.

Helander, Brock. *The Rock Who's Who*. New York: Schirmer Books, 1982.

Heller, Steven, and Chwast, Seymour. "Design & Style (No. 1): Jugendstil." New York: Mohawk Paper Mills and The Pushpin Group, 1986.

Henderson, David. *Jimi Hendrix*. New York: Doubleday, 1978.

Hennessy, Val. *In the Gutter*. New York: Quartet Books, 1978.

The Heritage of French Poster Art. Preface by René Salanon. Sponsored by Air France. Exhibition: June 21–July 19, 1966, IBM Gallery, New York.

Hewison, Robert. *Too Much: Art and Society in the Sixties*. London: Methuen, 1986.

Hilburn, Robert. *Springsteen*. New York: Rolling Stone Press/Scribner, 1985.

Hillier, Bevis. *Posters*. New York: Stein & Day, 1969.

———. *100 Years of Posters*. London: Pall Mall Press, 1972.

Hinckle, Warren. "A Social History of the Hippies." San Francisco: *Ramparts* 5, no. 9, March 1967.

Hirshey, Gerri. *Nowhere to Run*. New York: Times Books, 1984.

Hoare, Ian, ed. *The Soul Book*. London: Eyre Methuen, 1975.

Hopkins, Jerry. *Bowie*. New York: Macmillan, 1985.

Hopkins, Jerry. *Elvis*. New York: Simon & Schuster, 1971.

Hopkins, Jerry, and Sugerman, Daniel. *No One Here Gets Out Alive*. New York: Warner Books, 1980.

Hornung, Clarence P. *Handbook of Early American Advertising Art*. New York: Dover Publications, 1953.

"Howie Klein." San Francisco: *Damage*, January 1980.

Humphries, Patrick, and Hunt, Chris. *Springsteen: Blinded by the Light*. London: Plexus, 1985.

Hunter, Ian. *Diary of a Rock & Roll Star*. London: Panther, 1974.

Hutchison, Harold. *The Poster: An Illustrated History from 1860*. New York: Viking Press, 1968.

Images de la Revolte: 1965–1975. Paris: Musée de l'Affiche, 1975.

Images of an Era: The American Poster, 1945–1975. Washington, D.C.: The Smithsonian Institution and Cambridge, Mass.: The M.I.T. Press.

Iswell, Hook. "A Brain-Scan of the Club 88." Los Angeles: *Slash*, June 1979.

"In Loving Remembrance of Charles F. Tilghman, Sr." Oakland: privately printed, 1985.

Jackson, Blair. "The Collector" (article on Glenn Howard). Berkeley: *The Mix*, March 1984.

Jackson, Blair, and McMahon, Regan. "Howie Klein: On a Life in Music and Art That Matters." Oakland: *BAM Magazine*, July 15, 1983.

———. "Art for Fun's Sake: The Magical World of Alton Kelley." Oakland, Calif.: *The Golden Road*, Summer 1984.

"Jefferson Starship: Flight Log." Los Angeles/San Francisco: Grunt Records, ca. 1980.

"Jello Biafra." Los Angeles: *Slash*, May 1980.

"Jennifer Miro Communicates." San Francisco: *Search & Destroy* 1, 1977.

Johnson, J. Stewart. *The Modern American Poster*. New York: Museum of Modern Art/New York Graphic Society/Little, Brown, 1983.

Jugendstil, Modern Style, Art Nouveau. Hamburg, Basel, Vienna: Basilius-Press, 1966.

Jugendstil & Expressionism in German Posters. Exhibition organized by Herschel B. Chipp. Catalog by Brenda Richardson. Exhibition: University Art Museum, University of California, Berkeley, November 16–December 9, 1965.

Julien, Edouard. *The Posters of Toulouse-Lautrec*. Boston: Boston Book & Art Shop, 1966.

Kauffer, E. McKnight, ed. *The Art of the Poster: Its Origin, Evolution and Purpose*. New York: Albert & Charles Boni, 1928.

Keil, Charles. *Urban Blues*. Chicago: University of Chicago Press, 1966.

Kendall, Paul. *Led Zeppelin: A Visual Documentary*. New York: Omnibus, 1982.

King, Eric. *A Collector's Guide to the Numbered Dance Posters Created for Bill Graham and the Family Dog: 1966–1973*. Berkeley, Calif.: Svaha Press, 1980.

Klein, Howie. "The Ramones." San Francisco: *Psyclone*, March 1977.

———. "The Bay Area's #1 Problem: Crime." Oakland: *BAM Magazine*, September 1977.

———. "Cramps/Mutants at Napa State Hospital." *New York Rocker*, July–August 1978.

Klein, Joe. *Woody Guthrie*. New York: Knopf, 1980.

Kossatz, Horst-Herbert. *Ornamental Posters of the Vienna Secession*. New York: St. Martin's Press, 1975.

Kramer, Daniel. *Bob Dylan*. Newark, N.J.: Castle Books, 1967.

L'Amato, Will. "Screamers Play Orange." Los Angeles: *Slash*, September 1978.

LaLiberte, Norman. *The Book of Posters*. Blauvelt, N.Y.: Art Education, 1970.

Leadbitter, Mike, and Slaven, Neil. *Blues Records: 1943–1966*. London: Hanover Books, 1968.

Lee, Martin A., and Shlain, Bruce. *Acid Dreams*. New York: Grove Press, 1985.

Lewis, David L. *When Harlem Was in Vogue*. New York: Knopf, 1981.

Lewisohn, Mark. *The Beatles Live!* New York: Henry Holt, 1986.

Lomax, Alan. *Folk Song Style and Culture*. Washington, D.C.: American Association for the Advancement of Science, 1968.

Lydon, Michael. *Rock Folk*. New York: Dial, 1971.

———. *Boogie Lightning*. New York: Dial, 1974.

"Mabuhay." San Francisco: *Search & Destroy* 15, 1977.

Malone, Bill C. *Country Music, USA*. Austin: University of Texas Press, 1985.

Manna, Sal. "Pushing It to the Max." New York: *American Way*, June 25, 1985.

Marcus, Greil. *Mystery Train*. New York: Dutton, 1975.

Marcus, Greil, ed. *Rock & Roll Will Stand*. Boston: Beacon Press, 1969.

Margolin, Victor. *The Golden Age of the American Poster*. New York: Ballantine Books, 1976.

Marsh, Dave. *Born to Run: The Bruce Springsteen Story*. New York: Dolphin/Doubleday, 1979.

———. *Elvis*. New York: Rolling Stone Press/Times Books, 1982.

———. *Before I Get Old*. New York: St. Martin's Press, 1983.

Marsh, Dave, and Stein, Kevin. *The Book of Rock Lists*. New York: Rolling Stone Press/Dell, 1981.

Marsh, Dave, and Swenson, John, eds. *The Rolling Stone Record Guide*. New York: Rolling Stone Press/Random House, 1979.

———. *The New Rolling Stone Record Guide*. New York: Rolling Stone Press/Random House, 1983.

Marshall, Jim; Wolman, Baron; and Hopkins, Jerry. *Festival!* New York: Collier, 1970.

Max, Peter. *The Peter Max Poster Book*. New York: Crown, 1970.

McDonough, Jack. *San Francisco Rock: 1965–1985*. San Francisco: Chronicle Books, 1985.

McEwen, Joe. *Sam Cooke: The Man Who Invented Soul*. New York: Chappell Music, 1977.

McNeil, Legs, et al. "The 10th Anniversary of Punk." New York: *Spin* 1, no. 9, January 1986.

Medeiros, Walter Patrick. "San Francisco Rock Concert Posters: Imagery and Meaning." Unpublished M.A. thesis, University of California, Berkeley, 1972.

———. *San Francisco Rock Poster Art: A Catalog for the October 6–November 21, 1976 Exhibition*. San Francisco: The Museum of Modern Art.

Melly, George. *Revolt into Style*. London: Pan, 1971.

Meltzer, Richard. *The Aesthetics of Rock*. New York: Something Else Press, 1970.

Menten, Theodore. *Advertising Art in the Art Deco Style*. New York: Dover, 1975.

Metzl, Ervine. *The Poster: Its History and Its Art*. New York: Watson-Guptill, 1963.

Millar, Bill. *The Coasters*. London: W. H. Allen, 1975.

———. *The Drifters*. London: Studio Vista, 1971.

Miller, Jim, ed. *The Rolling Stone History of Rock & Roll*. New York: Rolling Stone Press/Random House, 1980.

Mitchell, George. *Blow My Blues Away*. Baton Rouge: Louisiana State University Press, 1971.

Morse, David. *Motown and the Arrival of Black Music*. New York: Macmillan, 1971.

Morthland, John. *The Best of Country Music*. New York: Dolphin/Doubleday, 1984.

Moscoso, Victor. "Artist Rights Today Information Pamphlet." Woodacre, Calif.: December 1, 1986.

Mouse, Stanley, and Kelley, Alton. *Mouse & Kelley*. New York: Dragon's World/Dell, 1979.

Mr. OK. "Plugz, Black Flag at the Masque X-Mas Party." Los Angeles: *Slash*, January/February 1980.

Mucha, Jir. *Alphonse Mucha: His Life and Art*. London: Heinemann, 1966.

Murgatroyd, Keith. *Modern Graphics*. London: Studio Vista, 1974.

Neff, Robert, and Connor, Anthony. *Blues*. Boston: David R. Godine, 1975.

Neill, Alex. "At War Over Rock Posters." San Rafael, Calif.: *Marin Independent-Journal*, February 23, 1987.

"1976 and All That: Retrospective Series on Punk." London: *New Musical Express*, January, February, March 1986.

Nolan, Dennis. "The Rock & Roll Poster Phenomenon." Unpublished paper, San Jose State University, ca. 1968.

Norman, Philip. *Shout!: The Beatles in Their Generation*. New York: Simon and Schuster, 1982.

Obituary: Charles F. Tilghman, Sr. *Oakland Tribune*, December 17, 1985.

Ochs, Michael. *Rock Archives*. New York: Dolphin/Doubleday, 1984.

Oliver, Paul. *Blues Fell This Morning*. London: Cassell, 1960.

———. *The Story of the Blues*. Philadelphia: Chilton, 1969.

Palmer, Myles. *New Wave Explosion*. New York: Proteus Books, 1981.

Palmer, Robert. *Deep Blues*. New York: Viking, 1981.

———. *The Rolling Stones*. New York: Rolling Stone Press/Doubleday, 1983.

Palmer, Tony. *All You Need Is Love*. New York: Grossman/Viking, 1976.

Pareles, Jon, and Romanowski, Patricia. *The Rolling Stone Encyclopedia of Rock & Roll*. New York: Rolling Stone Press/Summit, 1983.

Pascall, Jeremy. *The Illustrated History of Rock Music*. New York: Galahad Books, 1978.

Pearlman, Jill. *Elvis for Beginners*. New York: Writers & Readers/Unwin, 1986.

Peellaert, Guy. *Rock Dreams*. London: Pan, 1973.

"Penelope Houston." San Francisco: *Search & Destroy* 2, 1977.

Pennebaker, D. A. *Don't Look Back*. New York: Ballantine Books, 1968.

Perry, Charles. *The Haight-Ashbury*. New York: Rolling Stone Press/Random House, 1984.

"Personalities: 'Murphy' and Rick Griffin." Dana Point, Calif.: *Surfer* 3, no. 3, August–September 1962.

Peterson, Clark. "The Less Than Freaky Creators of the Furry Freak Brothers: Gilbert Shelton and Dave Sheridan." Brooklyn: *Relix* 5, no. 4, September 1978.

———. "It's David Singer, Not the Song." Brooklyn: *Relix* 8, no. 4, August 1981.

———. "A Hep Cat Named Mouse." Brooklyn: *Relix* 8, no. 4, August 1981.

Platt, John. "Rick Griffin: A Life of Art . . . And the Art of Life." London: *Zig Zag*, ca. 1971.

———. "Interview with Chet Helms." London: *Comstock Lode* 2, spring 1978.

———. "Notes on Kelley & Mouse; Quicksilver Family Tree." London: *Comstock Lode* 7, spring 1980.

———. *Yardbirds*. London: Sidgwick & Jackson, 1983.

———. *London's Rock Routes*. London: Fourth Estate, 1985.

Platt, John and Mary. "Big Brother Interview." London: *Comstock Lode* 3, summer 1978.

Pollack, Bruce. *When Rock Was Young*. New York: Holt, Rinehart & Winston, 1981.

———. *When the Music Mattered*. New York: Holt, Rinehart & Winston, 1983.

"Pop! Goes the Poster: Pop Art Portraits of Comic Book Favorites." *Newsweek*, March 29, 1965.

Poster Art of the World. Exposition: The Royal Ontario Museum, Toronto, Canada, 1960; catalog: University of Toronto Press, 1960.

"Printing . . . a Craft with Posterity in Mind" (article on David Goines). Berkeley: *Independent & Gazette*, April 6, 1980.

Progner, Jean, and Dreyfus, Patricia. "The Poster Revolution: Artifact into Art." New York: *Print*, July–August, 1971.

"Psychedelic Revival." Brooklyn: *Relix* 14, no. 1, February 1987.

Ramsey, Frederic, Jr. *Been Here and Gone*. New Brunswick, N.J.: Rutgers University Press, 1960.

Read, R. B. "These Are the Boys That Made the Art That Sparked the Scene . . ." San Francisco: *California Living*, November 20, 1966.

———. "Reply to John Luce" (letter to the editor). *Berkeley Barb*, ca. January 1967.

Reich, Charles, and Wenner, Jann. *Garcia: A Signpost to New Space*. San Francisco: Straight Arrow, 1972.

Reid, Jan. *The Improbable Rise of Redneck Rock*. San Antonio: Heidelberg Publishers, 1974.

Rennert, Jack, ed. *The Poster Art of Tomi Ungerer*. Greenwich, Conn.: New York Graphic Society, 1971.

———. *100 Poster Masterpieces*. New York: Phillips, 1981.

———. *19th and 20th Century Posters*. New York: Phillips, 1981.

———. *Posters: The Source Book for Collectors (1)*. New York: Posters Please, 1982.

———. *Posters: The Source Book for Collectors (2)*. New York: Posters Please, 1982.

———. *Posters: The Source Book for Collectors (3)*. New York: Posters Please, 1984.

Rice, Jo; Gambaccini; and Read, Mike. *The Guinness Book of Hit Singles* (5th ed.). London: Guinness Superlatives, 1985.

Richardson, John. "Symbols and Sacraments: The Poster Art of Gary Grimshaw." Detroit: *Metro Times*, April 17, 1985.

Rickards, Maurice. *Posters of the Nineteen Twenties*. New York: Walker, 1968.

———. *The Rise and Fall of the Poster*. Newton Abbott, Great Britain: David & Charles, 1971.

Rijff, Ger. *Elvis: Long Lonely Highway*. Amsterdam: Tutti Frutti Productions, 1985.

Ritz, David. *Divided Soul: The Life of Marvin Gaye*. New York: McGraw-Hill, 1985.

Robbins, Ira. A., ed. *The New Trouser Press Record Guide*. New York: Scribners, 1985.

"Robert Hanrahan Talks About the Deaf Club." San Francisco: *Damage*, July 1979.

"Rock 'n' Roll Band Impresario [Bill Quarry] Scores," Hayward, Calif.: *Daily Review*, May 14, 1967.

Rockwell, John. *All-American Music*. New York: Knopf, 1983.

Rohde, H. Kandy. *The Gold of Rock & Roll: 1955–1967*. New York: Arbor House, 1970.

Rolling Stone editors. *Lennon Remembers*. San Francisco: Straight Arrow, 1971.

———. *The Rolling Stone Record Review* (Vol. 1). San Francisco: Straight Arrow, 1971.

———. *The Rolling Stone Record Review* (Vol 2). San Francisco: Straight Arrow, 1974.

———. *The Rolling Stones*. San Francisco: Straight Arrow, 1975.

———. *The Who*. San Francisco: Straight Arrow, 1975.

———. *The Rolling Stone Interviews: 1967–1980*. New York: Rolling Stone Press/St. Martin's Press, 1981.

———. *The Rolling Stone Rock Almanac*. New York: Rolling Stone Press/Collier, 1983.

Rosenberg, Neil V. *Bluegrass: A History*. Urbana: University of Illinois Press, 1985.

Russell, Ethan. *Dear Mr. Fantasy*. Boston: Houghton Mifflin, 1985.

Sachs, Howard C. "The Paper Chase." Brooklyn: *Relix* 9, no. 4, August 1982.

Salberg, Lester S. "The San Francisco Psychedelic Dance Posters." Unpublished paper, University of California, Berkeley, 1969.

"San Francisco Memorabilia." Brooklyn: *Relix* 8, no. 2, April 1981.

Sandahl, Linda. *Rock Films*. New York: Facts on File, 1987.

Santelli, Robert. *Aquarius Rising*. New York: Dell, 1980.

Sawyer, Charles. *The Arrival of B. B. King*. London: Blandford Press, 1981.

Scaduto, Anthony. *Bob Dylan*. New York: Grosset & Dunlap, 1971.

Schaffner, Nicholas. *The Beatles Forever*. New York: McGraw-Hill, 1977.

———. *The British Invasion*. New York: McGraw-Hill, 1983.

Schiesel, Jane. *The Otis Redding Story*. New York: Doubleday, 1973.

Schiffman, Jack. *Harlem Heyday*. New York: Prometheus Books, 1984.

Schipper, Merle. "Yeah, I Know Exactly What You Mean: A Dialogue with Harry Kipper and John Van Hamersveld." Venice, Calif.: *Main* 1, no. 2, April 1986.

Schmutzler, Robert. *Art Nouveau*. New York: Harry N. Abrams, 1964.

Sculatti, Gene, and Seay, Davin. *San Francisco Nights*. New York: St. Martin's Press, 1985.

Selz, Peter. *Funk*. Exhibition catalog. Berkeley: University of California Art Museum, 1967.

———. "The Hippie Poster." New York: *Graphis*, 1968.

Shaw, Arnold. *The World of Soul*. New York: Cowles, 1970.

———. *The Rockin' 50's*. New York: Hawthorn, 1974.

———. *Honkers and Shouters*. New York: Collier, 1978.

———. *Black Popular Music in America*. New York: Schirmer Books, 1986.

Shelton, Cyril. *A History of Poster Advertising*. Detroit: Gale Publishing, reprint ed., 1937.

Shelton, Robert. *No Direction Home*. New York: Beech Tree/William Morrow, 1986.

Shelton, Robert, and Gahr, David. *The Face of Folk Music*. New York: Citadel Press, 1968.

Shemel, Sidney, and Krasilovsky, M. William. *This Business of Music* (5th ed.). New York: Billboard Publications, 1985.

Shore, Michael. *Music Video*. New York: Ballantine Books, 1987.

Shore, Michael, and Clark, Dick. *The History of American Bandstand*. New York: Ballantine Books, 1985.

"Sid and Nancy." New York: *New York Rocker*, November 1978.

Simmons, Jan; Gentry-Turrini, Rita; and McNally, Dennis. *Bill Graham Presents: 11 Years of Rock & Roll (1965–1976), Taken from His Calendars*. San Francisco: Bill Graham Presents, ca. 1976.

Simmons, Jan. *Bill Graham Enterprises & An Abbreviated History of Bill Graham Presents*. San Francisco: Bill Graham Presents, ca. 1986.

Sinclair, John. *Guitar Army*. New York: Douglas Books, 1972.

Snider, Burr. "How 'San Francisco Sound' Became America's Music." *San Francisco Examiner*, March 8, 1967.

Snyder, Don. *Aquarian Odyssey*. London: Liveright Publishing, 1979.

Snyder-Scumpy, Patrick. "Commander Cody Honky Tonks Deep in the Heart of Texas." New York: *Crawdaddy*, April 1974.

Southern, Eileen. *The Music of Black Americans*. New York: Norton, 1983.

Spitz, Robert S. *The Making of Superstars*. New York: Anchor Press/Doubleday, 1978.

———. *Barefoot in Babylon*. New York: Viking, 1979.

Stambler, Irwin, and Landon, Grelun. *The Encyclopedia of Folk, Country & Western Music*. New York: St. Martin's Press, 1984.

Stermer, Dugald. "Art: Posters for Peripatetics." *Ramparts* 5, no. 7, January 1967.

———. "Rock Posters." *Journal of Communications* 9, 1967.

Stokes, Geoffrey. *Starmaking Machinery*. New York: Bobbs-Merrill, 1976.

———. *The Beatles*. New York: Rolling Stone Press/Times Books, 1980.

Stokes, Niall, ed. *U2: In the Name of Love*. New York: Harmony, 1985.

Sugerman, Danny. *The Doors: An Illustrated History*. New York: Quill/William Morrow, 1983.

"Summer of Love: 20 Years Later." *San Francisco Chronicle*, April 9, 1987.

"Summer of Love: 20th Anniversary Issue." Brooklyn: *Relix* 14, no. 3, June–August, 1987.

"The Summer of Love: Yesterday and Today." *San Francisco Focus*, June 1987.

Tamarkin, Jeff. "Big Brother and the Holding Company: An Interview with David Getz." Long Island, N.Y.: *R.P.M.*, no. 9, ca. 1985.

Taylor, Derek. *As Time Goes By*. San Francisco: Straight Arrow, 1973.

Taylor, Derek. *It Was Twenty Years Ago Today*. New York: Fireside/Simon and Schuster, 1987.

Tennis, Cary. "All Punked Up and Nowhere to Go." San Francisco: *Calendar*, March 1986.

Territo, Joseph. "Alton Kelley: Spirit of the Sixties." Brooklyn: *Relix* 8, no. 4, August 1981.

Thompson, Toby. *Positively Main Street*. New York: Coward-McCann, 1971.

Thorgerson, Storm; Dean, Roger; and Hamilton, Dominy. *Album Cover Album*. New York: Dragon's World/A & W Visual Library, 1977.

Tobler, John, and Grundy, Stewart. *The Record Producers*. New York: St. Martin's, 1982.

Tomorrow, Tommy. "Tidal Wave Hits Winterland!" *New York Rocker*, September–October 1977.

Tonooka, Tim. "Black Flag." San Jose *Ripper*, no. 3, September 1981, and no. 6, December 1981.

Tosches, Nick. *Hellfire: The Jerry Lee Lewis Story*. New York: Delacorte, 1982.

———. *Unsung Heroes of Rock & Roll*. New York: Scribner, 1984.

———. *Country*. New York: Scribner, 1985.

Van Hamersveld, John. "The Endless Summer Image." Unpublished.

Vermorel, Fred and Judy. *Sex Pistols: The Inside Story*. New York: Omnibus, 1987.

"The Visitors, Fear, the Mutants, and the Dils at Bace's Hall." Los Angeles: *Slash*, November 1978.

Von Schmidt, Eric, and Rooney, Jim. *Baby, Let Me Follow You Down*. New York: Anchor Press/Doubleday, 1979.

BG 29. "The Sound"
Jefferson Airplane; Butterfield
  Blues Band
Winterland, 9/23–24, 30/66;
Fillmore Auditorium, 9/25,
10/2/66
Artist: Wes Wilson

BG 30. Butterfield Blues Band;
  Jefferson Airplane
Winterland, 10/7–8/66
Artist: Wes Wilson

BG 31. Butterfield Blues Band;
  Jefferson Airplane
Fillmore Auditorium,
10/14–16/66
Artist: Wes Wilson

BG 32. 10/21–22: Grateful Dead;
  Lightning Hopkins
Fillmore Auditorium, 10/21–23/66
Artist: Wes Wilson

BG 33. Yardbirds; Country Joe
  and the Fish
Fillmore Auditorium, 10/23/66
Artist: John H. Myers

BG 34. Captain Beefheart and
  His Magic Band; Chocolate
  Watchband
Fillmore Auditorium, 10/28–30/66
Artist: Wes Wilson

BG 35. Muddy Waters Blues
  Band; Quicksilver Messenger
  Service
Fillmore Auditorium, 11/4–6/66
Artist: Wes Wilson

BG 36. Bola Sete; Country Joe
  and the Fish
Fillmore Auditorium, 11/11–13/66
Artist: Wes Wilson

BG 37. "New Year Bash"
Jefferson Airplane; Grateful Dead
Fillmore Auditorium, 12/30–31/66
Artist: Wes Wilson

BG 38. Grateful Dead; James
  Cotton Chicago Blues Band;
  Lothar and Hand People
Fillmore Auditorium, 11/18–20/66
Artist: Wes Wilson

BG 39. Jefferson Airplane; James
  Cotton Chicago Blues Band
Fillmore Auditorium, 11/25–27/66
Artist: Wes Wilson

BG 40. Love; Moby Grape; Lee
  Michaels
Fillmore Auditorium, 12/2–4/66
Artist: Wes Wilson

BG 41. Grateful Dead; Big Mama
  Mae Thornton; Tim Rose
Fillmore Auditorium, 12/9–11/66
Artist: Wes Wilson

BG 42. Jefferson Airplane; Junior
  Wells Chicago Blues Band; Tim
  Rose
Fillmore Auditorium, 12/16–18/66
Artist: Wes Wilson; photographer:
  Herb Greene

BG 43. Otis Redding and His
  Orchestra; Grateful Dead
Fillmore Auditorium, 12/20–22/66
Artist: Wes Wilson

BG 44. Young Rascals; Sopwith
  Camel
Fillmore Auditorium, 1/6–8/67
Artist: Wes Wilson

BG 45. Grateful Dead; Junior
  Wells Chicago Blues Band
Fillmore Auditorium, 1/13–15/67
Artist: Wes Wilson

BG 46. Butterfield Blues Band;
  Charles Lloyd Quartet
Fillmore Auditorium, 1/20–22/67
Artist: Wes Wilson

BG 47. Butterfield Blues Band;
  Charles Lloyd Quartet
Fillmore Auditorium, 1/27–29/67
Artist: Wes Wilson

BG 48. Jefferson Airplane;
  Quicksilver Messenger Service
Fillmore Auditorium, 2/3–5/67
Artist: Wes Wilson

BG 49. Blues Project; Jimmy
  Reed
Fillmore Auditorium, 2/10–12/67
Artist: John H. Myers

BG 50. Blues Project; Mothers
Fillmore Auditorium, 2/17–19/67
Artist: Wes Wilson

BG 51. Otis Rush and His
  Chicago Blues Band; Grateful
  Dead
Fillmore Auditorium, 2/24–26/67
Artist: Wes Wilson

BG 52. B. B. King; Moby Grape
Fillmore Auditorium, 2/26/67
Artist: John H. Myers

BG 53. Otis Rush and His
  Chicago Blues Band; Mothers
Fillmore Auditorium, 3/3–5/67
Artist: Wes Wilson

BG 54. Jefferson Airplane; Jimmy
  Reed
Winterland, 3/10–11/67; Fillmore
  Auditorium, 3/12/67
Artist: Wes Wilson

BG 55. Chuck Berry; Grateful
  Dead
Winterland, 3/17–18/67; Fillmore
  Auditorium, 3/19/67
Artist: Wes Wilson

BG 56. Moby Grape; Chambers
  Brothers
Winterland, 3/24–25/67; Fillmore
  Auditorium, 3/26/67
Artist: Wes Wilson

BG 57. Byrds; Moby Grape
Winterland, 3/31–4/1/67; Fillmore
  Auditorium, 4/2/67
Artist: Wes Wilson

BG 58. Chambers Brothers;
  Quicksilver Messenger Service
Fillmore Auditorium, 4/7–9/67
Artist: Wes Wilson

BG 59. Howlin' Wolf; Country Joe
  and the Fish
Fillmore Auditorium, 4/14–16/67
Artist: Peter Bailey

BG 60. Howlin' Wolf; Big Brother
  and the Holding Company
Fillmore Auditorium, 4/21–23/67
Artist: Wes Wilson

BG 61. Buffalo Springfield; Steve
  Miller Blues Band
Fillmore Auditorium, 4/28–30/67
Artist: Wes Wilson

BG 62. Grateful Dead; Paupers
Fillmore Auditorium, 5/5–6/67
Artist: Wes Wilson

BG 63. Jefferson Airplane;
  Paupers
Fillmore Auditorium, 5/12–14/67
Artist: Bonnie MacLean;
  photographer: Herb Greene

BG 64. Martha and the Vandellas;
  Paupers
Fillmore Auditorium, 5/19–20/67
Artist: Bonnie MacLean

BG 65. Big Brother and the
  Holding Company; Steve Miller
  Blues Band
Fillmore Auditorium, 5/26–27/67
Artist: Bonnie MacLean

BG 66. Jim Kweskin Jug Band;
  Peanut Butter Conspiracy
Fillmore Auditorium, 6/2–3/67
Artist: Bonnie MacLean

BG 67. Doors; Jim Kweskin Jug
  Band
Fillmore Auditorium, 6/9–10/67
Artist: Bonnie MacLean

BG 68. Who; Loading Zone
Fillmore Auditorium, 6/16–17/67
Artist: Bonnie MacLean

BG 69. "Opening of the Summer
  Series"
Jefferson Airplane; Jimi Hendrix
Fillmore Auditorium, 6/20–25/67
Artist: Clifford Charles Seeley

BG 70. Chuck Berry; Eric Burdon
  and the Animals
Fillmore Auditorium, 6/27–7/2/67
Artist: Greg Irons

BG 71. Bo Diddley; Big Brother
  and the Holding Company
Fillmore Auditorium, 7/4–9/67
Artist: Bonnie MacLean

BG 72. Butterfield Blues Band;
  Roland Kirk Quartet
Fillmore Auditorium, 7/11–16/67
Artist: Bonnie MacLean

BG 73. Sam and Dave; James
  Cotton Blues Band
Fillmore Auditorium, 7/18–23/67
Artist: Bonnie MacLean

BG 74. "The San Francisco
  Scene in Toronto"
Jefferson Airplane; Grateful Dead
O'Keefe Center, Toronto,
7/31–8/5/67
Artist: James H. Gardner;
  photographer: Herb Greene

BG 75. Yardbirds; Doors
Fillmore Auditorium, 7/25–30/67
Artist: Bonnie MacLean

BG 76. Muddy Waters; Buffalo
  Springfield
Fillmore Auditorium, 8/1–6/67
Artist: Bonnie MacLean

BG 77. Electric Flag American
  Music Band; Moby Grape
Fillmore Auditorium, 8/8–13/67
Artist: Bonnie MacLean

BG 78. Count Basie; Chuck Berry
Fillmore Auditorium, 8/15–21/67
Artist: Jim Blashfield

BG 79. Paul Butterfield Blues
  Band; Cream
Fillmore Auditorium, 8/22–27/67
Artist: Bonnie MacLean

BG 80. Cream; Electric Flag
  American Music Band
Fillmore Auditorium, 8/29–9/3/67
Artist: Jim Blashfield

BG 81. "The San Francisco
  Scene in Los Angeles"
Jefferson Airplane; Grateful Dead
Hollywood Bowl, 9/15/67
Artist: Jim Blashfield;
  photographer: Herb Greene

BG 82. Byrds; Loading Zone
Fillmore Auditorium, 9/7–9/67
Artist: Jim Blashfield

BG 83. Electric Flag American
  Music Band; Mother Earth
Fillmore Auditorium, 9/14–16/67
Artist: Jim Blashfield

BG 84. Blue Cheer; Vanilla Fudge
Fillmore Auditorium, 9/21, 23/67;
  Cow Palace, 9/22/67
Artist: Bonnie MacLean

BG 85. Jefferson Airplane; Mother
  Earth
Fillmore Auditorium, 9/28/67;
  Winterland, 9/29–30/67
Artist: Greg Irons

BG 86. Donovan
Cow Palace, 9/22/67
Artist: Bonnie MacLean

BG 87. Quicksilver Messenger
  Service; Grass Roots
Fillmore Auditorium, 10/5–7/67
Artist: Bonnie MacLean

BG 88. Jefferson Airplane;
  Charlatans
Fillmore Auditorium, 10/11–12/67;
  Winterland, 10/13–14/67
Artist: Bonnie MacLean;
  photographer: Herb Greene

BG 89. Eric Burdon and the
  Animals; Mother Earth
Fillmore Auditorium, 10/19–21/67
Artist: Bonnie MacLean

BG 90. Pink Floyd; Lee Michaels
Fillmore Auditorium, 10/26–28/67
Artist: Bonnie MacLean

BG 91. Big Brother and the
  Holding Company; Pink Floyd
Fillmore Auditorium, 11/2/67;
  Winterland, 11/3–4/67
Artist: Bonnie MacLean

BG 92. Procol Harum; Pink Floyd
Fillmore Auditorium, 11/9/67;
  Winterland, 11/10–11/67
Artist: Nicholas Kouninos

BG 93. Doors; Procol Harum
Fillmore Auditorium, 11/16/67;
  Winterland, 11/17–18/67
Artist: Jim Blashfield

BG 94. Donovan; H. P. Lovecraft
Fillmore Auditorium, 11/23/67;
  Winterland, 11/24–25/67
Artist: Nicholas Kouninos

BG 95. Nitty Gritty Dirt Band;
  Clear Light
Fillmore Auditorium, 11/30–
  12/2/67
Artist: Bonnie MacLean

BG 96. Byrds; Electric Flag
Fillmore Auditorium, 12/7/67;
  Winterland, 12/8–9/67
Artist: Bonnie MacLean

BG 97. Mothers of Invention;
  Tim Buckley
Fillmore Auditorium, 12/14/67;
  Winterland, 12/15–16/67
Artist: Stanley Mouse

BG 98. Buffalo Springfield;
  Collectors
Fillmore Auditorium, 12/21–23/67
Artists: Alton Kelley, Stanley
  Mouse

BG 99. "Six Days of Sound"
Doors; Chuck Berry
Winterland, 12/26–31/67
Artist: Bonnie MacLean

BG 100. "New Year's Eve"
Jefferson Airplane; Big Brother and
  the Holding Company
Winterland, 12/31/67
Artist: Bonnie MacLean

BG 101. Vanilla Fudge; Steve
  Miller Band
Fillmore Auditorium, 1/4/68;
  Winterland, 1/5–6/68
Artist: Lee Conklin

BG 102. Chambers Brothers;
  Sunshine Company
Fillmore Auditorium, 1/11–13/68
Artist: Bonnie MacLean

BG 103. Butterfield Blues Band;
  Charles Lloyd Quartet
Fillmore Auditorium, 1/18–20/68
Artist: Jack Hatfield; photographer:
  Louis Sozzi

BG 104. Big Brother and the
  Holding Company; Electric Flag
Fillmore Auditorium, 1/25/68;
  Winterland, 1/26–27/68
Artist: Jack Hatfield

BG 105. "Flying Eyeball"
Jimi Hendrix Experience; John
  Mayall and the Blues Breakers
Fillmore Auditorium, 2/1, 4/68;
  Winterland, 2/2–3/68
Artist: Rick Griffin

BG 106. John Mayall and the
  Blues Breakers; Arlo Guthrie
Fillmore Auditorium, 2/8–10/68
Artist: Stanley Mouse

BG 107. Butterfield Blues Band;
  James Cotton Blues Band
Fillmore Auditorium, 2/15/68;
  Winterland, 2/16–17/68
Artist: Lee Conklin

BG 108. Who; Cannonball
  Adderly
Fillmore Auditorium, 2/22/68;
  Winterland, 2/23–24/68
Artist: Lee Conklin

BG 109. Cream; Big Black
Fillmore Auditorium, 3/3/68;
  Winterland, 2/29–3/2/68
Artist: Lee Conklin

BG 110. Cream; James Cotton
  Blues Band
Fillmore Auditorium, 3/7/68;
  Winterland, 3/8–10/68
Artist: Stanley Mouse

BG 111. Traffic; H. P. Lovecraft
Fillmore Auditorium, 3/14/68;
  Winterland, 3/15–16/68
Artists: Stanley Mouse, Alton
  Kelley; photographer: Bob
  Seidemann

BG 112. Moby Grape; Traffic
Fillmore Auditorium, 3/21/68;
  Winterland, 3/22–23/68
Artist: Lee Conklin

BG 113. Country Joe and the
  Fish; Steppenwolf
Fillmore Auditorium, 3/28–30/68
Artist: Dana W. Johnson

BG 114. Eric Burdon and the
  Animals; Quicksilver Messenger
  Service
Fillmore Auditorium, 4/4/68;
  Winterland, 4/5–6/68
Artist: Dana W. Johnson

BG 115. Big Brother and the Holding Company; Iron Butterfly
Fillmore Auditorium, 4/11/68; Winterland, 4/12–13/68
Artist: Patrick Lofthouse; photographer: Thomas Weir

BG 116. Love; Staple Singers
Fillmore Auditorium, 4/18/68; Winterland, 4/19–20/68
Artist: Patrick Lofthouse

BG 117. Albert King; Electric Flag American Music Band
Fillmore Auditorium, 4/25/68; Winterland, 4/26–27/68
Artist: Mari Tepper

BG 118. Moby Grape; Hour Glass
Fillmore Auditorium, 5/2–4/68
Artist: Mari Tepper

BG 119. Loading Zone; Crome Syrcus
Fillmore Auditorium, 5/9–11/68
Artist: Weisser

BG 120. Country Joe and the Fish; Incredible String Band
Fillmore Auditorium, 5/16–18/68
Artist: Weisser

BG 121. Yardbirds; Cecil Taylor
Fillmore Auditorium, 5/23–25/68
Artist: Lee Conklin

BG 122. Buffalo Springfield; Chambers Brothers
Fillmore Auditorium, 5/29–30/68; Winterland, 5/31–6/1/68
Artist: Lee Conklin

BG 123. Mothers of Invention; B. B. King
Fillmore Auditorium, 6/6/68; Winterland, 6/7–8/68
Artist: Bob Fried

BG 124. Big Brother and the Holding Company; Crazy World of Arthur Brown
Fillmore Auditorium, 6/13/68; Winterland, 6/14–15/68
Artist: Bob Fried; photographer: Jonathan Julian

BG 125. Chambers Brothers; Quicksilver Messenger Service
Fillmore Auditorium, 6/18–23/68
Artist: Lee Conklin

BG 126. Albert King; Ten Years After
Fillmore Auditorium, 6/25–30/68
Artist: Lee Conklin

BG 127. Creedence Clearwater Revival; Butterfield Blues Band
Fillmore Auditorium, 7/2–7/68
Artist: Lee Conklin

BG 128. "Blues Bash"
Electric Flag; Blue Cheer
Fillmore Auditorium, 7/9–14/68
Artist: Lee Conklin

BG 129. Big Brother and the Holding Company; Sly and the Family Stone
Fillmore–Carousel, 7/16–21/68 (Fillmore West at Market and Van Ness was known as the Carousel Ballroom before Bill Graham began presenting concerts there.)
Artist: Lee Conklin

BG 130. Moby Grape; Jeff Beck Group
Fillmore–Carousel, 7/23–28/68 (Fillmore West at Market and Van Ness was known as the Carousel Ballroom before Bill Graham began presenting concerts there.)
Artist: Lee Conklin

BG 131. 7/30–8/1: Butterfield Blues Band; Santana
Fillmore West, 7/30–8/4/68
Artist: Lee Conklin

BG 132. Chambers Brothers; Eric Burdon and the Animals
Fillmore West, 9/6–11/68
Artist: Lee Conklin

BG 133. Who; Creedence Clearwater Revival
Fillmore West, 8/13–25/68
Artists: Alton Kelley, Rick Griffin

BG 134. Steppenwolf; Grateful Dead
Fillmore West, 8/27–9/1/68
Artist: Lee Conklin

BG 135. Chuck Berry; Steve Miller Band
Fillmore West, 9/5–7/68
Artist: Lee Conklin

BG 136. "Heart and Torch"
Big Brother and the Holding Company; Santana
Fillmore West, 9/12–14/68
Artist: Rick Griffin

BG 137. "Bull's Eye"
Albert King; Creedence Clearwater Revival
Fillmore West, 9/19–21/68
Artist: Rick Griffin

BG 138. Super Session (Mike Bloomfield, Al Kooper, and Friends); It's a Beautiful Day
Fillmore West, 9/26–28/68
Artist: Lee Conklin

BG 139. Canned Heat; Gordon Lightfoot
Fillmore West, 10/3–5/68
Artist: Lee Conklin

BG 140A. Buck Owens and His Buckaroos
Fillmore West, 10/11–12/68
Artist: Pat Hanks

BG 140. Jimi Hendrix Experience; Buddy Miles Express
Winterland, 10/10–12/68
Artists: Rick Griffin, Victor Moscoso

BG 141. Iron Butterfly; Sir Douglas Quintet
Fillmore West, 10/17–19/68
Artists: Rick Griffin, Victor Moscoso

BG 142. Jefferson Airplane; Ballet Afro–Haiti
Fillmore West, 10/24–26/68
Artist: Lee Conklin

BG 143. Procul Harum; Santana
Fillmore West, 10/31–11/2/68
Artist: Lee Conklin

BG 144. Quicksilver Messenger Service; Grateful Dead
Fillmore West, 11/7–10/68
Artist: Lee Conklin

BG 145. Ten Years After; Country Weather
Fillmore West, 11/14–17/68
Artist: Lee Conklin

BG 146. Moody Blues; Chicago Transit Authority
Fillmore West, 10/21–24/68
Artists: Rick Griffin, Alton Kelley

BG 147. It's a Beautiful Day; Deep Purple
Fillmore West, 11/28–12/1/68
Artists: Alton Kelley, Rick Griffin

BG 148. Jeff Beck Group; Spirit
Fillmore West, 12/5–8/68
Artist: Lee Conklin

BG 149. Country Joe and the Fish; Sea Train
Fillmore West, 12/12–15/68
Artist: Lee Conklin

BG 150. Santana; Grass Roots
Fillmore West, 12/19–22/68
Artist: Wes Wilson

BG 151. Steve Miller Band; Sly and the Family Stone
Fillmore West, 12/26–29/68
Artist: Wes Wilson

BG 152. "New Year's Eve"
Grateful Dead; Quicksilver Messenger Service
Winterland, 12/31/68
Artist: Lee Conklin

BG 153. "New Year's Eve"
Vanilla Fudge; Youngbloods
Fillmore West, 12/31/68
Artist: Lee Conklin

BG 154. Grateful Dead; Blood, Sweat and Tears
Fillmore West, 1/2–4/69
Artist: Randy Tuten

BG 155. Country Joe and the Fish; Led Zeppelin
Fillmore West, 1/9–11/69
Artists: Randy Tuten, D. Bread; photographer: P. Pynchon

BG 156. Creedence Clearwater Revival; Fleetwood Mac
Fillmore West, 1/16–19/69
Artist: Lee Conklin

BG 157. Iron Butterfly; James Cotton Blues Band
Fillmore West, 1/23–26/69
Artist: Lee Conklin

BG 158. Chuck Berry; Jam (Mike Bloomfield, Nick Gravenites, Mark Naftalin, and Friends)
Fillmore West, 1/30–2/2/69
Artist: Randy Tuten

BG 159. Mike Bloomfield and Friends—Nick Gravenites and Mark Naftalin (Jam); Byrds
Fillmore West, 2/6–9/69
Artist: Randy Tuten

BG 160. Santana; Melanie
Fillmore West, 2/14–16/69
Artist: Greg Irons

BG 161. Move; Cold Blood
Fillmore West, 2/20–23/69
Artist: Greg Irons

BG 162. Grateful Dead; Pentangle
Fillmore West, 2/27–3/2/69
Artist: Lee Conklin; photographer: Herb Greene

BG 163. Spirit; Ten Years After
Fillmore West, 3/6–9/69
Artist: Lee Conklin

BG 164. Creedence Clearwater Revival; Jethro Tull
Fillmore West, 3/13–16/69
Artist: Randy Tuten

BG 165. Janis Joplin and Her Band; Savoy Brown
Winterland, 3/20–22/69; Fillmore West, 3/23/69
Artists: Randy Tuten, D. Bread

BG 166. Butterfield Blues Band; Michael Bloomfield and Friends
Fillmore Auditorium, 3/27–30/69
Artist: Greg Irons

BG 167. Procul Harum; Buddy Miles Express
Fillmore West, 4/3–6/69
Artist: Greg Irons

BG 168. Jeff Beck Group; Aynsley Dunbar Retaliation
Fillmore West, 4/10–13/69
Artist: Randy Tuten

BG 169. The Band; Sons of Champlin
Winterland, 4/17–19/69
Artist: Randy Tuten

BG 170. Led Zeppelin; Julie Driscoll, Brian Auger and Trinity
Fillmore Auditorium, 4/24, 27/69; Winterland, 4/25–26/69
Artist: Randy Tuten; photographer: P. Pynchon

BG 171. Jefferson Airplane; Grateful Dead
Fillmore Auditorium, 5/1, 4/69; Winterland, 5/2–3/69
Artist: Randy Tuten

BG 172. Albert King; It's a Beautiful Day
Fillmore West, 5/8–11/69
Artist: Lee Conklin

BG 173. Santana; Youngbloods
Fillmore West, 5/15–18/69
Artist: Lee Conklin

BG 174. Creedence Clearwater Revival; Northern California State Youth Choir with Dorothy Morrison
Fillmore West, 5/22, 25/69; Winterland, 5/23–24/69
Artist: Randy Tuten

BG 175. Steve Miller Band; Chicago
Fillmore West, 5/29–6/1/69
Artist: Randy Tuten

BG 176. Grateful Dead; Junior Walker and the All Stars
Fillmore West, 6/5–8/69
Artist: Randy Tuten

BG 177. Byrds; Joe Cocker and the Grease Band
Fillmore West, 6/12–15/69
Artist: Randy Tuten

BG 178. Who; Woody Herman and His Orchestra
Fillmore West, 6/17–22/69
Artist: David Singer

BG 179. Iron Butterfly; Spirit
Fillmore West, 6/24–29/69
Artist: David Singer

BG 180. Johnny Winter; Eric Burdon and His Band
Fillmore West, 7/1–4/69
Artist: David Singer

BG 181. B. B. King; Santana
Fillmore West, 7/8–13/69
Artist: David Singer

BG 182. B. B. King; Country Joe and The Fish
Fillmore West, 7/15–20/69
Artist: David Singer

BG 183. Ten Years After; Steve Miller Band
Fillmore West, 7/22–27/69
Artist: David Singer

BG 184. Canned Heat; Everly Brothers
Fillmore West, 7/29–8/3/69
Artist: David Singer

BG 185. Fleetwood Mac; Jr. Walker and the All Stars
Fillmore West, 8/5–10/69
Artist: David Singer

BG 186. Doors; Lonnie Mack
Cow Palace, 7/25/69
Artist: Randy Tuten

BG 187. Chuck Berry; Chicago Transit Authority
Fillmore West, 8/12–17/69
Artist: David Singer

BG 188. John Mayall; Mother Earth
Fillmore West, 8/19–21/69; Golden Gate Park, 8/22–24/69
Artist: David Singer

BG 189. Ten Years After; Spirit
Fillmore West, 9/26–31/69
Artist: David Singer

BG 190. Santana; Seatrain
Fillmore West, 9/4–7/69
Artist: David Singer

BG 191. Steve Miller Band; James Cotton Blues Band
Fillmore West, 9/11–14/69
Artist: Randy Tuten

BG 192. Taj Mahal; Buddy Guy
Fillmore West, 8/18–21/69
Artist: Randy Tuten; photographer: Jim Marshall

BG 193. Chuck Berry; Aum
Fillmore West, 9/25–28/69
Artist: Greg Irons

BG 194. Crosby, Stills, Nash and Young; Blues Image
Fillmore West, 10/2/69; Winterland, 10/3–4/69
Artist: Greg Irons

BG 195. Country Joe and the Fish; Albert King
Fillmore West, 10/9–12/69
Artist: Randy Tuten

BG 196. Joe Cocker and the Grease Band; Little Richard
Fillmore West, 10/16–19/69
Artists: David Singer, Randy Tuten

BG 197. Jefferson Airplane; Grateful Dead
Winterland, 10/24–25/69
Artist: Bonnie MacLean Graham

BG 198. It's a Beautiful Day; Ike and Tina Turner
Fillmore West, 10/30–11/2/69
Artist: Bonnie MacLean Graham

BG 199. 11/6–8: Led Zeppelin; Bonzo Dog Band
Winterland, 11/6–8/69; Oakland Coliseum, 11/9/69
Artist: Randy Tuten

BG 200. Crosby, Stills, Nash and Young; Cold Blood
Winterland, 11/13–16/69
Artist: Randy Tuten

BG 201. Rolling Stones
Oakland Coliseum, 11/9/69
Artist: Randy Tuten; photographer: Ron Raffaelli (misspelled "Rafaelli")

BG 202. Rolling Stones
San Diego International Sports
  Arena, 11/10–11/69
Artist: Randy Tuten; photographer:
  Ron Raffaelli (misspelled
  "Rafaelli")

BG 203. Jethro Tull; MC5
Fillmore West, 11/20–23/69
Artist: Randy Tuten

BG 204. Kinks; Taj Mahal
Fillmore West, 11/27–30/69
Artist: Randy Tuten

BG 205. Grateful Dead; Flock
Fillmore West, 12/4–7/69
Artist: David Singer

BG 206. Chambers Brothers; Nice
Fillmore West, 12/11–14/69
Artist: David Singer

BG 207. Santana; Grand Funk
  Railroad
Winterland, 12/18–21/69
Artist: David Singer

BG 208. Sly and the Family
  Stone; Spirit
Winterland, 12/26–28/69
Artist: David Singer

BG 209. Santana; Jefferson
  Airplane
Fillmore West, 12/31/69;
  Winterland, 12/31/69
Artist: Bonnie MacLean Graham

BG 210. Byrds; Fleetwood Mac
Fillmore West, 1/2–4/70
Artist: David Singer

BG 211. Chicago; Guess Who
Fillmore West, 1/8–11/70
Artist: David Singer

BG 212. B. B. King; Buddy Guy
Fillmore West, 1/15–18/70
Artist: David Singer

BG 213. Albert King; Savoy
  Brown
Fillmore West, 1/22–25/70
Artist: David Singer

BG 214. Steve Miller; Sha-Na-Na
Fillmore West, 1/29–2/1/70
Artist: David Singer

BG 215. Laura Nyro; The Band
Berkeley Community Theater,
  1/24, 31/70
Artists: Bonnie MacLean Graham,
  Pat Hanks

BG 215A. Moody Blues; Richie
  Havens
Berkeley Community Theater,
  4/2, 11/70
Artists: Bonnie MacLean Graham,
  Pat Hanks

BG 216. Grateful Dead; Taj
  Mahal
Fillmore West, 2/5–8/70
Artist: David Singer

BG 217. Country Joe and the
  Fish; Sons
Fillmore West, 2/12–15/70
Artist: David Singer

BG 218. Delaney and Bonnie and
  Friends with Eric Clapton; New
  York Rock and Roll Ensemble
Fillmore West, 2/19–22/70
Artist: David Singer

BG 219. Doors; Cold Blood
Winterland, 2/5–6/70
Artist: Randy Tuten

BG 220. Jack Bruce and Friends;
  Johnny Winter
Fillmore West, 2/26/70, 3/1/70;
  Winterland, 2/27–28/70
Artist: Randy Tuten

BG 221. Butterfield Blues Band;
  Savoy Brown
Fillmore West, 3/5–8/70
Artist: David Singer

BG 222. Jefferson Airplane;
  Quicksilver Messenger Service
Winterland, 2/23/70
Artist: David Singer

BG 223. Ten Years After; Buddy
  Rich and His Orchestra
Fillmore West, 3/12–15/70
Artist: David Singer

BG 224. It's a Beautiful Day;
  Chuck Berry
Fillmore West, 3/19–22/70
Artist: David Singer

BG 225. Chicago; James Cotton
  Blues Band
Fillmore West, 2/26, 29/70;
  Winterland, 3/27–28/70
Artist: David Singer

BG 226. Jethro Tull; Manfred
  Mann
Fillmore West, 4/2–5/70
Artist: David Singer

BG 227. Grateful Dead; Miles
  Davis Quintet
Fillmore West, 4/9–12/70
Artist: David Singer

BG 228. John Mayall; Larry
  Coryell
Fillmore West, 4/16–19/70
Artist: David Singer

BG 229. Joe Cocker; Van
  Morrison
Fillmore West, 4/23, 26/70;
  Winterland, 4/24–25/70
Artist: David Singer

BG 230. Pink Floyd
Fillmore West, 4/29/70
Artist: Pat Hanks (David Singer's
  name appears erroneously)

BG 230A. Pink Floyd
Fillmore West, 10/21/70
Artist: Pat Hanks

BG 231. Jethro Tull; Fairport
  Convention
Fillmore West, 4/30–5/3/70
Artist: David Singer

BG 232. Lee Michaels; Small
  Faces with Rod Stewart
Fillmore West, 5/7–10/70
Artist: David Singer

BG 232A. Incredible String Band
Fillmore West, 5/11, 13/70
Artist: Pat Hanks

BG 233. Spirit; Poco
Fillmore West, 5/14–17/70
Artist: David Singer

BG 234. No poster bearing this
  number was printed.

BG 235. B. B. King; Albert King
Fillmore West, 5/21–24/70
Artists: David Singer, Satty

BG 236. Country Joe and the
  Fish; Blues Image
Fillmore West, 5/28–31/70
Artist: David Singer

BG 237. Grateful Dead; New
  Riders of the Purple Sage
Fillmore West, 6/4–7/70
Artist: David Singer

BG 238. John Sebastian; Buddy
  Miles
Fillmore West, 6/11–14/70
Artist: David Singer

BG 239. Quicksilver Messenger
  Service; Don Ellis and His
  Orchestra
Fillmore West, 6/18–21/70
Artist: David Singer

BG 240. Sha-Na-Na; Pacific Gas
  and Electric
Fillmore West, 6/25–28/70,
  6/30–7/2/70
Artist: David Singer

BG 241. Traffic with Stevie
  Winwood, Chris Wood, and Jim
  Capaldi; John Hammond
Fillmore West, 6/30–7/2/70
Artist: David Singer

BG 242. Quicksilver Messenger
  Service; Mott the Hoople
Fillmore West, 7/9–12/70
Artist: David Singer

BG 243. Steve Miller Band;
  Bo Diddley
Fillmore West, 7/16–19/70
Artist: David Singer

BG 244. Lee Michaels; Cold
  Blood; Brethren
Fillmore West, 7/23–26/70,
  7/28–30/70
Artists: Satty, David Singer

BG 245. Ten Years After;
  Fleetwood Mac
Fillmore West, 7/28–8/9/70
Artist: David Singer

BG 246. Byrds; Led Zeppelin
Fillmore West, 8/13–16,
  20–26/70; Berkeley Community
  Theater, 8/30/70; Oakland
  Coliseum, 9/2/70
Artist: David Singer

BG 247. Iron Butterfly with Pinera
  and Rhino; John Mayall
Fillmore West, 8/24–9/1, 3–6/70
Artist: Alton Kelley

BG 247A. Jefferson Airplane
Fillmore West, 9/14–15/70
Artist: Pat Hanks

BG 248. Santana; Dr. John
Fillmore West, 9/10–13/70
Artist: Norman Orr

BG 249. Quicksilver Messenger
  Service; Buddy Miles
Fillmore West, 9/17–20/70
Artist: Norman Orr

BG 250. 9/24–27: Chuck Berry;
  Eric Burdon and War
Fillmore West, 9/24–27,
  10/1–4/70
Artist: David Singer

BG 251. Van Morrison; Captain
  Beefheart and His Magic Band
Fillmore West, 10/8–11/70
Artist: Norman Orr

BG 252. Leon Russell; Miles Davis
Fillmore West, 10/15–18/70
Artist: Norman Orr

BG 253. 10/22–25: Bo Diddley;
  Lightning Hopkins
Fillmore West, 10/21–25, 28/70
Artist: David Singer

BG 254. Procul Harum; Poco
Fillmore West, 10/28–11/1/70
Artist: David Singer

BG 255. Frank Zappa; Boz
  Scaggs
Fillmore West, 11/6–8/70
Artist: David Singer

BG 256. Kinks; Elton John
Fillmore West, 11/12–15/70
Artist: David Singer

BG 257. Love with Arthur Lee;
  James Gang; Sha-Na-Na; Elvin
  Bishop
Fillmore West, 11/19–22,
  26–29/70
Artist: Norman Orr

BG 259. Savoy Brown; Ry
  Cooder
Fillmore West, 12/3–6/70
Artist: David Singer

BG 260. Lee Michaels; Albert
  King
Fillmore West, 12/10–13/70
Artist: David Singer

BG 261. Butterfield Blues Band;
  Ravi Shankar
Fillmore West, 12/14, 16–20/70
Artist: Norman Orr

BG 262. Delaney and Bonnie and
  Friends; Voices of East Harlem
Fillmore West, 12/26–29/70
Artist: Norman Orr

BG 263. Cold Blood; Grateful
  Dead
Fillmore West, 12/31/70;
  Winterland, 12/31/70
Artist: David Singer

BG 264. Cold Blood; Boz Scaggs
Fillmore West, 12/31/70–1/3/71
Artist: Norman Orr

BG 265. Spirit; Elvin Bishop
  Group
Fillmore West, 1/7–10/71
Artist: Norman Orr

BG 266. Free; Bloodrock;
  Spencer Davis; Taj Mahal
Fillmore West, 1/14–17,
  21–24/71
Artist: David Singer

BG 268. Hot Tuna; Allman
  Brothers
Fillmore West, 1/28–31/71
Artist: Norman Orr

BG 269. B. B. King; Ballin' Jack
Fillmore West, 2/4–7/71
Artist: Norman Orr

BG 270. Fleetwood Mac;
  Steppenwolf
Fillmore West, 2/11–14,
  18–21/71; Winterland,
  2/12–13/71
Artist: Pierre

BG 271. New Riders of the Purple
  Sage; Boz Scaggs
Fillmore West, 2/25–28/71
Artists: David Singer, Satty

BG 272. Aretha Franklin; King
  Curtis and the Kingpins
Fillmore West, 3/5–7/71
Artist: David Singer

BG 273. Poco; Siegal Schwall;
  Sons of Champlin; Mark Almond
Fillmore West, 3/11–14,
  18–21/71
Artist: Norman Orr

BG 275. Eric Burdon and War;
  Santana
Fillmore West, 3/25–28,
  4/1–4/71; Winterland,
  3/26–27/71
Artist: David Singer

BG 276A. John Mayall; Johnny
  Winter
Fillmore West, 4/8–11, 15–18/71;
  Winterland, 8/9–10, 18/71
Artist: Willyum Rowe

BG 277. Taj Mahal; Stoneground
Fillmore West, 4/22–25/71;
  Winterland, 4/30–5/1/71
Artists: Randy Tuten, D. Bread

BG 278. Mike Bloomfield with
  Chicago Slim, Bola Sete and
  Mike Finnigan; Ten Years After
Fillmore West, 4/29–5/2/71;
  Winterland, 4/20–5/1/71
Artist: Randy Tuten

BG 279. Miles Davis; Elvin Bishop
  Group
Fillmore West, 5/6–9/71
Artist: David Singer

BG 280. Humble Pie; Swamp
  Dogg
Fillmore West, 5/13–16/71
Artist: David Singer

BG 281. Rascals; Grootna
Fillmore West, 5/20–23/71
Artist: Randy Tuten

BG 282. Cold Blood; Grateful
  Dead
Fillmore West, 5/27–30/71;
  Winterland, 5/28–29/71
Artist: Randy Tuten

BG 283. Albert King; Mott the
  Hoople
Fillmore West, 6/3–6/71
Artist: Willyum Rowe

BG 284. Cactus; Flamin' Groovies
Fillmore West, 6/10–13/71
Artist: Willyum Rowe

BG 285. Boz Scaggs; Tower of
  Power
Fillmore West, 6/17–20/71
Artist: David Singer

BG 286. Moby Grape; Spencer
  Davis and Peter Jameson
Fillmore West, 6/24–27/71
Artist: David Singer

BG 287. Boz Scaggs; Grateful
  Dead
Fillmore West, 6/30–7/4/71
Artist: David Singer

INDEX

The following constitutes a continuation of the copyright page.

The publisher wishes to express its thanks to the many individuals and institutions who have cooperated in making this book possible. Every effort has been made to reach copyright owners or their representatives. The publisher will be pleased to correct omissions or mistakes in future editions.

Photo Credits

Documentary photographs are by the following: Richard Alexander: p. 326; Gene Anthony: pp. 12, 86, 88; Jeff Berger: pp. 11, 15; Scott Dedenbach: p. 329; Herb Greene: pp. 74, 81; Jim Marshall: pp. 70, 77 (both), 323 (Joint Show II artists); Michael Ochs Archives: p. 24; Ron Schaeffer: p. 315; Bob Seidemann: pp. 13, 78, 323 (Joint Show I artists); Jon Sievert: pp. 19, 435; Michelle Vignes: p. 72; Cummings Walker: pp. 75, 80, 82, 84, 85.

Collection Credits

The posters for the Family Dog numbered series were photographed from the collections of Ben Friedman (Postermat), Paul Getchell, Dennis King, Eric King, Tim Patterson, and Randy Tuten. The posters for the Bill Graham numbered series were photographed from the collections of Harold Feiger, Ben Friedman (Postermat), Paul Getchell, Bill Graham Presents (BGP) Archives, Dennis King, Eric King, Ron Schaeffer, Jon and Wendy Sievert, David Singer, and Randy Tuten.

Other posters were photographed from the collections of Nancy Achilles: 4.267; Peter Albin: 1.97, 2.337, 2.344, 4.65; Ray Andersen: 2.25, 2.108, 2.113, 2.124, 2.156, 2.162, 2.163, 2.193, 2.199, 2.212, 2.237, 2.245, 2.317, 2.318, 2.333, 2.353, 2.364, 3.56, 3.105, 3.123, 3.183, 4.141; Zohn Artman: 4.263, 4.272; Tom Ballantyne: p. 320 (both), p. 430 (left); David Barker: 5.9, 5.36; Tim Barrett: p. 431, 5.21; Bob Barsotti: 4.259, 4.261, 4.290, 4.311, 4.322; Bay Area Music Archives: 1.88, 2.48, 2.87, 2.122, 2.167, 2.208, 2.232, 2.256, 2.290, 2.339, p. 252 (left), 3.28, 3.182, 4.1, 4.8, 4.18, 4.34, 4.75, 4.83, 4.85, 4.126, 4.130, 4.209, 4.225, 4.260, 5.4, 5.7, 5.12, 5.25, 5.99; Mark Behrens: p. 247, 3.128, 3.129, 4.86; Bill and Janice Belmont: 2.36, 2.83, 2.204, 2.272, 3.3, 3.159, 3.164, 3.168,

3.169, 3.178, 3.181, 3.186, 3.311, 4.107, 4.242, 4.246, 4.247, 4.262; Peter Belsito: 5.14, 5.15, 5.52, 5.53, 5.54, 5.57, 5.63, 5.64, 5.71, 5.74, 5.80, 5.83, 5.84, 5.85, 5.90, 5.91, 5.94, 5.95, 5.96, 5.97, 5.98, 5.100, 5.112, 5.113, 5.114, 5.116, 5.119, 5.131, 5.135, 5.140, 5.147, 5.152, 5.153, 5.154, 5.155; John Berns: 3.153, 4.62, 4.240, 4.253; Cara Bersani: p. 429, 5.123; Les Blank: 4.175, 4.177; Bill Bradt: 4.280; Stephen Braitman: 2.123, 2.223, 2.273, 2.291, 2.295, p. 250 (right), 3.34, 3.49, 3.51, 3.63, 3.75, 3.87, 3.90, 3.91, 3.93, 4.23, 4.26, 4.29, 4.37, 4.77, 4.282, 4.284, 4.285, p. 432 (left), p. 440 (right), 5.8, 5.11, 5.13, 5.19, 5.20, 5.23, 5.34, 5.35, 5.38, 5.39, 5.51, 5.55, 5.67, 5.72, 5.73, 5.77, 5.78, 5.86, 5.87, 5.92, 5.101, 5.102, 5.103, 5.106, 5.107, 5.108, 5.111, 5.121, 5.129, 5.144, 5.146, 5.148, 5.149; Jerilyn Brandelius: 3.166; Don Bratman: 2.200, 3.84, 4.223; Bread & Roses, Inc: 4.84; Steve Brown: pp. 67 (left), 69, 73, 76 (both), 79 (left), 2.141, 2.142, pp. 253 (left and right), 253, 3.100, 4.24, 4.132, 4.170, 4.237, 4.315; Nick Buck: 1.40, 1.54; Toby Byron: p. 88 (right); Mike Casey: 4.161; Sean Casey: 3.160; Art Chantry: 1.112, pp. 248 (right), 249 (right), 3.109, 4.135, pp. 437 (left), 437 (right), 438 (both), 438, 5.48, 5.49, 5.169; Evelyn Cipollina: 2.46, 2.47, 2.316; Bob Cohen: 2.322, 2.323, 2.324; Tom Constanten: 2.175, 2.176, 2.177; Chris Coyle: p. 67 (right), 2.2, 2.14, 2.58, 3.2, 3.167, 4.274, 5.2; Philip Cushway: 1.19, 4.252, p. 430 (right), 5.105; Bob Davis: 3.162; Richard Dorsett: p. 439, 440 (left), 442 (left), 5.161, 5.162; Harry Duncan: 4.27, 4.30, 4.174; Electric Factory: 4.210, 4.212, 4.213; Ray Etzler: 4.286, 4.300; Doug Fast: 3.106, 3.180; Harold Feiger: 1.106, 2.7, 2.74, 2.130, 2.131, 2.143, 2.173, 2.190, 2.203, 2.207, 2.216, 2.221, 2.254, 2.267, 2.269, 2.300, 2.329, 2.362, 2.365, 3.23, 3.24, 3.35, 3.52, 3.103, 4.55, 4.68, 4.123, 4.275; Robert Fletcher: 3.101, 4.106; Ben Friedman/Postermat: 2.126, 2.127, 2.128, 2.192, 2.357, 2.360, 3.22, 3.66, 3.116, 3.185, p. 322 (right), 4.46, 4.239; Lori Gates: 4.255; Paul Getchell: p. 16, 1.104, p. 87 (right), 2.28, 2.29, 2.31, 2.37, 2.53, 2.72, 2.78, 2.79, 2.82, 2.129, 2.135, 2.152, 2.158, 2.180, 2.185, 2.222, 2.224, 2.227, 2.228, 2.230, 2.235, 2.243, 2.251, 2.261, 2.268, 2.275, 2.276, 2.281, 2.288, 2.289, 2.292, 2.293, 2.302, 2.303, 2.304, 2.306, 2.307, 2.308, 2.310, 2.314, 2.330, 2.331, 2.332, 2.336, 2.340, 2.341, 2.356, pp. 243 (right), 244 (both), 245 (both), 248 (left), 255 (right), 3.12, 3.17, 3.20, 3.21, 3.25, 3.30, 3.32, 3.36, 3.37, 3.38, 3.39, 3.40, 3.44, 3.47, 3.50, 3.54, 3.61, 3.62, 3.78, 3.85, 3.92, 3.99, 3.102, 3.107, 3.112, 3.117, 3.121, 3.122, 3.125, 3.126, 3.131, 3.134, 3.137, 3.138, 3.140, 3.144, 3.145, 3.149, 3.150, 3.152, 3.155, 3.158, 3.173, p. 330 (right), 4.4, 4.5, 4.7, 4.51, 4.91, 4.113, 4.115, 4.116, 4.119, 4.122, 4.136, 4.199, 4.229, 4.234; David Getz: 3.57, 4.215; Globe Poster Printing Co.: 1.43, 1.44, 1.45, 1.47, 148; John Goddard/Village Music: 1.10, 1.16, 1.17, 1.18, 1.21, 1.23,